Principles of Financial Management

Corporate Finance, Investments, and Macrofinance

Seymour Friedland
York University

Questions and Problems Prepared by
William M. Lawson
Carleton University

Winthrop Publishers, Inc.
Cambridge, Massachusetts

Library of Congress Cataloging in Publication Data

Friedland, Seymour.
    Principles of financial management.

    Includes bibliographies and index.
    1. Corporations—Finance. 2. Business enterprises—
Finance. I. Lawson, William M., joint
author. II. Title.
HG4026.F75   658.1′5   77–13193
ISBN 0–87626–710–X

Interior design by Designworks, Inc.

10 9 8 7 6 5 4 3 2

to
Randy, Andrew, and Sharyn
because it's their turn

Contents

Annotated Table of Contents   ix
Preface   xxi

Part I   Introduction   1

Chapter 1   **The Functions and Objectives of Financial Management**   3

The Role of the Financial Manager   *3*
The Objectives of Financial Management   *3*
Financial Objectives for the Individual and Household—
Utility Maximization   *4*
Financial Objectives for the Firm   *6*
The Difference between Maximizing Profits and Maximizing
Share Values   *9*
Public Sector Decisions   *12*

Part II   An Introduction to Real and Financial Yields   17

Chapter 2   **The Yield on Real Assets: An Introduction to Capital Budgeting**   19

The Average or Bookkeeping Rate of Return   *20*
The Pay-Back Period   *28*
The Internal Rate of Return   *29*
The Benefit-Cost Ratio   *31*
Summary   35

Chapter 3 **The Yield on Debt Instruments**   **43**

Debt and Equity Claims *43*
Yields on Debt Instruments *45*
Special Yield Factors *55*
Summary 55

Chapter 4 **The Yield on Equity Instruments**   **63**

Preferred Stocks *64*
Convertible Preferreds *64*
Warrants *65*
The Price/Earnings Ratio *70*
Tax Treatment of Instruments *71*
Other Cost Factors *72*
Summary 74
Appendix A Yield Problems and Solutions 78

Chapter 5 **The Term Structure of Yields**   **83**

Expectations under Conditions of Certainty *85*
Expectations with Uncertainty *88*
Market Segmentation *91*
Portfolio Management Factors *92*
Summary 94

Chapter 6 **Introduction to Risk**   **99**

The Definition of Risk *100*
The Individual Determinants of Risk Premiums *104*
Managing Risk *107*
Efficient and Inefficient Portfolios *111*
Summary 113

Chapter 7 **The Market Price of Risk**   **119**

The Role of the Market *119*
The Capital Market Line *122*
Portfolio Risk Premium versus the Risk of
    Individual Assets *124*
Implications of Portfolio Risk Analysis for
    Financial Investors *129*
Implications of Portfolio Risk Analysis for
    Investors in Real Assets *130*
How Many Stocks Are Needed for Diversification *133*
Summary 133

Part III **Corporate Financial Management**   **141**

  Chapter 8 **An Introduction to Corporate Financial Management**   **143**

  Valuation *143*
  Individual Assets and Risk Premiums *145*
  Earnings Variability and Balance Sheet Management *146*
  Empirical Results and the Capital Asset
    Pricing Model (CAPM) *147*

  Chapter 9 **The Management of Liquidity**   **151**

  Liquidity and Risk *151*
  The Measurement of Liquidity *153*
  The Analysis of Working Capital Changes *156*
  The Cash Budget *159*
  Summary *166*

  Chapter 10 **Operating Leverage**   **173**

  Production Break-Even Analysis *174*
  Leverage Estimated from Income Statements *178*
  Summary *182*

  Chapter 11 **Financial Leverage and the Variability of Earnings**   **185**

  Leverage and the Rate of Return on Net Worth *185*
  Debt and Earnings per Share *189*
  Break-Even Ebit *190*
  The Degree of Financial Leverage *191*
  Combining Financial and Operating Leverage *192*
  The Effect of Financial Leverage on Beta *193*
  Taxes and Valuation *198*
  Summary *200*

  Chapter 12 **Dividend Policy**   **205**

  Review of Dividend Valuation Models *205*
  The Effect of Taxes on the Cost of Capital for
    Retained Earnings *208*
  Dividend Policy and Flotation Costs *209*
  The Demand for Dividends *210*
  Stock Dividends *212*
  Stock Repurchase *212*
  Summary *214*

Chapter 13 **The Cost of Capital**   **219**

Setting Target Rates *219*
The Costs of the Components of the Cost of Capital *220*
Is There an Optimal Capital Structure? *228*
Summary 230

Chapter 14 **Leasing Assets and Merger Policy**   **237**

Leasing *237*
Mergers *242*

Part IV **Some Macrofinancial Issues**   **251**

Chapter 15 **Financial Intermediation and the
                   Sources of Funds**   **253**

Sectoral Surpluses and Deficits *253*
Economic Impact of Surpluses and Deficits *254*
The Impact of Surpluses and Deficits on Yields *256*
Financial Intermediation *256*
Summary 259

Chapter 16 **Inflation and Yields**   **265**

Fixed-Return Instruments *266*
The Supply of Debt Instruments *271*
Cash Flow Inelasticity to Inflation *272*
Variable Return Instruments *274*
Effects of Inflation on Capital Budgets *279*
Summary 281

Chapter 17 **Some Aspects of International Finance**   **285**

The Balance of Trade and the Balance of Payments *285*
Can the United States Have an Independent
   Monetary Policy? *287*
Are Canadian and U.S. Interest Rates Movements Similar? *288*
Exchange Rate Hedging as an Equilibrium Mechanism *290*
Policies Creating Interest Rate and Monetary
   Policy Dependence *295*
The Role of Multinational Enterprise *295*
Summary 298

Index   **305**

Annotated Table of Contents

The book is aimed at the first course in financial management in both undergraduate and graduate business programs. It assumes that the student has some knowledge of statistics, accounting, and economics or is taking these courses simultaneously.

There are two ways in which this book differs from the major competitive texts in financial management:

I. This is a survey of the major areas of finance. It examines some of the more important elements that are factors of investments, particularly the determinants of yields. It covers the major aspects of corporate financial management. Finally, it considers the roles of financial institutions and certain significant macrofinancial problems such as international finance and inflation.

II. It integrates the capital asset pricing model as a key part of corporate financial management. The capital asset pricing model is not included merely as an appendix or other sort of addendum to the main part of the text, but is a main portion of the approach. A variety of readers have agreed that the treatment given in the text to the model manages to simplify it sufficiently so that students at the basic level can understand it, while at the same time doing justice to the capital asset pricing model.

Another noteworthy aspect of the text is the explicit concern for public sector financial management. Although this concern is limited to pointing out the similarities between the analysis for corporate financial managers and public financial managers (there is, for example, no presentation of the pros and cons of different concepts of the social cost of capital), the very nature of the book means that approximately two-thirds of the text is as appropriate for the public financial manager as for the corporate financial manager.

The overall layout of the book is relatively straightforward. Following an initial introductory chapter, which attempts to develop the objectives of financial management under conditions of risk, the remainder of the text is divided into three major sections: An Introduction to Real and Financial Yields; Corporate Financial Management; and Some Macrofinancial Issues.

The seventeen chapters provide adequate coverage for a semester course and permit the instructor some leeway in picking and choosing among the chapters and subjects. A brief description of each chapter follows:

Part I Introduction

Chapter 1 The Functions and Objectives of Financial Management

Financial managers are described as having three major functions: the translation of plans into the financial implications of these plans; the determination of the appropriate means for raising the funds; the development and application of measures to aid in the allocation of these funds. The major objective of financial management is cited as survival, particularly the avoidance of technical insolvency. Next, a detailed development of the profit-oriented goals by financial managers under riskless conditions is developed. First, the profit-oriented financial objectives for individuals and households are presented. Then, firms are dealt with. Under perfect competition, it is pointed out that the goals of survival and long-run maximization of profits really amount to the same thing. This relationship weakens, however, as we move to imperfect competition, particularly where private ownership exists. With publicly owned firms, something approaching profit maximization becomes significant because of the possibility of proxy fights or takeover bids if the firm deviates substantially from making reasonable rates of return. Next, the difference between maximizing profits and maximizing share values is discussed. At this point, the notion of risk is introduced by the simple and presumably familiar comparison of investments with different expected values and different standard deviations. Without going into great detail in the chapter, it is then put forth as reasonable that projects with larger standard deviations should be capitalized at higher rates than projects with lower standard deviations, resulting in value differences but reflecting the effect of risk. Finally, there is a brief discussion of the financial objectives of public sector decision-making units.

Following chapter 1, the text moves on to Part II, dealing with real and financial rates of return.

Part II   An Introduction to Real and Financial Yields

Chapter 2   The Yield on Real Assets: An Introduction to Capital Budgeting

This chapter is fairly standard in developing the various methods of measuring rates of return and compound interest. The order of presentation is a little unusual. The normal method of presentation is usually historical, starting with the average or bookkeeping rate of return and an explanation of its inadequacies, moving on to the payoff period, then to the internal rate of return and an explanation of its inadequacies, and finally on to present value. In the presentation in this chapter, I found that by discussing the inadequacies of the average or bookkeeping rate of return, I could then move immediately into present value. This is then compared to the internal rate of return, and the inadequacies of the internal rate of return can be developed somewhat more meaningfully in this way than with the usual historical discussion. A treatment of the "profitability index" is also included, with a discussion of its limitations. Finally, there is an explanation of the measurement of benefits and costs for capital assets including treatment of depreciation and taxation. Throughout the chapter, references are made to public sector capital budgeting decisions, and how they might differ or be the same as those in private capital budgeting.

Chapter 3   The Yield on Debt Instruments

The chapter opens with the distinction between internally and externally generated sources of funds and points out the importance of the internally generated sources. It then describes the relationships between financial instruments and external financing. It moves on to discuss the differences between debt and equity claims in terms of the priority of these claims to income and assets. The bulk of the chapter describes the yields on particular debt instruments, the debenture bond, the mortgage, and commercial paper. Notes are briefly described and it is pointed out that their yields on the short end are similar to those of commercial paper, while their yields on the longer end are similar to the yields on bonds. Next, we move on to a discussion of bonds, including the development of yields to maturity and holding period yields. An example of a bond yield book is included in the discussion. Next we move to mortgages pointing out that mortgages are similar to bonds. The amortization of mortgages is considered, as is the yield and present value of mortgages. Brief discussions are included on mortgage bonds and sinking fund bonds, with appropriate comparisons between the two classes of instruments. Finally, there is a discussion of commercial and sales finance company paper, showing how the discount yield is comparable to the yield to maturity for bonds.

Chapter 4   The Yield on Equity Instruments

This chapter begins with a descriptive discussion of the various classes of equity in terms of whether they are private stocks or public stocks, and if public, whether they are traded over the counter or on an organized exchange. This permits an early introduction of the Securities and Exchange Commission and its role in the registration of securities. Next comes a discussion of preferred stock, where the holding period yield is presented as a yield measurement and is compared to the market yield. The difficulties of the holding period yield are presented particularly in terms of determining the future value. A special discussion of convertible preferreds follows, and this permits a discussion of warrants, which goes beyond mere description into an analysis of why the price of the warrant will vary from what one would expect mathematically from the price of the underlying security. Common stocks are then treated, first descriptively, pointing out the need for determining holding period yields, and also indicating the freedom of the company in determining the dividend. The constant dividend growth model is developed as is the so-called super growth model, both of which are based on the definition of the value of common stock as the present value of the expected future dividends of the stock. The constant dividend model is also developed, since this permits an easy movement into a discussion of the price / earnings ratio. In the price / earnings ratio discussion, the shortcomings of the price / earnings ratio as a measure of value is analyzed, particularly under conditions where earnings are being reinvested profitably. A final brief section in this chapter deals with the tax treatment of instruments and how these tax effects may be reflected in yield differences. Special treatment for intercorporate dividend payments is considered, tax exempt bonds are considered, and "flower" bonds are also considered with the point being that often apparent anomalies in yield distributions really reflect differences in tax treatments.

Chapter 5   The Term Structure of Yields

This is the first of several analytic chapters on why yields differ. It begins with an example of the problems confronting a government borrower in determining whether to issue long or short term securities. It then moves into a fairly standard and reasonably straightforward discussion of the various theories of term structure differences, starting with expectations under conditions of certainty, and moving through expectations with uncertainty and the market segmentation theory of term structure differences. There is some discussion as to which of these theories is the "right" one, and although the trained analyst will not be completely satisfied with the presentation, we reach the conclusion that the market segmentation description is not an adequate description of the determinants of the term structure differences, even though it is appealing at a common sense level. The final section of the chapter deals with portfolio management factors in the term structure, and analyzes the behavior of bond prices when interest rates are changing, given different maturities and different coupon rates.

Chapter 6 Introduction to Risk

The initial aim of this chapter is to define risk by standard deviation or variance. This is done by a combination of graphic and numerical examples as well as by references to Latané's survey findings on risk attitudes, Michaelson's findings on government security yields, and Arditti's findings on the determinants of yield differences. Having defined risk, the next problem is to determine the size of the risk premium. This problem is emphasized by considering six numerical examples and assigning hypothetical yield differences, reflecting differences as standard deviation, which result in value differences. The next section goes into the individual determinants of risk premiums, considering the utility function and opportunity curve facing any individual. A risk-free asset is introduced, which helps determine the efficient portfolio line and also serves as an introduction to subsequent work on the capital market model. Next, the Markowitz approach to portfolio management is developed by showing how the correlation between assets in a two asset portfolio can reduce the standard deviation of the portfolio below that of the standard deviation of either of the two assets or a weighted average of the two assets. Finally, a series of numerical examples are considered of three asset portfolios, the aim being to develop the distinction between efficient and inefficient portfolios. The major point of all of this as being a meaningful definition of diversification is emphasized throughout the chapter.

Chapter 7 The Market Price of Risk

The purpose of this chapter is to fully develop the capital asset pricing model and the notion of betas. First, we present an example that illustrates how the market works in determining the risk premiums, given the demand schedule of several individuals and a fixed supply of securities. Next, the limitations of the Markowitz approach to portfolios are developed. Particularly, we concern ourselves with the problems of the risk of a security in the market being portfolio peculiar, that is, reflecting the existing composition of the individual's portfolio. Another problem considered is the number of calculations required in a Markowitz model. As a solution to the latter problem, we develop the distinction between systematic and diversifiable risk by making the Sharpe-Lintner assumption of insignificant intercorrelations among assets in a portfolio, with all significant relationships being between the assets and the market index. Next, the risk-free asset is reintroduced with the assumptions of a perfectly efficient market, so that the portfolio line becomes straight and identical for all investors. Considerable discussion develops about the underlying assumptions of market perfection. We move on to develop the notion of the portfolio risk premium versus the risk of individual assets, with a re-emphasis on the need for diversification even under the more sophisticated assumptions of the capital markets model. After this, the concept of risk premiums for securities is developed and the idea of the beta coefficient emerges. Again, we develop distinctions between portfolio betas and security betas, as well as between a capital markets line and a security line. In the next section, the implications of portfolio risk analysis for financial investors are developed. These implications are mainly the results of the notion of perfect knowledge and random walks and their impact on fundamental and technical analysis of security prices. The assumptions are not accepted whole, but are questioned. It is pointed out that at least in principle, even if the assumptions were true, there would be the possibility for profit if one could switch from high to low beta portfolios on the basis of market movements. In the next section, there is an attempt to develop implications of the foregoing analysis for investors in real assets; that is, corporations. It is suggested that asset betas may be developed with respect to the relationship between the variations and the returns of a particular asset and variations in the company's sales, industry sales, or some more aggregate measures, such as GNP. This provides a basis for discounting cash flows by different capitalization rates and an example of this is given. Next, we return to security analysis and a brief section is devoted to the statistical estimation of beta. Problems of the alpha value and variability of betas are discussed and the greater stability of portfolio betas as compared to security betas are also discussed. The final section of the chapter deals with the number of stocks needed for diversification in a portfolio, with the point being made that portfolios with as few as fifteen securities apparently reduce nonsystematic risk to zero. Reference is also made to the inefficiency of larger portfolios and more complex selection techniques in terms of the effects of increased costs and the subsequent impact on the net return of the portfolio.

This completes the material on yields and the portion of the overall survey that is concerned with investments. We now move to the section on corporate financial management.

Part III Corporate Financial Management

Chapter 8 An Introduction to Corporate Financial Management

This chapter is a transition between the investment section and the corporate financial management section. It is relatively brief and simply tries to tie the capital asset pricing model to corporate finance. The instructor might want to add some simple numerical examples of the impact of different asset class risks on a company's beta. The chapter starts out with the constant growth model as a convenient device. The valuation form of the model is used and then the relationship between the capitalization rate and the capital market equation is shown. The definition of beta is reviewed and the relationship between the standard deviation of the firm's rate of return and beta are developed very clearly. The point that is made is that variability of returns from the firm's asset portfolio will affect the firm's beta, and hence, will affect the value of the firm's stock. Numerical examples are given to demonstrate this. Relationships are developed verbally between individual assets and the risk premium, pointing out that the variability of returns of the individual asset are contributing factors to the overall variability of the firm's return. The point, however, is also made that the variability of the firm's return will depend upon the diversification; that is, the degree of independence of the probability distributions of the different assets. It is also pointed out, however, that there is relatively little leeway given for much diversification to be achieved in terms of the correlation among the different operating assets, with the exception of liquid assets. Finally, there is a discussion relating the variability of corporate earnings to the overall balance sheet of the firm. This section is essentially an introduction to the chapters that follow on corporate financial management, relating operating leverage and financial leverage to the firm's beta.

Chapter 9   The Management of Liquidity

First, liquidity is defined in a variety of ways. Next, the relationship between liquidity and risk is developed where liquidity is really compared to the risk-free asset in the capital asset pricing model. The following section attempts to measure liquidity explicitly, in terms of various accounting ratios, such as the average age of receivables, quick assets, the current ratio, the average age of inventories, and working capital. Next, working capital changes are analyzed in terms of the sources and uses of working capital. Following this we discuss the cash budget with a detailed numerical example of the development of the cash budget, starting from expected sales and continuing to actual net cash flows.

Chapter 10   Operating Leverage

The purpose of treating leverage is to demonstrate that the overall balance sheet structure can affect the variability of earnings, which in turn affects both the firm's beta and the market value of the firm's share. Operating leverage begins with typical production breakeven analysis handled both graphically and algebraically. We move from this to break-even levels in terms of sales rather than in terms of quantities, and here the analysis is extended to include a probability distribution for sales so that standard deviations can be computed explicitly.

Chapter 11   Financial Leverage and the Variability of Earnings

The treatment of financial leverage again is aimed not so much at showing the effect of financial leverage on the expected level of earnings as its effect on the variability of earnings. Algebraic, arithmetic, and geometric methods are used to demonstrate these effects and a specific section deals with the impact of financial leverage on the beta. The effect of financial leverage on value is introduced, using the net operating income and net income method. A final section develops measures of operating leverage and a degree of financial leverage and combines both effects to show the impact on beta, and the fact that firms with high operating leverage required by the production functions available to them, can offset this by low levels of financial leverage and vice versa.

Chapter 12 Dividend Policy

Since the previous chapter deals with debt policy, it is appropriate to now deal with the dividend policy. The section treats the issue of taxation and the value of dividends and the effect of taxes on dividend policy; namely, the bias existing tax laws give to shifting the distribution of a firm's income toward reinvestment and capital gains rather than toward dividend levels. The section also points out that the retention of earnings permits the firm to acquire funds without flotation costs. The next section treats the demand for dividends by shareholders and presents the perfect capital markets argument, which is that those who want dividends and hold shares in a company with a policy of high retained earnings can acquire the liquidity they need by borrowing on their shares. This position is criticized, since the risk of the shareholder borrowing on a share as collateral is quite different than the risk of a shareholder receiving a dividend. There is a discussion of the stability of dividend policy of the firm. Some comments are made on the empirical findings between the stability of dividend policy and the firm's beta. The final section of the chapter deals with stock dividends and makes clear that although a stock dividend conserves the firm's cash and allows it to capitalize a portion of its retained earnings, the relative ownership of the shareholders diminish if they dispose of their stock dividend. Stock repurchase plans are discussed. There is also a brief discussion comparing stock dividends to stock splits, including the impact of both of these on stock prices.

Chapter 13 The Cost of Capital

The cost of capital chapter first determines the cost of each component of the capital structure starting with common stock, and works through retained earnings, depreciation, preferred shares, and debt. In determining the cost of capital for common shares, the capital market equation is used and the relationship between the capital markets equation and the constant dividend growth model is developed. Retained earnings and depreciation are treated as having the same cost of capital as equity. The cost of capital of preferred shares are estimated at their dividend yield. In a discussion of debt, the cost of debt is treated as the after-tax cost. However, there is also a discussion of short-term debt and long-term debt. This provides the opportunity for distinguishing between temporary and permanent short-term debt as well as discussing the cost of failure to take trade discount terms. It also provides the opportunity to discuss the pros and cons of using coupon rates and current yields to maturity as the basis for determining the cost of capital, for debt. The conclusion is that the firm should ideally be using the interest rate that it expects will prevail when the funds have to be rolled over.

The chapter then moves to a discussion of the determination of appropriate weights, comparing market value weights with book value weights and points out their shortcomings. Again, it is pointed out that the firm should use the weights that reflect its desired capital structure, and provides the opportunity for some discussion of both the strategy and tactics of developing capital structure. The next section of the chapter raises the question of whether there is an optimal capital structure. The net operating income method is compared to the net income method, and we conclude that neither method of valuation provides the key to the optimal capital structure when taxes are taken into account. The conclusion is that the firm should have a target capital structure that reflects its willingness to absorb risk where the risk of the asset portfolio is reflected inversely to the risk of the capital structure.

Chapter 14 Leasing Assets and Merger Policy

The logic of this chapter is that both leasing and mergers are means of acquiring assets other than through the usually assumed means of the firm; that is, by buying assets from asset manufacturers or building assets. In the leasing discussion, we emphasize net leases and compare leasing and buying, with discounted cash flows providing the answers. There is also a discussion of the variety of leases and some of the reasons why leasing companies may be able to offer assets under more favorable terms than if the firms were to go out and buy the assets directly. With respect to mergers, the discussion begins by pointing out that the model for the merger decision is the same as that used for fixed assets; that is, the development of cash flows and the discounting of the same. The advantages and disadvantages of mergers as opposed to the firm adding up new assets are developed in terms of competition, costs, and taxation, with particular emphasis on capital gains taxation and the ability to consolidate losses, the economies of scale, etc. There is also a discussion of how various factors enter into determining the market value of each company's stock in the merger trade, and the role of minority stockholders is reviewed.

Part IV Some Macrofinancial Issues

Chapter 15 Financial Intermediation and the Sources of Funds

This chapter explains the process of savings and investments throughout the economy in terms of how the funds flow. Direct investment is compared to indirect investment, and in the process the student is introduced to the concept of financial intermediation and the justification for the existence of such intermediaries. Analysis is presented with reference to actual dollar flows for the major financial instruments in dictating the relative importance of institutions in each of the different parts of the financial markets.

Chapter 16 **Inflation and Yields**

This chapter discusses the differences between real and nominal yields and evaluates the so-called "Fisher Effect" where nominal yields are supposed to equal real yields and expected inflation. The initial analysis is in terms of fixed return instruments. After developing the relationship between real yields and the expected inflation rate in nominal yields, specific demands are developed for funds, particularly the demand institutions that are compelled to buy bonds even if their yields do not cover fully the expected inflation rate.

Such institutions include pension funds, which are tax-exempt, and therefore do not have to demand a full inflation premium, and insurance companies, which have to invest their funds in a fairly narrowly specified range of instruments, and therefore cannot demand the full inflation premium.

Further, there is a discussion of supply of funds and the fact that the effective inflation is not even among all sectors, so that certain borrowers may not increase the supply of bonds (and in fact may decrease the bonds they offer). Such borrowers include regulated utilities, where the regulatory authorities are unwilling to allow rate increases to match inflation.

The discussion next turns to variable return instruments and particularly common stocks. Here it is demonstrated that, unlike fixed return instruments, expected inflation rates will affect both the cash flows that may be available to the shareholders as well as their required rate of return. Again, inflation is uneven throughout the economy, and some firms may have increases in earnings greater than the rate of inflation, while other firms have earnings increases that are less than the rate of inflation. The impact of inflation on the constant dividend model is developed.

Finally, there is a discussion of the effects of inflation on capital budgets, where again the impact of inflation is shown in terms of its impact on cash flows as well as on its impact on the required rate of return. It is pointed out that if the cash flow elasticity to inflation is less than unity, the result of inflation may be to generate a smaller demand for fixed assets than if there were no inflation.

Chapter 17 **Some Aspects of International Finance**

The first section of this chapter deals with the difference between the balance of trade and the balance of payments. It discusses the recycling of deficits and surpluses and uses the oil deficits as a specific example as to how this is done.

The next section is concerned with the reduction in independence of monetary policy as a result of flexible exchange rates. The use of forward rates as well as spot rates are introduced and exchange rate hedging as an equilibrium mechanism is considered. It is pointed out, that as a result of such exchange rate hedging, countries should be allowed to have different interest rates and hence independent monetary policies even if there are no barriers to international capital flows.

In the process of this discussion, the student is exposed to the mechanisms by which financial managers can move funds across international borders, often profitably. Although exchange rate hedging should theoretically make this unprofitable, the existence of multinational corporations permits avoidance of normal exchange rate risk if multinational firms simply accelerate or slow down funds movements that would have occurred normally in any event. Hence, there is pressure on the value of currencies when interest rates across the world are not roughly similar.

At the end of each chapter, there is a selected bibliography, questions, and problems. In addition, we at York have used a set of outside projects, forcing the student into the "real" world. These include determination of term yield curves for actual securities, analysis of actual firms including an estimation of the firm's beta value, etc. These projects can be found in the book as appendix material and in the instructor's manual. The instructor's manual also includes classroom tested materials in the form of model solutions to the problems in the text as well as sample examination questions.

Preface

The typical first course in finance concentrates on corporate financial management. Though useful for those who subsequently major in finance, the course is less satisfactory for students whose primary interests lie in other areas. Large and important sectors of financial information are omitted. Students emerging from such a course have had little or no exposure to the area of investments, even though such knowledge would seem to be more personally useful than corporate financial management for most students. Students have had little exposure to the role of financial institutions, even though they will be consumers of their services. Despite the fact that the newspapers they read will periodically carry stories about currency crises, devaluations, and the like, they will have had no help from the financial management course in understanding these complex matters.

Those who major in finance may be in little better shape. With a limited number of electives, and the desire to specialize in a specific area of finance, they are unlikely to achieve a comprehensive coverage of finance. Further, finance majors may well be frustrated in finding suitable jobs as they emerge from programs with the usual emphasis on corporate financial management. The beginning financial manager often has primary skills in accounting, rather than financial management. In contrast, there are many financial institutions and governmental agencies interested in people with financial backgrounds in investment, capital markets, and international finance, as well as in corporate finance.

One of the remarkable changes that occurred during the sixties was the entrance of business students, both those with undergraduate degrees and M.B.A.'s, into government service. Partly, this reflects the general increase in government personnel. However, it also reflects the gradual acceptance of the applicability of some concepts of business management to public administration. We recognize this trend by pointing out the contrasts and similarities of the problems being discussed to those faced by a public sector manager. Of course, about half of the text is as applicable to public sector problems as it is to those of the corporation.

Finally, the extent to which this text has successfully accomplished the aims enunciated above reflects the dramatic advances in financial theory, particularly with respect to the analysis of risk and portfolio selection. These topics are still taught in advanced courses, as indeed they should be. However, the basic course must reflect these significant advances in the field, even if they cannot be presented in the depth achieved in advanced courses. In short, the basic course should have as one goal a survey of financial theory and practice. This is particularly true when the advances are not merely extensions of existing knowledge, but also tend to unify what have previously been unrelated topics. Risk analysis has permitted the integration of capital markets theory with capital budgeting. The risk coefficient has added new dimensions to cash budgeting and liquidity analysis, to mention only two areas of corporate finance affected by contemporary research.

The basic course has always been a tantalizing problem to me because of the need to apply contemporary theory to existing financial principles. The degree to which this has been successfully achieved will be determined by the reader.

For these reasons, we have written this text. It is designed for students taking their first course in finance, either as undergraduates or as candidates for the M.B.A. Although it is a beginning text, it does assume some preliminary background in financial accounting, macroeconomics, and statistics. With effort, students without such background also can complete the text.

Finally some words of thanks. This manuscript was typed and retyped patiently by Mrs. Dorothy Rochefort. In one version or another, it has been used for the basic finance course at York. Students have been very helpful in indicating errors and unclear portions of the text. My colleagues have been extremely generous in commenting on the material. Bill Lawson in particular has prepared the questions following each chapter, the appendices, and the instructor's manual. Nahum Biger and Dwight Grant have spent much time relaying their teaching experiences with the manuscript. Thanks also to Professor C. P. Jones of North Carolina State University and Professor T. Gregory Morton of the University of Connecticut for their extremely helpful suggestions and criticisms. While I thank these people for adding to the strength of the book, I am solely responsible for the weaknesses.

Seymour Friedland

Introduction

I

The Functions and Objectives of Financial Management

1

The Role of the Financial Manager

Financial managers have three major functions:

1. They translate the plans of the economic unit that they are managing into the amounts of funds that these plans require. For example, they translate production budgets into budgets for materials, labor, and capital required to fulfill the production budget, and to the cash required to buy the materials and capital goods and hire the labor.
2. They use the appropriate means for raising funds. This means they decide how much cash to raise by savings, by various forms of borrowing, or by selling additional shares of ownership. The financial manager must consider the firm's ability to repay loans, if money is borrowed, and other risks associated with the various means of finance.
3. They help determine how funds are allocated. Here, the financial manager must help to develop criteria for determining how to allocate funds among various uses. In effect, the financial manager is helping to assess the need for funds.

The Objectives of Financial Management

Survival

Most economic units, private or public, want to survive. The inability to pay currently maturing obligations, called *technical insolvency,* is a major cause of failure for both households (which can go into personal bankruptcy) and business firms. Nor are government organizations immune to technical insolvency. For example, New York City in 1975 faced a crisis of technical insolvency, since the city could not repay currently maturing obligations from its normal sources of cash, nor could it borrow the needed funds.

A good financial manager adopts planning and budgeting tools and utilizes appropriate financial instruments to avoid technical insolvency. The manager's job is made more difficult because the future is uncertain. However, for most economic units, a clear objective of financial management is to survive by avoiding technical solvency, that is, to have sufficient cash to pay currently due bills.

Other Goals

The popular view of the conservative financial manager reflects financial management's concern with survival. However, survival may simply constrain the financial manager's decisions, and the financial manager may have other goals to pursue.

For example, having adequate funds helps protect the firm against technical insolvency, but what constitutes an adequate amount of funds seems to vary with interest rates. As interest rates rise, the liquidity of most firms tends to decline. Clearly, something besides the concern with survival helps shape financial decisions.

Another example of the influence of other goals is the willingness of business firms to use debt. The interest rate on long-term debt is, in effect, a fixed charge against income. Since income varies, depending on business conditions, high levels of fixed debt are not consistent with the goal of survival.

Even short-term debt is a threat to survival. As short-term debt matures, a firm usually replaces, or "rolls over," the debt with new short-term debt. However, if credit is tight, the firm may not be able to refinance its short-term debt. It may not even have sufficient liquid assets to pay off the short-term debt. So the firm could become technically insolvent if it had high levels of short-term debt in changing credit conditions in the economy.

Yet firms tend to use more long-term debt during inflation than they do when prices are stable. When interest rates are high, firms tend to use more short-term debt than long-term debt. So you can see that influences other than survival shape the decisions of the firm. What are the other goals that help explain the financial behavior of economic units?

Financial Objectives for the Individual and Household—Utility Maximization

When a family invests or saves money, they are reducing their current consumption and increasing future consumption. But they will forego current consumption only if the increase in future consumption exceeds the sacrifice in current consumption. For this to be true, the interest rate on the savings must at least exceed zero.

Figure 1-1 shows how higher interest rates induce individuals and households to reduce current consumption. In this illustration, the household begins with current consumption of OD, and expected future consumption of OR. The curves marked U_0, U_1, U_2, and U_3 are indifference curves. The household does not care where it is on any indifference curve, but it prefers being on U_1 to being on U_0, and prefers U_2 to U_1, and U_3 to U_2. The interest rates are the straight lines marked i_0, i_1, and i_2. The steeper the straight line, the more future consumption it can have by foregoing current consumption, that is, the higher the interest rate, the steeper the line. A low interest rate, such as i_0, induces the household to forego the current consumption of CD in order to gain the future consumption of RS. However, at the higher interest rate i_1, the household gives up BD to get the additional future consumption of RT. Finally, at the highest rate, i_2, the household is willing to forego AD of current consumption in order to gain RU of future consumption. In each case, the household moves to its highest indifference curve. This analysis shows that the household adjusts its saving so that it is on the highest possible indifference curve. In other words, it maximizes its satisfaction or utility.

The idea that households maximize utility when they make decisions

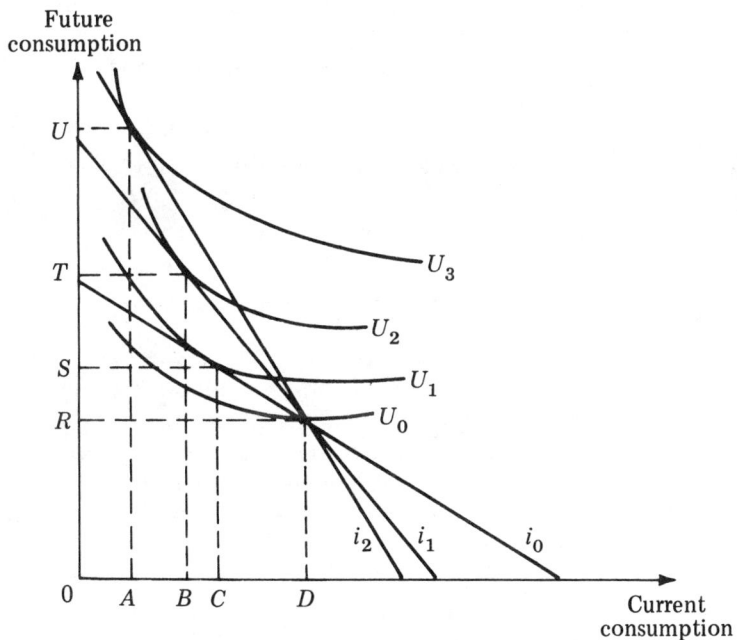

Figure 1-1
Determinants of Borrowing or Lending for the Individual

The Functions and Objectives of Financial Management

about consumption and investments is valid but it does not always predict the effect of interest rates on savings. Different households have differently shaped indifference curves. It would be relatively easy, for example, to draw a household with indifference curves sloped so that as interest rates rose, the amount saved declined. Even this behavior can be rationalized if we assume that the household has certain fixed future goals, such as attaining a level of future consumption large enough to enable the household to retire. At higher interest rates, this household would not have to forego as much current consumption in order to achieve the fixed goal.

Maximizing household utility is not necessarily the same as maximizing profits. Nonetheless, maximizing utility is conceptually a reasonably clear objective that, in addition to the constraint or objective of survival, helps explain the household's behavior. However, it is difficult to develop general rules of financial management under these conditions because of variations in utility functions and wealth.

Financial Objectives for the Firm

A firm may have many alternative goals, such as maximizing sales and gaining a certain share of industry as well as maximizing utility. Of the many possible goals, maximizing profit is of particular interest because the rules for doing so are reasonably well specified by the field of economics. Thus, we shall review various conditions of competition to determine whether maximizing profit is a necessary goal.

If a firm makes decisions that apply to more than one time period, as is often the case for financial decisions, the appropriate goal would be maximization of the firm's wealth, or net worth, rather than maximization of profits. These two goals are different because future outcomes are uncertain. For now, we shall assume that the firm is certain about the future outcome of its decisions. Under that assumption, maximizing profit is the same as maximizing net worth.

Perfect Competition

When competition is perfect, the firm will maximize profits in the long run. Perfect competition allows freedom of entry for competitors. Competitors enter the market as long as profits exceed the normal rate of return on capital invested. As new firms enter, the selling price of the product declines until average costs equal price and profits are zero. If the firm fails to maximize its profits, it will be generating losses and will leave the industry.

In effect, maximization of profit under perfect competition is really a disguise for the objective of long-run survival of the firm. Further, unlike the goal of maximizing utility, which is internally generated, the goal of maximizing profits in perfect competition is an externally generated goal. In contrast to the case for households, then, it is relatively easy to prescribe proper financial decisions for the firm under perfect competition because the idiosyncrasies of the individual economic unit do not affect the goal.

Imperfect Competition—The Large Numbers Case

Under conditions of perfect competition, the demand curve facing the individual firm is horizontal, since there is no product differentiation and complete freedom of entry. A very close relative of these conditions occurs when product differentiation is weak. Then the firm faces a negatively sloped demand curve on which marginal revenue is less than price. This would happen, for example, when a retail establishment has a favorable location so that the customer is willing to pay a little bit more for the convenience of shopping near home. But if price differentials between the neighborhood retail establishment and more distant firms grow too large, the customer would be willing to travel farther in order to pay the lower price.

Barriers to entry under these conditions are usually weak, so competitors can be easily attracted to areas that generate profits above the normal rate of return on invested capital. As a result of free entry, the demand curve facing the firm gradually shifts downward until price equals average cost. If it shifts to a point at which price is less than average cost in the long run, firms leave the industry until the demand curve shifts upward and the average cost equals price.

Because firms in these industries can enter freely, they face the same constraint as firms do under conditions of perfect competition. In the long run, profits will be zero. Hence, the firm has no choice but to make financial decisions that will maximize profit.

Privately Owned Oligopolies and Monopolies

When freedom of entry is restricted—because of advantages of unique location, strong product differentiation, or the economies of scale, profits in the long run can exceed zero. The goal or constraint of survival still applies, but it is not clear that such a firm must make decisions to maximize profit.

If the manager of the firm is also the owner, management is free, subject to the constraint of survival, to make decisions that do not necessarily maximize profits. For example, the firm may prefer to increase its market share or its physical size, even if such a decision is not consistent with profit maximization. For such firms, decisions are based upon the preferences of management, and managers make decisions that maximize their utility. Hence, the manager may choose to maximize profits, but is under no constraint to do so.

Under these conditions, we cannot determine a general set of optimal rules for financial management. Different firms in the same industry can survive even though they have different goals. However, it may still be useful to describe rules for financial management assuming that maximizing profit or wealth is a goal. Management can then use these rules to measure the costs of their decisions in terms of foregone profits.

Imperfect Competition with Public Ownership

The corporate form of business organization makes it possible to separate owners from management. The corporation itself is a legal entity, and usually owners can lose no more than they paid for their shares of ownership, the stock. The firm periodically declares dividends from its earnings and pays these to the shareholders. The value of the shares is the value of net worth. Hence, with no uncertainty about the future, maximizing profits is the same as maximizing share values.

There may be various classifications of shareholders. For example, some shareholders may have preference over others in terms of receiving dividends. However, at least one class of shareholder must also have voting rights. These shareholders vote, usually annually, for directors of the company, and this board of directors then appoints the management officers of the corporation.

The corporate form may be used under conditions of perfect competition or in the large-number case of imperfect competition. However, when used in those cases, the stockholder with the majority of voting rights is usually the manager of the company. In oligopolies and monopolies, managers often own only a small share of the corporation so that owners can be considered distinct from managers.

When the owners of a firm are not also its managers, what are the goals of financial management? The firm can survive even if profits are not maximized because of the structure of the industry. If the manager does not have a significant part of his personal wealth invested in the company, he or she has no personal incentive to maximize profits. And if no single owner controls a majority of the voting rights, as is often the case, it is difficult for individual owners to coerce managers to maximize profits.

Owners have two ways of coercing managers to maximize profits, even when ownership is largely separated from management and no single owner controls a majority of the votes of the owners.

1. *Proxy Fights* Voting rights can be transferred from the owner to anyone else if the owner signs a proxy statement—a revocable conferral of voting rights. In fact, management itself usually seeks proxies from the owners to support the existing board of directors and hence the existing management. If management has been operating the firm in a manner glaringly different from the way that would maximize profit, owners are more willing to assign their voting rights to corporate outsiders who promise to correct the management's policies. Presumably, correcting these policies leads to larger profits and hence in-

creases the value of the shares owned. However, proxy fights are very expensive in terms of legal costs and the costs of finding shareholders and convincing them to sign proxies. Further, it is not easy to prove that the existing management has not been maximizing profits if they have been making some level of profits. As a result, successful proxy fights are rare. Still, the threat of a proxy fight may push managers to adopt the interest of owners. Thus, even without proxy wars, owners can pressure managers to maintain a level of profits so as to avoid proxy fights.

2. *Takeover Bids* If management has been following principles that have led to lower share values than might otherwise be achieved, particularly if the firm has been losing money, other firms may attempt to take over the firm. Losses may attract an outside group because they can be used to reduce the profits, and hence the taxes, of the company making the takeover offer. The takeover bid may initially be a proposal to take over the company for a price above the market value of the company's shares. If management refuses this offer, the takeover company may then put out a public bid to shareholders to tender or offer their stock to the takeover company, again at a price in excess of the market value.

The price offered by the takeover company depends on its appraisal of what it can do with the absorbed company, and includes the value of any tax losses that can reduce the company's tax bill. The management of the company to be absorbed may counter with letters to shareholders explaining that takeover offers are actually well below the real value of the shares and that, if the shareholders refuse the offer, they can expect their share values to rise to higher levels in the future. Successful takeovers are more common than successful proxy fights. As with proxy fights, the threat of a possible takeover can coerce management into maximizing profits and hence maximizing the share values of their owners.

It is not clear whether the threat of proxy fights or takeovers is sufficient to make managements without significant ownership operate in the interests of the owners. However, the analysis that follows in this book is based on the assumption that managers operate companies to maximize share values.

The Difference Between Maximizing Profits and Maximizing Share Values

As we explained earlier, maximizing profits is consistent with maximizing share values under conditions of certainty. However, when risk and uncertainty exist, as is the case usually in the real world, there may be a difference between maximizing profits and maximizing share values.

We may define uncertainty as the condition in which the expected results of a decision have more than one value. We can distinguish risk from uncertainty, and define it as the condition in which the possible results of a decision can be described in the form of a probability distribution.

Consider the following possible results from investing in project A:

Possible profits ($)	Probability for project A
−2	.05
−1	.10
0	.15
1	.20
2	.25
3	.20
4	.05

The table shows that there is a 5% probability that the firm loses $2 if it invests in project A, a 10% probability of losing $1, and so on. The *expected value* is the mean of the possibilities weighted by their probabilities. For this investment, the expected value is $1.30. The risk of the investment measures the spread of possible outcomes around the expected value, and statistically, is the standard deviation. The following equation defines the expected value:

$$\sum_{i=1}^{n} p_i q_i = S \qquad (1\text{-}1)$$

where p represents the probabilities, q represents the possible outcomes, and S is the mean or expected value. The measure of variation that describes the risk of the investment can be defined as follows:

$$\left[\sum_{i=1}^{n} p_i (q_i - S)^2 \right]^{0.5} = SD \quad \text{(standard deviation)} \qquad (1\text{-}2)$$

Table 1-1 shows the actual figures for project A.

To see how considerations of risk may result in different decisions than if profit maximization and certainty were the rule, consider investment B:

Possible profits ($)	Probability for investment B
−2	.1
−1	.1
0	.1
2	.2
3	.3
4	.1

Table 1-1. Calculations for Project A

(1) Possible profits ($)	(2) Probability	(3) (1) × (2)	(4) S − (1)	(5) (4)²	(6) (5) × (2)
−2	.05	−.1	3.30	10.89	.5445
−1	.10	−.1	2.30	5.29	.5290
0	.15	0	1.30	1.69	.2535
1	.20	.2	.30	.09	.0180
2	.25	.5	− .70	.49	.1225
3	.20	.6	−1.70	2.89	.5780
4	.05	.2	−2.70	7.29	.3645

Expected value = Σ column 3 = $1.30
Variance = Σ column 6 $2.41
Standard deviation (SD) = $\sqrt{\text{variance}}$ $1.56

The expected value for investment B is $1.50 and its standard deviation, or measure of risk, is $1.86. Comparing the two investments, we have the following summary statistics:

	Investment A	Investment B
Expected value	$1.30	1.50
Risk (=SD)	1.50	1.86

If the firm were maximizing profits, it would clearly choose investment B because it has the higher expected value.

To see the effects of risk on value, assume that the return from each of the investments is received at the end of one year. However, because of the difference in risk, shareholders want a return of 10% from investment A and 30% from the riskier investment B. The effect of the required yield on value today, or present value (V), can be derived if:

$$(1 + i)V = S \tag{1-3a}$$

$$V = S\left[\frac{1}{1 + i}\right], \tag{1-3b}$$

where i = required rate of return. From (1-3b), the present value of investment A is V = $1.30 [1/1.1] = $1.18. The value of investment B is V = $1.50 [1/1.3] = $1.15. So, even though B generates a larger annual profit, the firm would maximize share value by choosing the lower annual return of the safer investment A because of the shareholders' attitudes toward risk. Note that the riskier investment is not always less desirable than the safer investment. For example, if investors required only a 12% return from investment B, its expected value would be $1.34. Hence, management must assess shareholders' attitudes toward risk in making investments for the firm. Clearly, the existence of risk considerably complicates the determination of rules for proper financial management.

Public Sector Decisions

Developing concepts of financial goals for governments and public institutions is even more complex than it is for households and business firms. Perhaps the simplest case is one of a dictatorship.

Presumably, the decisions made by the government of an absolute dictator are determined by the utility function of the dictator. There is some limit, determined by the judgment of the dictator, at which the citizenry rebels and overthrows the government.

In a democracy, the goals of government are less clear. If the absolute values of utility were known for each citizen, measuring the degree of satisfaction derived from a decision would simply involve adding up the numerical values of satisfaction for each citizen. However, no satisfactory way has been devised for measuring the absolute or cardinal values of utility for different individuals.

Hence, the decision-making goals in a democracy are subject to a political process. When a government makes financial decisions it considers the gains of those who benefit from the decision against those who have to pay taxes. The government makes comparisons in terms of political strength that is mobilized.

Some governments have developed cost-effectiveness techniques, which compare the benefits with the costs of particular projects, and select projects that generate the largest differences or net gains. This method provides an economic rationale for decisions, but critics of this approach argue that projects are needed for social welfare, whether or not the dollar equivalents make them desirable. Although political factors often determine complicated public sector decisions, one can nonetheless develop economically rational methods for analyzing the profitability of a public sector investment, even though the actual decisions may be determined by noneconomic factors. When we discuss the public sector in this text, we will assume economic rationality.

Review Questions

1-1   It can be argued that profit maximization for the firm and wealth maximization for the owners are equivalent objectives. Discuss. What are the assumptions in your argument?

1-2   Under what market circumstances might wealth maximization not be an operational decision criteria? Explain how the opportunity cost could be relevant in such circumstances.

1-3 Two projects require identical levels of investment and have the same life expectancy. The first project generates a profit stream having a greater present value than the second project. Should the first project necessarily be preferred? Discuss.

1-4 Describe examples of instances in which the directions taken by management may conflict with the shareholders' objectives.

1-5 What issues arise when management sets out to maximize shareholders' wealth?

Problems

1-6 A project is anticipated to generate one of the following equally likely levels of profit: $100, $200, $300, and $400. What is the expected profit? What is the variance of profit?

1-7 The possible levels of cash flow for a firm are described below:

Probability	Cash flows ($)
.2	1000
.3	2000
.3	4000
.2	5000

Determine the expected level of cash flow and standard deviation of cash flow for the firm.

1-8 Project A has an expected value of $40,000 with a risk (measured by standard deviation) of $20,000, whereas project B has an expected value of $50,000 with a risk of $30,000. Which project would you select? Discuss.

Glossary

Capital goods	Plant and equipment, machinery, etc.
Cardinal value	The absolute value.
Cost of capital	The rate of return that will leave the owner's wealth position unchanged.
Credit conditions	The conditions that face a firm interested in borrowing. For example, the cost of borrowing in terms of interest rates, and the willingness and ability of lenders to give loans generally.
Dividend	A payment to the owners of a corporation, normally in cash, but sometimes in shares.
Expected value	The mean (or average) possible future outcome deter-

	mined by weighting each possible outcome by the probability of its occurrence.
Legal entity	An entity recognized by the law and thus granted the rights and privileges of an individual (where that makes sense).
Liquid assets	Assets that may be readily exchanged for cash at their equilibrium (true) value. In fact, assets may be ranked in order of liquidity. For example, cash is the most liquid asset, while accounts receivable are less so, and inventory still less so.
Liquidity	Refers to a firm's cash position and its ability to meet maturing obligations.
Long-term debt	Obligations that take longer than five years to mature.
Losses	Less than the normal profit earned by the firm generating losses.
Marginal revenue	The contribution to total revenue of the last unit sold (where the last unit is the particular item under consideration).
Net worth	The capital and surplus of a firm—capital stock, capital surplus (paid-in capital), earned surplus (retained earnings), and occasionally certain reserves. For some purposes, preferred stock is included.
Normal return	The return producers require to remain in the industry; the accounting profit necessary to compensate producers for remaining in the industry.
Present value	The value of all future payments discounted at the yield required by shareholders.
Product differentiation	Differences between products sufficient that they cannot be called the same, although they may be very similar.
Profit	For accounting purposes, any excess of revenue over costs. In economics, profits are net of the normal rate of profit or return. Thus, a firm may earn an economic profit of zero and still have positive accounting profits.
Proxy statement	A document that permits a substitute for the owner of corporate stock to exercise the owner's rights, particularly the right to vote for directors.
Public organization	A government department, agency, division, or firm.
Refinance	To sell new debt to replace an existing issue.

Required yield	The return shareholders demand to compensate them for holding the stock; the yield that shareholders expect to receive on their stock.
Return on capital	The yield on the money invested in the firm by the owners (including profits retained and reinvested).
Risk	The probability that actual future returns will differ from expected returns. It is often measured by the standard deviation of returns.
Roll over	To replace, refund. See *refinance*.
Short-term debt	Obligations that mature within a year.
Standard deviation	A statistical term that measures the variability of a set of observations from the mean of the distribution.

$$\text{SD} = \left[\sum_{i=1}^{n} p_i (q_i - S)^2 \right]^{0.5}$$

where s = mean or expected value
q_i = possible outcomes
p_i = probability of each outcome

Stock	A share of ownership in a corporation.
Takeover bid	A proposal to management to obtain control of the company for a price above the market value of the company's shares.
Technical insolvency	The inability to pay currently maturing obligations.
Uncertainty	The condition under which the expected results of a decision have more than one value.
Utility	A measure of "satisfaction." Where satisfaction does not necessarily imply liking or happiness. (Thus a vaccination can be painful yet have utility because of the protection it provides.)
Utility function	The relationship between different amounts of some item (such as wealth) and the satisfaction it provides. A utility function is a summary statement of an individual's ranking of preferences with regard to the item in question.
Variance	The standard deviation squared.
Voting rights	The ability of the owners of a corporation to elect the directors of their company.
Yield	A rate of return.

Bibliography

ANTHONY, R. N., "The Trouble with Profit Maximization," *Harvard Business Review 38* (Nov./Dec. 1960), 126–134.

AUSTIN, D. V., "A Defense of the Corporation Pirate," *Business Horizons* (Winter 1964), 51–58.

BRANCH, BEN, "Corporate Objectives and Market Performance," *Financial Management 2* (Summer 1973), 24–29.

COASE, R. H., "The Nature of the Firm," *Economica 4* (Nov. 1937), 386–405.

COLE, A., *Business Enterprise in its Social Setting,* Cambridge: Harvard University Press, 1959.

DEALESSI, LOUIS, "Private Property and Dispersion of Ownership in Large Corporations," *Journal of Finance 28* (Sept. 1973), 839–851.

DONALDSON, G., "Financial Goals: Management vs. Stockholders," *Harvard Business Review 41* (May–June 1963), 429–451.

DUVALL, R. M., and D. V. AUSTIN, "Predicting the Results of Proxy Contests," *Journal of Finance 20* (Sept. 1965), 464–471.

ELLIOTT, J. W., "Control, Size, Growth, and Financial Performance in the Firm," *Journal of Financial and Quantitative Analysis 7* (Jan. 1972), 1309–1320.

GASKILL, WILLIAM J., "What's Ahead for Corporations in Social Responsibility?" *Financial Executive 39* (July 1971), 10–18.

GRABOWSKI, HENRY G., and DENNIS C. MUELLER, "Managerial and Stockholder Welfare Models of Firm Expenditures," *Review of Economics and Statistics 54* (Feb. 1972), 9–24.

HARTMANN, H., "Managers and Entrepreneurs: A Useful Distinction?" *Administrative Science Quarterly 3* (March 1959), 429–451.

KAMERSCHEN, D. R., "The Influence of Ownership and Control on Profit Rates," *American Economic Review 58* (June 1968), 432–447.

KERR, J. H., JR., and J. S. LETTS, "Appraisal Procedures for Dissenting Delaware Stockholders," *Business Lawyer 20* (July 1965), 1083–1097.

LEWELLEN, W. G., "Management and Ownership in the Large Firm," *Journal of Finance 24* (May 1969), 299–322.

MARSH, H., JR., "Are Directors Trustees?" *Business Lawyer 22* (Nov. 1966), 35–92.

MOAG, J. S., W. T. CARLETON, and E. M. LERNER, "Defining the Finance Function: A Model–Systems Approach," *Journal of Finance 22* (Dec. 1967), 543–555.

SIMON, H. A., "Theories of Decision-Making in Economics," *American Economic Review 49* (June 1959), 253–283.

"The Issues in Social Responsibility," *Financial Analysts Journal 27* (Sept./Oct. 1971), 26–34.

TRIVILI, GEORGE W., "Evaluation of Pollution Control Expenditures by Leading Corporations," *Financial Management 2* (Winter 1973), 19–24.

WESTON, J. FRED, "New Themes in Finance," *Journal of Finance 24* (March 1974), 237–243.

An Introduction to Real and Financial Yields

II

The Yield on Real Assets: An Introduction to Capital Budgeting

2

Organizations commonly have to choose among several alternative uses of a limited quantity of funds. Obviously, if funds were unlimited, they would not have to choose. Common sense suggests that they should prefer projects that provide the maximum gain.

Private organizations that have to choose among projects should prefer those that provide the largest difference between returns and costs, that is, the largest profit. Analogously, nonprofit organizations should prefer projects that provide the largest difference between benefits and costs. Even when projects are not being explicitly compared, an organization should undertake only projects whose returns equal or exceed their costs.

When the criterion is maximizing profit, or maximizing the difference between benefits and costs in the case of the public organization, it is difficult to evaluate projects whose useful lives are expected to extend over more than one period. How can a hospital finance committee compare the construction of a new wing with an improvement of kitchen facilities, if the construction of the new wing will involve cash outlays for the next three years and will not show any benefits until four years later, whereas the improvement in kitchen facilities might involve almost immediate benefits? A firm faces a similar problem when it has limited funds and it must choose between upgrading its machinery to achieve almost immediate savings and plowing funds into a research and development project that is not expected to generate benefits for many years in the future.

This problem has been of concern to the field of finance for many years. A number of methods of evaluation have been devised that appear to permit comparisons such as the difficult ones that we have described.

In this chapter, we shall review the applications and limitations of most of the important criteria for selecting projects.

The Average or Bookkeeping Rate of Return

The average return attempts to cut through the problems of comparing projects that have very different time distributions of costs and benefits. This method involves averaging the net benefits of the project, on the one hand, and the average invested cost on the other, and then taking the ratio of the two. If C = the original cost, S_1 = the first year's return, S_2, the second year's return, and so on, and N is the life of the investment, then the average rate of return is

$$r_a = \frac{\Sigma S/N - C/N}{C/2} \tag{2-1}$$

For example, say that project 1 returns \$100 annually for five years and costs \$300 at the beginning of the first year. In this case, the dollar returns for each year are the same, so averaging is not necessary, that is, the average annual return of project 1 is \$500/5 = \$100 per annum. Since this annual return is gross, we must subtract the annual estimate of depreciation; that is, we must subtract a portion of the original investment for each year that the project is expected to be useful. Hence, we must reduce the annual cash inflow of \$100 by \$60 (\$300/5). If we assume straight line depreciation, each year's depreciation is a constant that is equal to the original cost, less estimated salvage value, divided by the project's expected useful life.

On this basis, over the life of the investment, the firm has invested, on average, less than the original cost of \$300. For the first half of the life (2.5) the firm has more than \$150 invested, and for the second half the firm has less than \$150 invested. On average, the investment is half the original cost. Figure 2-1 shows this graphically, where C is the cost of the investment and N is the number of years of useful life of the investment. Hence the average return or bookkeeping return in this case is

$$\frac{500/5 - 300/5}{300/2} = \frac{40}{150} = 27\%$$

Now we can compare project 1 with project 2, which costs \$240 and is expected to return \$100 annually for four years. The average return on project 2 is

$$\frac{400/4 - 240/4}{240/2} = \frac{40}{120} = 33\tfrac{1}{3}\%.$$

Since project 2 has an advantage of above six percentage points over project 1, it appears to be desirable.

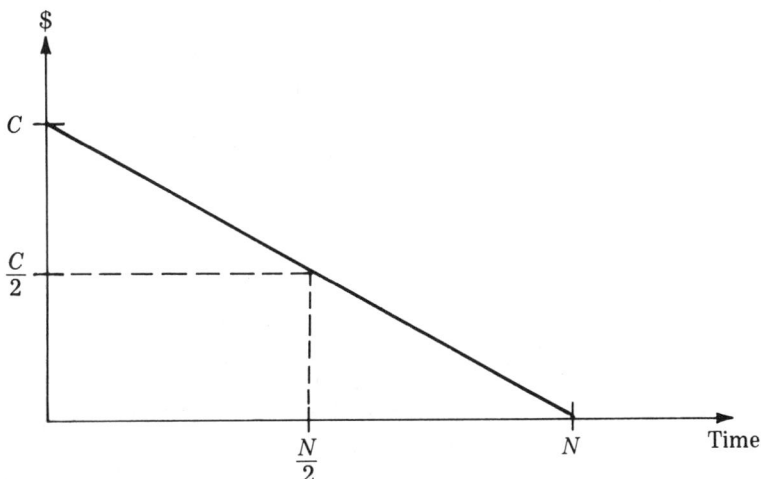

Figure 2-1
Diminution of Investment over Time

How Significant Is This Ratio?

Actually, the average return generates results of dubious significance. The two investment proposals have different lives, and the longer-lived proposal costs $60 more than the other, but generates an additional cash inflow of $100 in the fifth year. The question that is not answered by the average return is: Is it worth spending $20 more today in order to receive $100 in five years?

We can view the five-year proposal, proposal 1, as two investments. The first is essentially investment project 2 costing $240 and generating $100 a year gross, or $40 net of depreciation, for four years. The second project is the $60 incremental cost of project 1 over project 2, compared to the incremental benefits of project 1 over project 2, that is, $100 in the fifth year. One way to compare these projects is the following:

1. Estimate the organization's normal or minimally acceptable rate of return on cost of capital.[1]
2. Using that rate, calculate the amount that would have to be invested to yield the extra $100 gross in the fifth year.

The amount that would have to be invested at the normal rate of return to yield $100 in the fifth year is the *present value* of the $100. If the present value is less than $60, which is the extra amount that would be invested if project 1 were undertaken, the organization would be better off taking the four-year project and investing the $60 saved in normal investment opportunities, since the saved funds could generate more than

---

[1]This rate of return is called the cost of capital. We will discuss it in greater detail later. For now, we define it as the smallest rate that can be earned and leave the owners' wealth unchanged.

$100 in five years. On the other hand, if the firm's normal rate of return is so low that the present value of $100 in five years exceeds $60, the firm would be better off investing the $60 in project 1 and receiving the additional $100 at the end of five years.

Hence, an important inadequacy in the average rate of return, and a necessary component of any method of comparing projects with different lives and different distributions of returns and costs, is the firm's normal rate of return.

Calculating Present Value

If the firm's normal rate of return is 6% per year, how much would the firm have to invest at the normal rate of return to earn $100 in the fifth year? The return received in the fifth year includes the original amount invested, plus compound interest on the amount invested. If i is the normal rate of return, and V is the present value, the $100 received in the fifth year must equal:

V	Original investment
$+iV + i(iV) + i[i(iV)]$	
$+i[i(i)(iV)] + i[i(i)(i)(iV)]$	Compound interest for year 1
$+iV + i(iV) + i[i(iV)]$	(2-2a)
$+i[i(i)(iV)]$	Compound interest for year 2
$+iV + i(iV) + i[i(iV)]$	Compound interest for year 3
$+ iV + i(iV)$	Compound interest for year 4
$+iV$	Interest for year 5

Using the symbol S for the $100 in the fifth year and accumulating and simplifying the terms above, we have

$$S = V + 5(iV) + 4(i^2V) + 3(i^3V) + 2(i^4V) + i^5V \qquad (2\text{-}2b)$$

$$S = V(1 + i)^5 \qquad (2\text{-}2c)$$

To obtain the present value, we can revise equation (2–2c) so that

$$V = S[1/(1 + i)^5] \qquad (2\text{-}3)$$

We can solve equation (2-3) easily using logarithms. However, it is simpler to use a table of values of $1/(1 + i)^n$, such as Table A.

The column heads of Table A show interest rates, and the row heads show the number of years. For example, the value of $1/(1 + i)^7$ when i equals 8% is 0.583. In our example, the value of $S = \$100$, $n = 5$ years, and $i = 6\%$. We solve equation (2-3) for these values as follows:

$$V = \$100 \, \frac{1}{(1.06)^5}$$

or, using Table A,

$$V = \$100 \ (0.747) = \$74.70$$

At the normal rate of return, the firm would have to invest $74.70 in order to receive $100 in five years. However, with project 1, the firm can earn $100 in year 5 by investing only $60. Hence, project 1 is more profitable than project 2.

Note that the decision depends on the normal rate of return. With a 12% rate of return, the present value of $100 in five years is only $56.70 = $100 (0.567), and the firm would do better by undertaking project 2 and investing the $60 saving at 12%. The effect of different normal rates on the present value of $100 to be received in five years is shown in Figure 2-2.

From this example, we can formulate a general decision rule. Let C denote the actual cost of gaining a future return (in this case, the actual cost is $60). Then

Present value of $100 in 5 years

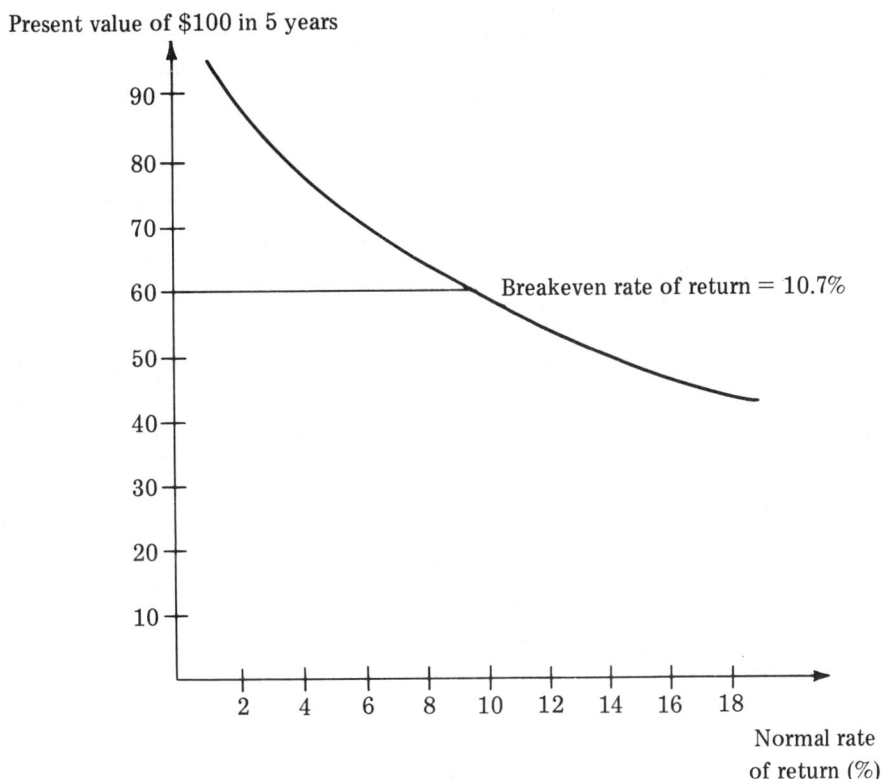

Breakeven rate of return = 10.7%

Normal rate of return (%)

Figure 2-2
Impact of Rate of Return on Present Value

The Yield on Real Assets: An Introduction to Capital Budgeting

$$C \leq V, \quad \text{undertake the investment}$$
$$C > V, \quad \text{reject the investment.}$$

Comparing the total present values at a 6% rate of return to the total costs of projects 1 and 2, we have for project 1,

$$V = \$100\left[\frac{1}{1.06}\right] + \$100\left[\frac{1}{(1.06)^2}\right]$$
$$+ \$100\left[\frac{1}{(1.06)^3}\right] + \$100\left[\frac{1}{(1.06)^4}\right] + \$100\left[\frac{1}{(1.06)^5}\right]$$

Although we could use Table A to calculate the present value for each of the years, we can use the fact that the annual receipts are identical for each year to factor the expression and simplify the calculations. Factoring and summing gives the expression

$$V = S \sum_{t=1}^{n} \frac{1}{(1 + i)^t} \tag{2-4}$$

Table B provides the summations for a variety of interest rates and for different years. Substituting numbers from project 1 into equation (2-4), we get

$$V = \$100 \sum_{i=1}^{5} \frac{1}{(1.06)^t}$$

Table B shows that the discount factor summed, that is, $\sum_{t=1}^{5} 1/(1.06)^t$ is 4.212. Hence,

$$V = \$100(4.212) = \$421.20$$

Using our decision rule, we have $V \geq C$, that is, $\$421.20 > \$300$. For project 2, the present value is

$$V = \$100 \sum_{t=1}^{4} \frac{1}{(1.06)^t}$$

or, using Table B,

$$V = \$100(3.465) = \$346.50$$

Once again, $V \geq C$, that is, $\$346.50 > \$240$, so project 2 also meets the decision rule. Thus, both investments should be undertaken if possible. However, they may be mutually exclusive alternatives. They may,

Table A. Present Value of $1 to Be Received at the End of N Years.

Discount Rate

N Years	2%	4%	6%	8%	10%	12%	14%	16%	18%	20%	22%	24%	26%	28%	30%
1	.980	.962	.943	.926	.909	.893	.877	.862	.847	.833	.820	.806	.794	.781	.769
2	.961	.925	.890	.857	.826	.797	.769	.743	.718	.694	.672	.650	.630	.610	.592
3	.942	.889	.840	.794	.751	.712	.675	.641	.609	.579	.551	.524	.500	.477	.455
4	.924	.855	.792	.735	.683	.636	.592	.552	.516	.482	.451	.423	.397	.373	.350
5	.906	.822	.747	.681	.621	.567	.519	.476	.437	.402	.370	.341	.315	.291	.269
6	.888	.790	.705	.630	.564	.507	.456	.410	.370	.335	.303	.275	.250	.227	.207
7	.871	.760	.665	.583	.513	.452	.400	.354	.314	.279	.249	.222	.198	.178	.159
8	.853	.731	.627	.540	.467	.404	.351	.305	.266	.233	.204	.179	.157	.139	.123
9	.837	.703	.592	.500	.424	.361	.308	.263	.225	.194	.167	.144	.125	.108	.094
10	.820	.676	.558	.463	.386	.322	.270	.227	.191	.162	.137	.116	.099	.085	.073
11	.804	.650	.527	.429	.350	.287	.237	.195	.162	.135	.112	.094	.079	.066	.056
12	.789	.625	.497	.397	.319	.257	.208	.168	.137	.112	.092	.076	.062	.052	.043
13	.773	.601	.469	.368	.290	.229	.182	.145	.116	.093	.075	.061	.050	.040	.033
14	.758	.577	.442	.340	.263	.205	.160	.125	.099	.078	.062	.049	.039	.032	.025
15	.743	.555	.417	.315	.239	.183	.140	.108	.084	.065	.051	.040	.031	.025	.020
16	.728	.534	.394	.292	.218	.163	.123	.093	.071	.054	.042	.032	.025	.019	.015
17	.714	.513	.371	.270	.198	.146	.108	.080	.060	.045	.034	.026	.020	.015	.012
18	.700	.494	.350	.250	.180	.130	.095	.069	.051	.038	.028	.021	.016	.012	.009
19	.686	.475	.331	.232	.164	.116	.083	.060	.043	.031	.023	.017	.012	.009	.007
20	.673	.456	.312	.215	.149	.104	.073	.051	.037	.026	.019	.014	.010	.007	.005
21	.660	.439	.294	.199	.135	.093	.064	.044	.031	.022	.015	.011	.008	.006	.004
22	.647	.422	.278	.184	.123	.083	.056	.038	.026	.018	.013	.009	.006	.004	.003
23	.634	.406	.262	.170	.112	.074	.049	.033	.022	.015	.010	.007	.005	.003	.002
24	.622	.390	.247	.158	.102	.066	.043	.028	.019	.013	.008	.006	.004	.003	.002
25	.610	.375	.233	.146	.092	.059	.038	.024	.016	.010	.007	.005	.003	.002	.001

Table B. Present Value of $1 to Be Received at the End of Each Year for N Years.

Discount Rate

N Years	2%	4%	6%	8%	10%	12%	14%	16%	18%	20%	22%	24%	26%	28%	30%
1	.980	.962	.943	.926	.909	.893	.877	.862	.847	.833	.820	.806	.794	.781	.769
2	1.942	1.886	1.833	1.783	1.736	1.690	1.647	1.605	1.566	1.528	1.492	1.457	1.424	1.392	1.361
3	2.884	2.775	2.673	2.577	2.487	2.402	2.322	2.246	2.174	2.106	2.042	1.981	1.923	1.868	1.816
4	3.808	3.630	3.465	3.312	3.170	3.037	2.914	2.798	2.690	2.589	2.494	2.404	2.320	2.241	2.166
5	4.713	4.452	4.212	3.993	3.791	3.605	3.433	3.274	3.127	2.991	2.864	2.745	2.635	2.532	2.436
6	5.601	5.242	4.917	4.623	4.355	4.111	3.889	3.685	3.498	3.326	3.167	3.020	2.885	2.759	2.643
7	6.472	6.002	5.582	5.206	4.868	4.564	4.288	4.039	3.812	3.605	3.416	3.242	3.083	2.937	2.802
8	7.326	6.733	6.210	5.747	5.335	4.968	4.639	4.344	4.078	3.837	3.619	3.421	3.241	3.076	2.925
9	8.162	7.435	6.802	6.247	5.759	5.328	4.946	4.607	4.303	4.031	38.76	3.566	3.366	3.184	3.019
10	8.983	8.111	7.360	6.710	6.145	5.650	5.216	4.833	4.494	4.192	3.923	3.682	3.465	3.269	3.092
11	9.787	8.760	7.887	7.139	6.495	5.938	5.453	5.029	4.656	4.327	4.035	3.776	3.544	3.335	3.147
12	10.575	9.385	8.384	7.536	6.814	6.194	5.660	5.197	4.793	4.439	4.127	3.851	3.606	3.387	3.190
13	11.348	9.986	8.853	7.904	7.103	6.424	5.842	5.342	4.910	4.533	4.203	3.912	3.656	3.427	3.223
14	12.106	10.563	9.295	8.244	7.367	6.628	6.002	5.468	5.008	4.611	4.265	3.962	3.695	3.459	3.249
15	12.849	11.118	9.712	8.560	7.606	6.811	6.142	5.575	5.092	4.675	4.315	4.001	3.726	3.483	3.268
16	13.578	11.652	10.106	8.851	7.824	6.974	6.265	5.669	5.162	4.730	4.357	4.033	3.751	3.503	3.283
17	14.292	12.166	10.477	9.122	8.022	7.120	6.373	5.749	5.222	4.775	4.391	4.059	3.771	3.518	3.295
18	14.992	12.659	10.828	9.372	8.201	7.250	6.467	5.818	5.273	4.812	4.419	4.080	3.786	3.529	3.304
19	15.679	13.134	11.158	9.604	8.365	7.366	6.550	5.877	5.316	4.843	4.442	4.097	3.799	3.539	3.311
20	16.352	13.590	11.470	9.818	8.514	7.469	6.623	5.929	5.353	4.870	4.460	4.110	3.808	3.546	3.316
21	17.011	14.029	11.764	10.017	8.649	7.562	6.687	5.973	5.384	4.891	4.476	4.121	3.816	3.551	3.320
22	17.658	14.451	12.042	10.201	8.772	7.645	6.743	6.011	5.410	4.909	4.488	4.130	3.822	3.556	3.323
23	18.292	14.857	12.303	10.371	8.883	7.718	6.792	6.044	5.432	4.925	4.499	4.137	3.827	3.559	3.325
24	18.914	15.247	12.550	10.529	8.985	7.784	6.835	6.073	5.451	4.937	4.507	4.143	3.831	3.562	3.327
25	19.524	15.622	12.783	10.675	9.077	7.843	6.873	6.097	5.467	4.948	4.514	4.147	3.834	3.564	3.329

for example, be two different ways of using the same factory space so that if one of the projects is undertaken, the second cannot. In that event, we must consider the differences between V and C, usually called net present value (NPV). For project 1,

$$NPV = V - C = \$421.20 - \$300 = \$121.20$$

For project 2,

$$NPV = \$346.50 - \$240 = \$106.50$$

Since $\$121.20 > \$106.50$, project 1 should be undertaken. This is the same result that was generated by considering the marginal returns and costs of projects 1 and 2.

If the normal rate of return were 12%, the NPV for each project would be

$$\$360.50 - \$300 = \$60.50, \quad \text{for project 1}$$
$$\$303.70 - \$240 = \$63.50, \quad \text{for project 2.}$$

Again, both projects are both profitable, but if they are mutually exclusive, project 2 is preferable to project 1 when the normal rate of return is 12%.

The Timing of Returns

Even when investment proposals have the same life, the distribution of returns may be different. This difference may not be reflected in the average rate of return, but it does show up in the present value. Consider the following examples:

	Project A	Project B
S_1	$100	$ 50
S_2	50	100
C	100	100

$$\text{Average rate of return on } A = \frac{(100 + 50)/2 - 100/2}{100/2} = 50\%$$

$$\text{Average rate of return on } B = \frac{(50 + 100)/2 - 100/2}{100/2} = 50\%$$

Assuming that the cost of capital is 10%, we have $NPV_A = \$32.20$ and $NPV_B = \$28.05$.

Some Basic Principles of Decision Making

The criticisms of the average return method of evaluating investment proposals and the development of the concept of present value generate two useful notions.

1. A bird in the hand *may* be worth two in the brush, since the values of returns depend in part on their distribution over time. Earlier returns are more valuable than equivalent amounts of late returns. Clearly, a bird in the hand is worth more than *at least one* in the brush.
2. The desirability of any future benefit depends on the price of the benefit and on the alternative yields that are available. A good criterion of investment alternatives embodies these ideas.

The Payback Period

The average rate of return does not have any of the qualities of a good device for evaluating investment proposals. It embodies neither of these two principles. The payback period is a substantial improvement over the average return method, although it does not embody both these principles.

The payback period is simply the ratio of the cost of an investment to its annual return. The ratio indicates the number of years it will take before the original cost is recovered. Therefore, the annual return is defined as gross of annual depreciation charges.

To see how payback works, consider the examples in the discussion of the average rate of return.

Project 1:

S = \$100   for 5 years,
C = \$300   where S is the annual cash flow gross of depreciation.

Project 2:

S = \$100 for 4 years
C = \$240

The payback period for project 1 is $300/100 = 3$ years, and for project 2 it is $240/100 = 2.4$ years.

If the investment proposals produce uneven annual cash flows, the payback period can be determined by summing the cash flows from the earliest on, until the sum of the cash flows equals the original cost.

Although the payback period considers the time distribution of returns and the cost of the benefits, it does not consider either returns that follow the payback period or the alternative rate of return available to the organization. It favors the shorter project simply because it has a shorter payback period.

As in the example of average rate of return, the shorter-lived investment is preferable only if the average rate of return available to the organization is 10.7% or more. Otherwise, despite its longer payback period, the five-year project is better.

Nonetheless, the payback period is often used, usually in conjunction with other methods of evaluating proposals. Its primary advantages are its simplicity and ease of calculation. It may also appeal to decision makers who are operating under conditions of extreme uncertainty and risk and are concerned with rapid recovery of capital.

The Internal Rate of Return

Although present value has all the features that make a criterion of investment merit desirable, it has one weakness. It lacks intuitive appeal to practical people. Business managers and public administrators are accustomed to thinking of rates of return. For this reason, they sometimes use a related measure to evaluate investment proposals, the *internal rate of return*. We may define it as the yield that sets the present value of a stream of future flows equal to its cost. Using the terminology developed before, we define it as the value of i that sets $V = C$. To distinguish the internal rate of return from any other interest rate, we'll let r stand for internal rate of return.

The internal rate of return can be found as follows:

$$C = \sum_{t=1}^{n} S \frac{1}{(1 + r)^t}$$

Since C, S, and n are known, the goal is to solve for r.

$$C/S = \sum_{t=1}^{n} \frac{1}{(1 + r)^t}$$

The right-hand terms are found in Table B. The left-hand term is the payback period. Hence, by looking in the appropriate n row for the discount factor equal to the payback period, one can determine r. We can find the internal rate of return for an investment costing $300 and paying $100 annually for five years by solving the following equation for r:

$$C/S = \frac{300}{100} = 3 = \sum_{t=1}^{5} \frac{1}{(1 + r)^t}$$

To determine the rate of return for a payback period of 3, we turn to Table B and look along the five-year row. The summation in the 18% column for five years is 3.127. It is 2.991 in the 20% column. Hence, the internal rate of return for project 1 is between 18% and 20%, or approximately 19%. We could determine the rate more accurately by interpolation, but projected future returns often have sufficient forecasting errors that a very precise estimate of the internal rate of return is unrealistic.

Having calculated the internal rate of return, how can we use it to evaluate an investment? The decision rule with internal rate of return is that if $r > i$, accept the proposal. If the internal rate of return is less than a minimally acceptable yield, reject the proposal. For example, if the organization considering the example proposal wanted at least a 25% return, it should reject Project 1. On the other hand, if they normally achieved a 10% rate of return, they should accept the project.

Measuring the internal rate of return when future flows are not equal is a little more complicated. Consider a proposal in which S_1 equals $75 and S_2 equals $50, while the cost of the investment (C) is $100. To determine the internal rate of return, we can use an iterative approach, which is simply a trial-and-error search for the appropriate rate of return. If a rate turns out to be too low, we try a higher rate of return. By interpolation, we can reach the internal rate of return fairly rapidly. In the example, we try

$$r = 20\%$$

$$C = S_1 \times \frac{1}{1 + r} + S_2 \times \frac{1}{(1 + r)^2}$$

Using Table A, we find

$$V_{20\%} = 75(0.833) + 50(0.694) = \$97.18 \quad \text{and} \quad NPV_{20\%} = -2.82$$

Since $r < 20\%$, we try 10%.

$$V_{10\%} = 75(0.909) + 50(0.826) = 109.48 \quad \text{and} \quad NPV_{10\%} = 9.48$$

So $r > 10\% < 20\%$. Thus to find r, we interpolate.

$$10\% + \frac{109.48 - 100}{109.48 - 97.18} (20\% - 10\%) = 10\% + \frac{9.48}{12.30} (10\%)$$

$$= 10\% + (0.77)10\%$$

$$= 17.7\%$$

Now to check, we try 18%.

$$(0.847)(\$75) + (0.718)(\$50) = \$99.425 \cong \$100$$

$$\text{and} \quad NPV_{18\%} \cong 0,$$

Thus $18\% \simeq r$, and further interpolation could lead to a more precise estimate.

Limits to the Internal Rate of Return

The internal rate of return has intuitive appeal because it seems to be a profit rate. It has the desirable characteristics for an investment criterion that we discussed earlier, that is, it considers the timing and distribution of future flows, the costs of alternatives, and the required rate of return. Nonetheless, the internal rate of return, too, has some flaws that limit its usefulness.

One of these flaws is that an investment proposal may sometimes have more than one internal rate of return. Mathematically, the internal rate of return is the root of the investment equation, and any equation may have more than one root. If so, we cannot find a unique internal rate of return.

Consider the following investment proposal:

$$C = \$60, \quad S_1 = \$110, \quad S_2 = \$20, \quad S_3 = \$10, \quad S_4 = \$-90$$

The negative flow in the fourth year could be considered unavoidable. For example, it might be the cost of restoring land surface after completing a strip-mining operation. In any event, calculating the internal rate of return for this equation yields at least two rates of return.

At 7%:

$$60 = 0.935(110) + 0.873(20) + 0.816(10) + 0.763(-90).$$

At 81%:

$$60 = 0.552(110) + 0.305(20) + 0.169(10) + 0.093(-90).$$

Another problem with the internal rate of return occurs with mutually exclusive investment alternatives. Using the internal rate of return, one would choose the alternative with the highest rate of return. However, that alternative may not generate the largest flow of benefits or profits. If one alternative generates 25% on $1000 of cost and another generates 100% on $5, using the internal rate of return as the criterion would lead us to choose the second, even though it seems clear that the first is preferable despite the second's higher internal rate of return.

The Benefit-Cost Ratio

In capital budgeting decisions, public sector administrators often use the benefit-cost ratio as a criterion of investment worthiness. The same measure in the private sector is called the profitability index. We can define the ratio (hereafter PI) as

$$PI = V/C = 1.$$

This is the same as $NPV = 0$, so normally, we should expect the same results whether we analyze projects in terms of net present value or the profitability index.

As with the internal rate of return, the exception to this occurs with mutually exclusive alternatives. For example, consider the following:

$$V_a = \$1,000,000 \qquad V_b = \$2,000,000$$
$$C_a = \$500,000 \qquad C_b = \$1,000,000$$
$$PI_a = 2 \qquad PI_b = 2$$
$$NPV_a = \$500,000 \qquad NPV_b = \$1,000,000$$

Although the profitability indexes are identical for the two projects, project b generates twice the wealth of project a. Since we have assumed that maximizing wealth is our objective, we should prefer project b even though the profitability indexes are identical. It would not be difficult to find an example in which project b has a lower PI and still has a substantially larger NPV.

Though net present value is as good as or better than the benefit–cost ratio, there are decisions in which the benefit–cost ratio may be a more sensible choice than NPV. Typically, it is better when there is some uncertainty about future events. Look at the following example.

$$V_c = \$1,000,000 \qquad V_d = \$5,000,000$$
$$C_c = \$800,000 \qquad C_d = \$4,700,000$$
$$PI_c = 1.25 \qquad PI_d = 1.06$$
$$NPV_c = \$200,000 \qquad NPV_d = \$300,000$$

NPV indicates that d is superior, although the PI indicates that c is better. If we were concerned only with maximizing wealth, we would choose d. Note, however, that to get the added \$100,000 in net present value from d, we'd have to invest \$3,900,000 more than we would with c. With uncertainty, it would be quite rational to prefer c, a project that has less at stake.

In general, net present value, that is, $V - C$, appears to be the best overall investment criterion. For purposes of presentation to decision makers, one may turn to other methods (such as the internal rate of return). However, if different decisions would be made under different investment criteria, the decision made under the net present value criterion is generally correct.

Benefits and Costs

Both in public and private projects, one of the more difficult tasks is measuring the benefits and costs of investments. Regardless of which criterion a firm uses, their decisions can be no better than the data on which they are based.

Costs should be defined to include all cash outflows that result from the investment. They should also include any reduction in resulting cash inflows. Costs should be deducted in the period in which the cash outflow or reduced inflow occurs, even if the deduction results in a negative net benefit for that period.

Many cost items are obvious, but not all. For example, a new, more productive machine may require a larger average investment in inventories. The added inventory is an investment cost and should be added to C. However, because the investment in inventory will be recaptured at the end of the project's life, even though the physical units are not the same, the inventory costs should be added to the cash inflow of the final year.

For example, suppose that a city is considering building a new zoo, and the roadways leading to the zoo have to be improved. The costs of improving the roads are properly assigned to the cost of the zoo if the only reason for improving the roads is to facilitate access to the zoo. However, if the roadways generally improve transit conditions, these benefits should be added.

On the other hand, there are items that may appear to be costs, but really are not. For example, if the added inventory in the previous example requires more floor space, it is appropriate to charge for this in the context of cost accounting. However, if the additional space has no alternative use, it is not a cost in the equation. The key is whether a cash flow is involved.

Many of the same cautions that apply to costs apply to benefits as well. Benefits must be true net additions to benefit flows. For example, building a canal may increase social benefits by increasing the flow of transport. The benefit is not the estimated value of shipping on the canal, but the expected value of shipping on the canal less the loss in value of shipping in an alternative means of transport, such as railroads.

In some instances, it may be difficult to estimate benefits using output figures such as sales. For example, suppose that a new machine requires less labor and materials for a given rate of output than an existing machine. We could calculate the costs and the benefits of the new machine on a differential basis. Then the cost of the new machine is its purchase cost less the value of any trade-in or alternative use of the old machine plus any costs in installing the new machine or removing the old machine. The benefits are the differences in after-tax cash flows due to changes in operating costs, including differences in depreciation. For example, if the depreciation on the old machine was $100 yearly and the new machine involves a depreciation charge of $175, the net benefit from depreciation is $75. The new machine should be adopted if the present value of these flows, after costs are deducted, is positive.

Capital Cost Allowances

Treatment of depreciation or capital cost allowances can be another problem for private firms. Depreciation is an allocation of original cost to taxable periods during the expected life of an investment. While depreciation is deductible for tax purposes, it is not a cash outflow. Still, since it reduces tax payments, it is appropriate to estimate the after-tax cash flow by adding depreciation back into after-tax income. For example, if the tax rate is 40%, earnings before depreciation and taxes are $1000, and depreciation is $200, we can estimate after-tax cash flow as follows:

Pretax and depreciation earnings	$1000
Less depreciation	200
Pretax income	$ 800
Taxes	320
After-tax income	480
Plus depreciation	200
After-tax cash flow (S)	$ 680

The significance of depreciation or capital cost allowances is not fully stated by considering only one year. The tax authorities can use capital cost allowances to stimulate or to discourage capital investments.[2] For example, consider an investment with an initial cost (C) of $1000 that will be recovered over the life of the investment. However, the capital cost allowances may be more or less valuable, depending on how rapidly the asset can be depreciated. Suppose that an asset has an expected life of five years, costs $1000, has estimated annual after-tax income of $480 annually, and is to be depreciated on a straight-line basis (where the annual depreciation is C/N). Then its annual cash flow is $680 annually for five years. At a normal return of 10%, the present value of the investment is $2577.88.

Suppose, however, that the tax authorities changed the regulations to permit a complete write-off of the investment in three years, with 40% of capital cost allowed in the first year and 30% for each of the next two years. If the tax rate is 40%, the annual cash flows are as follows:

[2]A similar effect can be achieved with an investment tax credit, whereby the firm can reduce its tax payable by some proportion of its capital expenditure.

	Years				
	1	2	3	4	5
Old after-tax income (Y)	$ 480	$ 480	$ 480	$ 480	$ 480
Before-tax income =					
$Y/(1 -$ tax rate)	800	800	800	800	800
+ Old depreciation =	200	200	200	200	200
Pretax and depreciation					
cash flow	1000	1000	1000	1000	1000
Less new depreciation	400	300	300	—	—
= New taxable income	600	700	700	1000	1000
Less tax	240	280	280	400	400
= New after-tax income	360	420	420	600	600
+ New depreciation	400	300	300	—	—
= New after-tax cash					
flow	760	720	720	600	600

At 10%, the present value of the new cash flows is $2608.60, an increase of $30.80 in present value. Clearly, a more liberal depreciation rate can make a difference in the acceptability of marginal projects.

In addition, note that the higher the normal rate of return, the larger the difference due to a higher depreciation rate. For example, at a 20% rate of return, the value of the old after-tax cash flows is $2033.88, and the value of the new after-tax cash flows is $2080.04. Although the present value of the cash flows under both depreciation systems is smaller with the higher rate of return, the difference between them is larger. At 20%, the more rapid rate of depreciation adds a present value of $46.16 to the investment value, larger than the $30.80 improvement at the 10% rate of return.

We shall return to certain aspects of capital budgeting later. Subsequent chapters will also treat the effects of inflation, the impact of risk, and the determinants of the normal rate of return of cost of capital.

Summary

Although a variety of means of evaluating investment projects exist, the net present value approach is generally superior. The internal rate of return is a measure that managers can perhaps identify with more readily, but it can also be misleading when alternatives are mutually exclusive (as is true also for the benefits–cost ratio). Moreover, some projects may not have unique internal rates of return.

As important as the method of evaluation is the selection of the data to be evaluated. The key is to allocate to the proper period the appropriate *cash* inflows or outflows. One should not be misled by arbitrary accounting allocations.

In this chapter, we have merely introduced the important topic of capital budgeting. We will cover other aspects of it later in this text.

Summary of Investment Valuation Measures

Name	Definition	Weaknesses
Average rate of return	Ratio of average annual cash flows less depreciation to average investment	Does not show that current dollars have different value from future dollars
Benefit–cost ratio	Ratio of present value of flows to project cash cost	In comparing mutually exclusive alternatives, will not necessarily pick alternative that maximizes share value
Internal rate of return	Rate that sets present value of cash flows equal to initial cash outlay	May give incorrect answer with mutually exclusive alternatives because it assumes cash outflows can be reinvested at internal rate. Also, a cash flow series may have more than one internal rate.
Net present value	Difference between present value of cash flows discounted at required rate of return, or cost of capital, and initial cash outlay	Generally useful
Payback period	Ratio of initial cash outlays to annual cash outflows until latter equals former.	Ignores cash inflows that occur after payback period.

Review Questions

2-1   As a consultant, what comments would you offer the management of a corporation that uses the average (bookkeeping) rate of return as the sole criterion for evaluating company projects?

2-2   Which project evaluation criteria implicitly assume that the rate of return can be earned on reinvested funds? How significant is this assumption?

2-3   Do any of the project evaluation criteria considered in this chapter explicitly allow for differences in risk among projects? How would you suggest handling risk?

2-4   When a firm compares two mutually exclusive projects of the same risk, how is the final selection influenced by the date (today or 10 years in the future) selected to evaluate cash flows?

2-5   How might the capital budgeting decision process be modified to allow for differences in risk between two mutually exclusive projects?

Problems

2-6   The Howe Company is considering a number of investments; however its capital budget is limited to $600.

a. Given the following information, which projects should they select?

Project	Expenditure ($)	NPV ($)
1	100	22
2	100	20
3	150	14
4	200	42
5	200	38
6	200	50

b. If we assume that Projects 4 and 6 are mutually exclusive, which projects should they select?

2-7   ABC Corporation is planning to get into the nursery business. They are considering two plans.

Plan 1: Build a modest greenhouse now and enlarge it later. The present construction cost is $300,000. The expected cost of the enlargement to be undertaken at the end of five years is $200,000. Maintenance during the first five years is expected to be $5000 per year (payable at the end of each year).

Plan 2: Build a large greenhouse now at a cost of $400,000. Maintenance is estimated at $8000 per year for the first five years.

The cost of capital for ABC is 10%. Ignore depreciation and tax effects. Which plan is most attractive to ABC?

2-8   The Federal Department of Agriculture is considering a proposal to dam the Moose River. Total federal construction costs for the dam are estimated at $55 million. The local government will have to spend another $9 million to reroute a freeway that currently passes near the dam site. Annual benefits from the project are expected to include power generated, worth $6 million, improved recreation, $600,000, improved navigation, $300,000, and flood control, worth $2,045,000. The project's share of departmental overhead is estimated at $50,000 per year. Elimination of the flood threat is expected to increase the value of farm lands in the valley below the dam by $20 million. The rerouted freeway will be slightly longer, and is expected to increase the cost of transportation to motorists using it by $1 million per year. Assume a life of 40 years and cost of capital of 10%.

a. Enumerate the benefits and costs of the project.

b. Should the federal government build the dam?

2-9 XYZ Corporation is considering the replacement of a machine that has zero book value but could be sold for $1000. The new machine costing $6000 would have a useful life of three years (the remaining life of the old machine), and it is estimated that it will have no salvage value at the end of three years. The new machine would result in cost savings of $2200 in each of the three years. Given that the cost of capital is 10%, should they purchase the new machine? (XYZ pays taxes at the 40% rate.)

2-10 Your employer has offered you one of the following fringe benefit schemes:

a. $4000 toward a one-month vacation after the next four years of employment.

b. An automobile-accommodation bonus of $800 per year for a four year period.

Ignoring tax effects, at what discount rate would you be indifferent between the two schemes?

2-11 The government of Oldfoundland, in an effort to encourage industrial expansion, offers a choice between one of the following incentives:

a. Full depreciation on a straight line basis of total project capital expenditures during the first half of the life of the project.

b. Depreciation on a straight line basis of 70% of project capital expenditures during the life of the project (with no other depreciation allowance) and a tax-free grant equal to 10% of project capital expenditures at the time that the project is begun.

The XYZ Company has decided to undertake a project requiring a capital outlay of $100,000 and having a life of 10 years. The cost of funds to XYZ is 10%, and it pays taxes at the 40% rate. Which incentive should they select? Does the selection depend on the amount of the capital expenditure?

Glossary

Average return   The ratio of average net benefits to average invested cost.

$$r_a = \frac{(S/N - C/N)}{c/2}$$

where S = annual benefit, C = cost, N = life of investment.

Benefit–cost ratio	See *profitability index.*
Capital budgeting	The process of planning expenditures on assets that yield returns for more than one year.
Capital cost allowance	The government's version of depreciation. It is more often a reflection of government policies (especially with regard to investment) than an attempt to allocate the cost of the investment over its useful life.
Compound interest	An interest rate that is applicable when interest in subsequent periods is earned on the principal and the accumulated interest. Compound interest thus differs from simple interest, which is earned only on the principal.
Cost of capital	The rate of return that, if earned, leaves the owners wealth position unchanged.
Depreciation	Deductions from income to account for the use of capital assets and to recover costs. The straight line method is frequently used:

$$\text{Annual charge} = \frac{\text{cost} - \text{salvage}}{\text{useful life}}$$

Internal rate of return	The rate of return on an asset investment. It is equivalent to the discount rate that equates the present value of future cash flows to the cost of the investment.
Iterative approach	A trial-and-error search for the appropriate rate of return.
Investment tax credit	A deduction from tax payable equivalent to same proportion of its capital expenditure.
Mutually exclusive alternatives	Projects that cannot be undertaken at the same time. Thus, if A and B are mutually exclusive, it is possible to undertake either A or B (or neither), but not both A and B.
Net present value	The present value of future returns, discounted at the normal rate of return, minus the present value of the cost of the investment.
Original cost	The amount paid for a capital asset, including necessary incidental expenditures such as those for installation.
Payback period	The number of years that will elapse before the origi-

nal cost of a project is recovered through the net revenues of that project.

$$\text{Payback period} = \frac{\text{project cost}}{\text{annual net revenue}}$$

Present value
The amount that would have to be invested today at a particular rate of return (often the normal rate of return) to yield a total of X after a certain number of years. Alternatively, the value of a future payment stream discounted at the normal rate of return.

Profitability index
Present value of future returns divided by the present value of the investment.

Bibliography

BAILEY, M. J., "Formal Criteria for Investment Decisions," *Journal of Political Economy 67* (Oct. 1959), 476–88.

BERNHARD, R. H., "Mathematical Programming Models for Capital Budgeting—A Survey, Generalization, and Critique," *Journal of Financial and Quantitative Analysis 4* (June 1969), 111–158.

BIERMAN, H., and S. SMIDT, *The Capital Budgeting Decision,* New York: Macmillan, 1966.

BROWN, H. P., "The Present Value Theory of Investment Appraisal: A Critical Analysis," *Bulletin Oxford University Institute of Economics and Statistics 31,* (May 1969), 105–131.

EDGE, C. G., *A Practical Manual on the Appraisal of Capital Expenditure,* Hamilton, Ontario: Society of Industrial and Cost Accountants of Canada, 1964.

ELTON, E. J., "Capital Rationing and External Discount Rates," *Journal of Finance 25* (June 1970), 573–584.

FOGLER, H. RUSSELL, "Ranking Techniques and Capital Rationing," *Accounting Review 47* (Jan. 1972), 134–143.

GONEDES, N. J., "A Test of the Equivalent-Risk Hypothesis," *Journal of Financial and Quantitative Analysis 4* (June 1969), 159–178.

GORDON, MYRON J., and ELI SHAPIRO, "Capital Equipment Analysis: The Required Rate of Profit," *Management Science 3* (Oct. 1956), 102–110.

JOHNSON, ROBERT W., *Capital Budgeting,* Belmont, Calif.: Wadsworth, 1970.

KLAMMER, THOMAS, "Empirical Evidence of the Adoption of Sophisticated Capital Budgeting Techniques," *Journal of Business 45* (July 1972), 387–397.

LEWELLEN, WILBUR G., HOWARD P. LANSER, and JOHN J. MCCONNELL, "Payback Substitutes for Discounted Cash Flow," *Financial Management 2* (Summer 1973), 17–23.

LORIE, JAMES H., and LEONARD J. SAVAGE, "Three Problems in Rationing Capital," *Journal of Business 28* (Oct. 1955).

MAO, JAMES C. T., "Survey of Capital Budgeting: Theory and Practice," *Journal of Finance 25* (May 1970), 349–360.

MERVILLE, L. J., and L. A. TAVIS, "A Generalized Model for Capital Investment," *Journal of Finance 28* (March 1973), 109–118.

QUIRIN, G. D., *The Capital Expenditure Decision,* Homewood, Ill.: Richard Irwin, 1967.

SARNAT, M., and H. LEVY, "The Relationship of Rules of Thumb to the Internal Rate of Return: A Restatement and Generalization," *Journal of Finance 24* (June 1969), 479–490.

SOLOMON, E., *The Theory of Financial Management,* New York: Columbia University Press, 1963.

————, *The Management of Corporate Capital,* Chicago: The Free Press of Glencoe, 1959. (An excellent collection of articles pertaining to Chapters 8 and 11. For the most part, articles in this collection are not listed elsewhere in this bibliography.)

TEICHROEW, D. A., A. ROBICHEK, and M. MONTALBANO, "An Analysis of Criteria for Investment and Financing Decisions under Certainty," *Management Science 12* (November 1965), 151–179.

WILLIAMS, JOHN DANIEL, and JONATHAN S. RAKICH, "Investment Evaluation in Hospitals," *Financial Management 2* (Summer 1973), 30–35.

The Yield on Debt Instruments

3

As we will see, an organization finances most of its spending, whether for current production or capital goods, from the normal cash inflows of the organization. For a private firm, normal sales revenues provide most of the financing necessary not only to cover production and distribution costs, but also to permit expansion of production facilities. For a government, tax receipts and other fees cover operating expenses as well as a substantial part of expenditures on highways, dams, and other long-lived projects.

If cash generated by current operations is insufficient, additional funds must be raised externally. In virtually all cases, raising the cash involves issuing some kind of financial instrument—a claim on the organization that someone is willing to buy. The net receipts from selling the instrument are then available to finance expenditures that exceed the funds available from normal operations. Purchasers of these financial instruments are obviously interested in the yields on the instruments, as well as in the risk associated with the instruments. In this chapter, we shall examine some of the more common types of instruments and their yields.

Debt and Equity Claims

Debt

Financial instruments may be classed broadly into two groups: debt instruments and equity instruments. Debt instruments involve money that is *owed* by the organization. The holder of the debt instrument is the creditor of the organization. When a business firm is unable to meet its obligations, creditors' claims have preference over owners' claims.

Within the group of creditors, there are special classes of precedence. For example, certain types of labor payment claims are called *statutory liens,* and payment of these liens or claims have priority over most other creditors' claims. Tax payments are a prior claim over most other creditors. Further, certain assets may have been pledged to the payment of the creditors' claims; for example, in a mortgage, real estate is pledged to the satisfaction of the mortgage loan. These secured creditors are entitled to the receipts from the sale of the pledged assets before other creditors have their claims satisfied.

Debt claims may be classified further in terms of priority of claims on income and, for redemption, on assets. Financial institutions commonly issue *subordinated debentures.* These are usually long-term, but they can claim interest only after interest has been paid on prior debt to which the debentures are subordinated. If a firm liquidates, the subordinated debentures are entitled to payment only after prior debt claims have been satisfied. The financial institutions that issue such claims rely mainly for their financing on very secure short- or long-term instruments, such as bank deposits or finance company paper (discussed in more detail later). They issue subordinated debentures because the quality of their primary sources of funds would be compromised if other kinds of debt were issued with the same priority. Nonfinancial organizations may issue subordinated debentures when they have other outstanding debt that contains a covenant or committment to limit issues of other debt of equal priority. The subordinated debt, in this instance, gives the firm additional long-term funds without violating its covenant.

Not all debt claims bear interest. Long-term claims, such as bonds and mortgages, usually do provide interest payments. Many short-term claims, such as bank loans, also provide interest. However, there is a broad class of short-term debt on which interest is not charged. These debts are referred to often as *accruals* and *payables.* They include such things as wages payable (wages owed but not yet paid, because the normal date for payment has not arrived), accounts payable (payments owed to merchants for goods that have been delivered), and taxes payable (payments owed to the government for taxes whose due date has not arrived).

Equity

Equity instruments imply ownership; hence governments do not issue equity. Even corporate instrumentalities of governments involved in business usually do not publicly issue equity instruments, since the equity is in effect held by the government. Normally, only nongovernmental corporations issue equity instruments.

The equity holder has the lowest priority in receiving income and in receiving satisfaction for a claim if the corporation becomes defunct.

Although the corporation must pay interest to creditors, it normally does not have to pay dividends (the designation of income payment made to owners). Since the owners are residual claimants both to income and assets, ownership instruments are usually more risky than the debt instruments of the same issuer. The best known ownership instrument is the common stock certificate. Preferred stock certificates provide the holder with more priority to income and the satisfaction of claims than is available to common stock holders, although still less security than is available to creditors. More detail on equity instruments appears in Chapter 4.

Yields on Debt Instruments

In this section, we consider three financial instruments. The first is the long-term note usually referred to as a *bond.* Sometimes these are known as *debentures,* particularly when the bonds have no specific assets pledged as collateral for the creditors. The second is also a long-term instrument called the *mortgage,* which has real estate as collateral to protect the creditors. The third is a short-term claim called *commercial paper.* Although the difference between the long-term and the short-term is essentially arbitrary, bonds and mortgages usually have maturities of five years or more. Commercial paper rarely matures beyond one year. In the intervening maturities, the instrument usually issued is referred to as a *note.* The yield on a note is determined in a fashion similar to that of a bond.

Bonds

Bonds pay interest periodically, usually quarterly or semiannually, and have a stated interest rate, referred to as the *coupon interest rate.* Bonds also have a principal or maturity value. The annual interest payment is the product of the coupon rate times the maturity value. Typically, bonds have maturity values denominated at $1000. If the coupon rate is 6%, the bond pays $60 per annum. The $60 may be divided into two or four installments.

The actual interest rate or yield on a bond is called its *yield to maturity.* This is not the ratio of annual interest payments to maturity value, unless the market value of the bond happens to equal the maturity value. When the bond is issued, the appropriate market rate of interest may be 6%, but at a later date the market rate might rise to 8%. At the higher market rate, the investor would have to pay less than $1000 in order to realize an 8% rate of return. Or, interest rates may have declined since the bond was issued, and the market rate might be 4% while the coupon rate is 6%. In that event, investors would be willing to pay more than the maturity value of the bond.

Further, the yield to maturity is not the current yield, the ratio of annual interest payments to market value. Such a ratio would ignore its term, the number of years remaining until the bond matures, which indicates the number of interest payments that will be made and the length of time to maturity. Two bonds paying $60 per year in interest and having maturity values of $1000 should not sell at the same price if one bond matures in one year and the other bond matures in 20 years (unless the market rate of interest happens to equal the coupon rate).

The yield to maturity of a bond is the internal rate of return that sets the present value of the stream of payments promised by that bond and its maturity value equal to the bond's market price. It is i in the following equation.

$$
\begin{aligned}
\text{Market value} = \ & (\text{Interest payments for year 1}) \times 1/(1 + i) \\
& + (\text{Interest payments for year 2}) \times 1/(1 + i)^2 \\
& + (\text{Interest payments for year 3}) \times 1/(1 + i)^3 \\
& \vdots \\
& + (\text{Interest payments for year } n) \times 1/(1 + i)^n \\
& + \text{Maturity value} \times 1/(1 + i)^n
\end{aligned}
$$

Of course, if interest payments are paid quarterly, this equation takes this into account by using, for example, $1/(1 + i)^{0.25}$ as a discount factor for the first quarter's payment, $1/(1 + i)^{0.5}$ for the second quarter's payment, and so on. If payments are made semiannually, the first semiannual payment would be discounted by the factor $1/(1 + i)^{0.5}$. Hence, given the market value of a bond, its coupon rate, its term to maturity, the periodicity of its interest payments, and its maturity value, one uses the equation for internal rate of return in order to determine its yield to maturity.

People who deal in bonds calculate yields to maturity throughout the day. Bond dealers have to be able to compare yields of similar bonds to make sure that the yields are consistent. Computing an internal rate of return using the iterative method is too cumbersome for such purposes.

To facilitate these calculations, bond yield tables have been prepared. Table 3-1 is a sample page from one of those tables. The upper percentage rate is the coupon rate. The designation of time, in the example 10 years and some months, refers to the period until the bond matures. In the body of the table are bond values expressed in bond points. One bond point equals $10, so 118.41 points is equal to $1184.10.

Thus a bond with a $7\frac{3}{4}\%$ coupon rate that matures in 10 years and 6 months and costs $922.60 has a yield to maturity of 8.90%. If the price of the bond is somewhere between values shown in the bond value table, you can determine the yield to maturity by interpolating. Since bond yield books show the yield to maturities for all coupon rates and terms to maturity, they are extremely thick books. The particular table shown in this exhibit calculates yield to maturity on the assumption that interest is paid semiannually and that coupon payments are reinvested at the yield to maturity.

Investors may be interested in knowing what the yield would be for a

Table 3-1. Yields to Maturity for Bonds with a 7¾% Coupon Rate, Maturing from 10 Years to 10 Years and 11 Months

7¾% Yield	Even	1 mo	2 mo	3 mo	4 mo	5 mo	6 mo	7 mo	8 mo	9 mo	10 mo	7¾% 11 mo
							10 Years					
2.00	151.88	152.27	152.66	153.05	153.43	153.82	154.21	154.60	154.98	155.37	155.75	156.14
2.10	150.72	151.10	151.48	151.86	152.23	152.61	152.99	153.36	153.74	154.11	154.49	154.86
2.20	149.58	149.94	150.31	150.68	151.04	151.41	151.78	152.14	152.51	152.87	153.23	153.60
2.30	148.44	148.80	149.15	149.51	149.87	150.22	150.58	150.93	151.29	151.64	151.99	152.35
2.40	147.31	147.66	148.01	148.35	148.70	149.05	149.40	149.74	150.08	150.42	150.77	151.11
2.50	146.20	146.53	146.87	147.21	147.54	147.88	148.22	148.55	148.88	149.22	149.55	149.88
2.60	145.09	145.42	145.74	146.07	146.40	146.73	147.06	147.38	147.70	148.02	148.35	148.67
2.70	144.00	144.31	144.63	144.95	145.27	145.58	145.90	146.22	146.53	146.84	147.15	147.47
2.80	142.91	143.22	143.53	143.83	144.14	144.45	144.76	145.06	145.37	145.67	145.97	146.28
2.90	141.84	142.14	142.43	142.73	143.03	143.33	143.63	143.92	144.22	144.51	144.81	145.10
3.00	140.78	141.06	141.35	141.64	141.93	142.22	142.51	142.80	143.08	143.36	143.65	143.94
3.10	139.72	140.00	140.28	140.56	140.84	141.12	141.40	141.68	141.95	142.23	142.51	142.78
3.20	138.68	138.95	139.22	139.49	139.76	140.03	140.31	140.57	140.84	141.10	141.37	141.64
3.30	137.64	137.90	138.16	138.43	138.69	138.95	139.22	139.48	139.73	139.99	140.25	140.51
3.40	136.62	136.87	137.12	137.37	137.63	137.89	138.14	138.39	138.64	138.89	139.14	139.39
3.50	135.60	135.84	136.09	136.33	136.58	136.83	137.08	137.31	137.55	137.80	138.04	138.28
3.60	134.59	134.83	135.06	135.30	135.54	135.78	136.02	136.25	136.48	136.72	136.95	137.18
3.70	133.60	133.82	134.05	134.28	134.51	134.74	134.97	135.20	135.42	135.64	135.87	136.10
3.80	132.61	132.83	133.05	133.27	133.49	133.71	133.94	134.15	134.37	134.58	134.80	135.02
3.90	131.63	131.84	132.05	132.26	132.48	132.69	132.91	133.12	133.33	133.54	133.75	133.96
4.00	130.66	130.86	131.07	131.27	131.48	131.69	131.90	132.09	132.29	132.50	132.70	132.90
4.10	129.70	129.89	130.09	130.29	130.49	130.69	130.89	131.08	131.27	131.47	131.66	131.86
4.20	128.75	128.93	129.12	129.31	129.50	129.70	129.89	130.08	130.26	130.45	130.64	130.83
4.30	127.80	127.98	128.16	128.35	128.53	128.72	128.91	129.08	129.26	129.44	129.62	129.80
4.40	126.87	127.04	127.21	127.39	127.57	127.75	127.93	128.10	128.27	128.44	128.61	128.79

Table 3-1. Yields to Maturity for Bonds with a 7¾% Coupon Rate, Maturing from 10 Years to 10 Years and 11 Months

7¾% Yield	Even	1 mo	2 mo	3 mo	4 mo	5 mo	6 mo	7 mo	8 mo	9 mo	10 mo	7¾% 11 mo
							10 Years					
4.50	125.94	126.11	126.27	126.44	126.61	126.79	126.96	127.12	127.28	127.45	127.62	127.79
4.60	125.02	125.18	125.34	125.50	125.67	125.83	126.00	126.15	126.31	126.47	126.63	126.79
4.70	124.11	124.27	124.42	124.57	124.73	124.89	125.05	125.20	125.35	125.50	125.65	125.81
4.80	123.21	123.36	123.50	123.65	123.80	123.95	124.11	124.25	124.39	124.54	124.68	124.83
4.90	122.32	122.46	122.60	122.74	122.88	123.03	123.18	123.31	123.45	123.59	123.73	123.87
5.00	121.44	121.57	121.70	121.83	121.97	122.11	122.25	122.38	122.51	122.64	122.78	122.91
5.10	120.56	120.68	120.81	120.94	121.07	121.20	121.34	121.46	121.58	121.71	121.84	121.97
5.20	119.69	119.81	119.93	120.05	120.18	120.30	120.43	120.55	120.67	120.79	120.91	121.03
5.30	118.83	118.94	119.06	119.17	119.29	119.41	119.54	119.65	119.76	119.87	119.99	120.10
5.40	117.98	118.08	118.19	118.30	118.41	118.53	118.65	118.75	118.86	118.96	119.07	119.19
5.50	117.13	117.23	117.33	117.44	117.55	117.65	117.77	117.86	117.96	118.07	118.17	118.28
5.60	116.29	116.39	116.48	116.58	116.68	116.79	116.90	116.99	117.08	117.18	117.28	117.38
5.70	115.46	115.55	115.64	115.74	115.83	115.93	116.03	116.12	116.20	116.30	116.39	116.49
5.80	114.64	114.72	114.81	114.90	114.99	115.08	115.18	115.26	115.34	115.42	115.51	115.60
5.90	113.83	113.90	113.98	114.06	114.15	114.24	114.33	114.40	114.48	114.56	114.64	114.73
6.00	113.02	113.09	113.16	113.24	113.32	113.40	113.49	113.56	113.63	113.70	113.78	113.86
6.10	112.22	112.28	112.35	112.42	112.50	112.58	112.66	112.72	112.79	112.86	112.93	113.00
6.20	111.42	111.48	111.55	111.62	111.68	111.76	111.83	111.89	111.95	112.02	112.08	112.15
6.30	110.64	110.69	110.75	110.81	110.88	110.95	111.02	111.07	111.13	111.19	111.25	111.31
6.40	109.86	109.91	109.96	110.02	110.08	110.14	110.21	110.26	110.31	110.36	110.42	110.48
6.50	109.09	109.13	109.18	109.23	109.29	109.35	109.41	109.45	109.50	109.55	109.60	109.66
6.60	108.32	108.36	108.41	108.45	108.50	108.56	108.61	108.65	108.69	108.74	108.79	108.84
6.70	107.56	107.60	107.64	107.68	107.73	107.77	107.83	107.86	107.90	107.94	107.98	108.03
6.80	106.81	106.84	106.88	106.91	106.96	107.00	107.05	107.08	107.11	107.15	107.19	107.23
6.90	106.07	106.09	106.12	106.16	106.19	106.23	106.28	106.30	106.33	106.36	106.40	106.44

Table 3-1 continued.

Table 3-1. Yields to Maturity for Bonds with a 7¾% Coupon Rate, Maturing from 10 Years to 10 Years and 11 Months

7¾% Yield	Even	1 mo	2 mo	3 mo	4 mo	5 mo	6 mo	7 mo	8 mo	9 mo	10 mo	11 mo 7¾%
						10 Years						
7.00	105.33	105.35	105.38	105.40	105.44	105.47	105.51	105.53	105.56	105.58	105.61	105.65
7.10	104.60	104.62	104.64	104.66	104.69	104.72	104.75	104.77	104.79	104.81	104.84	104.87
7.20	103.87	103.89	103.90	103.92	103.95	103.97	104.00	104.02	104.03	104.05	104.07	104.10
7.30	103.15	103.16	103.18	103.19	103.21	103.23	103.26	103.27	103.28	103.30	103.31	103.34
7.40	102.44	102.45	102.45	102.47	102.48	102.50	102.52	102.53	102.54	102.55	102.56	102.58
7.50	101.74	101.74	101.74	101.75	101.76	101.78	101.79	101.79	101.80	101.80	101.82	101.83
7.60	101.04	101.03	101.03	101.04	101.04	101.06	101.07	101.07	101.07	101.07	101.08	101.09
7.70	100.34	100.34	100.33	100.33	100.34	100.34	100.36	100.35	100.34	100.34	100.35	100.35
7.80	99.66	99.64	99.64	99.63	99.63	99.64	99.65	99.63	99.63	99.62	99.62	99.63
7.90	98.98	98.96	98.95	98.94	98.94	98.94	98.94	98.93	98.92	98.91	98.90	98.91
8.00	98.30	98.28	98.27	98.25	98.25	98.24	98.25	98.23	98.21	98.20	98.19	98.19
8.10	97.63	97.61	97.59	97.57	97.56	97.56	97.56	97.53	97.51	97.50	97.49	97.48
8.20	96.97	96.94	96.92	96.90	96.89	96.88	96.87	96.85	96.82	96.81	96.79	96.78
8.30	96.31	96.28	96.25	96.23	96.22	96.20	96.19	96.16	96.14	96.12	96.10	96.09
8.40	95.66	95.63	95.60	95.57	95.55	95.53	95.52	95.49	95.46	95.44	95.42	95.40
8.50	95.01	94.98	94.94	94.92	94.89	94.87	94.86	94.82	94.79	94.76	94.74	94.72
8.60	94.37	94.33	94.30	94.27	94.24	94.22	94.20	94.16	94.12	94.09	94.07	94.05
8.70	93.74	93.70	93.66	93.62	93.59	93.57	93.55	93.50	93.46	93.43	93.40	93.38
8.80	93.11	93.06	93.02	92.98	92.95	92.92	92.90	92.85	92.81	92.77	92.74	92.72
8.90	92.49	92.44	92.39	92.35	92.31	92.28	92.26	92.21	92.16	92.12	92.09	92.06
9.00	91.87	91.82	91.77	91.72	91.68	91.65	91.62	91.57	91.52	91.48	91.44	91.41
9.10	91.26	91.20	91.15	91.10	91.06	91.02	90.99	90.94	90.89	90.84	90.80	90.77
9.20	90.65	90.59	90.54	90.49	90.44	90.40	90.37	90.31	90.26	90.21	90.17	90.13
9.30	90.05	89.99	89.93	89.88	89.83	89.79	89.75	89.69	89.63	89.58	89.54	89.50
9.40	89.45	89.39	89.33	89.27	89.22	89.18	89.14	89.07	89.02	88.96	88.92	88.87

Table 3-1 continued.

period less than the maturity of the bond. In order to calculate this, they must first estimate the market value at the time they plan to sell the bond. They can then calculate the internal rate of return on the flow of interest payments and the expected sales price. That internal rate of return is not the yield to maturity; instead, it is referred to as an estimated *holding period yield*.

Institutional investors, such as life insurance companies and other large-scale investors in bonds, are concerned about very precise definitions of yield. As shown in the bond yield table, they go well beyond the percentage point level of accuracy. One hundredth of a percentage point could be significant to those dealing in millions of dollars. To simplify the confusion that might otherwise arise in referring to percentage points and percentage differences, we often refer to the yields on financial instruments in terms of *basis points*. One basis point is one hundredth of a percentage, that is, $1\% = 100$ basis points. Thus, when interest rates rise from 7% to 9%, one might confuse an increase of two percentage points with an increase in interest rates of about 28% from the previous level. To avoid such confusion, we can talk about an increase of 200 basis points.

Mortgages

A mortgage is a debt instrument similar to a bond. Both are promisory notes in which the debtor promises to make payments over a period of time to creditors. However, whereas a bond is usually one of many bonds that are issued and distributed among a group of creditors, a mortgage is the sole instrument for the entire proceeds of the loan. More important, a mortgage is secured by a pledge of real property that the creditors can seize if a debtor fails to comply with the terms of the mortgage agreement. A bond may or may not have collateral pledged.

Like interest payments for bonds, mortgage interest payments are determined by applying the interest rate specified in the mortgage instrument to the principal amount borrowed. Periodic payments may be set in any way that is agreeable to both the mortgagor (the debtor) and the mortgagee (the creditor). Since the Great Depression, the monthly payments of mortgages on private homes have included amortization of the principal of the loan as well as interest. As the principal is amortized, the amount owed by the mortgagor is reduced and so are the interest payments. However, most homeowners prefer a constant monthly payment to a diminishing payment, so monthly mortgage payments are usually set so that the payments are constant over the life of the loan. They include a growing component of amortization and a shrinking interest payment component. This prevents home buyers from buying as expensive homes as they could if the principal were not amortized. But it also enables mortgagors to own their homes at the end of the amortization period. Otherwise, they would be confronted with a large "balloon" payment covering the amount of unpaid principal at the end of the mortgage term.

In some jurisdictions, the term of the mortgage loan may be shorter than the amortization period. For example, the mortgage loan term may be for 5 years while the amortization period may be for 20 years. Under these conditions, the mortgage loan usually has a provision allowing extension of the loan, either at a specified interest rate or at the market rate current at the end of the mortgage note. In this case, although a "balloon" payment is due at the end of the five-year note, the mortgage contains a provision for refinancing it. So property owners will be worse off only if interest rates have increased over the period of the note. They will not be faced with a liquidity squeeze if tight monetary conditions at the end of the period of the mortgage note make it difficult to refinance the mortgage note. Further, after the amortization period has passed, they will not find themselves in the same position as many did in the 1930s before amortization was common. Many then had paid interest on property for several years without having established substantial equity in the property.

To determine the flat monthly payment that includes both interest and principal, you can use a mortgage payment table. This is similar to Table B in Chapter 2, except that Table B is based on the payments paid at the end of the year. A mortgage payment table would be based on payments paid at the end of the month. With monthly payments, the amount of principal owed at the end of the year is less than if payments were made annually. However, for illustration, let's use Table B. If C is the amount of the mortgage loan, i is the interest rate, n is the number of years (months, in the case of a mortgage payment table) of the note, and S is the annual payment, then the annual flat-sum payment that includes both principal and interest is

$$S = C \left/ \sum_{t=1}^{n} \frac{1}{(1 + i)^t} \right.$$

If the mortgage loan (C) is $20,000, the interest rate is 8%, and the term of the loan is 20 years, then

$S = \$20,000/9.818 = \$2,037.08$ per annum

Although mortgages are not usually sold in the open market as bonds are, they are negotiable instruments and can be traded. If sold, the market price of the mortgage is different from the original loan. Mortgages, unlike bonds, usually involve amortization payments so that the amount owed on a mortgage is less than the original loan. However, even without amortization, the value of the mortgage is less than the original loan if interest rates have risen between the time when the mortgage was originally issued and the time it was traded. On the other hand, the *value* of the mortgage may have risen since the time it was originally issued if interest rates decline during that period. One can determine the value of the mortgage when interest rates have changed by using a mortgage interest table. So if we use Table B as the annual equivalent, the formulation is as follows, with V as the market value.

$$V = S \sum_{t=1}^{n} \frac{1}{(1 + i)^t}$$

For example, suppose that we continue with the mortgage loan in the previous example of $20,000 at 8% for 20 years, for an annual payment of $2037.08. If, after 10 years, interest rates have remained the same, the value of the mortgage is $V_{8\%} = \$2037.08[6.710] = \$13,668.81$. However, if interest rates have risen to 10%, the value of the mortgage has declined by about $1150, to a value of $V_{10\%} = \$2037.08 [6.145] = \$12,517.86$.

The value at 8%, $13,668.81, is the present value of the remaining interest and unamortized portion of the mortgage to be paid over the remaining 10 years. The difference between that and the value at 10% is the erosion in value resulting from the increase in market interest rates. Note that despite the increase in interest rate, the monthly payment remains the same because this was set originally in the mortgage note.

Mortgage Bonds

In addition to bonds and mortgages there is a combination of bonds and mortgages called mortgage bonds. A company can issue bonds to the public that not only give the general creditor preference, but also pledge specific assets to guarantee payment. If the corporation defaults on agreed payments, the mortgage bondholders can seize the pledged assets. The proceeds from disposing of the assets are then available to pay the claims of the mortgage bondholders. If the proceeds exceed the claims of the mortgage bondholders, the remainder is used to pay other creditors. However, if the proceeds are less than the claims of the mortgage bondholders, they have the status of general creditors of the corporation for the unsatisfied portion of the debt.

Sinking Fund Bonds

Bonds also resemble mortgages in terms of amortization if the debtor corporation agrees to redeem portions of the bond issue before it matures. Such bond issues are often referred to as sinking fund bonds, because at one time, the debtor corporation instead of actually redeeming the bonds made payments into a sinking fund. This fund was then used to redeem the bond issue at maturity. Today, the debtor actually purchases and retires the bonds throughout the term of the bond issue.

With modern sinking fund bonds, the debtor corporation may also be able to redeem bonds at either the market price or at the *call price*, a price agreed on at the time of the bond issue. If the market price is below the call price, the corporation meets its redemption requirements by buying at the market price. On the other hand, if the call price is lower, the corporation "calls" the bonds. The privilege of exercising a call price can be reflected in the interest rate paid by the corporation. When interest rates are high, investors usually demand a higher interest rate for a callable bond than for a bond without the call feature because they anticipate that the bonds will be called when interest rates decline. Although the call privilege is usually a feature of sinking fund bonds, it may exist even if there are no provisions for amortizing the bond.

Other Types of Bonds

Debt instruments are designed to meet investors' needs, as well as those of the issuer. As a result, there are many kinds of long-term debt instruments, and the types that exist are always changing.

For example, convertible debentures permit holders to convert the bonds into common stock at a given ratio. The conversion ratio may be 10 to 1, that is, the owner may convert the bond into 10 shares of common. If the bond is worth $1000, the conversion price of the common stock is $100. If the market price of the common is less than $100, the convertible bond may still sell at a premium if investors believe that the price of the common may rise in the future. Certainly, the conversion privilege is reflected in the price of the convertible if the common stock is selling above the conversion price.

What motivates a firm to issue convertible debt? It may really want to issue common stock, but may be unwilling to do so because of market conditions. New issues of stock often depress the market price of common stock because of the temporary excess supply. With convertible debentures, there is no excess supply, and the debentures will be converted only as the price of the common rises. Further, management may believe that the price of their stock is below its "true" value so they may hesitate to sell stock at "bargain basement" prices. Again convertible debt lets a firm raise funds that can become equity without giving away new equity shares. Until the debt is actually converted, the firm can continue to deduct the interest costs of the debt from taxable income, whereas they cannot deduct dividends on stock.

Not all holders of convertible debt convert when the market price of the stock rises above the conversion price. By holding the convertible, they accomplish two things. First, they retain a debt instrument that has both income and asset preferences over an equity instrument. Second, they benefit from the appreciation of the common, since the price of the convertible reflects the value of the common. Their unwillingness to convert can be frustrating if management wants conversion.

To encourage holders to convert, management may set up the bonds so that the conversion ratio becomes smaller with time. For the first five years following issue, the conversion ratio may be 10 shares for 1 bond, a conversion price of $100. However, the ratio may decline to 8:1 after five years, increasing the conversion price to $125, and soon. In addition, they may specify that the convertible bonds are callable.

Another type of bond reflects fluctuations in interest rates over the past decade. To protect investors from further increases in interest rates (which, of course, decrease the value of their bond holdings) and still enable firms to issue long-term debt, firms may use *extendible bonds*. These bonds permit the holder to redeem the bond at a fixed time after issue at an agreed price (usually maturity value). So an investor could extend 20-year bonds at the end of five years. If interest rates have risen, the investor will probably redeem the bond at the end of five years. If rates have declined, he or she will hold the bond beyond the five-year period.

The other side of the coin is the *retractible bond*. With these bonds, the issuer can redeem the bond at some stated period and price before its stated maturity value. Usually, the issuer takes this option if interest rates have fallen enough to cover the costs of issuing new debt at lower interest rates. Bonds may be both extendible and retractible. Obviously, since extendible bonds give the investor an option, they sell at lower yields than similar bonds without the extendible provision. However, retractible bonds are like callable bonds; they sell at a discount, reflecting the advantage to the issuer.

Commercial Paper

Commercial paper is a form of debt that is marketable and usually matures in less than one year. Investors in commercial paper are usually financial institutions such as banks and other institutions seeking a safe, but very liquid (hence short-term), investment. Recently, large industrial corporations have also invested in commercial paper as an alternative to holding cash that would otherwise earn no interest in checking accounts or currency. Governments may also invest in short-term paper as a means of earning interest on cash balances that are currently not needed. Although commercial paper is generally a very safe investment, investors have to be certain that the issuing corporation is safe. This is not always possible. For example, when the Penn Central collapsed, many large investors were left holding millions of dollars of commercial paper of highly questionable value.

Sales finance paper is very similar to commercial paper, but it is issued by sales finance companies instead of industrial corporations. Once again the quality of the issuer is an important factor. In the 1960s, many sophisticated institutional investors were left with worthless finance paper issued by the Atlantic Acceptance Corporation.

Governments may also issue the equivalent of commercial paper, normally known as treasury bills.

Commercial paper, sales finance paper, and treasury bills differ from most long-term debt in that they are sold on a *discount* basis. The bills have a maturity value and a term to maturity. Buyers pay less than the maturity value, and the difference between what they pay and what they receive at maturity determines the interest rate. For example, suppose that an investor wanted to buy commercial paper with a maturity value of $1000 and a term of 90 days to yield 6% per year for 90 days. Thus

$$\text{Price} = \frac{1}{(1 + i)^{0.25}} \, (\$1000)$$

If $i = 6\%$

$$\text{Price} = \frac{1}{(1.06)^{0.25}} \, (\$1000) = (0.98554)(\$1000) = \$985.54$$

As with any other financial instrument, the value of commercial paper varies inversely with the interest rate. If interest rates change, one can recalculate the value of a treasury bill, sales finance paper, or commercial paper by taking the applicable interest rate, the maturity value, and the amount of time remaining. Tables are available to facilitate these calculations. Those who specialize in trading these short-term financial instruments have to recalculate the value of these instruments throughout the day.

Special Yield Factors

Yields on bonds issued by states and local governments usually sell at considerably lower yields to maturity than other debt, even debt of the federal government. The reason for this is that the state and local bonds are tax exempt. If the interest rate for taxable instruments of comparable risk is 8%, someone in the 40% tax bracket would be willing to pay a price yielding 4.8 percent. Of course, the investor still has to consider the quality of the debt issue, as unwary investors discovered during New York City's financial crisis.

Federal inheritance and estate taxes may be paid with U.S. government securities. For these purposes, the securities are valued at par value even though their market value may be far below par. These bonds are often referred to as *flower bonds,* (because flowers are usually sent to funerals), and their yield to maturity is lower than would be expected if this special feature did not exist.

Thus, yields vary for a variety of reasons, and investors should be wary of so-called anomalies in bond yields. Two apparently similar bonds may sell at different yields for many good reasons. Securities markets are usually efficient enough that yield anomalies are rare.

Summary

An organization usually issues financial instruments when they need more funds to invest in assets or to repay financial claims than they can generate internally by normal operations. The instruments may be debt (a fixed claim), or equity (an ownership instrument).

Creditors have preference over owners, that is, creditors receive interest or redemption payments before owners. However, among the creditors, certain classes of creditors have priority over others.

Debt instruments may have a coupon rate, which indicates the rate paid on the maturity value of the instrument. However, when market interest rates vary from coupon rates, the price of the debt instrument falls (when market rates exceed coupon rates) or rises (when market rates are less than coupon rates). Under these circumstances, the most common interest rate is the *yield to maturity*. This is the internal rate of return that sets the present value of the stream of expected interest payments and the redemption of principal equal to market price. Investors who are not interested in holding the instrument for its life, may estimate a *holding period yield*. This is the internal rate of return that sets the expected interest payments for the period over which the investor plans to hold the instrument, plus the estimated market price of the instrument at the end of the holding period, equal to the current market price.

Some types of debt are amortized in whole or in part over their lives. Mortgages are one such type of debt, and so-called sinking fund bonds are another. Such gradual redemption gives greater assurance to the creditor that claims will be repaid and reduces repayment or refinancing problems for debtors.

Some debt, particularly short-term marketable debt, sells on a discount basis rather than having a coupon interest rate. The yield to maturity on such instruments is the internal rate of return that sets the present value of the redemption value of the debt equal to its current selling price.

Review Questions

3-1 Discuss the difference between holding period yield and yield to maturity.

3-2 How can it be the case that the dividend yields on equity instruments are typically less than the yields on debt instruments when the latter subject the investor to less risk?

3-3 Under what market conditions might a firm prefer to raise funds by issuing convertible debentures rather than common stock?

3-4 Describe the general relationship among yield, coupon, and price for a bond.

3-5 What are the implications for both the investor and the issuer of a mortgage if the mortgage has a variable interest rate tied to prevailing market rates?

Problems

3-6 Find the value of an 8%, $100 bond redeemable in 6 years to yield 10%.

3-7 A $20,000 mortgage has a 10-year term and calls for an annual payment of $3571. The first payment is to be made one year from today. What is the interest cost of the mortgage?

3-8   A company is considering investing in a project that requires a cash outlay of $1000 and results in cash inflows of $200, $1200 and $500 after two, three, and four years, respectively. The equipment required for the project is expected to have no salvage value when the project is terminated in four years. Determine the net present value of the project and its internal rate of return. The company expects to earn a minimum of a 10% return on its projects. Should they undertake this project?

3-9   What is the effective annual yield on the commercial paper of XYZ Corporation if the paper has a maturity value of $50,000, can be purchased for $44,500, and will mature in 18 months?

3-10   Determine the after-tax yield (using an exact method) for an individual in the 40% marginal tax bracket on the following bond held to maturity: Price = $900, par value = $1000, coupon = 6% (annual), maturity = 8 years.

Glossary

Accruals and payables	Short-term debt on which interest is not charged, and which may or may not be currently due.
Actual interest rate	See *yield to maturity.*
Amortization	To liquidate on an installment basis. In the case of a loan, amortization is the payment of installments of principal before the maturity of the obligation.
Balloon payment	If a debt is not fully amortized, the final payment is larger than the previous amounts and thus is called a "balloon" payment.
Basis point	One hundredth of a percent. For example, 1% = 100 basis points.
Bond	A long-term note. "Long term" is often considered to be any period greater than five years. See also *note, commercial paper.*
Bond point	One bond point equals $10.
Callable bond	A bond that may be redeemed before its normal maturity. The call price is a price agreed on at the time of the issue and normally equals face value plus a "call premium."
Collateral	Assets pledged as security to a creditor.
Commercial paper	Unsecured, short-term (less than one year) debt instruments issued by large firms.

Common stock	A share of ownership of a corporation that is not a fixed claim to dividends. When a firm liquidates, holders of stock receive any residual after the payment of all prior claims.
Convertible debentures	Debentures that permit holders to exchange debt instruments for common stock at their own option. The number of shares obtained for a debenture is the conversion ratio or rate, while the conversion price is the face value of the debenture divided by the conversion ratio.
Coupon interest rate	The stated rate of interest on a debt instrument.
Covenant	A legally binding promise contained as part of a contract designed to serve other purposes. For example, a contract for the sale of a business may prohibit the seller from establishing a competing firm.
Current yield	The ratio of annual interest payments to market value.
Debenture	An unsecured long-term debt instrument. A subordinated debenture is one that provides a claim to interest, or the proceeds of liquidation, which is of lower priority than the claim of a previous debt issue.
Debt instrument	Representation of a corporation's financial obligation to another party.
Discount basis	A bond sold on a discount basis is sold at less than face value and does not bear interest. The difference between the initial selling price and the maturity value determines the interest rate.
Equity instrument	Representation of ownership of a corporation.
Extendible bonds	The holder may choose between redeeming the bond at a given time and at an agreed on price (usually maturity value), or holding for an additional (extended) term.
Finance company paper	Commercial paper issued by a finance company.
Flower bonds	U.S. government securities that can be used to pay federal inheritance and estate taxes. For that purpose they are valued at par values, not market prices. Thus their yield tends to be lower than it would be without such a special privilege.

General creditors	Creditors without specified security.
Holding period yield	The internal rate of return on a bond sold before it matures.
Liquidation	Conversion of a noncash asset into cash, usually by sale.
Liquidity squeeze	A shortage of liquid assets, in particular, cash.
Market rate of interest	The interest rate that may be earned in the market on similar instruments.
Maturity	The length of time until a debt must be paid completely.
Mortgage	A long-term debt instrument usually secured by real estate.
Mortgage bonds	Bonds secured by the pledge of specific real assets.
Negotiable instrument	A written security that may be transferred by endorsement and delivery or merely by delivery. The person to whom it is given obtains all the legal rights attached to the security.
Net receipts	Proceeds from the issuance of a financial instrument after deducting the costs of issuing it.
Note	A debt instrument, usually unsecured and usually maturing in more than one year but less than five years.
Par value	The face or nominal value of a financial instrument.
Pledge	Assets are pledged to secure a loan if the lender has been granted a prior claim to the proceeds of the disposition of that asset.
Preferred stock	A share of ownership that has a superior claim to earnings and the proceeds of liquidation to that of common stock, but a lesser claim than is provided to creditors.
Principal (maturity) value	The face value of a debt instrument.
Refinance	Issuance of new debt to replace a previous obligation.
Retractible bond	A bond that the issuer may redeem before maturity at a stated price.

Secured creditors	Lenders whose claims are insured by the pledging of assets. See *pledge*.
Sinking fund bonds	Bonds that the debtor agrees to redeem gradually before maturity. This is a form of amortization.
Statutory lien	A legal claim to payment that has special priority because of its statutory force.
Tax-exempt bonds	The interest on tax-exempt bonds is not taxable as income in the hands of the bondholder. These are issued by state and local governments.
Yield to maturity	The internal rate of return that sets the present value of interest payments and maturity value equal to the market price.

Bibliography

BAXTER, N. D., *The Commercial Paper Market,"* Princeton, N.J.: Princeton University Press, 1964.

BIERMAN, H., JR., and R. BROWN, "Why Corporations Should Consider Income Bonds," *Financial Executive 35* (Oct. 1967), 74ff.

BOWLIN, O. D., "The Refunding Decision: Another Special Case in Capital Budgeting," *Journal of Finance 21* (March 1966), 55–68.

BRIGHAM, E. F., "An Analysis of Convertible Debentures: Theory and Some Empirical Evidence," *Journal of Finance 21* (March 1966), 69–76.

BUSE, A., "Expectations, Prices, Coupons and Yields," *Journal of Finance 25* (Sept. 1970), 809–818.

CHRISTIE, R. A., "New Developments in the Commercial Paper Market," *Industrial Banker 35* (Aug. 1969), 10–13ff.

EVERETT, E., "Subordinated Debt—Nature and Enforcement," *Business Lawyer 20* (July 1965), 953–987.

FRAINE, H. G., and R. H. MILLS, "Effect of Defaults and Credit Deterioration on Yields of Corporate Bonds, *Journal of Finance 16* (Sept. 1961), 423–434.

LITZENBERGER, ROBERT H., and DAVID P. RUTENBERG, "Size and Timing of Corporate Bond Flotations," *Journal of Financial and Quantitative Analysis 8* (Jan. 1972), 1343–1359.

MEYER, A. B., "Designing a Convertible Preferred Issue," *Financial Executive 36* (April 1968), 42ff.

Money Market Instruments, Cleveland, Ohio: Federal Reserve Bank of Cleveland, 1965.

POENSGEN, O. H., "The Valuation of Convertible Bonds. I, II," *Industrial Management Review 7* (Fall 1965, Spring 1966), 77–92, 83–98.

POGUE, T. F., and R. M. SOLDOFSKY, "What's in a Bond Rating?" *Journal of Financial and Quantitative Analysis 4* (July 1969), 201–228.

ROBINSON, R. I., *Money and Capital Markets,* New York: McGraw-Hill, 1964.

SCHADRACK, F. C., JR., "Demand and Supply in the Commercial Paper Market," *Journal of Finance 25* (Sept. 1970), 836–852.

SHAPIRO, ELI, and CHARLES R. WOLF, *The Role of Private Placements in Corporate*

Finance, Boston: Division of Research, Graduate School of Business Administration, Harvard University, 1972.

SELDEN, R. T., *Trends and Cycles in the Commercial Paper Market,* New York: National Bureau of Economic Research, 1963.

STEVENSON, R. A., and J. LAVELY, "Why a Bond Warrant Issue?" *Financial Executive 38* (June 1970), 16–21.

VAN HORNE, JAMES C., "Implied Fixed Costs in Long-Term Debt Issues," *Journal of Financial and Quantitative Analysis 8* (Dec. 1973).

WEIL, R. L., JR., J. E. SEGALL, and D. GREEN, JR., "Premiums on Convertible Bonds," *Journal of Finance 23* (June 1968), 445–464.

WEINGARTNER, H. M., "Optimal Timing of Bond Refunding," *Management Science 13* (March 1967), 511–524.

WERNER, G. F., and J. J. WEYGANDT, "Convertible Debt and Earnings per Share: Pro Pragmatism vs. Good Theory," *Accounting Review 40* (April 1970), 280–289.

WINN, WILLIS J., and ARLEIGH HESS, JR., "The Value of the Call Privilege," *Journal of Finance 14* (May 1959), 182–195.

The Yield on Equity Instruments

4

Equity instruments represent the ownership of the organization. As such, they are usually restricted to private enterprise. The type of equity in which we are mainly interested is restricted to corporations, which issue transferable shares of equity called *shares of stock*.

Fairly large and well-known corporations may have their shares of stock traded on public exchanges, such as the New York Stock Exchange or the Midwest Stock Exchange. If it is a public stock, approved by an appropriate government authority, such as the Securities and Exchange Commission in the United States, it can be traded without being listed on an exchange. In this case, it is traded "over the counter" rather than on a listed exchange. If the stock is privately held, it may not be traded publicly.

Thus, if stocks are *public* and *listed*, they may be traded among the general public and they are listed on an organized securities exchange. If they are *public* and *unlisted*, they may be traded among the members of the public, but not on an organized exchange. Finally, if they are private, the general public may not buy shares, since the company has not been authorized to trade its shares publicly.

Owners of companies have only residual claims to income and assets; they are paid only after all creditors, including government tax debts, are paid. If the company fails, the stockholders' claims are satisfied only after all creditors' claims have been met. However, some stockholders may have preference for receiving income or the distribution of assets if a firm fails. Such shares are called *preferred shares*. The remaining shares are normally called *common shares* or *common equity*.

Preferred Stocks

Preferred shares usually have a prior claim to income and have a stated dividend or dividend rate. If there is a dividend rate, it is applied to the par value, normally $100. Hence, a 7% preferred stock usually pays a $7 dividend each year. However, the dividend is not a legal obligation of the company. Normally, all it means is that the preferred stockholders must receive their dividends before common stockholders receive anything. Often the preferred stock is cumulative. This means that the preferred stockholder must receive any unpaid dividends from preceding years, as well as the current dividend, before the common stockholders can receive anything.

Since preferred stock normally does not have a maturity value or limited life, the overall rate of return on preferred stock is difficult to calculate. We can compute the dividend yield. This is the annual dividend as a ratio of the stock's market price. It does not include any changes in the capital value or price of the preferred stock. The true measurement of yield would be a holding period yield for the preferred stock, that is, an internal rate of return on the expected dividend flows for the period during which the investor expects to hold the preferred stock, and on the market price that is expected at the end of the holding period. But the holding period yield is difficult to determine because the receipts of future preferred dividends are uncertain and estimates of the future market price of preferred stock are subject to large errors. Thus the expected holding period yield is almost meaningless. So we may reasonably take holding period yield as the yield on a perpetual stream of dividends, $i = D_0/P_0$, where i is the yield, D_0 is the dividend, and P_0 is the cumulative.

Convertible Preferreds

Sometimes preferred stocks, like bonds, are convertible. If a preferred stock is worth $100 and can be converted into 10 common shares, its convertibility adds to its value if the common stock is selling or is expected to sell at more than $10 a share.

For example, consider a 7% preferred stock that sells at $100 without a conversion privilege. If it has a conversion privilege allowing the shareholder to convert the preferred share into 10 shares of common stock, and the common is selling at $12 per share, the value of the convertible preferred is $100 plus the $20 added value of the conversion privilege ($2 per share × 10 shares). However, if the common is selling at $10 or less per share, the conversion privilege is worthless except to someone willing to speculate that the price of the common will rise about $10. To a speculator, it might seem safer to hold funds in convertible preferred stock until the common price rises than to buy the common directly. Hence, the yield on a convertible preferred could be less than it would be if the conversion feature was omitted. Like convertible bonds, convertible preferreds may also be callable to force conversion when the market price of the common stock exceeds the conversion price.

Warrants

Warrants or stock options are similar to the conversion privilege. The holder of a preferred stock with warrants can exercise the warrants to buy common stock at a predetermined price. But warrants usually permit the stockholder to retain the preferred share after exercising the warrants, whereas with convertible preferred, the preferred stockholder gives up the preferred stock when converting. Warrants are also attached to debt instruments, in effect combining elements of debt and equity.

A 7% preferred that is worth $100 and has warrants permitting the preferred shareholder to buy 10 shares of common at $10 per share is worth $120 if the market price of the common is $12 per share.

Warrants may also be detachable, that is, they may be sold separately from the preferred shares. If the exercise price of the warrant is $10 and the market price of the common is $12, then the value of the warrant is $2, or slightly more since you don't have to pay brokerage commissions if you buy common by exercising a warrant.

Further, the warrant can have a value even if the market price of the common is less than the exercise price of the warrant. The reason for this is that losses are more limited with a warrant than with a direct purchase of common. Suppose that the common stock has a market price of $8 and the exercise price of the warrant is $10. A speculator who believes that the common price will rise to more than $10 has to risk $8 per share to buy the common directly, since the price of the common could fall to zero. Under these circumstances the investor might prefer to pay $1 for a one-share warrant, even though the exercise price exceeded the market price of the common, in order to limit the maximum potential loss to $1 per warrant rather than $8 per share.

A warrant with an exercise price above the market price of the common can also have value if speculators can "lever" their returns with warrants. By levering their returns, they can get larger returns on their investments than they could if they bought the common directly. Given an exercise price of $10 and a market price of the common of $8, an investor with $1000 can buy either 125 shares of common or, assuming a warrant price of $1, 1000 warrants. If the stock price moves to $12 per share, the investor would have a return of 50% from an investment in common (the $1000 investment would be worth $1500). Had this investor purchased 1000 warrants, they would be worth $2000 if the market price of the common rose to $12, yielding a 100% return on an investment of $1000.

As a result, preferred stock or bonds with attached warrants can sell at a higher price or lower yield than similar securities without warrants.

Common Stocks

Determining the yield on common stocks is even more difficult than determining the yield on preferred stock. At least with preferred stock, the dividend is known. With common stock, the firm has complete legal freedom to determine the dividend. Although firms seem reluctant to vary dividends substantially, most investors don't count on receiving the same dividend for very long from any but the most established and stable firms.

Constant Dividend. Even if the dividend were constant and known, the value of the common share at the time the investor plans to sell is, of course, unknown. Common stock prices tend to vary much more than the values of preferred shares or bonds, so the uncertainty of the price at the end of a holding period is greater than with the other less risky instruments. In any event, the yield on a common share is the internal rate of return that sets the present value of the stream of expected dividends and the market price expected to prevail at the end of the holding period equal to the current market price.

Anyone making such a calculation has to estimate future dividends and the future price. The basic equation is

$$P_0 = \frac{D_1}{1 + i} + \frac{D_2}{(1 + i)^2} + \frac{D_3}{(1 + i)^3} + \cdots + \frac{D_n + P_n}{(1 + i)^n} \qquad (4\text{-}1)$$

where P is market price or present value, D is annual dividend, i is the internal rate of return or holding period yield of the stock, and the subscripts refer to time periods.

In the simplest case, suppose that dividends are expected to remain constant forever. A stockholder who never planned to sell the stock would value the stock as follows:

$$P_0 = \frac{D_1}{1 + i} + \frac{D_2}{(1 + i)^2} + \cdots + \frac{D_x}{(1 + i)^x} \qquad (4\text{-}2)$$

We can simplify this to the following:

$$P_0 = D/i \qquad (4\text{-}2a)$$

If the dividend is $1 per share and the market price is $10, the yield on the share is

$$i = D/P_0 \quad \text{or} \quad 10\% = \$1/10 \qquad (4\text{-}3)$$

Suppose that the holder of such a stock waited to sell it in one year. The expected selling price could be $10 in one year given the constant expected dividend. The yield would be determined as follows:

$$P_0 = (D_1 + P_1) \frac{1}{1 + i} \qquad\qquad (4\text{-}4)$$

or

$$\frac{P_0}{D_1 + P_1} = \frac{1}{1 + i} \qquad\qquad (4\text{-}4a)$$

or

$$\frac{D_1 + P_1}{P_0} - 1 = i \qquad\qquad (4\text{-}5)$$

With a current market price of \$10, an expected market price of \$10 in one year, and a \$1 dividend, the yield is

$$\frac{\$10 + \$1}{\$10} - 1 = 10\%$$

This is the same yield that a stockholder who planned to hold the stock forever would get. If we assume a constant dividend, the yield on the stock is 10% no matter what the holding period is. Hence, the value of a stock paying a constant dividend is

$$P = D/i \qquad\qquad (4\text{-}2a)$$

and the yield is

$$i = D/P \qquad\qquad (4\text{-}3)$$

regardless of the expected holding period.

In this case, we have implicitly assumed that all earnings are paid out as dividends, that is, that $E = D$, where E is earnings per share. So we can restate the yield as

$$i = E/P \qquad\qquad (4\text{-}6)$$

where the right-hand term is the earnings/price ratio.

Constant Growth. In reality, most corporations retain a portion of earnings for reinvestment. Reinvested profitably, these earnings generate additional earnings that permit the corporation to increase future dividends. We can determine the effect that these increases have on price by using the present value equation. They reduce the apparent yield, measured by the internal rate of return that sets the present value of the dividend stream plus expected future price equal to the current price. However, in reality, the expected growth rate of future dividends reduces actual yield, if the growth is not included in computing the yield. As we will show later, a true required yield of 17% could appear to be 12% if we ignore the expected growth of dividends.

The growth rate is the product of the proportion of reinvested earnings and the rate of return on the reinvested earnings:

$$G = br \qquad (4\text{-}7)$$

where G is the growth rate, b is the proportion of earnings being reinvested, and r is the rate of return on these reinvested earnings.

One widely used growth model is based on some fairly straightforward, simple assumptions. Basically, it assumes that the earnings of the firm, the firm's assets, and the dividends paid by the firm all grow at an identical and constant rate. Under these assumptions, the current value of a share equals

$$P = D/(i - G) \qquad (4\text{-}8)$$

where P is price, i is the yield on the stock, and $G = br$. Manipulating this expression algebraically gives the following expression for the yield of the stock.

$$i = D/P + G \qquad (4\text{-}9)$$

This equation says that the yield of a common stock is equal to its expected dividend yield plus its growth rate. Note that if we assume that a stock does not grow, the yield on a stock is exactly equal to the dividend yield. Without some growth, there is no reason to believe that the value of a share at the end of a holding period will be any different from the price paid today.

Suppose that earnings are currently $10 per share and that 60% of these earnings are paid out as dividends. Assume also that the current market price of a share is $50 and that the rate of return on reinvested earnings is $12\frac{1}{2}\%$. G is then $0.4 \times 0.125 = 5\%$, and the stock yield is

$$i = 6/50 + 0.05 = 0.17 = 17\%$$

If growth is really constant, earnings in the next year will rise from $10 to $10.50. Price should be $52.50 instead of the current $50, and the yield is

$$i = 6.30/52.50 + 0.05 = 0.17 = 17\%$$

However, if the expected growth rate falls to 1%, the yield falls substantially. At a 1% expected growth rate with a $6 dividend currently and a $50 price, the yield on this stock is yield $= 6/50 + 0.01 = 0.13 = 13\%$

But if investors required an equity yield of 17% when it was expected to grow at a 5% rate, why would they be willing to accept an even lower yield if the expected growth rate is smaller? This does not make sense, and would not occur. If the expected growth rate declined, it is more likely that the price, rather than the yield, would decline. Assuming that investors wanted to earn 17%, even at the lower growth rate, the current price of the stock would become

$$P = \frac{6}{0.17 - 0.01} = \$37.50$$

Conversely, an increase in the expected growth rate would not raise the required yield, but would increase the price.

The validity of this method of determining common stock yields depends on whether the earnings, dividends, and assets of the shares in question grow at a constant rate. Not all, and perhaps not even most, common stocks do this. We can formulate other methods of valuation if we can assume that the patterns of future dividends and prices have some regularity. However, when we cannot make this assumption, we must fall back on a straightforward estimation of future dividends and future stock prices in order to determine a holding period yield. Although the constant growth rate model is convenient, we have to be careful not to apply it when its assumptions do not hold. Among its limitations is that we cannot apply it to companies that pay no dividends or to companies with a growth rate in excess of i.

Super-Growth. In some cases, growth is so rapid that the growth rate (G) exceeds the required rate of return on the common (i). As we noted before, we cannot use the constant growth model to determine the value of a share for such a firm. Obviously, this does not mean that no value exists.

During the period of super-growth, the value of the share reflects the present value of dividends, as with any stock valuation model. Suppose that dividends are expected to grow 20% annually for five years in a company that has a required rate of return on equity of 10% and pays a current dividend of $1.00. The value of the five years of dividend growth is

$$\sum_{t=1}^{n} \frac{D_0(1 + G)^t}{(1 + i)^t} = \sum_{t=1}^{n} \frac{1(1.2)^5}{(1.1)^5} = \$6.54 \qquad (4\text{-}10)$$

Though management and investors often like to think that super-growth will continue forever, even constant growth is difficult to maintain for long periods of time. Suppose that at the end of the super-growth period, growth disappeared and a constant dividend was maintained. The full value of the firm would then be

$$\sum_{t=1}^{n} \frac{D_0(1 + G)^t}{(1 + i)^t} + \frac{D_0(1 + G)^t}{i} \frac{1}{(1 + i)^t} = 6.54 + (2.49/0.1)\,0.621$$

$$= \$22.03 \qquad (4\text{-}11)$$

If the super-growth period was expected to be followed by a period of 5% constant growth, the value of the share would be

$$\sum_{t=1}^{n} \frac{D_0(1 + G)^t}{(1 + i)^t} + \frac{D_0(1 + G)^t}{i - G'} \frac{1}{(1 + i)^t} = 6.54 + \left(\frac{2.49}{0.1 - 0.05}\right)\,0.621$$

$$= \$37.47 \qquad (4\text{-}12)$$

where G' refers to the lower normal growth rate. In both cases, the value expected in five years has been reduced to its present value by multiplying by $1/(1 + i)^5 = 0.621$

The Price/Earnings Ratio

The valuation of common stocks is a source of continual concern to investors, security analysts, and companies that issue the securities. The difficulties of valuation are such that one can easily succumb to the temptation of using a simple but inappropriate method. The constant growth model is certainly not the simplest approach to share valuation. One that is far more commonly used is the price/earnings (P/E) ratio. With this ratio, one tries to compare firms that are similar (perhaps they belong to the same industry) by looking at the ratio of price to earnings per share. All else equal, the stock with the lowest ratio of price to earnings is presumed to be the best buy. If in fact the stock is equivalent to stock of companies with higher price/earnings ratios, either the price of the stock with the low P/E ratio will rise or the other prices will fall.

But, as is often the case, the simple method is also treacherous. Certainly, the use of the price/earnings ratio is treacherous. Two companies in the same industry could have different price/earnings ratios because of differences in their dividend policies or differences in their growth rates.

And, of course, firms in the same industry can have different expected growth rates. Take the case of very homogeneous firms, say electric utilities. An electric utility serving a rapidly growing area has a higher growth rate of earnings than one serving an area having smaller population growth. Even when they serve the same market, companies may have different growth rates. This is the case, for example, with automobile companies. However, let us illustrate the problem of using the price/earnings ratio by examining a concrete example.

If $i = D/P + G$ (equation 4-9) and $D = (1 - b)E$, where E is earnings, b is the rate of retained earnings, (and $(1 - b)$ is the dividend payout ratio, the relative share of earnings paid out as dividends), then

$$i = \frac{(1 - b)E}{P} + G \qquad (4\text{-}10)$$

$$i - G = \frac{(1 - b)E}{P} \quad \text{(by subtracting } G) \qquad (4\text{-}11)$$

$$\frac{1}{i - G} = \frac{P}{(1 - b)E} \quad \text{(by inverting)} \qquad (4\text{-}12)$$

$$\frac{1 - b}{i - G} = \frac{P}{E} \quad \text{(by multiplying by } 1 - b) \qquad (4\text{-}13)$$

If $b = 0.6$, $i = 0.1$, and $G = 0.05$, then

$$\frac{P}{E} = \frac{0.4}{0.1 - 0.05} = 8$$

But if b falls to 0.4, G also falls since $G = br$. Assuming $r = 0.0833$, the decline in b reduces G to 0.033. As a result of the increase in the dividend payout ratio, P/E also rises to $0.6/(0.1 - 0.033) = 8.96$.

If the rate of return on reinvested earnings falls from $8\frac{1}{3}\%$ to 2%, G falls to 1.2% (0.6×0.02) and P/E $= 0.4/(0.1 - 0.012) = 3.99$. In this case, the change in P/E ratio reflects a change in dividend policy (a decline in payout resulting in a decline in expected growth), and the company is *not* more valuable with a P/E ratio of 3.99 than it was with a P/E ratio of 8.

Differences among price/earnings ratios are not the end of analyzing stock evaluation, but rather the beginning. Although it is always possible for two identical stocks to be priced differently in the market, it is safer to assume that if the prices are different, something else is different also.

Tax Treatment of Instruments

In general, tax treatment of debt instruments is different from equity instruments. This affects their yields, since investors are willing to accept lower before-tax yields when they get better after-tax yields. Interest payments on debt instruments are deductible as business expenses to the debtor, but are fully taxed as ordinary income to the creditor. On the other hand, the company issuing the stock may not deduct dividends as a business expense, but investors pay less taxes on dividends than on interest payments since a tax credit is permitted on dividends. Further, 85% of dividends paid by one corporation to another are not subject to taxation. Hence, corporations in the 50% tax bracket can buy preferred stock paying a 6% dividend yield and have an after-tax net yield of 5.55%. Thus the 6% dividend is equivalent to 12% interest, on which the corporation would have to pay 50% tax.

Since different taxpayers are in different tax brackets, it is difficult to estimate the impact of taxation on yield differences. Nonetheless, rational investors consider the relative tax burdens of different forms of investment income in determining their required yields.

Other Cost Factors

In addition to the required rate of return, the issuer of securities encounters other costs, particularly if the issue is public. Table 4-1 summarizes these costs, classified by type of security and size of issue.

Since many of these costs decline with the size of the issue, they must be fixed. Further, all else equal, debt seems to be cheaper to float than preferred stock, and preferred stock cheaper than equity.

The underwriting costs are compensation to investment bankers for the costs of distributing the securities (compensating salesmen, and so on) and may include a premium for risk taking. The investment banker often guarantees a net price to the corporate issuer of the securities before the securities are actually offered for sale. Such an issue is said to be *underwritten*. The investment banker or underwriter takes the risk that market conditions will not permit the sale of the securities at a price high enough to cover costs, a reasonable profit, and the net price guaranteed to the issuer. The investment banker usually finances the underwritten advance by an interest-bearing bank loan and is thus under considerable pressure to distribute the security rapidly, even under adverse market conditions. Delaying the distribution is unwise since market conditions may not improve and interest continues to mount on the loan. Thus, the risk is real and is contained in the underwriting fee.

The other expenses include legal and other professional fees involved in the preparation of the legal documents required by the Securities Act of 1933. This legislation applies to all issues (except government bonds and bank stocks) exceeding $500,000. A registration statement must be filed with the Securities and Exchange Commission at least 20 days before the public offering. This statement provides details on the financial, legal, and technical aspects of the company. As an aid to the investor, a summary of the registration statement, called a prospectus, must also be prepared and filed with the registration statement. If the SEC needs more time to check information or wants more information, the 20-day waiting period may be extended. However, selling efforts can begin during the waiting period, but these efforts are limited to a preliminary or "red-herring" prospectus. This must be labeled as neither an offer to sell nor a solicitation of an offer to buy the securities. Even after the waiting period, purchasers may sue the corporation, its officers and directors, the underwriter, and any of those participating in the preparation of the registration statement for misrepresentations or omissions. Since the penalties for such misrepresentations are severe, much care

Table 4-1. Costs of Flotation, 1961–1965
(as % of gross receipts)

Size of Issue (Millions of Dollars)	Debt			Preferred Stock			Common Stock		
	Underwriting Commission	Other Expenses	Total Costs	Underwriting Commission	Other Expenses	Total Costs	Underwriting Commission	Other Expenses	Total Costs
Under 0.5	7.4	8.0	15.4	7.9	8.0	16.0	11.3	7.3	18.5
0.5–0.9	7.2	3.1	10.3	8.0	3.1	11.1	9.7	4.9	14.6
1.0–1.9	7.0	3.4	10.4	8.0	3.4	11.4	8.6	3.0	11.6
2.0–4.9	4.2	1.2	5.4	4.8	1.2	6.1	7.4	1.7	9.1
5.0–9.9	1.5	0.6	2.1	1.0	0.6	1.6	6.7	1.0	7.6
10.0–19.9	1.0	0.4	1.4	1.4	0.4	1.8	6.2	0.6	6.9
20.0–49.9	1.0	0.4	1.4	2.7	0.4	3.1	4.9	0.8	5.6
50.0 and over	0.8	0.3	1.1	1.4	0.3	1.7	2.3	0.3	2.6

SOURCES: For common and preferred stocks: Securities and Exchange Commission, *Cost of Flotation of Registered Equity Issues, 1963–1965*, Washington, D.C.: U.S. Government Printing Office, March 1970, Tables 3 and 10. For debt: Underwriting costs estimated on basis of Irwin Friend, et al., *Investment Banking and the New Issues Market*, Cleveland, Ohio: World Publishing Company, 1967, Table 7–1, pp. 408–409. Because of rounding errors, totals may not equal the sum of the parts. Preferred stocks were used infrequently, and because of the small sample size the figures for this group are suspect.

and expense are taken in the preparation of both registration statement and prospectus.

Summary

Although preferred stocks are equity in the sense that the preferred stockholder has a weaker claim to income or assets than creditors, determining the yield on stock is similar to determining the yield on debt instruments of indefinite maturity. In both, the yield is the ratio of the income to the price.

However, preferred stock may have additional features that affect their values and, hence, yields. They may be convertible, that is, they may be exchanged for common stock at a set price. Thus, if the market price of the common exceeds the conversion price, the price of the convertible preferred reflects the conversion value.

Similarly, preferred stock, or debt, may have options to buy common stock, called warrants. If the price at which these warrants are exercised is less than the price of the common, the warrants add value to the security to which they are attached. Warrants may be issued separately from debt or preferred stock. Investors buy such warrants even when the market price of the common is below the exercise price on the warrant because losses are more limited with a low-priced warrant than with a common share. Further, if the price of the common rises, warrant holders realize a larger percentage gain on their warrants than they would if they had bought the common outright.

The yield on common stocks is more difficult to determine since the dividends are neither stated nor required of the firm. However, expected dividends are the basis for common stock yields, and the present value of expected dividends is the price of the common. If dividends are constant, or are assumed to grow at a constant rate, simplified models can be used to value and determine the yields of common shares. The use of price/earnings ratios as an indicator of value, though fairly common, is fraught with error since identical stocks with different dividend policies can have different prices. The investor who buys the cheaper stock on the basis of the price/earnings ratio may simply be buying a smaller dividend stream.

Taxation also affects yields. Certain government issues are tax free and hence sell at lower yields than they would if the interest was taxed. Similarly, only 15% of intercorporate dividends are subject to taxation, so that preferred stock may sell at lower yields than taxable interest-bearing bonds, even though the latter may be less risky.

In addition to yields, security issuers have other costs. A publicly issued instrument is subject to Securities and Exchange Commission regulations. There are distribution costs, including selling costs of investment bankers and, perhaps, a price guarantee by the investment banker. These costs are the costs of flotation. They tend to be a larger percentage of small issues, reflecting fixed charges, and they are larger for riskier instruments.

Review Questions

4-1 What, if any, are the differences in the tax treatments of bonds common stock?

4-2 What factors would enter a model for determining the price of a warrant?

4-3 What are the differences in the claims of holders of commercial paper, preferred stock, and common stock issued by the same corporation?

4-4 What are the essential differences between preferred stock and bonds?

4-5 Under what conditions does the price/earnings ratio equal the yield on the stock?

Problems

4-6 You are an investment banker trying to price a stock that has never been traded before, although the company has been in business for 50 years. Over this time, the company has maintained an annual growth rate in earnings of 10%. Its payout ratio is 40%. What more do you need to know to estimate the price of the stock? Explain.

4-7 The ABC Steel Company expects its earnings per common share to be $3 during the next year. Their dividend payout ratio has typically been 40%, and dividends have been paid annually. For this company, and the steel industry generally, the price/earnings ratio has been consistently near 9. If the stock is to yield 10% over the next year, what must its current price be?

4-8 The earnings for da Costa Corporation are expected to grow at the rate of 10% for the next two years; thereafter they are expected to grow at 5% forever. Earnings for the current year are expected to reach $10 per share. Da Costa will start paying dividends (at the rate of 50% of earnings) three years from now; the stock is currently selling for $103.47 per share. What return to the stockholders is consistent with this price?

4-9 The 7% preferred stock of XYZ Corporation (par value $20) is expected to be selling at $23 two years hence. What would be the two-year holding period return on the stock if it can be purchased for $20.64 today?

4-10 ABC Corporation expects growth of 4% per year to continue for the foreseeable future. The company has a 60% dividend payout policy. Investors in ABC require a 10% return. What is your estimate of the current price/earnings ratio for ABC?

Glossary

Cumulative dividend	A protective feature on preferred stock that requires all past preferred dividends to be paid before dividends are paid on common stock.
Dividend payout ratio	The proportion of earnings that the corporation pays in dividends.
Dividend yield	The ratio of the current dividend to the current price of a share of stock.
Earnings/price	Inverse of the price/earnings ratio. See *price/earnings ratio*.
Flotation costs	The costs of issuing new securities.
Investment banker	One who underwrites and distributes new securities and generally helps firms to obtain funds.
Lever	The investment of fixed return funds at a rate in excess of the fixed return. The surplus accrues to the owners, *levering* their earnings.
Listed	A stock is listed if it has been approved for trading by a public exchange.
Over-the-counter market	All facilities provided for trading in unlisted securities, especially the telephone.
Price/earnings ratio (P/E)	The ratio of price per share to earnings per share. It is often considered a reflection of the characteristics of the stock.
Prospectus	A document that describes a new security issue. The prospectus is verified by the SEC. Until the SEC approves the prospectus, a preliminary, or red-herring, prospectus may be distributed.
Public exchange	An organized and centralized market for corporate securities such as the New York Stock Exchange.
Public stock	One that may, as a result of government approval, be freely traded. Private stocks are those not so approved, and thus not available to the general public.
Retained earnings	Net income not paid out in dividends. The balance sheet figure includes all such amounts during the history of the company.
Retention rate	The proportion of earnings that the corporation retains.
Required yield	The rate of return that investors expect to receive on an investment in common stock.

Super-growth	Growth at a rate above the corporation's normal long-term rate.
Tax credit	A deduction from taxes payable.
Terminal price	The price at which a security is sold at the end of the holding period.
Underwriting	The process of issuing new corporate securities. Underwriters bear the risk of adverse price movement during the period in which the securities are being distributed.
Warrant	A long-term option to buy a stated number of shares of common stock at a specified price. The specified price is referred to as the exercise price. Warrants are detachable if they may be sold separately from the underlying share.

Bibliography

BACON, PETER W., "The Subscription Price in Rights Offerings," *Financial Management 1* (Summer 1972), 59–64.

BAUMOL, W. J., B. G. MALKIEL, and R. E. QUANDT, "The Valuation of Convertible Securities," *Quarterly Journal of Economics 80* (Feb. 1966), 48–59.

BIERMAN, H., JR., and R. WEST, "The Acquisition of Common Stock by the Corporate Issuer," *Journal of Finance 21* (Dec. 1966), 687–696. "Further Comments," *Ibid. 23* (Dec. 1968), 865–869.

BLACK, FISCHER, and MYRON SCHOLES, "The Valuation of Option Contracts and a Test of Market Efficiency," *Journal of Finance 27* (May 1972), 399–417.

BRIGHAM, E. F., "The Profitability of a Firm's Purchase of Its Own Common Stock," *California Management Review 7* (Winter 1964), 69–76.

CHANG, E. C., "Accounting for Stock Splits," *Financial Executive 38* (March 1969), 79–80ff.

CHEN, ANDREW H. Y., "A Model of Warrant Pricing in a Dynamic Market," *Journal of Finance 25* (Dec. 1970), 1041–1059.

CRETIEN, P. D., JR., "Convertible Premium vs. Stock Prices," *Financial Analysts Journal 25* (Nov.–Dec. 1969), 90–96.

DONALDSON, G., "In Defense of Preferred Stock," *Harvard Business Review 40* (July–August 1962), 123–126.

ELSAID, H. H., "Non-Convertible Preferred Stock as a Financing Instrument, 1950–1965: Comment," *Journal of Finance 24* (Dec. 1969), 939–941.

ELTON, EDWIN J., and MARTIN J. GRUBER, "The Economic Value of the Call Option," *Journal of Finance 27* (Sept. 1972), 891–902.

FERGUSON, D. A., "Preferred Stock Valuation in Recapitalizations," *Journal of Finance 13* (March 1958), 48–69.

FISCHER, D. E., and G. A. WILT, JR., "Non-Convertible Preferred Stock as a Financing Instrument, 1950-1965, *Journal of Finance 23* (Sept. 1968), 611–624.

HAYES, S. L., III, and H. B. REILING, "Sophisticated Financing Tool: The Warrants," *Harvard Business Review 47* (Jan.–Feb. 1969), 137–150.

HOLLAND, D. M., and W. G. LEWELLEN, "Probing the Record of Stock Options," *Harvard Business Review 40* (March–Apr. 1962), 132–150.

JOHNSON, K. B., "Stock Splits and Price Change," *Journal of Finance 21* (Dec. 1966), 675–686.

KEANE, SIMON M., "The Significance of the Issue Price in Rights Issues," *Journal of Business Finance 4,* No. 3 (1972), 40–45.

LOGUE, DENNIS E., "On the Pricing of Unseasoned Equity Issues: 1965–1969," *Journal of Financial and Quantitative Analysis 8* (Jan. 1973), 91–104.

McDONALD, J. G., and A. K. FISHER, "New Issue Stock Price Behavior," *Journal of Finance 27* (March 1972), 97–102.

MELICHER, RONALD W., "Financing with Convertible Preferred Stock: Comment," *Journal of Finance 26* (March 1971), 144–147; and GEORGE E. PINCHES, "Reply," *Ibid.,* 150–151.

PINCHES, G. E., "Financing with Convertible Preferred Stocks, 1960–1967," *Journal of Finance 25* (March 1970), 53–64.

SCHWARTZ, W., "Warrants: A Form of Equity Capital," *Financial Analysts Journal 26* (Sept.–Oct. 1970), pp. 87–101.

SOLDOFSKY, R. M., "Convertible Preferred Stock: Renewed Life in an Old Form," *Business Lawyer 24* (July 1969), 1385–1392.

———, "Yield-Rate Performance of Convertible Securities," *Financial Analysts Journal 27* (March–Apr. 1971), 61–65.

SPRECHER, C. RONALD, "A Note on Financing Mergers with Convertible Preferred Stock," *Journal of Finance 26* (June 1971), 683–686.

STEVENSON, RICHARD A., "Retirement of Non-Callable Preferred Stock," *Journal of Finance 25* (Dec. 1970), 1143–1152.

STOLL, HANS R., and ANTHONY J. CURLEY, "Small Business and the New Issues Market for Equities," *Journal of Financial and Quantitative Analysis 5* (Sept. 1970), 309–322.

VAN HORNE, J. C., "Warrant Valuation in Relation to Volatility and Opportunity Cost," *Industrial Management Review 10* (Spring 1969), 19–32.

———, "New Listings and Their Price Behavior," *Journal of Finance 25* (Sept. 1970), 783–794.

WALTER, JAMES E., and AGAUSTIN V. QUE. "The Valuation of Convertible Bonds," *Journal of Finance 28* (June 1973), 713–732.

WEINGARTNER, H. MARTIN, "Optimal Timing of Bond Refunding," *Management Science 13* (March 1967), 511–524.

YOUNG, ALAN, and WAYNE MARSHALL, "Controlling Shareholder Servicing Costs," *Harvard Business Review 49* (Jan.–Feb. 1971), 71–78.

Appendix A

Yield Problems and Solutions

Given i, the rate of interest per period, if an investment has a value of $\$P$ at any time, then its value n periods forward from this date is found by multiplying $\$P$ by $(1 + i)^n$, and its value n periods back from this date is found by multiplying $\$P$ by $(1 + i)^{-n}$.

The principal P that must be invested now at a given rate of interest in order to amount to a given sum F on some future date is called the *present value* of F, $F = P(1 + i)^n$.

Example 1a   It is estimated that a given project will result in cash flows of $100 two years from now and $200 three years from now. What is the present value (PV) of these cash flows if the interest rate for the period is 6% per annum?

Example 1b   The project in Example 1a entails an outlay of $222 now. Determine the net present value (NPV) of the project.

Example 1c   Determine the internal rate of return (IRR) of the project in Example 1a.

Example 2   Find the future value of $1000, invested for 10 years at 12% per annum.

An *annuity* is a succession of periodical payments. An annuity in which the payments continue forever is called a *perpetuity*.

Example 3   Payments of $100 each are to be made at the end of each year for four consecutive years. If the rate of interest is 8% per annum, find the value of the following payments.
   (a) One year before the first payment is due.
   (b) Immediately after the third payment is due.

Example 4   If the interest rate is 10% per annum, what is the present value of a perpetuity of $100 whose first payment is to be received one year hence.

Example 5   A man is entitled to receive $1000 at the *end* of each year forever. He wishes to exchange this for a payment of $R made at the *beginning* of each year for 20 years. Find R at 8% per annum.

Example 6   Find the value of a 6%, $100 bond redeemable in five years to yield 8%.

Example 7   A 9% bond of par value $1000 can currently be purchased for $956. The bond matures in six years. What is its yield to maturity?

Example 8   An individual plans to hold a 7%, $100 bond for three years. The bond matures in ten years. The bond can currently be purchased for $100.50, and its price after three years is expected to be $104. Determine the three-year holding period yield of the bond.

Example 9   A common stock can be purchased for $12 per share. During the coming year, equal semiannual dividends totaling $0.50 per share will be paid. The best estimate of the stock price one year hence is $14. What is the estimated one-year holding period return? Neglect brokerage costs.

Example 10   A company's stock sells for $10 per share and is expected to appreciate at a rate of 8% per annum. At that rate, what should its price per share be at the end of five years?

Solutions to Examples

Example 1a
$$PV = 100(1 + i)^{-2} + 200(1 + i)^{-3}$$
$$= 100(1.06)^{-2} + 200(1.06)^{-3}$$
$$= (100 \times 0.89) + (200 \times 0.84)$$
$$= 89 + 168$$
$$= \$257$$

b NPV = (present value of cash in flows) – (present value of cash outflows)
$$= 257 - 222$$
$$= \$35$$

c Solve for i: $222 = 100(1 + i)^{-2} + 200(1 + i)^{-3}$
Technique: Try different values of i
For $i = 12\%$, the right-hand side $= (100 \times 0.797) +$
$(200 \times 0.712) = 222.10$
Therefore $IRR \cong 12\%$

Example 2 $F = 1000(1.12)^{10} = 1000/(1.12)^{-10} = 1000/0.322 = \$3100$

Example 3

$$a = 100(1.08)^{-1} + 100(1.08)^{-2} + 100(1.08)^{-3}$$
$$+ 100(1.08)^{-4}$$
$$= 92.60 + 85.70 + 79.40 + 73.50 = \$331.20$$
$$b = 100(1.08)^{2} + 100(1.08)^{1} + 100 + 100(1.08)^{-1}$$
$$= 100/0.857 + 100/0.926 + 100 + 92.60 = \$417.30$$

Example 4
$$PV = 100(1.10)^{-1} + 100(1.10)^{-2} + 100(1.10)^{-3}\ldots$$
$$= 100[(1.10)^{-1} + (1.10)^{-2} + (1.10)^{-3}\ldots]$$

$$= 100 \frac{(1.10)^{-1}}{1 - (1.10)^{-1}} = 100 \frac{1}{1/(1.10)^{-1}} = 100 \frac{1}{1.10 - 1}$$

$$= 100 \frac{1}{0.10} = \frac{100}{0.10} = \frac{\text{payment}}{\text{rate}} = \$1000$$

Recall: For a geometric progression
$$\text{Sum} = a + ar + ar^2 + ar^3 + \ldots = \frac{a}{1 - r} \quad \text{for} \quad r < 1$$

Example 5 Present value of perpetuity $= \dfrac{1000}{.08} = \$12,500$

Present value of annuity $= R + R(1.08)^{-1} + R(1.08)^{-2}$
$$+ R(1.08)^{-3} + \cdots + R(1.08)^{-19}$$
$$= R + R(9.604) = \$10.604R$$
Therefore, $R = \dfrac{12,500}{10.604} = \$1,179$

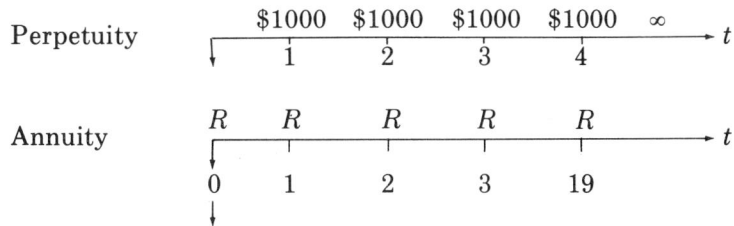

Perpetuity

$$\begin{array}{ccccc} \$1000 & \$1000 & \$1000 & \$1000 & \infty \\ 1 & 2 & 3 & 4 \end{array} \quad t$$

Annuity

$$\begin{array}{cccccc} R & R & R & R & R \\ 0 & 1 & 2 & 3 & 19 \end{array} \quad t$$

Example 6 $V = 100(1.08)^{-5} + 6\left[\displaystyle\sum_{j=1}^{5} (1.08)^{-j}\right]$

$= 68.10 + 6(3.993)$

$= \$92.06$

Example 7 Solve for i: $95 = 1000(1 + i)^{-6} + 90\left[\displaystyle\sum_{j=1}^{6}(1 + i)^{-j}\right]$

For $i = 10\%$, the right-hand side $= 564 + 90(4.355) = 955.95$

Therefore, yield to maturity $\cong 10\%$

Example 8 Solve for i: $100.50 = 104(1 + i)^{-3} + 7\left[\displaystyle\sum_{j=1}^{3} (1 + i)^{-j}\right]$

For $i = 8\%$, the right-hand side $= (104 \times 0.794) + (7 \times 2.577) = 100.515$

Therefore, holding period yield $\cong 8\%$

Example 9 Let i = one-year holding period return.

$\$12 = 0.25(1 + i)^{-0.5} + 0.25(1 + i)^{-1} + 14(1 + i)^{-1}$

For $i = 20\%$, right-hand side $= 0.25(0.914)$

$+ (0.25 + 14)(0.833) = 12.09$

Note: $(1 + i)^{-0.5} = [(1 + i)^{-1}]^{0.5}$

Therefore, the one-year yield on this stock is expected to be approximately 20%.

Example 10 $P(5 \text{ years hence}) = 10(1.08)(1.08)(1.08)(1.08)(1.08)$

$$= 10(1.08)^5 = 10\left(\frac{1}{0.681}\right) = \$14.70$$

The Term Structure of Yields

5

At the end of Chapter 4, we reviewed some of the factors that create differences in yields on financial assets. In this and the next few chapters, we shall present some systematic approaches explaining the differences in yields among financial instruments. First, we shall attempt to explain why securities with essentially the same risk of default (the risk that the issuer will not fulfill all promises), but with different terms to maturity, should have different yields.

Though this inquiry certainly seems pedestrian compared to exploring the differences in yields among common stocks, some understanding of differences in term structure is important. Differences in yield caused solely by term factors are found mainly among securities issued by governments, since few corporations have a large number of debt issues that are identical except for their terms.

Government has literally billions of dollars of outstanding debt, issued by international (such as the World Bank), national, and subnational units of government. Much of the public debt is not retired when it matures. Instead, it is refunded or "rolled over," with new debt issued to replace the old. Either in issuing new debt or refunding existing debt, government financial managers and their advisors in the investment and banking industries must consider the term to maturity of the new issue.

As a partial illustration of the problem, consider Table 5-1. Faced with the problem of refunding an existing issue in January of 1974, the U.S. Treasury might well have decided to take advantage of the unusual situation in which the average yield on three-to-five–year notes was less than the yield on 90-day treasury bills and issue notes, a condition characteristic of early 1974 and all of 1973. However, if they wanted to

Table 5-1. Shifting Advantage of Going Long

	U.S. 90 Day Treasury Bills	U.S. 3–5 Year Notes	Spread in Basis Points	Spread/ T Bill Rate
Jan. 74	7.77%	6.94%	−93	−12%
Dec. 74	7.15	7.22	7	1
Feb. 75	5.65	6.92	127	23
July 75	6.01	7.62	161	27
Feb. 76	4.85	7.17	232	48
July 76	5.41	7.40	199	37

SOURCE: Board of Governors of the Federal Reserve System.

minimize interest rate costs, the data in Table 5-1 show that they would have been better off issuing treasury bills over the entire period, ignoring the higher total issue costs because of the larger number of rollovers of the shorter-term treasury bills. Note that both the absolute and relative advantage of staying in the short end of the market increased over the time span in the table.

Thus, market movements over even a short period of $2\frac{1}{2}$ years are difficult to forecast. The Treasury may have had goals other than minimizing government interest costs and growth of issue costs. But the wide absolute and relative differentials shown in Table 5-1 indicate how difficult it is to make a prudent decision regardless of criterion. It also shows the potential value of understanding what determines the differences in yields of securities from the same issuer with different maturities.

A financial institution investing part of its portfolio in debt may have made similar mistakes, but in the opposite direction. In 1974, it might have preferred the short end of the term structure, given the differential. In one year, it would have reinvested funds in notes. However, the value of the notes would have declined over the next two years as rates on three-to-five–year notes rose, with long-term rates rising sharply, while short-term rates fell. As we shall point out later, an increase in interest rates affects long-term security prices far more severely than short-term security prices. Figure 5-1 illustrates the dynamics of the term structure, showing how it can even become negative at times.

We don't know of any formulas that would have avoided these hypothetical mistakes, but some appreciation of the reasons for differences in term structure yields is clearly helpful. These examples show that an investor could err by choosing the highest yielding of a group of securities that have identical risks of default but different terms.

Explanations of term differences fall into two major groups:

1. Explanations that emphasize the impact of expected future short-term rates on the current differential between long-term and short-

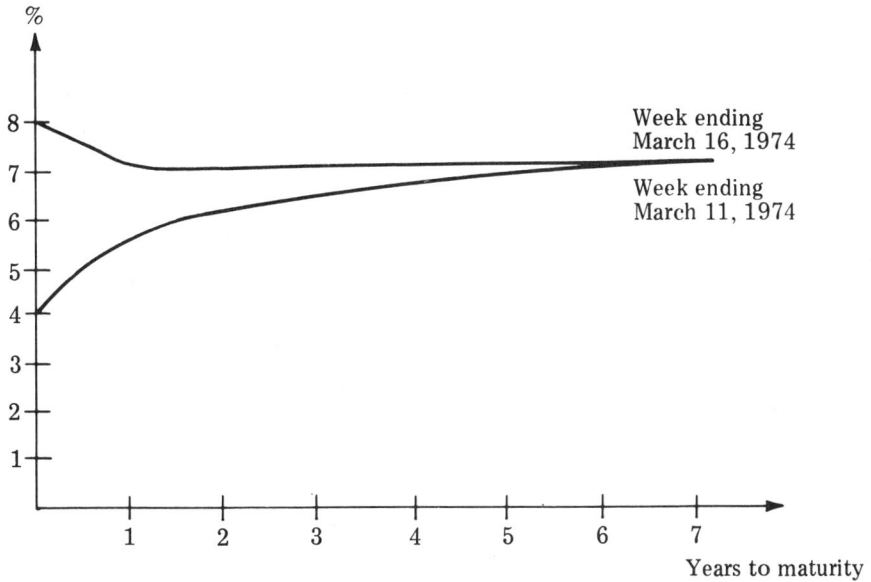

Source: *Board of Governors of the Federal Reserve System.*

Figure 5-1
Term Structure of Yields on U.S. Treasure Securities

    term rates. A variant of this explanation includes consideration of the additional risk of investing in a long-term security.

2. An explanation that emphasizes the segmentation of debt markets. Institutions involved in long-term investment (such as life insurance companies) invest primarily in the long end of the market, while institutions involved primarily in shorter-term investments (such as banks) dominate short markets. Thus, the term structure of interest differences reflects different growth rates for the different kinds of institutions. That is, if life insurance companies are growing more rapidly than banks, the demand for long-term bonds increases more rapidly than the demand for short-term securities. As a result, the difference between long- and short-term yields narrows.

Expectations under Conditions of Certainty

    The pure expectations theory is probably the oldest explanation of term structure differences. It assumes that there exists a generally accepted set of expectations about future short-term interest rates. Given these expectations, one can compare returns from a strategy of short-term investment (reinvesting proceeds from maturing short-term claims into new short-term claims) with the strategy of investing in long-term securities. In this theory, costs of making transactions are ignored. The return on the short-term strategy equals the average of the current and expected future short-term rates. This average return can be compared to the current long-term rate of return that is available by investing in the long-term security now, and not having to replace the security over the planning period of the portfolio. According to this theory, if the average short-term return is larger than the long-term yield, investors buy short-term securities, thus driving up short-term prices and pushing down their yields. They avoid long-term securities, and as a result, long-term security prices fall and long-term security yields rise. This pressure continues until the average yield expected from reinvesting in short-term investments over the planning period of the portfolio equals the currently available long-term yield.

As an illustration of this theory, consider the following. The current one-period interest rate R_1 is 10%, the one-period interest rate expected at the end of the current period for the next period (r_2) is 10%, and $100 is to be invested. What must the current rate for a two-period investment equal?

At the end of two years, the expected future value is

$$(1 + r_2)(1 + R_1)(100) = (1.1)(1.1)(100) = 121$$

If R_2 is the annual two-period interest rate, R_2 must equal 10% per year, since an investor can earn 10% annually from the short-term security. The expected future value from investing in a two-period security is

$$(1 + R_2)^2(100) = (1.21)(100) = \$121$$

and, by arbitrage,

$$(1 + R_1)(1 + r_2)100 = (1 + R_2)^2(100) \,^{\textstyle .}$$

or $\qquad\qquad\qquad\qquad\qquad\qquad\qquad\qquad\qquad\qquad$ (5-1)

$$(1 + R_1)(1 + r_2) = (1 + R_2)^2$$

or

$$1 + R_2 = \sqrt{(1 + R_1)(1 + r_2)} \qquad\qquad\qquad (5\text{-}1a)$$

So, in the example, $R_2 = 10\%$.

The current rate for a three-year security would be R_3 and

$$1 + R_3 = [(1 + R_1)(1 + r_2)(1 + r_3)]^{1/3} \qquad\qquad (5\text{-}2)$$

In general

$$R_n = [(1 + R_1)(1 + r_2)(1 + r_3) \cdots (1 + r_n)]^{1/n} - 1 \qquad (5\text{-}3)$$

Hence, with the pure expectations approach to term structures, the long-

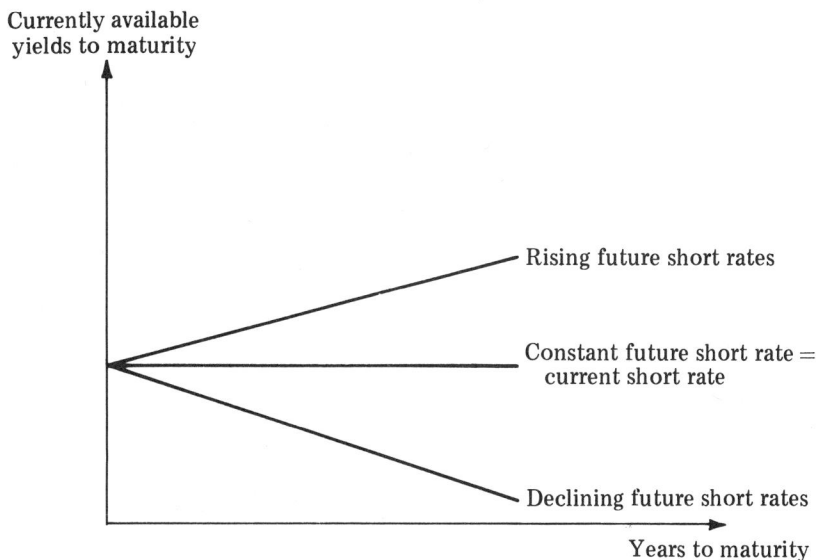

Currently available
yields to maturity

Rising future short rates

Constant future short rate =
current short rate

Declining future short rates

Years to maturity

Figure 5-2
Yield Curves with Certainty

term interest rate is the geometric mean[1] of expected future short-term rates.

In this example, expected short-term rates are constant. Is the formulation affected by differences in future short-term rates? Suppose that next period's short-term rate is expected to be 12%, although the current one-period rate is 10%. What is the value of the current two-period rate?

Investing in the short-term strategy would yield $(1 + R_1)(1 + r_2) - 1$, so the rate on a two-year security (R_2) must also equal this or

$$1 + R_2 = \sqrt{(1.1)(1.12)} = 1.11 \quad \text{or} \quad R_2 \cong 11\%$$

If r_3 is expected to be 14%, what is the value of R_3, the current three-period yield?

$$\begin{aligned}
1 + R_3 &= [(1 + R_1)(1 + r_2)(1 + r_3)]^{1/3} \\
&= [(1.1)(1.12)(1.14)]^{1/3} \\
&\cong 1.123 \quad \text{or} \quad R_3 \cong 12.3\%
\end{aligned}$$

In the two-period example, if r_2 is expected to decline to 8%, then

$$R_2 = \sqrt{(1.1)(1.08)} - 1 = \sqrt{1.188} - 1 \cong 0.09$$

[1]The geometric mean is the antilog of the arithmetic mean of the logs of the data, i.e. geometric mean = $[(X_1)(X_2) \ldots (X_n)]^{1/n} - n$.

So yield curves can rise or fall depending on the expected short-term rate.

The yield curves in Figure 5-2 show the differences in yields on securities of different maturities available in the market today. With the rising yield curve, long-term rates exceed short-term rates, since future short-term rates are expected to rise. If future short-term rates are expected to remain constant, the yield curve is flat, and current short-term rates equal current long-term rates. Finally, a declining yield curve indicates that current long-term rates are less than current short-term rates because future short-term rates are expected to decline.

Expectations with Uncertainty

The notion that long-term rates can be less than short-term rates goes against the grain of even financial novices. However such differences have occurred. From approximately the end of the Civil War to 1898, short-term rates in the United States tended to exceed long-term rates. Since then, there have been brief periods during which short-term rates have exceeded long-term rates. The most recent such period in the United States occurred during the second half of 1973.

The fact that long-term interest rates generally exceed short-term interest rates does not negate the pure expectations theory. When investors expect future short-term rates to rise, yield curves have positive slopes, that is, long-term rates exceed short-term rates. However, some have argued that the tendency for long-term rates to exceed short-term rates reflects, in addition to expectations about future short-term rates, the greater degree of uncertainty confronting long-term investors. In effect, this modification removes the very strong assumption of the pure expectations theory that investors must be certain about the future. Individual investors are *not certain* about their expectations. Hence, a rate higher than the average of expected future short-term rates may be needed to entice them into long-term markets. This uncertainty gives rise to a yield premium above that justified by expectations alone. The premium can be viewed as a premium for undertaking uncertainty. Sometimes, it is referred to as a liquidity premium because long-term investors are foregoing the liquidity they would have had with short-term investments. However, since bonds are marketable, long-term bonds can be considered as liquid as short-term bonds, provided that there is an active secondary bond market (market dealing with securities other than those newly issued).

To see how the uncertainty premium operates in a simple illustration, consider the following example. Let $R_1 = 10\%$, and $r_2 = 10\%$, but the investor wants a premium for being tied into a two-period investment contract. So

$$(1 + R_2)^2 = (1 + R_1)(1 + r_2 + L_2), \qquad (5\text{-}4)$$

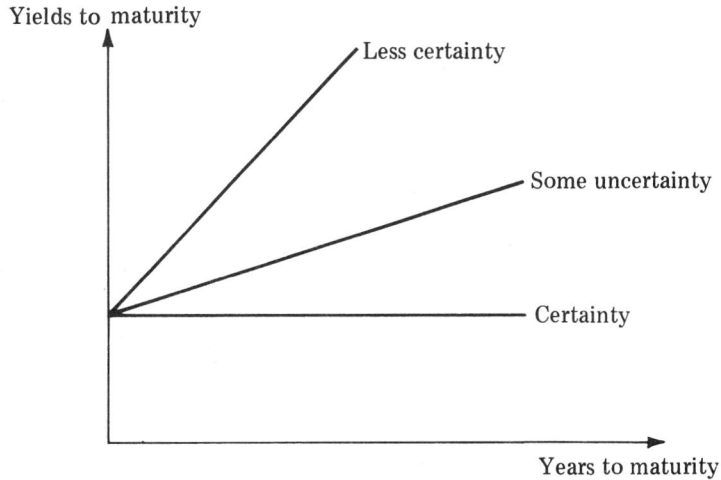

Figure 5-3
Yield Curves with Uncertainty

where L_2 is the premium for being tied to an investment in future years. If $L_2 = 4\%$, then

$$1 + R_2 = \sqrt{(1.1)(1.1 + 0.04)} = \sqrt{(1.1)(1.14)} = \sqrt{1.254} = 1.12$$

Because of uncertainty premiums, the curve relating yields over time tends to be positively sloped, with the curve becoming steeper as the future becomes less certain. Suppose that future short-term rates are expected to be constant. With no uncertainty, the yield curve in Figure 5-3 is shown by the horizontal line labeled "perfect certainty." As uncertainty grows, the yield curve becomes steeper.

We can determine the multiperiod yield when expected future short-term rates are not constant as follows. If $r_2 = 12\%$, $L_2 = 2\%$, and $R_1 = 10\%$, then substituting these values into

$$1 + R_2 = \sqrt{(1 + R_1)(1 + r_2 + L_2)}$$

yields

$$1 + R_2 = \sqrt{(1.1)(1.12 + .02)} \cong 1.13 \quad \text{or} \quad R_2 \cong 13\%$$

If $r_2 = 8\%$, $L_2 = 2\%$, $R_1 = 10\%$, then substituting yields

$$1 + R_2 = \sqrt{(1.1)(1.08 + .02)} = 1.10 \quad \text{or} \quad R_2 = 10\%$$

Thus, uncertainty premiums bias the yield curve upward, and one cannot derive expected future rates mathematically from the yield curve because of this bias.

The Term Structure of Yields

The Consistency of Yields

Now we investigate whether one can take advantage of the term structure of yields. We might do this, for example, by buying a two-year security when it has a higher interest rate than a one-year security, and then selling it at the end of the first year. In this fashion, it may be argued, we earn the higher two-year rate for the first year and are better off than if we had purchased a one-year security.

In general, this is not possible. Although the investor in the two-year security receives more interest the first year because of the higher interest rate, the price of the two-year security is below its maturity value at the end of the first year. The net yield, therefore, is exactly the same as that for a one-year security.

For example, if $R_1 = 10\%$ and $r_2 = 12\%$, then $R_2 \cong 11\%$, assuming no uncertainty. Thus buying a two-year security and selling it after one year yields

$$i = \frac{\text{interest} + \text{market value at end of year}}{\text{cost at beginning of year}} - 1$$

The expected market value at the end of one year is the present value of the security for the second year (V).

$$V = \frac{\text{interest during second year} + \text{maturity value}}{1 + r_2}$$

Now suppose that the cost at the beginning is $100. Then the interest during the second year is R_2 (maturity value) or $0.11 \times 100 = \$11$. If the maturity value is $100, the holder for the second year receives $11 in interest + $100 maturity value or $111. So

$$V = \$111 \times \frac{1}{1.12} = \$111 \times 0.89286 = \$99.10$$

at the end of the first year. The holding period yield for the first year is then

$$i = \frac{\$11 + 99.10}{100} - 1 = \frac{110.10}{100} \cong 10\%$$

If an uncertainty premium exists for the second year, the one-year holder receives it. This is fair since this holder assumed the risk of holding a two-period security for the earlier period to which the premium applied.

Market Segmentation

The market segmentation explanation of term differences is based on institutional factors. Savers who deposit money in institutions such as banks and trust companies receive claims that are very liquid. As a result, the institutions issuing such claims tend to invest in assets that are equally liquid. They therefore tend to invest in the short end of the market.

Other institutions such as life insurance policies and retirement pension funds issue longer-term claims. As a result, these institutions operate in the long end of the market and buy such things as mortgages and bonds.

Business borrowers, it is argued, need long-term funds to finance capital spending and hence cannot move easily among the various term instruments even if the short end of the market offers yield advantages. Thus, some argue that term structure differences reflect the differential rate of growth for financial institutions primarily in the long-term market. If savings placed in short-term claims issued by deposit institutions grow at a more rapid rate than those placed in life insurance companies, banks will be buying substantial quantities of short-term assets, thus depressing short-term interest rates, and the term structure of yields will become steeper. On the other hand, if savers increase the growth rate of funds flowing into retirement funds and life insurance companies, the demand for long-term claims by these institutions will grow. Thus long-term yields will decline relative to short-term yields, generating flatter yield curves. Figure 5-4 illustrates the flow patterns that are expected.

Like most institutional arguments, this one is persuasive to a degree rarely matched by theoretical arguments. However, the data do not clearly support the argument that the market is firmly segmented, with deposit institutions in the short end and long-term financial institutions in the long end. Although financial institutions undoubtedly match the

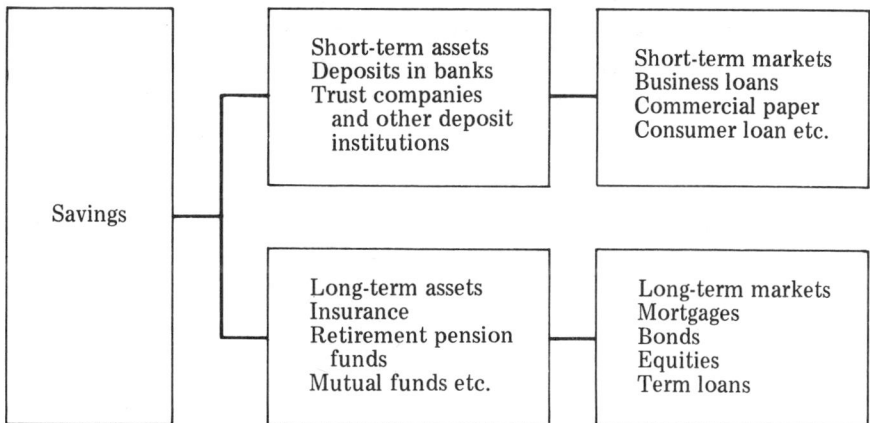

Figure 5-4
Financial Market Segmentation

terms of their assets with those of their liabilities to some degree, they do respond to yield differences, particularly as savers become more sophisticated and compare the net returns of different claims issued by the different financial institutions.

The precise matching of asset and liability terms assumed in this theory is somewhat naive. After all, although on any given day some depositors withdraw their funds from a deposit institution, other depositors deposit new funds. Thus, even though deposits turn over, deposit institutions can count on a more or less permanent level of deposits that they can feel free to invest in long-term assets. (Of course, an institution must first provide for unforeseen variations in the demand for deposit withdrawals.) Hence, deposit institutions can follow higher long-term yields despite the short-term nature of their liabilities.

On the other hand, long-term institutions are not as free from withdrawals as their name might imply. Life insurance companies, for example, often offer policyholders the right to borrow money on their insurance policies. Such policy loans are effectively temporary withdrawals of funds from the institution. Policyholders usually take these loans when market interest rates rise above the rates that the insurance company charges on policy loans. Thus, the life insurance company can face substantial drains, and in this way, its situation is similar to a bank's. Hence, prudent life insurance companies do not go fully into long-term assets; instead, they retain some funds in relatively short-term assets.

Even business borrowers are not constrained to finance long-term assets with long-term funds. If the short-term rate is well below the long rate, the firm may find it profitable to use short-term funding despite the higher refinancing costs of short-term funds and the greater risk that refinancing funds may not be available. Thus, profit maximizing behavior on the part of financial institutions and borrowers, combined with a recognition that the need for liquidity is not restricted solely to deposit institutions, suggests that the market segmentation argument is not a complete description of the way that financial institutions operate. So it is probably not an adequate description of the determinants of yield differences.

Portfolio Management Factors

Do practical applications exist for term structure considerations? As we pointed out at the beginning of this chapter, knowledge that some relationship exists among the yields of securities with different terms to maturity prevents borrowers from blindly issuing claims with the lowest interest rates, or investors from buying claims at the highest interest rates.

Further, investors may make money by knowing the term structure if they can discover an anomaly, that is, a yield significantly off the yield curve. If the yield is substantially above the yield curve, it is a good buy. If the yield is well below the yield curve, that security should be sold. However, investors have to be certain that anomalies are true anomalies and not merely shifts in the yield curve. The term structure theories do not explain shifts in the yield curves.

Knowing how prices of securities with different terms to maturity behave when interest rates change has a number of practical applications. For example, consider the following problem. Two bonds both have a coupon rate of 1% paid annually, but one matures in five years and the other in ten years. Which is better if interest rates are expected to fall from 10% to 8%?

Term	Price at 10%	Price at 8%	Dollar gain	Appreciation (%)
5-year	685.91	720.97	45.06	5.1
10-year	447.45	530.10	82.65	18.7

The prices behave differently because the longer-term bond has more years for discount factors to be affected by the change in interest rate. If interest rates rise instead of fall, the ten-year bond would show a larger loss than the five-year bond. Thus this illustration shows *not* that it is more profitable to hold longer-term bonds, but that it is more *risky* to hold longer-term bonds, since their values fluctuate more widely when interest rates change.

Next consider the effect of the coupon interest rate. Two bonds both mature in five years, but one has a 5% coupon and the other has a 10% coupon. Which is better if interest rates are expected to rise from 8% to 10%?

Coupon	Price at 8%	Price at 10%	Dollar loss	Loss (%)
5%	880.65	810.55	70.10	8
10%	1080	1000	80	7.4

Their prices behave differently because, although both have the same yield to maturity, most of the returns for the 5% coupon bond are in the maturity value rather than in interest. Interest on the 5% coupon bond is $50 per year, whereas it is $100 per year for the 10% coupon bond. Hence, the returns are weighted further out in the future for the 5% coupon bond.

A shift from 8% to 10% in market interest rates is more extreme the further into the future one moves. Consider the denominator of the discount factor $1/(1 + i)^n$. The larger the value of n, the more that any change in i affects the discount factor.

Now let's return to Table A in Chapter 2. Moving from 8% to 10%, we find that the discount factor for the first year declines 0.017. By the fifth year, however, the decline is 0.060. Since most of the returns on the

5% coupon bond occur later in its life, the present value of these returns is more severely affected by a shift in interest rates than if the returns were close to the current period.

Once again, we cannot conclude from this example that the investor should avoid low-coupon bonds. After all, if interest rates decline, the return on investment would be correspondingly higher for low-coupon bonds. What we can conclude is that when interest rates are volatile, low-coupon bonds tend to generate more variable returns than high-coupon bonds. More succinctly, low-coupon bonds tend to be riskier than high-coupon bonds in terms of price volatility.

Thus, knowledge of the factors determining the term structure of yields may not make a fortune for either issuers or investors. However, such knowledge helps both avoid following "anomalies" that are really part of the term structure.

Summary

The term structure of yields is significant particularly for large borrowers, such as governments, as well as for investors. One should not necessarily issue short-term securities because they have lower yields than longer-term ones. When the short-term issue matures, it may have to be refinanced (replaced) with debt at interest rates even higher than the long-term rates available originally. Similarly, investors who lock themselves into long-term debt because of higher yields may see the value of their holdings decline as interest rates rise.

Unfortunately, we don't know of any theory that allows us to avoid these errors and accurately foretell interest rates. However, existing theories of interest rate differentials explain the relationships among similar instruments of different term. The oldest of these is the pure expectations theory. This theory states that interest rates on long-term investments equal the geometric mean of the expected future short-term rates over the life of the long-term security. Thus, long-term rates can be above or below current short-term rates.

A modification of this theory adds a premium to the long-term yield for "illiquidity" or uncertainty about the direction of future rates. Thus, long-term investors get some compensation if they misjudge the direction of future rates.

Finally, there is an institutional theory of interest rate differences. Certain institutions, such as banks, issue short-term claims (demand deposits, for example). They tend to invest these funds in short-term instruments. Other institutions, such as life insurance companies, issue long-term claims and, hence, can buy long-term instruments. According to this theory, interest rate differentials reflect the growth rates of the different kinds of institutions. Borrowers are assumed to prefer long-term funds, since they tend to invest in long-term assets. Hence, the term structure of yields rises with term. There are many problems with this theory. Despite the temporary nature of a bank deposit, the overall level of deposits for a bank may be constant, so that banks can invest in long-term securities. On the other hand, insurance companies may be subject to policy loans when the loan rate is below the market rate for loans, so that their funds are considerably less long-term than might be expected. Finally, borrowers have short-term needs, although they can finance long-term assets by "rolling-over" short-term debt when the interest rate differential is large enough to justify the risk.

Investors should recognize that bonds with varying coupon rates and maturities have different risks even though there may be no question that the issuer will meet all the terms of the debt instrument. The price of short-term bonds tends to be less volatile than that of long-term bonds. Low-coupon bonds tend to have more volatile prices than high-coupon bonds.

Review Questions

5-1 What are the principle factors that influence the yield on a bond?

5-2 An insurance company sells an annuity contract that yields 8% (term 20 years). The company has an opportunity to buy a 20-year instrument that will yield $8\frac{1}{4}\%$. Short-term rates are currently 10%. Should the company go into the short or long end of the market?

5-3 Are the expectations and market segmentation theories of interest rate term structure mutually consistent? Discuss.

Problems

5-4 Reconstruct the example of Table 5-1 using more recent data. Would the same argument apply?

5-5 Given:

$R_1 = 10\% =$ actual interest rate for the current year

$r_2 = 12\% =$ expected one-year rate for the year beginning one year from now.

$r_3 = 14\% =$ expected one-year rate for the year beginning two years from now.

a. Find R_2, the actual rate for the next two years.

b. Find R_3, the actual rate for the next three years.

c. At what price would an investor who had money for only one year and who purchased a two-year bond (coupon = 8%, yield = 10.99%) be able to sell the bond at the end of the year? What would be the yield during the second year to the purchaser of the bond?

5-6 a. Compare (i) the prices of $5\frac{1}{2}\%$ bonds of various maturities to yield 5% and 6% with (ii) the prices of $5\frac{1}{2}\%$ bonds of various maturities to yield 7% and 8%. What do you find from these two comparisons?

b. A one-year bond bought today yields 4%, and yield rates on one-year bonds are expected to go to 5% next year and to stay at that level for the following three years. An investor wants to buy a longer maturity bond and hold it for the next four years. What yield should the investor expect?

5-7 If 25-year bonds yield 6%, and 10-year bonds of the same risk class yield 8%, what is the expected 15-year rate 10 years hence under the pure expectations hypothesis?

5-8 The following riskless bonds are available:

Yield	Maturity
7%	4 years
8%	5 years
9%	6 years

Investors require a liquidity premium of 0.04% to lend for two years instead of one ($L_2 = 0.04\%$), and this premium grows at a compound rate of 5% per year for each additional year they must lend long.

a. What is the expected one-year rate four years from now?

b. What is the expected one-year rate five years from now?

Glossary

Anomaly	An asset with a yield significantly different from that indicated as appropriate by the yield curve.
Arbitrage	The process of selling overvalued and buying under-valued assets to ensure that all assets are properly valued such that equilibrium exists.
Default risk	The risk that the issuer of a security (generally debt) will fail to fulfill his obligation.
Liquidity (yield) premium	An excess of yield above that justifiable by expectations to compensate the long-term investor for the loss of liquidity.
Market segmentation	The delineation of different customer groups.
Policy loan	A loan made against a life insurance policy.
Pure expectations theory	The theory that argues that the yield on a bond is the geometric mean of the expected short-term or one-period rate over the term of the bond.
Rolled over	Refunded. To refund is to sell new debt to replace a previous issue.

Short end	The part of the term structure that involves short-term securities.
Term structure	The pattern of yields on obligations of different maturities.
Treasury bills	A short-term, usually less than six-months, government security issued at a discount.
Uncertainty premium	See *liquidity premium.*
Yield curve	A graph of yields against years until maturity.
Yield spread	The difference between the yields on two securities.

Bibliography

CONARD, JOSEPH W., *Introduction to the Theory of Interest,* Part II. Berkeley, Ca: University of California Press, 1959.

CULBERTSON, J. M., "The Term Structure of Interest Rates," *Quarterly Journal of Economics,* Nov. 1957, 489–504.

JOHNSON, R. E., "The Term Structures of Corporate Bond Yields as a Function of Risk of Default," *Journal of Finance 22* (May 1967), 313–345.

KESSEL, R. A., *The Cyclical Behavior of the Term Structure of Interest Rates,* New York: *National Bureau of Economic Research,* 1965 (occasional paper 91).

MALKIEL, BURTON G., *The Term Structure of Interest Rates: Expectations and Behavior Patterns,* Princeton, N.J.: Princeton University Press, 1966.

———, *The Term Structure of Interest Rates: Theory, Empirical Evidence,* New York: McCaleb-Seiler, 1970.

MEISELMAN, DAVID, *The Term Structure of Interest Rates,* Englewood Cliffs, N.J.: Prentice-Hall, 1962.

MICHAELSEN, J. B., "The Term Structure of Interest Rates: Comment," *Quarterly Journal of Economics 77* (Feb. 1963), 166–174.

SILBER, WILLIAM, "The Term Structure of Interest Rates," in Polakoff et al., *Financial Institutions and Markets,* Boston: Houghton Mifflin, 1970.

WOOD, J. H., "Expectations and the Demand for Bonds," *American Economic Review 59* (Sept. 1969), 522–530.

Introduction to Risk

6

Although it is extremely important to understand why securities with different terms to maturity may offer different yields, term structure analysis is considerably simpler than risk analysis. Everyone recognizes that the future is uncertain and that today's decision may have more than one outcome. Yields should reflect differences in the degree of uncertainty among assets.

Hence, an analysis that explains differences in yields due to risk is valuable. If a business firm can determine the relative risks of two capital spending proposals, either the riskier proposal must have a larger net present value or it must be discounted by a larger required rate of return. Similarly, a government agency may require a higher ratio of expected benefits to cost from an unfamiliar proposal whose effectiveness is uncertain than it would from a familiar proposal whose outcome is more certain. These responses by business and public agencies are ways of managing risk. One of the purposes of this chapter is to appraise the appropriateness of such managerial responses to risk.

It is probably easier to recognize the role of risk in determining yield differences among financial assets than among real assets. A financial investor's ability to determine the reasons for differences in yields is crucial in developing a successful investment strategy. The investor who does not know that the term to maturity of an investment affects yield differences, or that risk may be related to yield differentials, may treat any difference in yield as a promise of unusual profits. Since term to maturity factors, differences in risk, or technical differences such as those described at the end of Chapter 4 explain most yield differences, an investment strategy that ignores these determinants is unlikely to generate even a normal rate of return, to say nothing of an above-average rate.

In this chapter, we shall attempt first to define risk. Then we shall develop a system of managing risk that we can apply to all kinds of assets, real or financial, private or public. In Chapter 7, we present a method of controlling risk that is applicable solely to financial assets.

The Definition of Risk

Probability Distribution

Whenever the outcome of a decision is not certain, that is, when several outcomes are possible, we say that *uncertainty* exists. If we can describe the uncertainty more precisely by specifying the kinds of outcome that may occur and the likelihood of their occurrence, then we move from generalized uncertainty to *risk*. Risk is related to the variability of the distribution of possible future outcomes.

Consider the investment alternatives in Figure 6-1. Which invest-

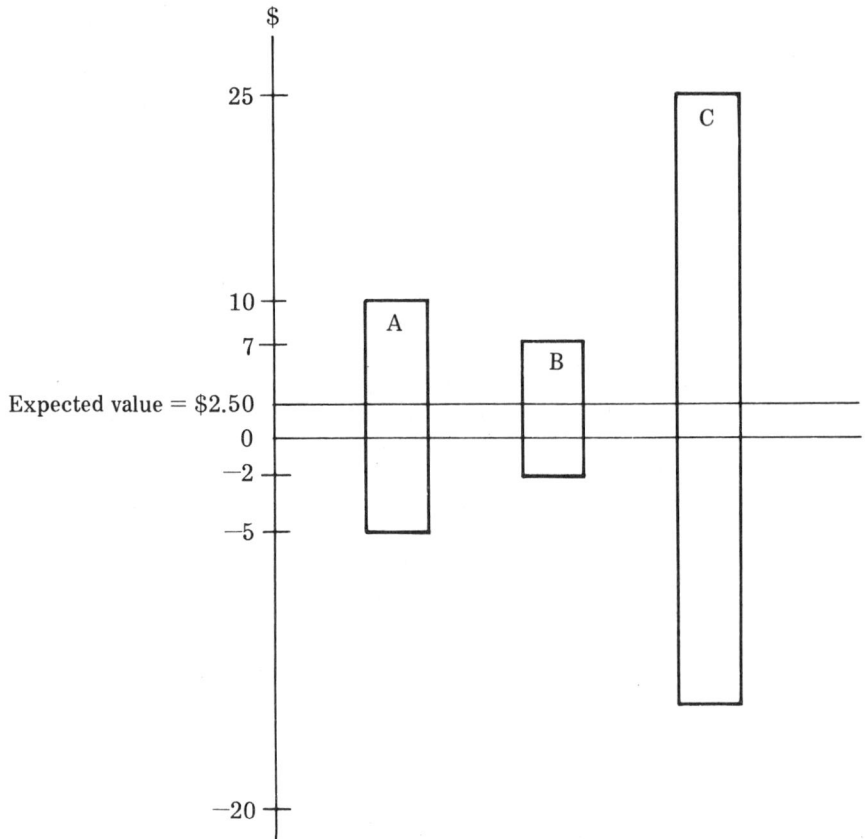

Figure 6-1
Possible and Expected Values of Three Investment Portfolios

An Introduction to Real and Financial Yields

ment portfolio do you prefer? On average, each of the portfolios returns the same value, $2.50. Yet it is unlikely that investors would pay the same price for each investment portfolio. Investors with limited resources might be reluctant to undertake portfolio C, which could lose as much as $20. They might prefer portfolio B, where the maximum loss is only $2.00.

In a series of experiments conducted among graduate business students at the University of North Carolina, Latané (see reference 2) discovered that most students confronted with portfolios similar to those in Figure 6-1 preferred portfolio B to portfolio C, assuming that both portfolios had identical prices. This suggests that investors may be averse to variations in returns. Thus, if variability is a measure of risk, these students behaved as if they were risk averse.

Standard Deviations

A widely used statistical measure of variability is *variance,* or its square root, *standard deviation.* The formulas for measuring the variance and its application to portfolios A, B, and C are as follows:

Standard deviation = square root of variance (Var)

$$\text{Var} = \sum \frac{(x - \bar{x})^2}{N}, \text{where } \bar{x}_A = \bar{x}_B = \bar{x}_C = \quad (6\text{-}1)$$
arithmetic mean $(\bar{x})$ or expected value of each portfolio.

So, using these definitions, we can find the variance of each portfolio.

	A		B		C	
	$x - \bar{x}$	$(x - \bar{x})^2$	$x - \bar{x}$	$(x - \bar{x})^2$	$x - \bar{x}$	$(x - \bar{x})^2$
	-7.5	56.25	-4.5	20.25	-22.5	506.25
	7.5	56.25	4.5	20.25	22.5	506.25
	$\Sigma (x - \bar{x})^2 =$	112.5		40.5		1012.5
Var =						
$\sum \frac{(x - \bar{x})^2}{N}$		56.25		20.25		506.25
$\sigma = \sqrt{\text{Var}}$		7.5		4.5		22.5

$$(6\text{-}2)$$

Thus, using variability as a measure of risk, B is the safest of the three alternatives and C is the most risky, even though they all have the same expected value.

The three portfolios are peculiar in the sense that they have probability distributions with only two values. So even though the expected value for each is $2.50, investors cannot expect to get $2.50 from any portfolio. However, an investor who undertook a large number of invest-

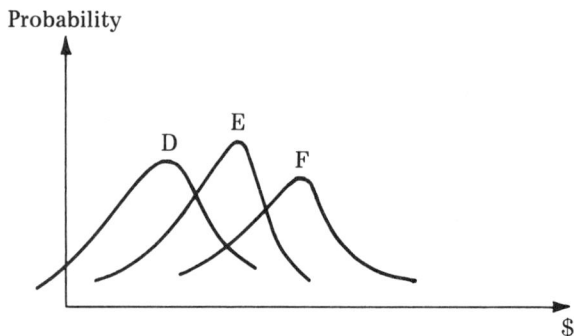

Figure 6-2
Probability Distributions of Three Different Investments

ments such as A would average $2.50 over the long run. In each case, however, the investor would either lose $5.00 or make $10.00.

More commonly, investments offer a multivalued range of outcomes like those in Figure 6-2. Portfolios D, E, and F have ranges of outcome that can be described by the probability distributions shown in Figure 6-2. Their ranges are summarized by the first two moments of the distribution—the expected value (*EV*) and the standard deviation—as Table 6-1 shows. In this case, the differences in expected return and risk complicate the choice. Now it is more difficult to choose among the portfolios than it was when they had the same expected values.

However, a description of investor behavior based purely on maximizing returns or on minimizing risk is incomplete. It seems reasonable to assume that investors are concerned both with return and risk, and thus might prefer to rank investment portfolios by some composite measure such as the ratio of risk (as measured by the standard deviation) to the expected return. This ratio is the *coefficient of variation*. For the example in Figure 6-1, we would then have the following coefficients:

Portfolio	D	E	F
Coefficient of variations (SD/EV)	3.16/10 = 0.316	2.24/20 = 0.112	3.16/30 = 0.105

Under this criterion, investors would probably choose the portfolio with

Table 6-1. Portfolio Characteristics

Portfolio	*Expected Value (EV)*	*Standard Deviation (SD)*
D	10	3.16
E	20	2.24
F	30	3.16

An Introduction to Real and Financial Yields

the least risk per dollar of return, in this example, F. Portfolio D would be the least desirable portfolio according to this criterion.

Implicit in the criterion of coefficients of variation is that investors require larger returns from riskier portfolios. This seems reasonable, and there exists considerable evidence that investors do behave in this way. In Chapter 5, we noted that the prices, and hence the returns, of longer-term bonds vary more than those of shorter-term bonds when interest rates change. In a study of the United States government securities market, Michaelson (see reference 4) showed that the standard deviations of longer-term securities were larger than those of shorter-term. This difference appears to be a manifestation of another aspect of the uncertainty premium theory of term structure. It is also consistent with the notion that risk-averting investors require a risk premium in order to undertake the risk, or variability of return, of longer, term securities.

In studying the determinants of differences in rates of return on common stock, Arditti (see reference 1) showed that differences in standard deviation are important in explaining differences in the yields on common stocks. The relationship between yield and standard deviation is positive—the larger the standard deviation, the larger the rate of return on the common stock. This supports the notion that standard deviation, or variance, is a reasonable measure of risk, and that investors in general are risk averters who require a premium in order to undertake risk.

How are risk premiums determined? Clearly, individual investors do not determine the premium as individuals. Rather, they play a role in determining such risk premiums as components of market demand and supply. As an example, let us use the six portfolios that we developed in Figures 6-1 and 6-2. Their risk/return characteristics are summarized in Table 6-2.

From Table 6-2, we see that portfolio F has the lowest ratio of variance to expected value. Risk-averting investors would probably prefer F to the other portfolios. As a result, the price of portfolio F would increase as market prices adjust toward equilibrium. As its price rises, the difference between its expected value and its cost (the net expectation)

Table 6-2. Risks and Returns of

Six Portfolios

Portfolio	EV ($)	SD ($)	SD/EV
A	2.50	32.50	13
B	2.50	4.5	1.8
C	2.50	22.5	9
D	10.00	3.16	0.316
E	20.00	2.23	0.112
F	30.00	3.16	0.105

Table 6-3. Risk/Return Characteristics of Six Investments

Portfolio	SD/EV	Price	Yield
A	13	$ 1.67	50%
B	1.8	1.78	40
C	9	1.50	67
D	0.316	7.50	33
E	0.112	16.67	20
F	0.105	27.27	10

declines, and the ratio of risk to return increases, making F less desirable.

Suppose that investors wanted at least a 10% yield on portfolio F. In that event,

$$\text{the price of F} = EV \times \frac{1}{1 + 0.10} = \$30(0.909) = \$27.27$$

Thus, if the price of F rises to $30.00, a number of investors might prefer a riskier alternative with a higher yield. Despite its relative safety, there is a maximum price that investors are willing to pay for portfolio F.

We could make a similar argument for portfolio E and for every other portfolio. The market might well develop the range of prices and yields for the six investment portfolios portrayed in Table 6-3. The yields are based on the assumption that the projects are all one-period projects whose expected values occur at the end of the period. Hence, each yield is simply the internal rate of return necessary to set price equal to the expected value. Comparing the risk/return ratio column to the yield column, we see that these hypothetical portfolios are consistent with the findings that investors generally require higher returns from riskier proposals.

The Individual Determinants of Risk Premiums

The size of risk premiums is determined in the market place by the interplay of individuals who have different ideas of what an appropriate premium is for a given portfolio. In this section, we shall consider the determinants of an individual's willingness to accept a given risk premium.

A fundamental factor underlying an individual's willingness to accept a risk premium is that person's basic attitude toward risk. Some investors are prone to gambling and others are conservative. Such differences are shown in Figure 6-3. Parts of the preference functions between

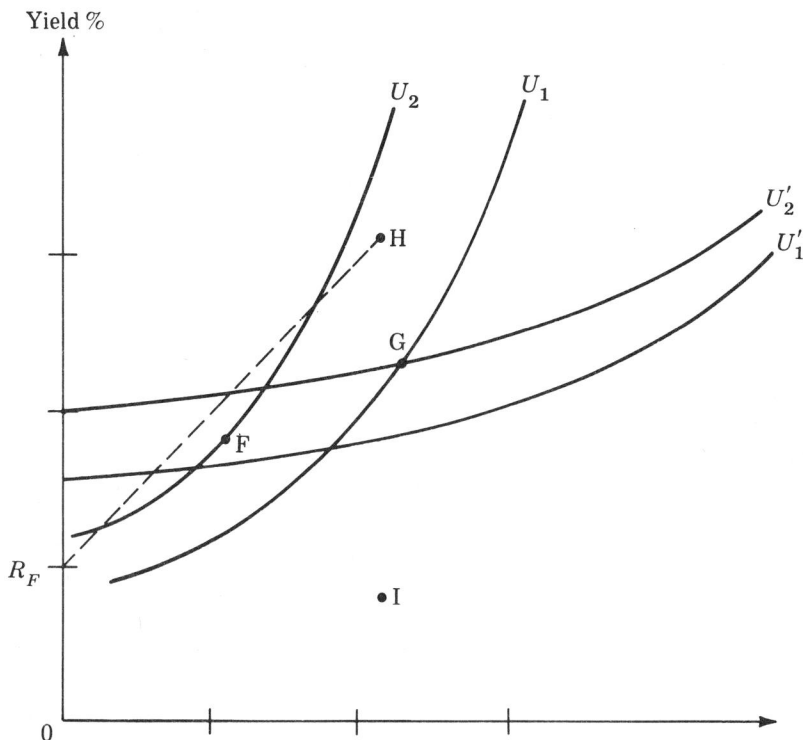

Figure 6-3
Standard Deviation of Portfolio Choices Given Risk of Return Preferences

risk and return for two different investors are shown in this figure. The steep curves designated U_1 and U_2 represent the preference of the more conservative investor, whereas the curves labeled U_1' and U_2' represent the preference of the more risk-prone investor. The curves are indifference curves, that is, the investor does not care where he is on a curve. However, the more conservative investor prefers any point on U_2 to any point on U_1, since for a given level of risk he has a higher yielding portfolio on U_2 than on U_1. Similarly, the more risk-prone investor prefers any point on U_2' to any point on U_1'. Thus, the slopes of the indifference curves reflect the basic attitudes of individual investors. Risk aversion still applies, as long as the indifference curves have positive slopes.

The shapes of the indifference curves also reveal something about investors' attitudes toward risk. We may refer to these slopes as *marginal rates of substitution* between yield and risk. Note that as investors reach levels of high risk, the curves become steeper. The increasing slope indicates that the investor requires a larger risk premium to stay on the indifference curve as the level of risk increases.

Figure 6-3 shows four investment portfolios, F, G, H, and I. It seems reasonable to expect the investor to prefer the portfolio highest on the indifference curve. Although this figure shows only two representative preference curves for each investor, many other preference curves fall between and beyond these sample curves. You can see clearly the effects of the different shapes of the preference curves on the ranking of investment portfolios.

Conservative (steeper line)	Gambler (flatter line)
F	H
H	G
G	F
I	I

Thus, the orderings are quite different, except for I, which is the least preferred portfolio alternative for both investors.

Preference functions alone do not determine the preferred portfolio. Another important factor is the alternative yield available. Suppose that we have a risk-free security, that is, one whose returns are certain. Such security is marked R_F on the yield axis of Figure 6-3. This asset has zero variance, which is appropriate for a risk-free asset. Now we can construct a new portfolio by combining any one of the other portfolios, say H, with the risk-free asset. The return and risk of the resulting combined portfolio vary, depending on the proportion of H and the risk-free asset in the portfolio. However, these combinations fall along the dashed line connecting the risk-free rate and H. Although the more conservative investor prefers portfolio F to portfolio H, he prefers some combination of H and the risk-free asset to F. However, that preference depends on the risk-free rate level. For example, suppose that the risk-free asset has a zero rate of return. If we draw a line connecting the origin, which denotes the zero yield of the risk-free asset, to portfolio H, we see that the more conservative investor does not prefer a combination of H and the risk-free asset to portfolio F under these circumstances. By experimentation, you can find a number of positive rates of return for the risk-free asset that are still too low to change the original orderings of the portfolio preferences. For now, the relevant point is that a risk-free asset combined with an undesirable portfolio may become a desirable portfolio.

Thus, introducing the risk-free asset has complicated the analysis of the risk premium. The only time that the risk-free asset does not affect the size of the risk premium is when it has a very low yield relative to the yield on riskier portfolios. More commonly, the risk-free asset's yield is sufficiently large that it *reduces* risk premiums. It has this effect because combining the risk-free asset with a risky portfolio can create a new portfolio offering either less risk and the same return, or the same risk with a larger return, than a portfolio that does not include the risk-free asset. Under these circumstances, the risk for a given portfolio decreases when it is combined with the risk-free asset, and the lower risk justifies a lower premium.

Managing Risk

Managing risk generally involves creating new and more desirable portfolios. Insurance companies have a similar way of managing risk. They use mortality tables to describe the percentage of given groups (usually designated by age and sex) that will die within some specified time period, say a year. We can view this percentage as the probability of someone in that group dying. For an individual the table is meaningless, since the individual will either live or die. But the probabilities do apply to a group of *unrelated* individuals. For example, the probabilities are invalid for soldiers in the same military unit or for firefighters in the same fire station.

Say that 10% of a given age group will die over the next 12 months. If 1000 of these people each wanted a one-year life insurance policy for $10,000 each, the insurance payments due to loss of life would be

$$0.10 \times 1000 \times \$10,000 = \$1,000,000$$

If we ignore the cost of running the insurance company, then the insurance company would have to charge each person a $1000 premium for a $10,000 policy. Thus, if 1000 people each contribute $1000, the pool of funds available to make payments would be $1,000,000—exactly equal to the payment requirements that are expected.

What the insurance company has done is to *diversify*. It has used a large group of unrelated factors, or people in this case. By combining them, it has reduced risk to zero. In effect, the uncertainties of death have been converted to certain and known cost. Diversification is the basic principle of risk management.

Although two assets with identical expected values and variances appear identical, they may not vary in the same direction. Specifically, when asset A takes on a high value, it does not follow that asset B also takes on a high value, even though their expected values are identical. The coincidence of values of assets A and B determines how risky the portfolios are and whether a combination of A and B results in diversification.

First, assume that A and B move together as shown in Table 6-4. In this case, combining A and B leads to a portfolio that behaves exactly as the individual assets do. We combined two assets and diversified, but no effect of diversification is apparent. In the insurance company, this would be equivalent to insuring two circus acrobats sitting at either end of a seesaw suspended 100 feet above the ground. If one slips and falls off the seesaw, the other will almost certainly fall. Hence, there is no diversification effect.

Statistically, the relationship between two series is sometimes referred to as the *degree of correlation* between them. Correlation considers not only the amount of variance in each of the distributions, but also the direction of their variance. If two variables change in the same

Table 6-4. Portfolios with Perfect Positive Correlation

	When A is	Then B is	Portfolio 0.5A + 0.5B
	20%	20%	20%
	10	10	10
	0	0	0
EV	10	10	10
Var	1	1	1

direction and by the same proportion, the coefficient of correlation between them is +1, and the coefficient is called perfect and positive. Under such conditions, no effective risk management is possible.

On the other hand, it is possible to have perfectly negative correlation. In our example, when A takes a value 10% above its mean and B's value is 10% below its mean, their correlation is perfectly negative. An example of a portfolio of half A and half B with perfectly negative correlation is shown in Table 6-5. Figure 6-4 shows this combination graphically. In this case, diversification is easy because the two assets have identical standard deviations and are perfectly negatively correlated. We can reduce the variance to zero by taking equal proportions of their two distributions. Note that the return or expected value is still the same as it would be if the investor invests in only one of the assets.

The correlation coefficient can range from +1 (perfect positive correlation) through 0 (no correlation at all) to −1 (perfect negative correlation). Negatively correlated assets obviously provide very powerful diversification effects and can reduce risk sharply. However, most economic events, including the values of assets, tend to be positively correlated. Fortunately, risk reduction is possible as long as the assets are not *perfectly* positively correlated. Indeed, we can reduce portfolio risk to zero by combining many different assets that are positively but not

Table 6-5. Portfolios with Perfect Negative Correlation

	When A is	Then B is	Portfolio 0.5A + 0.5B
	20%	0%	10%
	10	10	10
	0	20	10
EV	10	10	10
Var	1	1	0

Returns

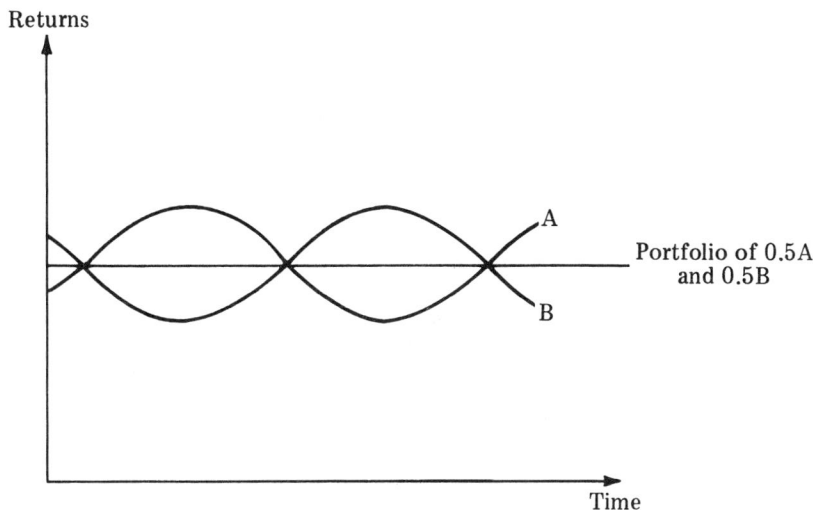

Portfolio of 0.5A
and 0.5B

A

B

Time

Figure 6-4
Impact of Negatively Correlated Yields on Portfolio Risk

perfectly correlated, provided that we place an arbitrary limit on the variance of any single asset.

The relationship between the variance of a portfolio and the variances of its assets is neither simple nor direct. We cannot arrive at the portfolio of half A and half B in the previous example simply by averaging the variances of each asset. We also have to take the correlation into account. The *covariance* is a measure that considers both the variances of two assets and their correlation. The covariance of any two assets is defined as follows:

$$\text{covariance } AB = (\sigma_A \sigma_B)(\text{correlation coefficient}_{AB}) \qquad (6\text{-}8)$$

Note that the covariance reflects risk relations between the two assets by considering the products of their standard deviations, as well as the degree to which they tend to vary together.

With the covariance, we can compute the variance of a portfolio by using the following equation:

$$
\begin{aligned}
\text{Var port} = \ & a[\text{Var}_A + b\,\text{Cov}_{AB} + c\,\text{Cov}_{AC} + \cdots + n\,\text{Cov}_{AN}] \\
& + b[\text{Cov}_{BA} + b\,\text{Var}_B + c\,\text{Cov}_{BC} + \cdots + n\,\text{Cov}_{BN}] \\
& \vdots \\
& + n[a\,\text{Cov}_{NA} + b\,\text{Cov}_{NB} + c\,\text{Cov}_{NC} + \cdots + n\,\text{Var}_N]
\end{aligned}
$$
$$(6\text{-}9)$$

where Cov is covariance and a, b, c, and n refer to the percentage distribution of the assets in the portfolio. This equation simplifies to

$$\text{Var port} = a^2 \text{Var}_A + b^2 \text{Var}_B + \cdots + n^2 \text{Var}_N$$
$$+ 2ab \, \text{Cov}_{AB} + 2ac \, \text{Cov}_{AC}$$
$$\vdots \qquad\qquad\qquad\qquad (6\text{-}10)$$
$$+ 2bc \, \text{Cov}_{BC} + \cdots + 2mn \, \text{Cov}_{MN}$$

Thus, the variance of a portfolio is the sum of its weighted variances and covariances. The form of the equation in (6-10) allows us to compute the variance of a portfolio that has more than two assets. For example, there are three assets in Table 6-6.

Note that in the correlation matrix the correlation of A to A is 1. Further, the covariance of each asset to itself is the variance of the asset. The left-hand side of the correlation matrix is left blank since the correlation of B and A is the same as the correlation of A and B, that is, 0.5. We have computed the covariances by using equation (6-10). As with correlation, the covariance between A and B is the same as the covariance between B and A, so there are blanks in these spots in the covariance matrix.

If we assume that each asset makes up one-third of the portfolio, then the variance of the portfolio is

$$\text{Var port} = (0.33)^2 0.01 + (0.33)^2 0.04 + (0.33)^2 (0.09)$$
$$+ 2(0.33)^2 0.01 + 2(0.33)^2 0.024 + 2(0.33)^2 0.036$$
$$= 0.031$$

Note that the variance 0.031 is well below the average of the variances of A, B, and C. The average of these variances is 0.047, more than 50% above the actual variance of the diversified portfolio. Thus, although all these assets are positively correlated, combining them has reduced the risk. The yield, however, is a weighted linear combination or weighted mean of the three yields; in this example, it is 15%, if we weight each asset equally.

Table 6-6. Computation of the Variance of a Portfolio with Three Assets

Assets	Var	Correlation A	B	C	Covariance A	B	C	Yields
A	0.01	1	0.5	0.8	0.01	0.01	0.024	0.10
B	0.04		1	0.6		0.04	0.036	0.15
C	0.09			1			.09	0.20

An Introduction to Real and Financial Yields

Efficient and Inefficient Portfolios

The risk and return of a portfolio depend on the proportion of each asset in the portfolio. For example, if the investor in the previous illustration chooses to hold no A, 80% of the portfolio in B, and 20% in C, the variance of the portfolio rises to 0.041, but the return also rises to 16%. Hence, the investor can trade off between risk and return by shifting the weights assigned to the various assets. Five other portfolios formed from assets, A, B, and C are shown in Table 6-7. These portfolios are just a few of the many possible combinations of these assets. They are ranked in order of diminishing yields. For the first three portfolios, risk decreases as portfolio yield decreases. However, portfolio 4 provides the same yield as portfolio 3, but with more risk. Hence, rational investors prefer portfolio 3 to portfolio 4, that is, portfolio 3 dominates portfolio 4. We can make this statement without having to refer to any investor's specific preference function. Further, comparing portfolio 5 with portfolio 3, we see that portfolio 3 also dominates portfolio 5, since portfolio 5 provides only $12\frac{1}{2}\%$ return at a greater risk than portfolio 3. Again, one can state that portfolio 3 dominates portfolio 5, without referring to the individual investor's preference function.

Of the five alternatives, portfolio 3 is an efficient portfolio. No other portfolio in the example offers as high a yield at as little risk. Portfolios 4 and 5 are examples of *inefficient* portfolios. An inefficient portfolio offers either more risk and the same return as another portfolio, or the same risk and a lower return. Clearly, no rational investor wants an inefficient portfolio. However, even after eliminating inefficient portfolios, we still have many asset combinations that generate efficient portfolios. Computing all these combinations is formidable. Nonetheless, schedules of efficient portfolios can be developed.

Figure 6-5 is a graphic representation of the results of the computations. The graph shows three inefficient portfolios, A, B and D, as well as three efficient portfolios, C, E and F. The lines linking the efficient portfolios is the *efficient portfolio line.* Such a line connects adjacent

Table 6-7. Yield and Risk Characteristics
of a Three-Asset Portfolio

Asset	Weights			Yield port (%)	Var port
	a	*b*	*c*		
1	0.25	0.25	0.50	16.25	0.042
2	0	0.80	0.20	16.00	0.041
3	0.33	0.33	0.33	15.00	0.031
4	0.50	0	0.50	15.00	0.037
5	0.50	0.50	0	12.50	0.033

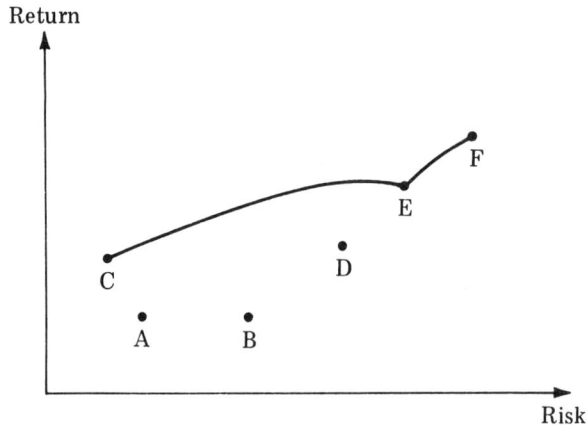

Figure 6-5
Efficient Frontier

efficient portfolios. Combinations of adjacent efficient portfolios are also
efficient portfolios. In Figure 6-5, the line represents combinations of
portfolios C and E to the left of portfolio E, and combinations of E and F
to the right of portfolio E. We can show mathematically that these combinations of efficient portfolios are also efficient.

We began this chapter with the concern that inadequate attention
would be paid to risk differences that result in yield differences. Certainly, we have seen that risk differences should be reflected in yield
differences and that the wary investor must review the risk of an investment that promises an unusually high rate of return.

On the other hand, an investment that should be undertaken may be
rejected. Portfolio analysis indicates that the contribution of a single
asset to the risk of a portfolio is less than the risk of the asset itself,
provided that the correlations between the new asset and the assets already in the portfolio are less than perfectly positive. Indeed, in the unusual case of negative correlation, the addition of a risky asset can work
to reduce the risk of the portfolio. Failure to consider the impact of a
single asset on the overall risk of the portfolio could lead an investor
to reject an asset that might be quite acceptable if its diversification effect were considered.

With securities portfolios, an overall view of assets is common. However, this is less common in the world of real asset portfolios. Hence,
precautions must be taken to make certain that the penalties attached to
risky proposals reflect the marginal risk, that is, the risk added to the
overall portfolio of assets held by the organization.

Both private and public organizations have procedures that include
overall reviews of spending proposals. In corporations, these may be
embodied in the activities of capital budgeting committees. Often these
committees are subcommittees of the board of directors. Similarly, public organizations have high-level committees that review capital spending
and budgets. But often these committees do not have the chance to con-

sider proposals that have been rejected because of their individual risk. Thus they may not get to evaluate a proposal that might be acceptable as part of the organization's overall activity.

Thus, an organization should probably not require different rates of return for proposals that have different risks. Rather, they should require a single rate of return for the organization as a whole, so that projects are not eliminated too early. If they do this, they can evaluate risky projects in the context of overall portfolios.

Also important in the management of portfolios of real assets is the quantification of returns and the probability distribution of returns. Often it is difficult to generate a single-valued estimate of a project's worth, to say nothing of an *accurate* probability distribution of returns. Even if an organization could estimate the probability distribution, most organizations would still find it difficult to determine the correlation between different projects. However, it does not follow that the concepts underlying portfolio management are useless unless the quantitative requirements can be fulfilled.

Often the organization has an intuitive grasp of the riskiness of an individual project and how its outcome interrelates with the outcomes of other projects. Yet they may not be able to quantify the intuitive "feel" without making unjustified assumptions. Great care must be taken in making such "hard" number estimates, since others may invest them with a degree of accuracy that is totally insupportable. It may be better to operate nonquantitatively under such circumstances. Still, the principle of diversification can and should be applied, even if it must be limited to as simplistic a principle as "Don't put all your eggs in one basket."

Summary

Although we can measure the risk of an asset by its standard deviation, we can usually reduce the risk of this individual asset by combining it with others whose variations partially offset the variation of the initial asset. The combination of assets is a portfolio. The degree to which the riskiness of the asset is reduced by being combined with others in a portfolio depends on the riskiness of the asset itself, its correlation with the other assets, and the riskiness of the other assets. We can usually generate portfolios that offer the same yield at a lower risk or a larger yield for the same risk as an individual asset.

It is also possible to combine a risk-free asset with other assets to form new combinations of portfolios that dominate most portfolios not containing the risk-free asset. Portfolios that dominate others, that is, those that offer lower risk for a given return or greater return for a given risk level, are efficient portfolios. Appropriate combinations of efficient portfolios generate other efficient portfolios.

In the end, the risk premium that investors can receive depends only partly on the riskiness of the individual asset. If they fail to combine assets, including perhaps a risk-free asset, to generate an efficient portfolio, then the risk premium they receive will be less than it would be for an efficient portfolio of equal risk. Or they could have a safer portfolio for the same risk premium that they earn with an inefficient portfolio.

Review Questions

6-1 The government is about to issue a bond whose coupon is 1% above the yield on comparable bonds already outstanding. What effects might be anticipated?

6-2 What might be the risk management practices of a bank and a mortgage company? Discuss.

6-3 What do we mean when we say that a portfolio is efficient?

Problems

6-4 The probability distribution of the return R during the coming year on the stock of the ABC Corporation is given below. Calculate the expected return and the standard deviation of the return.

Return	Probability
0.02	0.1
0.03	0.2
0.05	0.4
0.07	0.2
0.09	0.1

6-5 We wish to analyze the portfolios that we can construct with the following two securities:

	Expected return	Standard deviation of return
Security 1	$E_1 = 6\%$	$\sigma_1 = 0.2$
Security 2	$E_2 = 8\%$	$\sigma_2 = 0.3$
Covariance of returns $= \sigma_{12} = -0.01$		

a. Graph the relationship between portfolio risk (σ_p) and the proportion (X_1) of the available funds invested in security 1.

b. Graph the relationship between portfolio risk (σ_p) and portfolio expected return (E_p) for different X_1.

6-6 The following tables give the realized yields, standard deviations of yields, and the correlation matrix of yields of four securities, A, B, C, and D.

Correlation Matrix

	A	B	C	D	*Standard Deviation*	*Yield*
A	1	0.8	0.8	0.3	0.01	0.10
B		1	0.9	0.7	0.02	0.08
C			1	0.5	0.04	0.06
D				1	0.05	0.04

a. Calculate the variance and yield of a portfolio containing 25% of each security. What is the extent, if any, of diversification?

b. Which security offers the most diversification? What are the variance and the yield of a portfolio containing 70% of that security and 10% each of the other three?

c. Do the yields indicated suggest that variance of the security is major determinant of risk premiums? Explain.

Glossary

Coefficient of variations
The ratio of risk (standard deviation) to expected return.

Correlation
The relationship between two series that considers the amount of variance in each series and the coincidence of the direction of their variance. If two variables move in the same direction and by the same proportion, the coefficient of correlation is +1 (perfect positive correlation)

$\rho_{ij} = \sigma_{ij} / \sigma_2 \sigma_j$
ρ_{ij} = correlation of series 2 and j
σ_{ij} = covariance of 2 and j
σ_2 = standard deviation of 2

Covariance
Measure of the degree to which two variables move together. A positive value means that, on average, they move in the same direction.

$\sigma_{ij} = \rho_{ij} \sigma_1 \sigma_j$
σ_{ij} = covariance of 2 and j
ρ_{ij} = correlation of 2 and j
σ_2 = standard deviation of 2
$\sigma_{ij} = \Sigma (x_2 - \overline{x}_i)(x_j - \overline{x}_j) P(x_2, x_j)$
$\quad x_2$ = return on 2
$\quad \overline{x}_2$ = expected value of 2
$\quad P(x_2, x_j)$ = joint probability of i and j.

Diversification
The spreading of investments over more than one com-

pany or industry to reduce the uncertainty of future returns caused by unsystematic risk.

Dominate	Exhibits a more desirable combination of risk and return.
Efficient portfolio	A fully diversified portfolio. For any given rate of return, no other portfolio has less risk; and for any given level of risk, no other portfolio provides better returns.
Efficient portfolio line	Line linking the various efficient portfolios.
Indifference curve	A curve that represents combinations of two items, for example, risk and return, that are equally valued.
Inefficient portfolio	See *efficient portfolio.*
Marginal rate of substitution	The slope of an indifference curve.
Marginal risk	Risk added to the overall portfolio of assets by the inclusion of a particular asset.
Moment	A characteristic of a distribution that may be used to describe it. The expected value and the standard deviation are the first two moments.
Portfolio	A combination of assets.
Preference curves	See *indifference curves.*
Risk aversion	Risk-averse investors are concerned with risk and do not like it. Thus, they require proportionately more return for an increase in risk.
Risk-free security	A security with a single possible future return, as opposed to a probability distribution of future returns.
Risk management	Involves the creation of new, more desirable, portfolio combinations.
Risk premium	The difference between the required rate of return on a risky asset and the return on a riskless asset with the same expected life.

Variance of a portfolio

$$\text{Var}_{\text{port}} = a^2 \text{Var}\,A + b^2 \text{Var}_B + \cdots + n^2 \text{Var}_n$$
$$+ \ 2ab\,\text{Cov}_{AB} + 2ac\,\text{Cov}_{AC} + \cdots$$
$$+ \ 2_{bc}\,\text{Cov}_{BC} + \cdots + 2_{mn}\,\text{Cov}_{mn}$$

Cov = covariance
$a, b, c, \ldots, m$ = proportion of portfolio in assets $a, b, c, \ldots, m.$

Weighted mean　　A linear combination of returns weighted by the proportion of the portfolio in each asset.

Bibliography

ARDITTI, F. D., "Risk and the Required Return on Equity," *Journal of Finance 22* (March 1967), 19–36.

LATANE, H., "Criteria for Choice among Risky Ventures," *Journal of Political Economy 67* (Apr. 1959), 144–155.

MARKOWITZ, H. M., "Portfolio Selection," *Journal of Finance 7* (March 1952), 77–91.

――――, *Portfolio Selection,* New York: Wiley, 1959.

MICHAELSON, J. B., "The Term Structure of Interest Rates and Holding Period Yields on Government Securities," *Journal of Finance X* (Sept. 1965), 310–323.

SHARPE, WILLIAM F., *Portfolio Theory and Capital Markets,* New York: McGraw-Hill, 1970.

TOBIN, JAMES, "Liquidity Preference as Behavior toward Risk," *Review of Economic Studies* (Feb. 1958).

TREYNOR, J. L., "How to Rate Management of Investment Funds," *Harvard Business Review 43* (Jan.-Feb. 1965), 63–75.

The Market Price of Risk

7

Risk analysis and portfolio management apply to all assets with variable outcomes. But risk analysis in the portfolio management of common stock has received special development. This development undoubtedly has been fostered by the potential of practical applications, particularly in the management of large equity funds, such as pension and mutual funds. Although it is difficult to estimate the impact of risk analysis on decision making in the management of large institutionalized equity funds, the data required for such management are becoming increasingly available. Many articles written by fund managers advocate the use of risk analysis and have fostered its development. Although risk analysis is still in its development stage, the portfolio management risk techniques and concepts that we shall describe in this chapter are likely to find ever increasing use over the years.

The Role of the Market

Let's first consider how risk premiums are determined, using the variance–covariance analysis developed in Chapter 6. Each investor has an individual risk–return preference function. If we assume that the demand for financial assets is similar to the demand for nonfinancial assets, an increase in yield of an asset with a given risk increases the demand for that asset. (Remember that when the yield of an asset increases, its price declines.) Suppose that the market is made up of the demands of three individuals, A, B, and C, and that their demand schedule for a financial asset with specific risk is as shown in Table 7-1. The total market demand, shown in the last column to the right, is simply a summation of the quantities demanded at the different yields. If supply is constant at

Table 7-1. Demand Schedules for Three Individuals and the Entire Market

	Demand Schedules			
	Individuals			Market
	A	B	C	Total
Yield	Q_A	Q_B	Q_C	Q
0.16	5	4	8	17
0.14	4	2	7	13
0.12	3	0	6	9
0.10	0	0	5	5

13 units, it equals demand at a yield of 14%. The risk premium is the difference between 14% and the yield on a risk-free asset. If the risk-free rate is 6%, the risk premium is 8 percentage points or 800 basis points.

Problems in Estimating General Risk Premiums

The key to developing individual demand schedules, such as those in Table 7-1, is an efficient portfolio line. Given this and the individual's preference function between risk and return, we can determine the composition of the portfolio. The actual quantities of risky assets are determined by the total number of dollars in the portfolio. As with all demand functions, estimating demand is not simple, since one must consider income, the prices of other assets and goods, current consumption, shifts in preferences between consumption and saving, and so on.

The Individual's Problems

In analyzing portfolios, the problems of determining demand and hence risk premiums are even greater. Two problems are particularly bothersome. The first is that the *risk that a particular asset adds to a portfolio depends on the characteristics of that portfolio.* If the assets already in the portfolio are highly correlated with the new asset, the new asset's contribution to the risk of the overall portfolio is larger than if its return is only weakly correlated with the returns of securities already in the portfolio.

However, even if the correlation relationships are not remarkable, the risk added also reflects the standard deviations of the existing assets. This is true because covariance is the product of the new stock's standard deviation, each of the existing securities' standard deviations, and their correlation coefficients. If the risk that a stock adds to a portfolio is "portfolio-peculiar," the market risk premium reflects the nature of the portfolios in which the stock is held as much as it reflects any characteristic of risk inherent in the stock itself. Hence, changes in the risk premium may reflect changes in portfolio composition rather than any change in the stock's inherent risk.

Computational Complexity

Another problem in determining risk premiums has to do with the number of calculations. Using the model developed in Chapter 6, we see that for a portfolio with 5 assets, we have to use 15 variances and separate covariances to compute the risk of the portfolio. When the portfolio has 6 assets, the number of variances and covariances goes up to 21. A portfolio with 7 assets has 28 variances and separate covariances. For a portfolio with 20 risky assets, 210 separate variances and covariances must be considered. In general, the number of variances and separate covariances in a portfolio equals $N(N + 1)/2$, where N is the number of securities in a portfolio. Even with special computational methods such as quadratic programming and the use of the computer, the time needed to compute sets of efficient portfolios is very expensive when the portfolios include many risky assets.

A firm dealing in assets that are not traded very often may be able to bear the cost of computing an efficient set of portfolios, since they will do it infrequently. However, unlike the manager of a portfolio of real assets, the manager of a portfolio of financial assets may be continually changing the composition of the portfolio. Further, the prices of many negotiable securities change rapidly. With each price change, the assets' yields also change, and the old efficient portfolio line is no longer valid. A new portfolio line must be calculated. Thus, the computational problem is not trivial for portfolio managers of even very large funds of financial assets. With highly volatile common stocks, the model developed in Chapter 6 is almost totally unworkable. Thus, the first step in making portfolio analysis a practical management tool for financial asset portfolios was to reduce the time and cost of computation.

Systematic versus Diversifiable Risk

The simplification was accomplished by dividing the variance of stocks into two components. The first is a systematic variation due to the overall movements of the stock market, that is, average price or price index. Thus, when stock prices generally rise, the price of a particular stock is expected to rise also, although not necessarily as much as the general increase in stock prices. The remaining variation, after the general stock market effect is removed, is assumed to be unsystematic or random. Hence, if we consider only the relationship between the stock and the overall market, we can safely ignore the remaining variation, provided that there are many stocks in the portfolio. If each stock's variations are random after the stock market effect is removed, the variations offset each other. In other words, we can eliminate the unsystematic or nonstock market risk by diversifying.

Although this simplification has had profound effects on financial research, its original purpose was to reduce computational complexity by permitting one to ignore all the covariances among stocks. With a portfolio of 10 stocks, for example, there are 10 variances for each of the stocks, and an additional 10 covariances of each stock with the market. The market covariance is

$$\text{Cov}_{xM} + (\sigma x)(\sigma m)(\text{Cor}_{xM}) \qquad (7\text{-}1)$$

where x refers to the yield on stock x, and m to the yield on the market index. Instead of having to study 55 variances and separate covariances, as we have to if we use the model developed in Chapter 6, we need only consider 20 variances and covariances. Instead of 210 variances and covariances, a 20-security portfolio has only 40 variances and covariances.

Although the computational problems are still formidable, they are considerably simpler than before. The equation for the variance of a portfolio is quite similar to that in the last chapter:

$$\begin{aligned} \text{Var}_{\text{port}} = {} & a^2 \text{Var}_A^2 + b^2 \text{Var}_B + \cdots + n^2 \text{Var}_N \\ & + a^2 \text{Cov}_{AM} + b^2 \text{Cov}_{BM} + \cdots + n^2 \text{Cov}_{NM} \end{aligned} \qquad (7\text{-}2)$$

where M refers to the market index.

Perhaps more remarkable than reducing the number of calculations is the use of the market relationship to determine a risk measure for an individual stock regardless of the composition of the portfolio. With the market index relationships, a portfolio manager can view the risk of a stock independently of a portfolio, since covariances are related only to the market index which is common for all portfolios. Thus, the change in Var_{port} from adding stock A is $a^2[\text{Var}_A + \text{Cov}_{AM}]$.

The Capital Market Line

So far, we have not examined the theoretical content of risk analysis very deeply. The only theoretical content in Chapter 6 was the risk-aversion behavior of investors. The rest was essentially mechanical, statistical manipulation of data. In many ways, this focus is desirable, since analytic tools based extensively on strong theoretical assumptions have little practical use when theoretical assumptions do not apply. Now, however, we are going to describe a step that has a strong theoretical assumption. Not surprisingly, this step may be the weakest link in the development of risk analysis for equity portfolios.

The next step *appears* straightforward. We assume that there exists

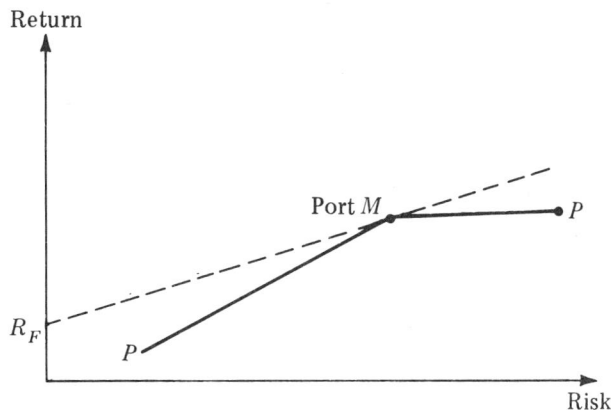

Figure 7-1
Contrast between Markowitzian-Efficient Portfolio and Efficient Capital Markets Line

a risk-free asset. As an example, treasury bills are often used.[1] These instruments have virtually no default risk and, because of their very short term, are almost invulnerable to interest rate risk.

If a risk-free asset is available, investors can combine it with a risky portfolio to generate a new portfolio with less risk and a somewhat lower return. Since the asset is risk free, the risk of the combined portfolio is reduced by the proportion of the portfolio still invested in risky assets, times the standard deviation of the portfolio without the risk-free asset. For example, if a portfolio without a risk-free asset has a portfolio standard deviation of 20%, the risk of that portfolio, with 10% of the assets invested in the risk-free asset, is 18%; i.e. $[0.9(0.2) = 0.18]$. In general, the standard deviation declines linearly as the proportion of the risk-free asset in the portfolio increases.

Note that the relationship between the risk of the portfolio without a risk-free asset and its risk with the risk-free asset is now linear. The return relationship is obviously linear, simply a weighted average of the returns of all the assets including the risk-free asset. Figure 7-1 graphically portrays the alternatives now confronting an investor.

In the graph, Port M is an efficient portfolio representing a price index of stocks. We can construct the stock price index in a number of ways. However, it is common to use either Standard and Poor's Index or the Dow Jones. Standard and Poor's Index contains a 500-stock sample and Dow Jones has 65 stocks, but both move similarly. Port M is one of the efficient portfolios that exist on the PP line, which is the efficient portfolio line in the absence of the risk-free assets. However, a rational investor prefers combinations of R_F and the market portfolio to any of the

---

[1] The use of treasury bills as the risk-free rate has been questioned because, except for the government, no one can borrow at the risk-free rate. Instead, it has been suggested that a zero beta portfolio be used. See Fischer Black's "Capital Market Equilibrium with Restricted Borrowing," *Journal of Business* (July 1972).

portfolios lying between P and Port M. In other words, because a risk-free asset is available, all the previously efficient portfolios to the left of Port M are now inefficient.

We further assume that the investor cannot only lend at the risk-free rate, but also borrow at the risk-free rate. Hence, we can extend the line connecting R_F and Port M to the right of Port M. Effectively, the investor is expanding the market portfolio and financing the expansion by borrowing at the risk-free rate. Under these conditions, all the portfolios on the old efficient line, except the market portfolio, become inefficient.

Now let's assume that entry to capital markets is perfect, so that most investors can either borrow or lend at the risk-free rate. This is a very strong assumption, since few borrowers other than the federal government can borrow at the risk-free rate. However, to the extent that it holds, such conditions mean that every investor faces a straight efficient portfolio line beginning at the risk-free rate and running tangent to the market portfolio. Since the risk–return relationships for the market portfolio are the same for all investors, and the risk-free rate is the same for all investors, all investors face exactly the same efficient portfolio line.

However, this line represents only demand, not supply. With investors buying combinations of the market portfolio and the risk-free asset, the demand for individual securities may not equal supply. In some cases, demand for a security may exceed supply, and in other instances, supply may exceed demand. Hence, in the market place, stock prices move up or down, affecting the demand–supply relationship. As the prices of these stocks move, their yields move inversely. Though these shifts do not necessarily affect the risk-free rate, they do affect the market portfolio, as well as all other portfolios. The slope of the straight line running through the market portfolio therefore changes as the market portfolio's risk–return combination changes. These shifts occur until stock prices and yields balance supply and demand.

Portfolio Risk Premium versus the Risk of Individual Assets

Thus, the efficient portfolio line for all investors is linear. Enough efficient portfolios other than the market portfolio fall on this line, so that supply for each security equals demand. Otherwise, the line shifts. Figure 7-2 illustrates portfolio choice under these conditions. The investor picks the portfolio on the capital markets line that is tangent to his indifference curve.

Choices still exist. Investors with steep indifference curves (strong risk-aversion) choose portfolios toward the risk-free rate. More venturesome investors choose portfolios further up the line, perhaps financing them with borrowings at the risk-free rate.

Some other significant changes have affected risk premiums. The

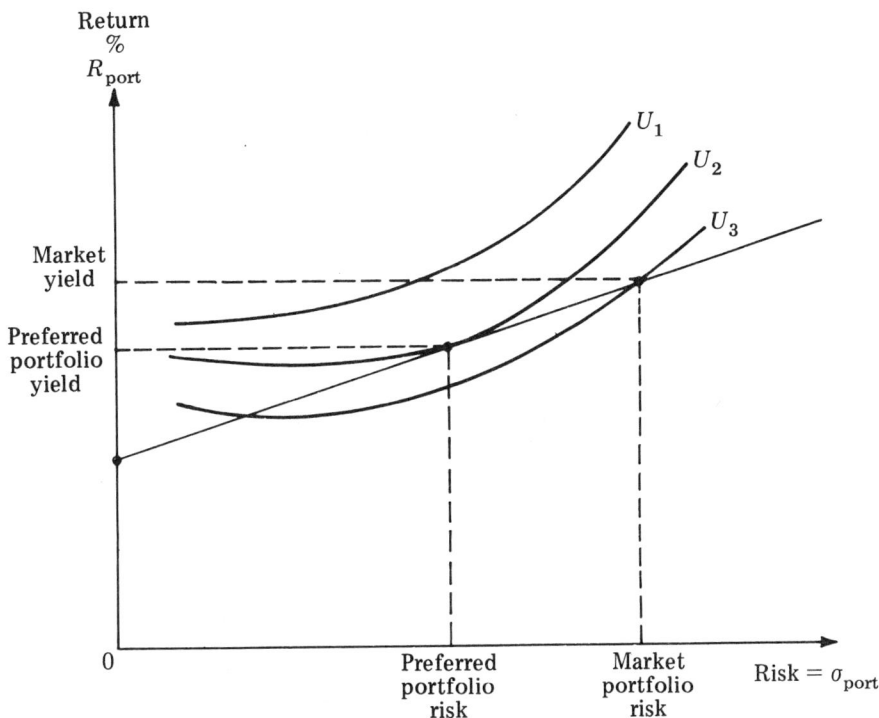

Figure 7-2
Choice of Portfolio with Risk-free Rate, Market Portfolio, and Perfect Capital Markets

equation for the new linear efficient portfolio line shown in Figure 7-1 is

$$R_{port} - R_F = K'\sigma_{port} \qquad (7\text{-}3)$$

where R_{port} is the return on the portfolio, R_F is the risk-free rate, K' is a constant reflecting the slope of the portfolio line $(\Delta R_{port}/\Delta\text{Risk})$, and σ_{port} is the standard deviation of the portfolio. The left-hand term is the risk premium that is a function of the risk of the portfolio.

Is the risk of the portfolio the same now as under the Markowitz portfolio approach that we developed in Chapter 6? The answer to this lies in the assumption about the relationship between individual security yields and market yields. Since the only important relationship is between securities and the market, rather than among securities, we cannot remove the market risk by diversification.

However, we can remove the variation that is not attributable to risk by diversification. If we can do so, then it is not appropriate or realistic to expect the market to provide a risk premium to compensate for such avoidable risk. Even if an investor is too unskilled, too lazy, or too ignorant to use diversification, other investors will diversify. They are willing to pay higher prices for securities, or accept lower prices in order to sell securities, than the undiversified investor. Market prices reflect the effects of diversification, and the only risk premium is due to market-related risks. As a result, the risk premium is not a function of the standard deviation of the portfolio, which reflects both market risk and unsystematic variations. Rather it is a function of the part of the variation that is due to the undiversifiable market relationship. In other words, instead of being a function of a portfolio's standard deviation, the risk premium is a function of the covariance of the stock with the market. We can state this as an equation.

$$R_{\text{port}} - R_F = K \operatorname{Cov}_{\text{port}M} \tag{7-4}$$

To distinguish this equation from the one we used for efficient portfolio lines in Chapter 6, we can refer to this new equation as the equation for the capital markets line. The *capital markets line* relates the undiversifiable risk (the market risk) of a portfolio to the return on that portfolio. It says that the risk premium is a function only of market risk, and not of the remaining risk that we assume is random and hence diversifiable. It follows that any undiversified portfolio is inefficient, since the risk absorbed by the investor is greater than the market is willing to pay as compensation for risk. In other words, there is another portfolio that has the same risk as the undiversified portfolio, but it offers a larger yield.

Risk Premiums for Securities

The comments in the preceding section apply primarily to portfolios. However, it is not difficult to extend the reasoning to securities. If we can reduce nonsystematic risk, that is, the risk not associated with market price movements, by diversifying the portfolio, then the investor is not entitled to expect compensation for holding unsystematic risk, and yields on individual stocks should contain risk premiums that reflect only risk associated with overall stock market movements, rather than with the total variability of the stock's yield. The risk premium for an individual stock should be a function of its covariance with the market, rather than its total variance. Hence,

$$R_Z - R_F = K \operatorname{Cov}_{ZM} \tag{7-5}$$

where Z is a stock and K is a constant like the one in equation (7-4). It seems intuitively reasonable that the systematic risk for a *portfolio* should have the same relationship to its risk premium as the systematic risk of a *security* to its risk premium. Hence, the constant K seems the same, and we can show mathematically that this is so. In that case, it is useful to define K more explicitly.

Deriving Beta

For a more explicit definition of K, consider the risk premium for the market portfolio.

$$R_M - R_F = K\operatorname{Cov}_{MM} = K\operatorname{Var}_M \qquad (7\text{-}6)$$

By algebraic manipulation, we can define K as

$$K = \frac{R_M - R_F}{\operatorname{Var}_M} \qquad (7\text{-}7)$$

Thus the definition of K contains only terms that relate to the market portfolio and the risk-free asset. So we can apply it to all other portfolios and securities as a constant term. Using this new expression for K in the equation for the risk premium of a security, we have

$$R_Z - R_F = \frac{R_M - R_F}{\operatorname{Var}_M}\operatorname{Cov}_{ZM} \qquad (7\text{-}5a)$$

Now the K term that we have derived is the same for all securities and portfolios. However, by algebraic manipulation we can get a new term, which is different for different securities and portfolios.

$$R_Z - R_F = \frac{\operatorname{Cov}_{ZM}}{\operatorname{Var}_M}(R_M - R_F) \qquad (7\text{-}8)$$

This ratio of the covariance to market variance has some interesting features, primarily, that it is scalar. If the systematic risk of a stock exceeds that of the market portfolio, its covariance with the market is greater than the variance of the market. Hence, the ratio exceeds one. On the other hand, if the stock is less risky than the market, its covariance with the market is less than the variance of the market, and the ratio is less than one. This ratio for a particular stock or portfolio, commonly called the *beta* value, describes the relative systematic risk of a stock or portfolio.

Though beta is obviously an important characteristic of a stock, we should not forget the assumptions that we have made in arriving at the beta value. We have assumed that the nonrandom elements of individual stock variations are due to variations in the stock market price index. Further, we have assumed that a risk-free security exists and, more importantly, that the risk-free rate is available to most investors either for borrowing or lending. To the extent that these assumptions are not correct, the beta estimate is also incorrect. With an incorrect beta, the investor could buy a low-beta stock, assuming that it also has low risk, only to find out that the stock has a much larger risk. Fortunately, a number of empirical studies suggest that the beta estimate is a useful and usable measure, particularly for portfolios, despite its drawbacks. Stock betas alone appear to be less stable.

Portfolio and Security Betas

Although beta is calculated the same way for both portfolios and securities, its application to securities is substantially different from its application to portfolios. Consider, for example, a portfolio consisting solely of a single stock with a beta of one (equivalent to the risk for a market portfolio). Would this portfolio have the same risk as a diversified portfolio that also had a beta of one?

Portfolio betas are the weighted sum of the security betas, taking into account the weight of the riskless asset. Even though a beta can be computed for any portfolio, it does not follow that any portfolio is efficient. An efficient portfolio generates the lowest beta for the expected return. In order to do this, the portfolio must be well diversified, so that all nonsystematic risk has been removed from the portfolio.

Thus, a single-stock portfolio with the same beta does not necessarily offer the investor less risk than the diversified portfolio. Since the variability of the single stock includes both its relationship to the market

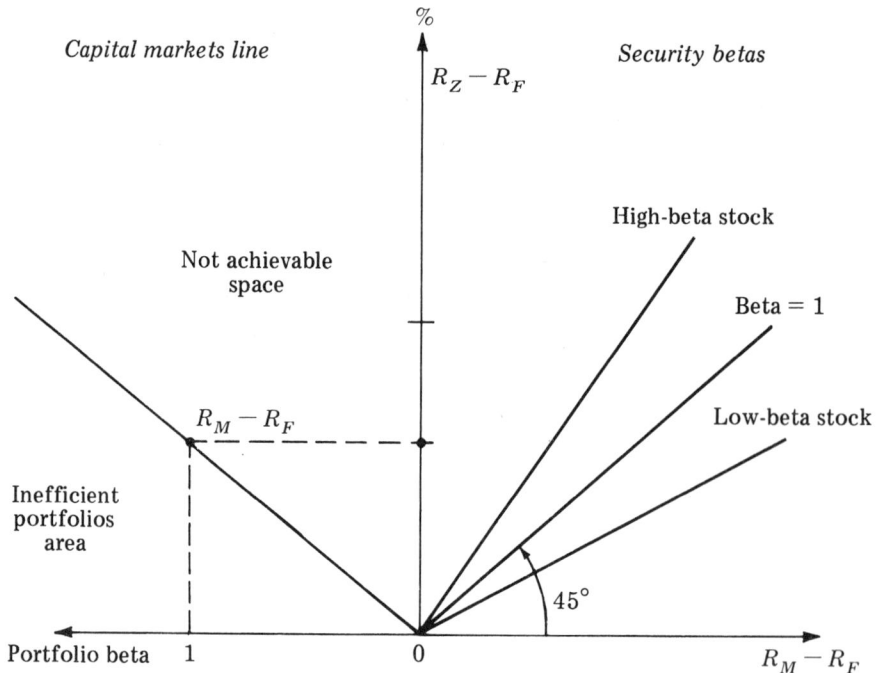

Figure 7-3
The Capital Markets Line and Security Betas

yield and its nonsystematic variations, a portfolio consisting of a single stock would vary considerably more than the beta suggests. As a result, it is unlikely that a single-stock portfolio is efficient, regardless of the beta of the stock. Relationships are shown in part in Figure 7-3.

The right-hand graph shows rays for three different stocks with different betas. (Remember that the beta only reflects the covariance of the stock.) On the left-hand side, the capital markets line, which is the relationship between a portfolio beta and the risk premium, is shown. Inefficient portfolios fall in the area underneath the capital markets line. The area above the portfolio line is not achievable, given market yields. Except in the rare instance of a stock having a nonsystematic risk of zero, the stock beta falls in the area underneath the efficient portfolio line. Hence, diversification is necessary even with the use of betas. This approach to portfolio analysis is often referred to as the *capital asset pricing model*.

Implications of Portfolio Risk Analysis for Financial Investors

Our analysis so far suggests that financial investors choose securities for a portfolio so that the weighted beta of the securities equals the desired beta for the portfolio and reflects the investor's willingness to take risks. We have not discussed any attributes other than the betas of the securities. However, there exist two large bodies of analysis for selecting securities. The first is *fundamental* analysis, which deals with the effect of expected variables such as changes in dividends and changes in the growth rate of earnings on share values. The second is *technical* analysis, which attempts to forecast future stock values on the basis of past price changes.

Some have argued that one can ignore both these bodies of analysis if one believes that capital markets are *efficient* in the sense that market participants have *perfect knowledge,* that is, that they have all the information about a security almost immediately.

In the case of fundamental analysis, those who believe in perfect knowledge argue that any change in the fundamentals of a stock are immediately available to all investors, who can thus immediately sell the stock if the fundamentals have deteriorated, or buy the stock if the fundamentals have improved. As a result, share prices immediately reflect the impact of the changes in fundamentals. Thus, they argue that an analyst in an efficient market who attempts to improve stock selection by analyzing a firm's fundamentals is wasting time and money. With efficient markets, the market price reflects all fundamentals and is the best estimate of the present value of the share.

With perfect knowledge, share price immediately reflects all relevant information. This not only makes fundamental analysis useless, but it also means that technical analysis only adds to the costs of managing the portfolio without improving selection. Past changes in stock prices reflect past market information. If such information was sometimes favorable and other times unfavorable, past price changes for a stock took on the nature of a *random walk*. Statistically, this implies that past changes in share prices are independent of each other and do not predict future price changes. Of course, the news that has affected price changes often has a trend—one piece of good news may follow other good news. In such cases, price changes do seem serially correlated. However, after correction for the trend in news, the pattern of price changes from a random walk.

Even if we weaken the assumption of perfect information by saying that news is not available to some investors, the random walk principle holds as long as enough investors know the news so that share prices fully reflect all information. Since large institutional investors have excellent sources of information, the assumption of perfect information seems reasonable. Certainly, some statistical tests suggest that even if considering either fundamental or technical information improves selection, the cost of acquiring such information appears to exceed the improvement in portfolio performance. This has been reasonably well established by comparing the net returns of a "buy-and-hold" strategy, in which the investor simply does not trade the portfolio, with the net returns (after brokerage costs) of some other strategy that involves switching the portfolio on the basis of technical information.

This argument is not yet settled. There are many proponents of fundamental analysis. However, most of the statistical tests have been aimed at technical analysis. But the ability to predict markets could be profitable, since such an ability would enable managers to switch their portfolios to high-beta securities when the market is about to rise, and to low-beta stocks when it is about to decline. They could achieve the same effect by varying the portion of the portfolio invested in the risk-free asset—increasing the proportion when markets are expected to decline, and decreasing the proportion when markets are expected to rise. Unfortunately, most studies indicate that managers do not have a consistent ability to forecast markets correctly. In that event, the costs of forecasting the market are likely to exceed its benefits, so the portfolio manager is still better off with a "buy-and-hold" strategy.

Implications of Portfolio Risk Analysis for Investors in Real Assets

In Chapter 6, we indicated that risk analysis is applicable to the management of a real asset portfolio (including machinery, investory, and other physical assets). However, because we have to consider the covariances among all assets in order to assess the risk of a specific asset, we argued that risk analysis should be used only at an organizational level high enough to deal with the total asset portfolio. Clearly, this restriction results in a heavy workload at high levels of management, since they have to review all projects that have been accepted on a net present value basis by lower echelons. Two approaches can be taken to introduce risk at lower levels.

Real Asset Beta

If we could find the real asset equivalent of the market index for financial assets, we could analyze the risk of individual real assets without having to worry about all the covariances. Suppose, for example, that we assumed that the variability of individual real assets was correlated with a company's sales, and that any remaining variation was random. Then we could estimate the risk of an individual asset by considering only its variance and its covariance with sales. This would not only simplify our task, but would also permit us to evaluate an asset's profitability and its risk at a lower level of management than if we had to consider the full range of covariance. How do various real assets relate to sales?

Inventory value is highly correlated with sales. However, accounts receivable has a weaker relationship to sales, since the collections of accounts receivable reflect *past* sales and the ability of customers to pay their debts. Plant and equipment have a still weaker relationship to current sales because the yield on long-term assets is affected by future expected sales as well as by current sales. Financial assets such as cash or negotiable securities probably have an even weaker relationship to sales because their value to the firm is based at least in part on the interest rate for financial assets, which should be weakly correlated with sales.

Sales is not the only possible basis for an index of risk. Industry data such as total sales may be better than an individual firm's sales. For some firms, changes in gross national product may be a good index for risk analysis. Statistical tests can establish the best indicator by measuring correlation of the assets with the indicator and considering whether the variation of the asset returns after taking out the indicator's effect is random.

Once we have determined an appropriate indicator, we could then compute real asset betas by measuring the ratio of covariance of each asset's returns with the indicator to the variance of the indicator. We could then obtain consistent estimates of risk by having top management specify a schedule of discount rates and betas. For example, consider the following:

If beta is	Discount cash flows by
1.5–2.0	20%
1.0–1.5	16
0.5–1.0	12
0.0–0.5	8
−0.5–0.0	4

This schedule would permit risk evaluations to affect the discount rate at any level of the organization and still treat risk consistently.

Capital Markets Beta

An even better approach, though more difficult to implement, is to discount the assets at a rate that reflects the asset's effect on the firm's true beta. The difficulty with this method, however, is estimating the asset's effect on the firm's beta at a relatively low level in the organization. However, if an asset investment is expected to increase the firm's beta, the asset's required rate of return should reflect the growth needed to offset its adverse effect on the value of the firm's stock. If the investment is expected to reduce the firm's beta, the required rate of return could be very low, since it would have a favorable effect on the firm's stock price. While it may not be feasible to develop risk premiums and discounts for real asset investment by considering the impact on true beta, this approach is conceptually useful in developing a schedule of discount rates such as the preceding one.

Statistical Estimation of Beta

For statistical reasons, estimating beta by calculating the ratio of the covariance between the firm's rate of return and the market's rate of return to the variance of the market's rate of return can lead to biased results. A more desirable approach is to use regression analysis to solve for beta in the following equation:

$$R_j - R_f = \alpha + \beta(R_m - R_f). \tag{7-9}$$

The data can be based on monthly or quarterly estimates, and the more the better. Remember that

$$R_j = \frac{P_1 + D}{P_0} - 1. \tag{7-10}$$

where P is price. In months or quarters in which no dividend is paid, the dividend value should be zero. Further, the market values must be taken from some index such as Standard and Poor's Index. Of course,

$$R_m = \frac{MP_1 + D}{MP_0} - 1 \tag{7-10a}$$

where MP is market price plus dividends paid during the period to the stocks included in the index. The risk-free rate is usually taken as the rate on three-month treasury bills, which can be found in the *Federal Reserve Bulletin,* among other sources.

The theoretical value of alpha is zero, but alpha in fact often has a value significantly different from zero. There has been much discussion about the implications of this difference, but for our purposes, an important result is that beta is cardinally unstable. By this we mean that the beta estimated for one time period differs from that coming from earlier or later periods. For portfolios of stocks, the ordinal rankings of beta seem relatively stable, so if portfolio A has a higher beta than portfolio B as of 1977, A's beta is likely to be above B's in 1978, although the absolute values of the two betas may change.

There are a variety of sources of security beta values. Wells Fargo is one organization that calculates betas for listed stocks.

How Many Stocks Are Needed for Diversification?

Diversification in the framework of the beta approach involves reducing the nonsystematic risk of the portfolio to zero. If doing so required 500 stocks, many private investors would be unable to achieve real diversification. However, if they need only 10 or 15 stocks, the advantages of diversification would be available to many shareholders. Determining the number of stocks needed for diversification on analytic grounds is not possible. Instead, we must resort to simulations of experience. These simulations have been conducted in American markets.

One test involved random selections of stocks to make up portfolios of different sizes. Then returns for portfolios of the same size were computed, and the standard deviation of these returns measured. When these measures were compared to the standard deviation of the market's return, it was found that portfolios of 15 securities effectively reduced nonsystematic risk to zero. Larger portfolios did not improve the diversification effect.

Even when stocks were selected from different industries so that the diversification was less naive than a simple random selection, the results were very much the same. Portfolios of eight stocks reduced nonsystematic risk to zero, and the results were little better than the simple random selection of stocks.

One thing that did change as larger portfolios and more complex selection techniques were adopted was the cost of the selection process. In most cases, the returns of these portfolios did not grow as rapidly as the costs. The larger the portfolio, the more expensive it is to continue reviewing the portfolio's contents.

Summary

In determining risk premiums, two problems arise. First, in addition to the intrinsic riskiness of the asset, the premium reflects the composition of the portfolios of all investors. Second, computing a portfolio's risk is difficult simply because a large number of calculations is involved when the covariances among all assets are considered.

Although it has profoundly changed financial theory, a simple assumption about the covariances of common stocks has reduced the number of computations. The assumption is that the correlation between individual stocks and a market index or average of stocks can replace the correlation among the individual stocks. Thus, the remaining relationship among stocks is zero after the market relationship is removed. This means that the only covariance needed for a stock is its relationship to the market. The result is not only a reduction in computations, but also the development of a risk premium that depends on the volatility of the stock relative to the volatility of the market index. Thus, the risk premium is independent of the composition of individual portfolios. The risk ratio is called the *beta coefficient*. The risk of a portfolio is the weighted sum of its beta values.

When we add the risk-free asset, efficient portfolios form a straight line relating risk to return. This is called the *capital markets line* and contains all the efficient security portfolios. It is based on the assumptions that investors in capital markets have perfect information and that they can borrow and lend at the risk-free rate. Neither of these assumptions may be completely accurate, but the theoretical model does well empirically, particularly with respect to portfolios.

To apply risk analysis to real (in contrast to financial) assets, we would have to develop a real beta coefficient for specific assets such as machinery and inventories that would relate their volatility to the volatility of some index such as company sales, industry activity, or even gross national product. Then we could treat the results like financial portfolios. Or we could estimate the impact of a specific asset on the firm's stock beta. If the asset has an effect, we would discount the expected returns of the risky asset by the higher rate of return implied by the increase in beta. The net present value of the risky asset would have to be large enough to offset the decline in the value of the firm's other assets that would result from the increase in beta and the required rate of return.

Although beta is a valuable concept, it does not replace diversification. A low-beta stock does not make a low-beta portfolio. Simulation experiments have shown, however, that effective diversification can be achieved with as few as 15 securities.

Review Questions

7-1   Does the market yield on a security compensate for the total risk of return of the security? Discuss.

7-2 How does diversification affect the return characteristics of a portfolio of securities?

7-3 What are the implications of the existence of a risk-free security for the set of efficient portfolios?

Problems

7-4 Given the following return data, which security should sell at the higher yield? Explain?

Security	A	B
Standard deviation	0.04	0.06
Correlation with market	0.8	0.6

7-5 The following 12 portfolios are representative of the total set of portfolios that can be constructed using varying quantities of the different stocks listed on the Toronto Stock Exchange.

Portfolio	Expected return, E_p (%)	Standard deviation of return, σ_p (%)
1	8	0.6
2	4	0.26
3	8	0.4
4	10	0.9
5	11	1.3
6	13	1.1
7	13.6	1.5
8	11	0.7
9	7	1.0
10	9	0.5
11	8	1.2
12	6	0.3

a. Plot these portfolios on a diagram of $E_p - \sigma_p$.

b. Determine the set of efficient portfolios.

c. If the risk-free rate of interest (R_f) is 6%, plot the *efficient portfolio line* and determine its equation. Note that the general form of this equation is $E_p = R_f + r\sigma_p$, where r = price of risk reduction for efficient portfolios.

d. If an investor's indifference curves have the form $k = E_p^2 - 133\sigma_p$, determine the optimal investment strategy.

7-6 The annual realized rates of return on the common stock of XYZ Corporation for the years 1959 to 1970 are given in the following table. The realized rates of return on the market portfolio are also shown.

a. Calculate the value of beta for XYZ common stock.

Year	R_{xyz}	R_M (%)
1959	5.0	6.0
1960	6.0	6.0
1961	3.0	2.0
1962	2.0	1.0
1963	7.0	5.0
1964	9.0	10.0
1965	12.0	10.0
1966	16.0	12.0
1967	0.0	4.0
1968	−3.0	2.0
1969	2.0	6.0
1970	4.0	7.0

b. Would you say XYZ common is a risky stock? Why?

Glossary

Beta	A measure of the degree to which a security or portfolio is sensitive to and varies with the market.

$$\beta = \frac{\mathrm{Cov}_{zm}}{\mathrm{Var}_m}$$

z = return on z
Cov = covariance
Var = variance

Buy-and-hold strategy	The investor does not change the portfolio by trading.
Capital market line	A graphical relationship between risk and the required rate of return.

$$R_{\mathrm{port}} - R_F = K\,\mathrm{Cov}_{\mathrm{port}\,M}$$

R_{port} = return on portfolio

R_F = risk-free rate

$K = \Delta R_{\mathrm{port}} / \Delta_{\mathrm{risk}}$

Cardinal instability	The value estimated is cardinally unstable if its American value changes over time.
Default risk	The risk that the firm will be unable to meet its maturing obligations.

Diversifiable risk	Unsystematic or random variability not explained by the market as a whole. Since it can be diversified away, it is not found in an efficient portfolio.
Diversification	Spreading investments over more than one company or industry to reduce the uncertainty of future returns caused by unsystematic risk.
Equity fund	A mutual fund that concentrates on equities.
Financial assets	Paper that has little or no value in and of itself, but obtains its value because it represents a claim on another individual or firm.
Fundamental analysis	In-depth study of the company and industry to determine the effect of expected changes in dividends, earnings, and so on, on share values.
Interest rate risk	The risk that the value of a security will change because of a change in the level of interest rates.
Market covariance	The relationship between the variability of a security's return and the variability of the market.

$$\text{Cov}_{xm} = (\sigma_x)(\sigma_m)(\text{Cor}_{xm})$$

x = yield on stock x
m = yield on market index
Cov = covariance
Cor = correlation

Market portfolio	Includes all risky assets in proportion to their market value. In the capital asset pricing model, it is the optimum portfolio of risky assets for all investors.
Mutual funds	A managed portfolio in which the investor can buy shares instead of buying the stock directly and managing the individual portfolio.
Nonfinancial (real) assets	Actual items such as inventory or machinery.
Perfect knowledge	All information about any security is virtually immediately known to market participants.
Portfolio composition	The makeup of a portfolio in terms of the various securities and the relative amounts of each.
Quadratic programming	A mathematical (normally computerized) procedure for solving quadratic equations (equations with a squared variable).

Random walk	Without a particular pattern that would enable forecasting future price movements on the basis of past trends.
Rational investor	One who always prefers more return to less at a given level of risk.
Risk aversion	The investor is concerned with risk and does not like it. Thus, he requires a proportionately greater increase in return to compensate him for undertaking more risk.
Risk-free rate	The return on an asset that is riskless in terms of default or interest rate risk.
Risk premium	The difference between the required rate of return on a risky asset and the rate of return on a riskless asset of the same life.
Serial correlation	Successive changes are statistically independent if the serial correlation is zero.
Systematic risk	Volatility of rates of return on securities or portfolios associated with changes in the rates of return on the market as a whole.
Technical analysis	The attempt to ascertain patterns in the past price movements of a stock in order to provide a basis for forecasting the future of the stock.

Bibliography

ARROW, K. J., and R. C. LIND, "Uncertainty and the Evaluation of Public Investment Decisions," *American Economic Review 60* (June 1970), 364–378.

BALL, R., and P. BROWN, "An Empirical Evaluation of Accounting Income Numbers," *Journal of Accounting Research 6* (Autumn 1968), 159–178.

BLACK, FISCHER, "Capital Market Equilibrium with Restricted Borrowing," *Journal of Business* (July 1972), 17–23.

BLACK, FISCHER, MICHAEL C. JENSEN, and MYRON SCHOLES, "The Capital Asset Pricing Model: Some Empirical Tests," in Michael C. Jensen, ed., *Studies in the Theory of Capital Markets,* New York: Praeger, 1975.

BLUME, MARSHALL, "On the Assessment of Risk," *Journal of Finance 26* (March 1971), 1–10.

BREALEY, RICHARD A., "An Introduction to Risk and Return from Common Stocks," Cambridge, Mass.: The MIT Press, 1969.

BRENNAN, J. J., "Capital Market Equilibrium with Divergent Borrowing and Lending Rates," *Journal of Financial and Quantitative Analysis 6* (Dec. 1971), 1197–1205.

CASS, D., and J. E. STIGLITZ, "The Structure of Investor Preference and Asset Returns, and Separability in Portfolio Allocation: A Contribution to the Pure Theory of Mutual Funds," *Journal of Economic Theory 2* (June 1970), 122–160.

CHEN, H. Y., "Valuation under Uncertainty," *Journal of Financial and Quantitative Analysis 2* (Sept. 1967), 313–325.

EVANS, J., and S. H. ARCHER, "Diversification and the Reduction of Dispersion: An Empirical Analysis, *Journal of Finance* (Dec. 1968), 761–767.

FAMA, EUGENE, "Risk, Return, and Equilibrium," *Journal of Political Economy 79* (Jan./Feb. 1971), 30–55.

FAMA, EUGENE, and M. H. MILLER, *The Theory of Finance,* New York: Holt, Rinehart & Winston, 1972.

FARRAR, D. E., *The Investment Decision under Uncertainty,* Englewood Cliffs, N.J.: Prentice-Hall, 1962.

FRANCIS, J. C., and S. H. ARCHER, *Portfolio Analysis,* Englewood Cliffs, N.J.: Prentice-Hall, 1971.

HAMADA, R. S., "Portfolio Analysis, Market Equilibrium and Corporation Finance," *Journal of Finance 24* (March 1969), 13–32.

HERTZ, D. B., "Risk Analysis in Capital Investment," *Harvard Business Review 42* (Jan./Feb. 1964), 95–106.

HILLIER, F. S., "The Derivation of Probabilistic Information for the Evaluation of Risky Investments," *Management Science 9* (Apr. 1963), 443–457.

JENSEN, MICHAEL C., *The Foundations and Current State of Capital Market Theory,* Studies in the Theory of Capital Market, New York: Praeger, 1971.

————, "The Performance of Mutual Funds in the Period 1945-64," *Journal of Finance 23* (May 1968), 389–416.

JENSEN, A. C., "Capital Markets: Theory and Evidence," *The Bell Journal of Economics and Management Science 3* (Autumn 1972), 103–120.

KING, BENJAMIN F., "Market and Industry Factors in Stock Price Behavior," *Journal of Business* (Jan. 1966).

————, "Market and Industry Factors in Stock Price Behavior," *Journal of Business 23* (Jan. 1966, supplement), 151.

LINTNER, JOHN, "The Valuation of Risk Assets and the Selection of Risky Investments in Stock Portfolios and Capital Budgets," *Review of Economics and Statistics 47* (Feb. 1965), 13–37.

————, "Security Prices, Risk, and the Maximal Gains from Diversification," *Journal of Finance 20* (Dec. 1965), 587–615.

————, "The Aggregation of Investors' Diverse Judgement and Preferences in Perfectly Competitive Security Markets," *Journal of Finance and Quantitative Analysis* (Dec. 1969), 80–95.

LORIE, JAMES H., and LAWRENCE FISHER, "Some Studies of Variability of Returns on Investment in Common Stocks," *Journal of Business 42* (Apr. 1970), 99–134.

MAO, J. C. T., and J. F. HELLIWELL, "Investment Decisions under Uncertainty: Theory and Practice," *Journal of Finance 24* (May 1969), 323–338.

MASICEK, OLDRICH A., and R. MCQUOWN, "The Efficient Market Model," *Financial Analysts Journal* (Sept.–Oct. 1972), 27–35.

MARKOWITZ, HARRY. "Portfolio Selection," *Journal of Finance 8* (March 1952), 89.

MERRETT, A. J., and A. SYKES, *The Finance and Analysis of Capital Projects,* New York: Wiley, 1963.

MILLER, MERTON H., and MYRON SCHOLES, "Rates of Return in Relation to Risk: A Reexamination of Some Recent Findings," unpublished memorandum (July 1970).

MOSSIN, JAN, "Equilibrium in a Capital Asset Market," *Econometria 34* (Oct. 1966), 768–783.

ROBICHEK, A. A., and S. C. MYERS, "Conceptual Problems in the Use of Risk-Adjusted Discount Rates," *Journal of Finance 21* (Dec. 1966), 727–730.

SCHOLES, M. S., "The Market for Securities: Substitution Versus Price Pressure and the Effects of Information on Share Prices," *Journal of Business 45* (Apr. 1972), 178–194.

SHARPE, WILLIAM F., "A Simplified Model for Portfolio Analysis," *Management Science 9* (January 1963), 277–293.

_____, *Portfolio Theory and Capital Markets,* New York: McGraw-Hill, 1970.

_____, "Capital Asset Prices: A Theory of Market Equilibrium under Conditions of Risk," *Journal of Finance 9* (Sept. 1964), 425–442.

SOLOMON, M. B., JR., "Unvertainty and Its Effect on Capital Investment Analysis," *Management Science 12* (Apr. 1966), B334–B339.

TREYNOR, JACK "Toward a Theory of Market Value of Risky Assets," unpublished memorandum (1961).

Corporate Financial Management

III

An Introduction to Corporate Financial Management

8

In Chapter 1, we argued that a reasonable goal for the corporation is the maximization of share price, but we did not have sufficient background at that time to discuss the tools that corporate financial managers need to achieve that goal. Now, however, we can discuss in detail the means of maximizing share value. This discussion is of interest not only to potential corporate managers, but to public managers as well. Certainly, the concepts are useful to public managers who have to deal with the private sector—such as managers of government units that provide grants to business firms—pension fund managers, and those involved in the regulatory processes that apply in the fields of taxation, public utilities, and so on.

Valuation

We have already used the constant growth model of share valuation. Admittedly, the assumptions underlying the model do not apply to all or even to most firms. Nonetheless, this simple model includes most of the significant variables useful to financial managers. Recall that it is formulated as (equation 4-8)

$$V = D/(i - G),$$

where V is the present value or price of the share, D is the current year's dividend to common shareholders, i is the required nominal rate of return on common shares (and is the same as R_j in Chapters 6 and 7), and G is the annual expected growth rate of earnings and dividends, which is assumed to be both constant and less than i.

Dividend policy is reflected in the numerator of the valuation model. The growth rate reflects the firm's asset portfolio. We may define the required nominal yield for firm j as

$$i_j = R_F + \beta_j(R_M - R_F). \qquad (8\text{-}1)$$

Although the firm can do little to affect the return on the market (R_M) or the risk-free rate (R_F), it can affect the beta coefficient. Recall that the firm's risk coefficient (beta) is

$$\beta_j = \frac{\text{rate of return } (\text{Cov}_{jM})}{\text{variance of the market's rate of return } (\text{Var}_M)} \qquad (8\text{-}2)$$

and that $\text{Cov}_{jM} = \text{correlation coefficient}_{jM}(\sigma_j)(\sigma_M)$.

The firm can do little to affect either the variance or the standard deviation of the market's rate of return, but by its choice of assets it can have a limited effect on the correlation of the firm's rate with the market's rate. In addition, it can affect the standard deviation of its rate of return by its asset selection and its choice of capital structure (the structure of the firm's liabilities and net worth).

To see how the firm's standard deviation is affected, consider the following data:

	A	B
Standard deviation (σ)	0.1	0.2
Correlation with market (Cor)	1.0	1.0
Dividend (D)	$1	$1
Growth (G)	0	0

$R_F = 0.06, R_M = 0.1,$ and $\sigma_M = 0.1$

Now

$$i_A = R_F + \beta_A(R_M - R_F)$$

$$= 0.06 + \left[\frac{(0.1)(0.1)}{0.01}\right](0.1 - 0.06) = 0.10$$

so

$$V_A = D/i_A = 1/0.10 = \$10.00$$

Similarly,

$$i_B = 0.06 + \left[\frac{(0.2)(0.1)}{0.01}\right](0.1 - 0.06) = 0.14$$

so

$$V_B = D/i_B = 1/0.14 = \$7.14$$

Hence, variability of returns matters.

If B tried to improve share value by taking on a risky venture, share value would rise only if the risk/return ratio were favorable. For example, if the venture increased D_B to \$1.50, had no impact on G, but raised σ_B to 0.3, then

$$V_B = \frac{1.50}{0.06 + [(0.3)(0.1)/0.01](0.1 - 0.06)} = \frac{1.50}{0.18} = 8.33$$

so B's shareholders would be better off. However, if the venture had only increased D to \$1.25 and σ_B to 0.3, then

$$V_B = \frac{1.25}{0.18} = \$6.95$$

and B's shareholders would have been better off with the smaller, but safer, old dividend.

In the example, note that the investment earns the required rate of return when B's management takes on the risky venture with the \$1.25 dividend only if one ignores the impact of the increase in risk on β. However, would B's management have undertaken the risky venture had they foreseen the decline in share value? Not if their objective is to maximize share value.

Individual Assets and Risk Premiums

Each of the components of the firm's portfolio of assets has earnings or costs subject to a probability distribution. Earlier, we gave examples of capital budgeting decisions that would result in asset portfolio growth as fixed assets were acquired. To illustrate the discounting process and the development of criteria of investment desirability, we treated the cash flows associated with the sample projects as if they were certain flows. That is, for each time period, we considered only one flow. Obviously, this is an oversimplification, since the firm cannot know for certain the value of the cash flow in a future period. Indeed, if future economic conditions turn out to be quite different from those anticipated, the flow could be substantially different from the flow estimated at the time of investment. It seems reasonable to treat a range of probability distributions of flows, generating a range or probability distribution of present values. These would give rise to variances and standard deviations.

As we pointed out earlier, the variability associated with asset components applies to assets other than the fixed assets. When the firm holds inventory, it expects to sell the inventory in the future. Hence, the inventory has an expected value. However, the sales may not occur or, if they do, they may not occur when the firm expects them to, thus reducing the profit because of added carrying charges for the inventory. Or, the inventory may not sell at the price at which the firm had hoped to sell it. In any event, we probably cannot treat the expected value of an inventory investment as if it were certain, even if the inventory investment is for a very short period of time. So we have to consider alternative values and again generate probability distributions and standard deviations.

Accounts receivable are another asset with a variable return. A firm offers credit to its customers when it could not make the sales without credit or when it would have to lower the price substantially in order to make a cash sale. However, the customer may not pay as originally agreed, reducing the firm's net profit because of the lengthened collection period. Indeed, to get the money, the firm may have to absorb legal costs, further reducing its net gain. Hence, the returns from accounts receivable are also subject to a probability distribution, from which we can generate a standard deviation.

The firm's risk depends not only on the risks of the individual assets, but also on the diversification of the assets, or the degree of independence of their probability distributions. If the probability distributions are substantially independent, the standard deviation for the overall asset portfolio is small, even if individual assets have large standard deviations. However, in general, firms cannot really choose the independence of probability distributions. Usually, there is a high degree of dependence among its assets. Perhaps the cheapest form of diversification possible in that case is to hold low-return/low-risk assets, such as bank deposits, fixed-term savings certificates, or commercial paper.

Nonetheless, the nature of the asset portfolio is determined by the nature of the firm's business. Mining exploration companies in general tend to be riskier than public utilities, and this difference is reflected in the standard deviations of their assets, as well as in the standard deviation of the asset portfolio as a whole.

Earnings Variability and Balance Sheet Management

The variability of corporate earnings partly reflects variations in demand. When sales decline, the firm may not be able to reduce costs as rapidly, resulting in reduced earnings. When sales increase, the reverse may occur with costs not rising as rapidly, generating increased earnings. Although firms may moderate some fluctuations in demand by marketing techniques such as advertising and developing product lines designed to offset seasonal variations in demand, they cannot completely offset variations in demand due to changes in general economic conditions. Such shifts affect some industries more seriously than others. For example, recessions affect producers of capital goods more severely than producers of nondurable consumer goods. So the firm has only limited control over the variability of its earnings and hence its beta coefficient. Most of the effect is determined by the nature of its business.

Even so, the firm can develop the structure of its balance sheet to magnify or diminish the impact of demand fluctuations on the variability of earnings. Firms subject to extreme variations in the demand for their products may structure their balance sheets to offset the effects of such demand variations on their earnings. Firms that face fairly stable demand may adopt balance sheet structures that increase the effect of such shifts on earnings. The balance sheet devices that serve to amplify or diminish the impact of external events or risk on earnings are subject to internal control. In this and in the next few chapters, we shall review three general classes of such internally controlled modulators: (1) *liquidity* policy, (2) fixed operating costs on earnings, called *operating leverage*, and (3) fixed financial charges on earnings, called *financial leverage*. We shall also consider the impact of dividend policy on the risk and the required rate of return, and we shall discuss some other topics, including leasing and mergers.

To complete the section on corporate financial management, we shall consider the determinant of the firm's overall required rate of return, its cost of capital. As we have already stated, the firm's required rate of return on equity is determined by its risk premium. However, the firm's overall cost of capital has to include the costs of debt and internally generated funds as well as the cost of shares. Among the important questions in financial theory is whether a firm's overall cost of capital can be changed by the composition of its liabilities and net worth. Specifically, do firms with large proportions of debt in their capital structures have the same overall cost of capital as firms with lower debt proportions? Or do firms that finance extensively with retained earnings have different overall costs of capital than firms that pay out net earnings as dividends? In short, do many of the techniques of financial management have any impact on the firm's overall required rate of return?

Empirical Results and the Capital Asset Pricing Model (CAPM)

Much of the subsequent analysis is based on the capital asset pricing model, the portfolio valuation model developed in Chapter 7. Yet most of the applications of this model have been in investments, not in corporate financial management. Fortunately, most of the applications of the model to corporate financial management lead to conclusions similar to those derived from older analytic techniques. For example, high liquidity, low operating leverage, and low financial leverage are all associated with low risk. Nonetheless, it may be useful to review the empirical findings of attempts to link the capital asset pricing model to financial management.

Most of these tests compare the relationship between accounting ratios that measure liquidity, operating leverage, financial leverage, and dividend policy to beta for individual stocks or portfolios of stock.

The earliest work was undertaken by Beaver, Kettler, and Scholes in their 1970 article (see reference 1). Though they did not consider operating leverage, they did include asset size, growth, and two variability measures that we have ignored. They also included financial leverage and liquidity. Their primary aim was to determine whether accounting values show the same risk characteristics as market risk measures. Since many financial decisions are based on accounting data, the empirical work is highly significant.

They studied two periods, 1947–1956 and 1957–1965. The simple correlation coefficients had the expected signs, except that liquidity in the second period not only had the wrong sign, but was statistically insignificant. Except for leverage, the correlation coefficients were markedly smaller in the later period than in the early. Further, the partial correlation coefficients for liquidity and leverage were near zero. Thus, this study is slightly disappointing.

Using accounting variability measures has been a dominant approach in these studies, despite the problem of separating independent from dependent variables and the difficulty of expressing expected variability and covariability measures. For examples of these approaches, see Gonedes and Thompson (reference 2).

Where the relationships between ordinary accounting ratios and beta have been measured, the results have beem mixed. See for example, Breen and Lerner (reference 3). In that study, although some ratios had the expected signs, the explanatory power of the equations was low. This and a number of the other studies (see, for example, reference 4), lack a theoretical underpinning, so that even the a priori expectations are not always clearly based on the capital asset pricing model. It is difficult, for example, to understand why we should expect the dividend payout ratios to be negatively related to beta on the basis of the portfolio model. Dividends are mentioned specifically, because in some form they usually turn out to have a reasonably strong relationship to beta.

Two studies have utilized the capital asset pricing model explicitly in developing the analytic base. The first, by Lev (reference 5), showed that beta and operating leverage are positively related. The second, by Hamada (see reference 6), developed a test for the financial leverage relationship and found significant results showing the expected positive relationship between systematic risk as measured by beta and financial leverage.

Except for Breen and Lerner, whose work covers 1970, none of these empirical tests go beyond 1968. Hence they may be overly affected by the bull market of the 1960s, and they may fail to reflect the high rates of realized and expected inflation of recent years. Certainly, low expected growth and high expected inflation are likely to affect the attitudes of both corporate financial managers and investors toward liquidity, operating leverage, financial leverage, and dividend coverage.

In summary, the empirical findings so far do not completely support the applicability of the capital asset pricing model to problems of liquidity management, operating leverage, financial leverage, and dividend policy, but such shortcomings are not uncommon in empirical studies. Certainly, the results are at least as definitive as any available on alternative approaches to financial management.

Review Questions

8-1 What is the relevance of a firm's common stock beta to the management of the firm?

8-2 Suggest an alternative to the corporate objective of maximizing share value. Discuss.

8-3 Discuss the relationship between diversification and the covariance of returns among individual assets.

Problems

8-4 You have been assigned the task of determining whether Bell Telephone is making an excessively large yield on its common stock. The Bell people argue that the yield is reasonable when risk is considered.
   a. What data would you need to compute the risk premium on Bell's shares, and how would you use the data?
   b. What contribution would knowledge of the risk-free rate and Bell's risk premium make to the controversy?

8-5 Assume that the capital asset pricing model holds and that security I and the market portfolio have the following characteristics:

Standard deviation, market portfolio	0.12
Standard deviation, security I	0.25
Expected return, market portfolio	0.08
Covariance between returns on security I and the market portfolio	0.027
Risk-free rate	0.05

   a. What is the expected return on security I?
   b. What would happen to this return if the risk of security I were greater? What would happen if the covariance were less?
   c. What is the value of beta for security I? What does beta tell us both in general terms and specifically about security I?

8-6 XYZ Corporation is planning to pay the first common dividend in its history at the end of the current period. Earnings for the period are expected to be $144,000. The common stock of the company is currently trading at $10 per share and there are 216,000 shares outstanding. The company anticipates long-run growth of 6% each year. What maximum dividend payout policy is consistent with keeping the cost of equity funds below 10%? If this maximum dividend payout ratio were exceeded by 50%, what would happen to the cost of equity funds? (Assume that the current market price of the common remains unchanged.)

Glossary

Capital structure	The financing of the firm by debt, preferred stock, and net worth (including capital, capital surplus and retained earnings).
Carrying charges	The costs of holding inventory, such as warehousing costs, and the interest paid on the funds used to finance the inventory.
Collection period	The average length of time between the sale of a good and the receipt of payment for that good.
Financial leverage	The effect of fixed financial charges on equity earnings.
Fixed-term savings certificate	A certificate representing the depositor's agreement to leave funds on deposit for a fixed period of time.
Liquidity policy	The firm's policy with regard to its level and mix of cash and other liquid assets.
Nominal yield	The return in monetary terms, not adjusted for any change in the price level.
Operating leverage	The effect of fixed operating costs on earnings before interest and taxes.
Risk/return ratio	The ratio of risk (as measured by standard deviation) return (as measured by the yield).

Bibliography

BEAVER, W., P. KETTLER, and M. SCHOLES, "The Association between Market-Determined and Accounting-Determined Risk Measures," *Accounting Review* (Oct. 1970), 654–682.

GONEDES, M. J., "Evidence on the Information Content of Accounting Numbers: Accounting-Based and Market-Based Estimates of Systematic Risk," *Journal of Financial and Quantitative Analysis* (June 1973), 407–443.

BREEN, W. J., and E. M. LERNER, "Corporate Financial Strategies and Market Measures of Risk and Return," *Journal of Finance* (May 1973), 339–351.

THOMPSON, D. J., II, "Sources of Systematic Risk in Common Stocks," *Journal of Business* (Apr. 1976), 173–188.

LEV, B., "On the Association between Operating Leverage and Risk," *Journal of Financial and Quantitative Analysis* (June 1974), 27–35.

HAMADA, R. S., "The Effect of the Firm's Capital Structure on the Systematic Risk of Common Stocks," *Journal of Finance* 27 (May 1972), 435–452.

The Management of Liquidity

9

Liquidity is a complex condition. It may indicate simply the amount of cash available, or it may be broadened to include many of the noncash assets, such as marketable securities, that can be converted to cash rapidly. The definition may be broadened even further to include operating assets of the firm that it expects to convert into cash shortly in the normal cycle of business activities. For example, accounts receivable becomes cash when they are collected, and merchandise inventory becomes liquid when it is sold for cash; it is only two steps removed from cash if it is sold on credit terms.

We may also define liquidity more narrowly by differentiating between a firm's total liquidity and the portion that is not needed to pay current liabilities, such as accounts payable, wages payable, and other short-term accruals.

In this chapter, we shall be concerned first with the importance of liquidity in determining the firm's risk. Next we shall consider the measurements of liquidity, and finally we shall review methods of planning liquidity needs.

Liquidity and Risk

Some liquid assets are required for the operations of the firm. These assets, which include operating cash, accounts receivable, and inventory, should meet the rate of return or present value hurdle applied to nonliquid assets such as plant and equipment.

Liquid assets have characteristics in addition to rate of return. Generally, the expected yields on such assets tend to have lower variances than on fixed assets. For example, the firm can rid itself of excess cash without difficulty by buying securities, investing in other earning assets, or redeeming debt. The expected risk on receivables is small (though not zero), since the payment of these receivables is a legal obligation of the firm's creditors. The expected return on inventory tends to be more variable than the returns on many other liquid assets, but is less than the variability of the rate of return on most fixed assets. Inventory, after all, very quickly generates cash inflows. In contrast, the factors contributing to the return on a machine depend more on *future* demand than on *current* conditions.

Further, the returns of many liquid assets are only weakly correlated, if at all, with the returns on other assets. If the firm were holding treasury bills or commercial paper instead of holding excess cash, the yield on these liquid assets has only the most tenuous relationship to the expected yield on inventories or fixed assets. Even the return on accounts receivable tends to be weakly correlated with the returns on other earnings assets, since the former depends directly on the liquidity and honesty of a customer, rather than on business conditions.

The low standard deviation for the individual liquid asset, combined with its usually weak correlation to the returns of other assets, permits the firm to adopt a lower risk portfolio when liquid assets exceed operating needs than it can without such "excess" liquidity. Under some conditions—for example, when the yields on relatively illiquid portfolios are low or when the correlation between the yields on liquid assets and nonliquid assets is zero or negative—portfolios with "excess" liquidity may have superior risk/return characteristics than portfolios without such liquidity.

Figure 9-1 shows some of these possibilities. *PP'* represents the efficient portfolio frontier confronting a firm if it holds no excess liquid assets. *LP'* is the same earning asset combinations with the addition of a relatively high-yielding, low-risk liquid asset. *RTP'* is a firm's efficient frontier if, it has a low-return, *risk-free* liquid asset such as a treasury bill instead of the high-yielding, low-risk liquid asset. Whether *LP'* is generally superior to *RTP'* depends on how high the yield is relative to the risk on the liquid asset included in *LP'*. With high risk and a relatively lower yield than in the figure, *RTP'* is generally superior to *LP* . More important, the availability of liquid assets usually makes the range of low-risk/return portfolios that include liquid assets superior to those without liquid assets (beyond operating needs), but this is not always the case. A high ratio of standard deviation to return for liquid assets could make a frontier such as *PP'* superior to portfolios that include liquid assets.

In short, varying the liquid assets held offers a means of managing risk in real asset portfolios when risk is generally dictated by the nature of the business. To be an effective means of risk management, liquid assets must have either (1) no risk or very small risk or (2) no correlation or very weak correlation with other assets.

As the yield on liquid assets rises, the desirability of holding them as

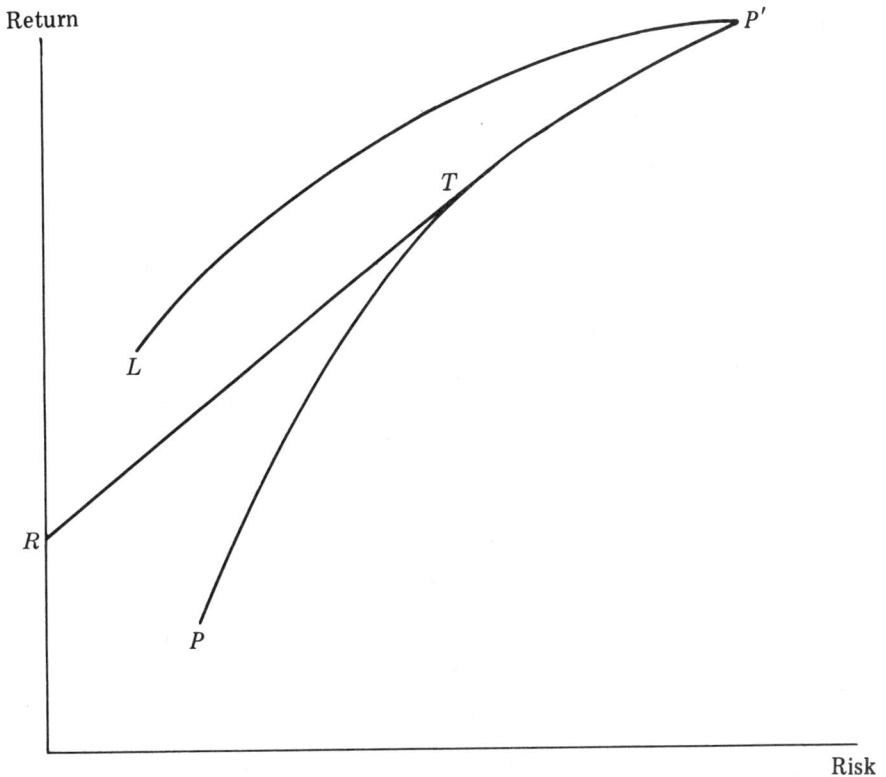

Figure 9-1
Possible Effects of Adding Excess Liquidity to Earning Asset Portfolio

operating assets increases, even if these two conditions are not met. However, under such circumstances, the motive for holding excess liquidity is more likely to be to gain returns rather than to reduce asset portfolio risk.

The Measurement of Liquidity

Defining liquidity is not simple. The most straightforward definition is cash on hand and cash in checking accounts. However, many firms also hold term deposits in financial institutions, which may or may not be negotiable, as well as marketable securities. Since these are quite safe and usually can be converted into cash very rapidly, shouldn't they be included in liquidity?

Once the definition of liquidity is broadened, it is difficult to stop. There are a number of other assets in a firm's balance sheet that are less liquid than cash, but can generate cash in a relatively short period. Traditionally, such assets are normally included in liquidity measures. For example, accounts receivable become cash immediately upon collection. Inventory also becomes liquid once the inventory is sold and the

Exhibit 1. ABC Manufacturing Corporation

Balance Sheet

	December 31, 1976		June 30, 1977	
Assets				
Cash	$100		$180	
Accounts receivable, net	200		250	
Merchandise inventory	300		330	
Total current assets		$ 600		$ 760
Fixed assets, gross	$500		$550	
Less accumulated depreciation	100		120	
Net fixed assets		400		430
Total assets		$1000		$1190
Liabilities and Net Worth				
Accounts payable	$ 40		$ 60	
Bank loan payable	60		50	
Current portion of term loan	60		60	
Other accruals payable	100		140	
Total current liabilities		$ 260		$ 310
Term loan payable*		240		180
Total liabilities		$ 500		$ 490
Paid-in capital	$300		$300	
Retained earnings	200		400	
Total net worth		$ 500		$ 700
Total liabilities and net worth		$1000		$1190

Income Statement for Six Months Ending June 30, 1977

Sales	$2000
Less cost of goods sold**	1200
Gross income	$ 800
Other expenses	200
Net income before taxes	$ 600
Income taxes	310
Net income after taxes	$ 290
Dividends	90
To retained earnings	$ 200

*Term loan is repaid in semiannual installments of $60.
**Includes depreciation of $50

sales are collected. To see this more clearly, consider the balance sheet and income statement in Exhibit 1.

How liquid are the accounts receivable in this balance sheet? As a first step, compute the rate of turnover of the accounts receivable. On average, net accounts receivable were $225 for the six months illustrated. If we assume that the $2000 of sales were all credit sales, accounts receivable turned over 8.888 times ($2000/$225). To determine the time that it took to turn over the inventory 8.888 times, we can divide the number of months to which the turnover rate applies by the turnover rate to get an "average age of receivables" in months. The average age of receivables is 0.675 months (6/8.888), or about 21 days.

Although the accounts receivables are not cash, they will be collected quickly in this instance, and hence it is common to include accounts receivables with marketable securities and cash. We define this total as the *quick* assets of the firm.

Since the firm receives no cash from inventory until the sales are collected, inventory is generally considered less liquid than accounts receivables and cash. However, since it is clearly more liquid than fixed assets, it is generally included in some definitions of liquidity if it is expected to generate cash in the current period. Thus, to see whether we should include inventory, we have to determine the speed with which the inventory is typically converted into sales. We can do this by computing the average inventory turnover and dividing this into some period of time. In our example, inventory turnover is the ratio of cost of goods sold to average inventory and equals 3.81 ($1200/$315) for six months. Thus, the average time required to convert inventory into sales is 1.575 months (6 months/3.81), or about 47 days. Combining the 47 days that it takes on average to sell inventory with the average collection period, we see that it takes about 68 days on average to convert inventory into cash. Since the inventory is likely to be collected during the current period, we can combine it with the quick assets. We usually refer to the total as *current assets*.

However, when we are defining liquidity, we cannot consider just liquid *assets*. We also have to consider liabilities that must be paid within the current period, since these represent a claim on the firm's liquidity. If we subtract from the current assets, the remainder is the firm's liquidity, often referred to as the firm's *working capital*. In our example, the working capital for the end of 1976 is the difference between the total current assets and the total current liabilities, or $340. It had risen to $450 by the end of June 1977.

Working capital measured absolutely is not a satisfactory measure of the firm's liquidity, if liquidity connotes safety. Suppose that the ABC Manufacturing Corporation borrows $500 on July 1, 1975, payable on demand; this increases its total current assets and its current liabilities by $500. Working capital is unaffected. However, once they convert the cash proceeds of the loan into other assets—even if these other assets are inventory or other current assets—the firm's relative liquidity is less, because its current obligations have increased $500.

To capture this change, the ratio of current assets to current liabilities, called the *current ratio,* is often used as a measure of liquidity. The current ratio of the ABC Manufacturing Corporation was 2.31 at the end of December 1976 (600/260) and rose to 2.45 by the end of June 1977 (760/310). If they take the $500 demand loan on July 1, their current ratio on July 1 would be 1.56 (1260/810), even though their working capital is still $450.

Another measure of liquidity is the ratio of quick assets to current liabilities, sometimes known as the *acid-test ratio.* The acid-test ratio of the ABC Manufacturing Corporation at the end of December is 1.15 (300/260) and 1.39 at the end of June (430/310).

The Analysis of Working Capital Changes

Techniques of analyzing the factors changing working capital are useful, either for determining the causes of past changes or for translating the impact that the firm's operating plans may have on their working capital for some period in the future. One of the more widely used techniques is flow-of-funds analysis or sources-and-uses of working capital changes analysis. This type of analysis is now so common that most published annual reports of corporations include statements of the factors affecting working capital changes along with their income statements and balance sheets.

In flow-of-funds analysis, the simplest and most basic rule is that any change in a noncurrent asset is a use of working capital, and any change in a noncurrent liability or an equity item is a source of working capital. Using data from ABC Manufacturing Corporation's balance sheet, we can devise a simple flow-of-funds, or sources-and-uses, statement by listing the sources and uses of working capital as follows:

Beginning working capital			$340
Plus sources:			
Change in retained earnings	$200		
(Reduction in term loan payable)	−60		
Total sources		$140	
Less uses:			
Change in net fixed assets	30		
Total uses		30	
Net change in working capital			110
Ending working capital			$450

Though this statement is useful, more detail would increase its value. For example, the change in retained earnings is the result of a combination of income earned by the company less the dividends paid. It would be useful to separate them, since the net income after taxes is a source of funds and the dividends are a use. The net effect on working capital would be the same, since the dividends (a use) would be subtracted from income (a source). In other words,

Net income after taxes	$290
Less dividend	90
Change in retained earnings	$200

Additional details for the changes in fixed assets would be quite useful, but they are considerably more complex than adding net income. The change in net fixed assets of $30 reflects a combination of three kinds of changes. First, the gross fixed assets, or original cost of the fixed assets, have decreased as the accumulated depreciation account has risen to reflect the additional depreciation charges during the first half of 1977. However, the change in accumulated depreciation is only $20, whereas the depreciation charges for the period are $50. The difference between these two changes is an estimate of the book values of the assets retired during the first half of the year, the second source of change in the net fixed assets account. Finally, the total additions and replacements of fixed assets during the period, which are of interest since they reflect changes in working capital, reflect the retirements of fixed assets, the depreciation charges against fixed assets that have not been retired, and the assets that are true net replacements. These changes affect the statement as follows:

Retirements of fixed assets:		
Beginning accumulated depreciation		$100
Plus depreciation changes during period		50
Total		$150
Less ending accumulated depreciation		120
Estimated book value of retirement		$ 30
Ending fixed assets, gross		$550
Beginning fixed assets, gross	$500	
Less estimated retirements	30	
Book value of assets less retirements before additions		$470
Total expenditures on replacements and additions to fixed assets		$ 80

With the additional details, the sources and uses statement becomes

Beginning working capital		$340
Plus sources:		
Net income after taxes	$290	
(reduction in term loan payable)	−60	
Depreciation charges	50	
Total sources		$280

Table 9-1. Flow of Funds Analysis for ABC Manufacturing Corporation for 6 Months Ending June 30, 1975

Account	Trial Balance, December 31, 1974		Adjustments To Nonworking Capital Accounts		Trial Balance, June 30, 1975	
	Dr	Cr	Dr	Cr	Dr	Cr
Fixed assets	500	—	80[e]	30[d]	550	
Accumulated depreciation	—	100	30[d]	50[c]	—	120
Term loan	—	240	60[f]	—	—	180
Paid-in capital	—	300	—		—	300
Retained earnings	—	200	90[b]	290[a]	—	400
Working capital	340	—	110[g]	—	450	
Totals	840	840	370	370	1000	1000

	Adjustments to Working Capital	
	Sources	Uses
After-tax profits	290[a]	
Dividends	—	90[b]
Depreciation	50[c]	
Fixed asset acquisitions	—	80[e]
Term loan payment	—	60[f]
Totals:		
Sources of working capital	340	
Uses of working capital	—	230
Net increase in working capital	—	110[g]
Totals	340	340

NOTES:

[a] To record net income after taxes.

[b] To record dividends.

[c] To record depreciation charged.

[d] This is the difference between the sum of the December accumulated depreciation total plus depreciation for the six-month period and the June accumulated depreciation. It is an estimate of the fixed assets that have been disposed of and written off the books. Therefore, it reduces both accumulated depreciation and fixed assets.

[e] To record the gross additions to fixed assets, i.e. gross of writeoffs.

[f] To record amortization of term loan, not interest.

[g] To transfer excess of sources of working capital over uses for six-month period to working capital account.

Less uses:			
Replacements and additions to fixed assets	$ 80		
Dividends	90		
Total uses		170	
Net change in working capital			$110
Ending working capital			$450

Note that we have included depreciation charges as a source of funds. We can view this as offsetting the replacement of fixed assets that have been included in the revised sources-and-uses statement. Another way of viewing this inclusion is to recognize that we have deducted depreciation from sales in arriving at net income after taxes. Unlike most other expenses, depreciation expenses do not reflect a cash or working capital change during the accounting period. Instead, depreciation, is an allocation of the original cost of the assets spread over their lives, according to formulas acceptable to the tax authorities. Hence, during the first half of 1977, expenses rose by $50 because of depreciation charges, but cash did not decrease by $50. Thus, working capital generated from the operations of the business increased by more than the net income after taxes. In fact, it increased by the sum of net income after taxes and the depreciation for the period.

If you are familiar with accounting procedures, you may find it useful to analyze flow of funds in terms of ordinary accounting procedures. Table 9-1 details the accounting changes that generate the sources-and-uses statement.

The Cash Budget

The best laid plans of business often go astray because of inadequate attention to the plans' impacts on cash. Even profitable operation can lead a firm to severe problems if it does not have sufficient cash to meet its current obligations. We call such a situation *technical insolvency*. If it does not have sufficient cash to meet its payroll, the firm may lose its work force and be forced to cancel otherwise profitable operations, or the tax authorities may create difficulties if the firm can't pay its tax bills. How can this happen to a profitable firm?

Consider an exaggerated case in which a firm expects to receive $100,000 during a period and to spend $80,000. This leaves a $20,000 profit. However, if all the $80,000 expenses occur at the beginning of the period and all the receipts occur at the end, the firm will not have enough cash unless it has arranged with its creditors to wait for the $80,000 of expenses. Or, the firm could borrow the necessary funds until they receive the $100,000. Expense flows that do not match revenue flows in timing are not usually a problem if they are foreseen. The firm can arrange to finance its temporary cash deficit. If it cannot make such arrangements, or if it can make them only under such onerous terms that their operation would be unprofitable, advance planning would at least prevent the firm from entering into untenable operations.

The major tool in such planning is the cash budget. It is an integral part of an overall budgeting system, if the firm is operating on such a sophisticated system. Often, however, smaller firms do not use a full budgeting system that includes sales and production planning, budgets for capital acquisitions, and so on. Smaller firms may have simpler problems that require less coordination. Nonetheless, even small firms need some plan to determine their cash needs. For these purposes, it is necessary to distinguish between the time that a sale is made and the time that the cash from that sale is received. The latter increases cash, while the former does not affect cash at all. On the other side of the ledger, distinctions must be made between the time that an expense is incurred and the time that cash payment must be made. For example, tax liabilities incurred during the accounting period may not have to be paid until some later time. Such expenses are not cash disbursement.

Hence, the firm must thoroughly review its plans for the period. In a technical sense, the firm must anticipate the type of accounting entry associated with each element of the budgeting system or plan of the firm. If these elements do not involve debits or credits to the cash account, they do not appear in the cash budget. On the other hand, if they do involve a cash account, they do affect cash. The firm may not have to pay the tax liability it is currently incurring during this period, but it may have to reflect in its cash budget the payment of a *previous* tax liability.

Although the process of cash budgeting is deceptively simple, it is

Exhibit 2. XYZ Manufacturing Corporation
Projected Income Statement for Year
Ending December 31, 1976
(Thousands of Dollars)

Sales		14,000
Less		
Wage and salary expense	6,520	
Materials costs	5,090	
Depreciation	1,970	
Operating expenses		13,580
Gross income		420
Less interest expense		114
Net income before taxes		306
Income taxes		159
Net income after taxes		147
Dividends		100
To retained earnings		47

Exhibit 3. XYZ Manufacturing Corporation Projected Monthly Income Statements for 1976
(In Thousands of Dollars)

Account	Jan.	Feb.	Mar.	Apr.	May	June	July	Aug.	Sept.	Oct.	Nov.	Dec.	Total
Sales	1,000	900	900	1,100	1,200	1,400	900	600	1,200	1,400	1,600	1,800	14,000
Less wages and salaries	550	500	500	550	560	570	500	500	560	570	580	580	6,520
Materials	360	350	350	380	400	500	350	200	400	500	600	700	5,090
Depreciation	125	135	140	140	150	160	170	180	180	180	205	205	1,970
Interest	10	10	10	10	10	10	9	9	9	9	9	9	114
Net income before tax	-45	-95	-100	20	80	160	-129	-289	51	141	206	306	306
Quarterly taxable income	—	—	-240	—	—	260	—	—	-367	—	—	653	306
Previous loses	—	—	—	—	—	-240	—	—	—	—	—	-367	
Net tax	—	—	0	—	—	11	—	—	0	—	—	148	159

tremendously important. At a fundamental level, nothing in this book is a more important tool of financial management than cash budgeting. As a statement of estimates reflecting the planned operations of a firm or as an integral part of a highly sophisticated budgeting system, cash budgets are a sine qua non of proper financial management.

To illustrate the importance of cash budgeting, the following example of the development of a cash budget may be useful.

Exhibit 2 presents a projected income statement for a hypothetical firm. Exhibit 3 shows the same information by months. Underlying these projections are the sales forecasts, inventory and production-scheduling decisions, and trade credit decisions.

Income statements alone, however, give only limited information about cash flows. We know, for example, that depreciation expense is not a cash outflow. Exhibit 4 provides another example of the difference between profit flows and cash flows. Here, sales are translated into actual cash collections. It has been assumed that the firm expects to collect 20% of sales in the month in which the sale is made. It expects to collect 40% in the month following the sale, and 30% two months after the sale. The remaining 10% will be collected three months after the sale.

Thus, during the first three months of the year, the firm expects to collect not only from sales made during 1976, but also from sales made in 1975. At the end of the projection, part of the sales for the last three months are not expected to be collected until 1977. Since total expected collections are less than total expected sales, the investment in accounts receivable at the end of 1976 will be larger than at the end of 1975.

Exhibit 5 takes the collection information and combines it with monthly details on cash disbursements. Here, too, the timing of cash flows does not coincide with the profit flows. We assume that wage and salary payments lag a half month behind the period in which they are earned. Thus, one-half of the $500 allotted for January's wage and salary payments was incurred in January and the other half was incurred in December.

We have assumed that this firm pays for materials one month after they are delivered. Thus, January's bills are shown in February. Just as the unpaid portion of the wage and salary expenses is reflected in the current liability "accrued wages and salaries," unpaid bills are reflected in accounts payable.

We assume that corporations pay taxes quarterly, six months after incurring the tax liability. Thus, the tax liability incurred over the first two quarters of 1976 is not reflected in the cash flow schedule until it is paid in December 1976. No tax payment is shown in September, since the firm expects to show a loss for the first quarter of 1976. Losses may be carried forward to offset profits for as long as five years, or carried back by recalculating past tax liabilities for one year. The firm could have planned equal quarterly payments of 25% of the 1976 estimated tax liability, with the first payment starting in September 1976. The pay-

Exhibit 4. Collections from Sales for 1976
(In Thousands of Dollars)

	Jan.	Feb.	Mar.	Apr.	May	June	July	Aug.	Sept.	Oct.	Nov.	Dec.	Total
Cash sales	200	180	180	220	240	280	280	120	240	280	320	360	
Previous month	640	400	360	360	440	480	560	360	240	480	560	640	
2 months ago	360	480	300	270	270	330	360	420	270	180	360	420	
3 months ago	100	120	160	100	90	90	110	120	140	90	60	120	
Totals	1,300	1,180	1,000	950	1,040	1,180	1,210	1,020	890	1,030	1,300	1,540	13,640

Exhibit 5. XYZ Manufacturing Corporation Monthly Cash Flows for 1976
(In Thousands of Dollars)

Account	Jan.	Feb.	Mar.	Apr.	May	June	July	Aug.	Sept.	Oct.	Nov.	Dec.	Totals
Collections	1,300	1,180	1,000	950	1,040	1,180	1,210	1,020	890	1,030	1,300	1,540	13,640
Wage and salary payments	500	525	500	525	555	565	535	500	530	565	575	580	6,455
Materials payments	600	360	350	350	380	400	500	350	200	400	500	600	4,990
Interest payments	—	—	—	—	—	60	—	—	—	—	—	54	114
Tax payments	—	—	10	—	—	125	—	—	—	—	—	11	146
Term loan amortization	—	—	—	—	—	200	—	—	—	—	—	200	400
Bank loan repayment	—	—	—	—	50	—	—	—	—	—	—	—	50
Dividend payment	25	—	—	25	—	—	25	—	—	25	—	—	100
Fixed asset acquisitions	310	470	200	—	400	—	510	—	220	—	420	—	2,530
Net cash flow	-135	-175	-60	50	-345	-170	-360	170	-60	40	-195	95	-1,145

ments planned for March and June of 1976 are for tax liabilities in curred in the last half of 1975.

Although interest is incurred over the year, actual payments are made semiannually. We have assumed that the interest is paid on the term loan.

Before we turn to items that do not appear on the income statement, but which do affect cash flow, we should make one other point about the effect of income statement items on cash. In the example, we have assumed that the firm does not plan to either increase or diminish the investment in inventory. Had the firm planned to increase inventory investment, the labor, materials, and depreciation used for the inventory accumulation would not have been shown in the income statement, but would have been reflected in the cash flow schedule. On the other hand, if the firm had planned to reduce inventory investment, the cost of the goods produced in the past but sold in 1976 would be shown in the planned income statement. The cost would not affect cash in 1976, however, since the cash expenditures would have been made when the goods were produced.

The installment payment on the term loan, the bank loan repayment, and the cash expenditures for the acquisition of fixed assets are not shown directly in the income statement. The loan payments do reduce interest, and the acquisition of fixed assets does increase depreciation expense. However, the information needed to reflect the cash impact of these transactions is not in the income statement.

The dividend payments shown in the planned disbursement for January 1976 reflect profits earned in 1975. Dividend payments for the last quarter of 1976 will not be made until 1977. Firms commonly keep dividends at a stable level, even though profits fluctuate.

Exhibit 5 shows the cash flow by months. If the firm preferred to ignore the monthly schedules and take only the annual cash flow into account, difficulties might ensue. Over the year, the firm expects to disburse $1,145,000 more than it receives from operations. If the firm plans to have $100,000 cash available each month to take care of the average monthly net outflow, it will run short of cash in each of the six months when the net cash outflow exceeds $100,000.

Even if the firm plans for cash on a monthly basis, it may have cash shortages. Suppose that the disbursements of $1,435,000 planned for January take place in the first half of the month, but the collections do not occur until the end of the month. If the firm plans on starting January with a cash balance equal to the expected net outflow for the month, $135,000, a substantial shortage will occur well before January 15.

To avoid shortages during a planning period, the firm must choose a time period short enough to avoid such fluctuations. The shorter the budget period, the less likely the net cash outflow for any period will exceed the net cash outflow for the period as a whole. On the other hand, the shorter the period, the more expenses are incurred in preparing budgets for the year. Preparing daily budgets would make little sense. The costs would be enormous, and for most disbursement items, the firm will not incur severe penalties if it makes payments one day late. Weekly budgets would be less expensive, and the penalties for late payment are likely to be more severe if the payment is one week late than one day late. However, even weekly budgets may be unnecessary if disbursements come at the end of the week and receipts come at the beginning, or if receipts and disbursements are faily well matched.

In the example, we have assumed that the firm has decided to use a monthly planning period. This decision implies that the probability of a cash deficit greater than the net cash flow's occurring within the month is small.

Summary

The management of liquidity is probably the most important survival skill required in financial management. Without adequate liquidity, the firm can become technically insolvent and the rest of the apparatus of financial analysis becomes redundant.

However, measuring liquidity is not simple. The firm does not know whether an asset other than cash is really liquid until it tries to convert the asset into cash. However, assets payable within a short period (such as accounts receivable) or those expected to be sold soon (inventory) are usually included in liquidity measures. Offsetting these are the liabilities that must be paid in the near term.

Liquidity not only ensures survival by averting technical insolvency, it may also act as a risk-free asset in a firm's portfolio since the risks of many liquid assets are usually low and only weakly correlated with the returns expected from longer-term assets. Thus, the greater the proportion of truly liquid assets in the portfolio, the lower the overall portfolio risk.

The usual summary measure of liquidity is working capital, the difference between current assets and current liabilities. Measuring expected working capital changes over a planning period is an important part of the planning process. Analysis of working capital changes is now required in a public firm's historic reporting and stands on a par with the traditional operating statements in the company's annual report.

To avoid technical insolvency and to minimize high-cost emergency cash-raising operations, a firm should prepare cash budgets as well. These budgets recognize the expected delays in converting noncash assets into cash, and they consider the effects of accruals and other disbursements and receipts that may not be included in the income statement. While working capital planning can be made for periods as long as a year, cash budgets are usually for shorter periods, typically a month.

Review Questions

9-1 What elements of a corporate manager's job are similar to those of an investment portfolio manager? Explain.

9-2 Present a scenario of the possible effects of an increase in working capital on the price of a firm's common stock. What are the potential weaknesses of your argument? (Keep other variables in your analysis constant.)

9-3 What are some of the limitations of ratio analysis?

9-4 How might portfolio considerations affect the liquidity management practices of a firm?

9-5 What implications does a seasonal sales pattern have for liquidity management policy?

Problems

9-6 For the ABC Manufacturing Company whose balance sheet appears in Exhibit 1 (this chapter) determine the following financial ratios:

Ratio	Industry norm
Sales/total assets	2 times
Net profit/sales	4%
Net profit/total assets	3%
Net profit/net worth	8%

Do your findings suggest any errors in the management practices of ABC?

9-7 Carry out a flow-of-funds analysis for Flint Corporation.

Flint Corporation

Comparative Balance Sheets

Year ending Dec. 31, 1972 (in millions)

Assets	1971	1972	Liabilities and Net Worth	1971	1972
Cash	$ 6	$ 3	Notes payable	$20	$ 1
Marketable securities	5	7	Accounts payable	5	8
Accounts receivable	10	15	Accrued wages	2	2
Inventories	12	15	Accrued taxes	3	5
Fixed assets, net	50	55	Long-term debt	0	15
Other assets	7	5	Common & surplus	60	69
Total assets	$90	$100	Total liabilities and net worth	$90	$100

Flint Corporation
Statement of Income and Retained Earnings
Year Ending Dec. 31, 1972

Net sales		$50,000,000
Expenses:		
Cost of goods sold	$25,000,000	
Selling, general, and		
administrative expense	5,000,000	
Depreciation	5,000,000	
Interest	1,000,000	36,000,000
Net income before taxes		14,000,000
Less: Taxes		7,000,000
Net income		7,000,000
Add: Retained earnings at 1/1/72		40,000,000
Subtotal		47,000,000
Less: Dividends	3,000,000	
Loss on sale of fixed assets*	2,000,000	5,000,000
Retained earnings at 12/31/72		42,000,000

*The assets were sold at the beginning of 1972 for $11,000,000. The accumulated depreciation on these assets was $4,000,000.

9-8 What was the after-tax cash flow for Flint Corporation for the year ending Dec. 31, 1972? Determine the following ratios for Flint (1972): receivables turnover, average age of receivables, quick ratio, current ratio, inventory turnover. Which, if any, of these indicate areas needing attention?

9-9 The ACE Corporation has asked you to prepare its cash budget for the first three months of 1978. Schedules of cash receipts, cash disbursements, and cash balance are required. The following information is available:

1. *Sales (actual 1977)*   *Sales (forecasted 1978)*

November	$100,000	January	$ 80,000
December	130,000	February	80,000
		March	100,000
		April	110,000

2. Sales are 50% cash and 50% credit. Forty percent of credit sales are collected after one month and the remainder are collected after two months.
3. The gross margin on sales is 50%.
4. Purchases are made one month before anticipated sales and are paid for one month after purchase.

5. The wages and salaries paid each month equal $5000 plus 2% all sales over $90,000 for the month.
6. Rent is $2000 per month.
7. Taxes are paid at the end of each quarter and are 10% of the period's gross margin.
8. The firm currently (Dec. 31, 1977) has a cash balance of $15,000 (minimum desired cash balance). Bank borrowing will be arranged at the start of any month to ensure that cash balances do not fall below the *minimum* during the month.

Glossary

Accounts receivable turnover	$$\frac{\text{credit sales}}{\text{average net accounts receivable}}$$ where average $= \dfrac{\text{beginning} + \text{end values}}{2}$
Acid-test (quick) ratio	$$\frac{\text{current assets} - \text{inventory}}{\text{current liabilities}}$$
Accumulated depreciation	The total of all previous amounts taken as depreciation expense on an asset or asset class.
Balance sheet	A statement of the company's assets and liabilities at some point in time (normally the end of the fiscal period, which is usually one year).
Book value	The value stated in the accounting records of the firm. It is either original cost, or original cost less depreciation (if the asset is depreciable) for an asset. For a liability or equity item, it is also the historical value.
Cash budgeting	The process of planning cash flows (receipts and disbursements) for a specified period of time.
Current liabilities	Debts due within one year.
Current ratio	$$\frac{\text{current assets}}{\text{current liabilities}}$$
Flow-of-funds analysis	An analysis of the factors affecting working capital, using the working capital.
Gross fixed assets	Fixed assets are noncurrent, such as plant and equipment. "Gross" means that depreciation has not been deducted.
Income statement	A record of the company's revenues and expenses over the period in question (normally a year).

or	Inventory turnover	$\dfrac{\text{cost of goods sold}}{\text{average inventory}}$

where average $= \dfrac{\text{beginning} + \text{end value}}{2}$

Liquidity	The cash position of a firm and its ability to meet its currently maturing obligations.
Marketable securities	Investments in interest-earning assets by the firm to absorb cash not currently needed in the business.
Net fixed assets	Fixed assets net of accumulated depreciation. *See gross fixed assets.*
Nonliquid asset	An asset that cannot readily be converted into cash at its equilibrium (true) value. For example, machinery.
Operating assets	The assets a firm requires in the conduct of its business.
Quick assets	The most liquid assets in the firm. They consist of cash, accounts receivable, and marketable securities.
Sources-and-uses of funds	See *flow-of-funds analysis.*
Trade credit	Credit provided by suppliers by not demanding payment on delivery.
Working capital	Current assets less current liabilities. It is considered a measure of the liquidity available to the firm.

Bibliography

ALTMAN, E. I., "Financial Ratios, Discriminant Analysis and the Prediction of Corporate Bankruptcy," *Journal of Finance 23* (Sept. 1968), 589–609.

ARCHER, S. H., "A Model for the Determination of Firm Cash Balances," *Journal of Financial and Quantitative Analysis 1* (March 1966), 1–11.

BAUMOL, W. J., "The Transactions Demand for Cash: An Inventory Theoretic Approach," *Quarterly Journal of Economics 66* (Nov. 1952), 545–556.

BEAVER, W. H., "Financial Ratios as Predictors of Failure," *Empirical Research in Accounting, Selected Studies, 1966* (Institute of Professional Accounting, January, 1967), 71–111.

BENISHAY, HASKEL, "Economic Information on Financial Ratio Analysis," *Accounting and Business Research 2* (Spring 1971), 174–179.

BRUNNER, K., and A. H. MELTZER, "Economies of Scale in Cash Balances, Reconsidered," *Quarterly Journal of Economics 81* (Aug. 1967), 422–436.

CALMAN, R. F., *Linear Programming of Cash Management: Cash Alpha*, Cambridge, Mass.: The MIT Press, 1968.

COATES, J. P., "Trade Credit: A Case Study," *Journal of Industrial Economics* (June 1965), 205–213.

DONALDSON, G., "Strategy for Financial Emergencies," *Harvard Business Review 47* (Nov.–Dec. 1969), 67–69.

FREIMER, M., and M. J. GORDON, "Why Bankers Ration Credit," *Quarterly Jou* *of Economics 79* (Aug. 1965), 397–416.

GREENLEAF, R. W., *Introduction to Corporate Financial Statements* (rev. ed.) Indianapolis: Orchard House Press, 1965.

HARRIS, D. G., "Rationing Credit to Business: More than Interest Rates," *Business Review, Federal Reserve Bank of Philadelphia* (Aug. 1970), 3–14.

HURLEY, E. M., "Business Financing by Business Finance Companies," *Federal Reserve Bulletin 64* (Oct. 1968), 815–827.

JOHNSON, G. L., "Funds-Flow Equations," *Accounting Review 41* (July 1966), 510–517.

LERNER, E. M., "Simulating a Cash Budget," *California Management Review 11* (Winter 1968), 79–86.

LEVY, F. K., "An Application of Heuristic Problem-Solving to Accounts Receivable Management," *Management Science 12* (Feb. 1966), B236–B244.

MILLER, M. H., and D. ORR, "A Model of the Demand for Money by Firms," *Quarterly Journal of Economics 80* (Aug. 1966), 413–425.

ROBICHEK, A. A., D. TEICHROEW, and J. M. JONES, "Optimal Short-Term Financing Decision," *Management Science 12* (Sept. 1965), 1–36.

WESTON, J. F., "Financial Analysis: Planning and Control," *Financial Executive 33* (July 1965), 40–42ff.

WHALEN, E. L., "An Extension of the Baumol–Tobin Approach to the Transactions Demand for Cash," *Journal of Finance 23* (March 1968), 113–134.

al

Operating Leverage

10

One reason that corporate earnings vary is that certain components of cost remain constant even though revenues vary. When revenues increase, these costs remain unchanged, so total costs increase less rapidly than revenues, and hence profits increase more rapidly than revenues. On the other hand, when revenues decline, total costs fall less rapidly, so profits decline more rapidly than revenues. Such variability in the distribution of earnings is reflected in its standard deviation, and hence in the firm's beta. If all other factors are equal, one would expect firms with relatively large fixed components in their cost structures to have larger betas (larger risk premiums) than firms with relatively small fixed-cost components. This does not mean that the share values of firms with large fixed-cost components would be less than similar firms with low fixed-cost components. Firms with many fixed costs may be more profitable on average, even though they are also more risky.

The relationship of profit volatility to fixed costs is often referred to as *leverage*. The term derives from the fact that profits are "levered up" more rapidly than revenues, when revenues are growing. We shall discuss two kinds of leverage. The first deals with fixed costs associated with production and distribution. The most obvious of these are the depreciation and maintenance charges associated with plant and equipment. Also included are other fixed costs, such as management and supervisory personnel salaries, and all other operating costs that do not fluctuate with revenues. Since these costs are associated with the firm's operations, we can refer to this type of leverage as *operating leverage*.

Whereas many of the fixed-cost components of operating leverage are assets, such as plant and equipment, the fixed costs of the second type of leverage are the liabilities of the firm. This type of leverage is called *financial leverage*, because it deals with the impact of fixed financial charges on the earnings available to shareholders. We shall examine financial leverage in Chapter 11. Large quantities of fixed liabilities affect the volatility of shareholders' earnings, and hence the risk premium required on the share return.

Production Breakeven Analysis

Perhaps the most familiar type of operating leverage analysis is the determination of breakeven points for production processes. The *breakeven point* is the level of output at which total costs equal total revenues, or where profits are zero. We can use such analysis to assess the risk of an operation by comparing the normal range of output to the breakeven level. The risk is large if the normal range of output is close to the breakeven point.

We can also use breakeven analysis to compare production alternatives. A new production method may increase fixed costs and reduce variable cost per unit. For example, machinery may replace labor, or more efficient machinery may reduce waste. In either case, one way to compare the proposed new method with the old method is to calculate their breakeven points.

When we analyze the breakeven point of a production process, we usually assume that the price per unit of output is constant and that variable costs per unit are also constant. This may be an unreasonable assumption over wide ranges of output, since the firm would probably have to reduce the price of an item in order to sell twice as many units. Per-unit variable costs may not be constant if output is doubled. But the purpose of breakeven analysis is not to determine the actual profit at different levels of output. Rather, its purpose is to determine the reduction in output than can be tolerated under existing price/variable-cost relationships before losses are incurred. In other words, breakeven analysis is a device to assess risk rather than to determine profitability.

Now we shall describe this analysis on a formal level

$$\text{revenue} - \text{costs} = \text{profit}$$

Revenues are price (p) times quantity (Q). Costs are fixed costs (FC), which do not vary with output, and total variable costs, which are per unit variable costs (vc) times quantity. Then we have

$$pQ - FC - (vc)Q = \text{profits} \qquad (10\text{-}1)$$

Breakeven quantity $(\overline{Q})$ occurs when profits are zero. Figure 10-1 shows this graphically. We can also express this relationship in an equation.

$$p\overline{Q} - (vc)\overline{Q} - FC = 0 \qquad (10\text{-}1a)$$

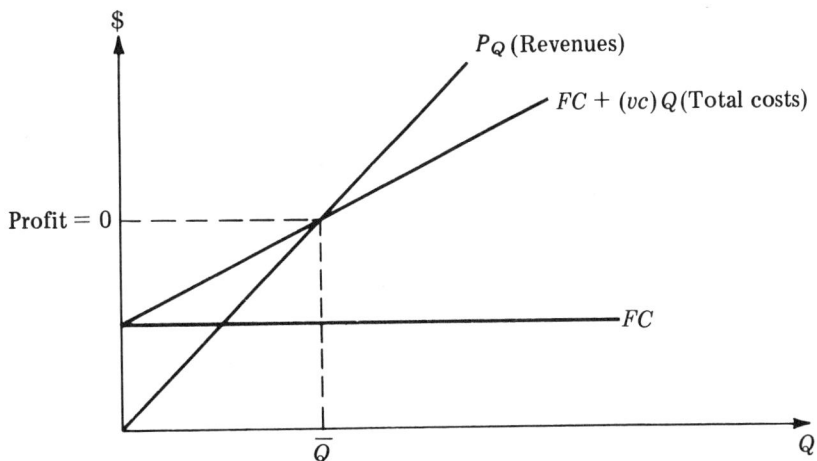

Figure 10-1
Breakeven Chart

or

$$\overline{Q} = \frac{FC}{p - vc} \qquad (10\text{-}1b)$$

Thus the breakeven quantity $\overline{Q}$ is the ratio of fixed costs to the margin between price and per unit variable costs.

Let's look at some specific numbers. If $p = 10$, $vc = 8$, and $FC = 100$, then $\overline{Q} = 100/(10 - 8) = 50$. At 50 units, revenue is $500, fixed costs are $100, and total variable costs are $400.

To see the leverage effect of fixed costs on profits, consider the profits in this example for a selected range of outputs:

Q	Profits ($)
10	−80
20	−60
30	−40
40	−20
50	0
60	20
70	40
80	60
90	80

The profit equation is

$$\text{profits} = 2Q - 100 \qquad (10\text{-}2)$$

We can show this graphically, as in Figure 10-2.

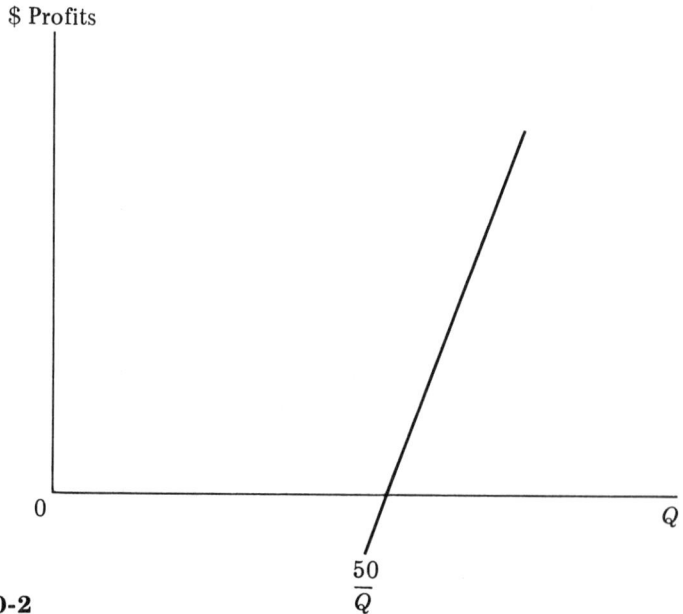

Figure 10-2
Profit Function under Breakeven Analysis

Various production conditions limit the application of breakeven analysis.

1. More than one product is produced in the fixed facilities.
2. The relative importance of each product can and does change.
3. The margin for each product is different, that is, $p - vc$ is different for each product.

There can be as many breakeven points as there can be combinations of products in total output.

As a measure of risk, breakeven analysis is quite limited, since it concentrates on only one aspect of risk, namely the level to which output may fall before profits become losses. To see the limitations of break-even analysis as a measure of risk, consider an example. The probability distribution of sales to a firm is shown in Table 10-1. The standard deviation of the probability distribution of profits is $36.06, similar to the calculation shown in Chapter 1. If the firm can reduce vc to $5 by increasing FC to $200, what impact will this have on return and risk?

$$\overline{Q} = \frac{200}{10 - 5} = 40 < \text{old } \overline{Q} \text{ of } 50.$$

So on the basis of breakeven analysis, the new proposal is less risky. However, the proposal's standard deviation is almost three times that of the old project. Thus, the standard deviation implies that the new proposal is riskier.

Table 10-1. Conditional Profit Example

(1)	Probability Distribution of Sales (2)	Profits are: (3)				(4) = (2) × (3)
Q	Probability	$(10Q)$ − pQ	$(8Q)$ − $(vc)Q$	100 − FC	$= Profits$ $= Profits$	Partial Expectations
20	0.05	200	160	100 =	−60	−3
30	0.10	300	240	100 =	−40	−4
40	0.15	400	320	100 =	−20	−3
50	0.20	500	400	100 =	0	0
60	0.20	600	480	100 =	20	4
70	0.15	700	560	100 =	40	6
80	0.10	800	640	100 =	60	6
90	0.05	900	720	100 =	80	4

Expected value = $10

To appreciate the relationship between leverage and risk, note that a riskless profit occurs only if profits are constant at all levels of output. (See Table 10-2.) The more responsive profits are to output variations, the larger the standard deviation of profits, and hence the greater the volatility of rate of return. In terms of the profit equation, this means that the slope for riskless profits is zero. The slope for the existing system in the example was 2. The proposed system's slope is still $p - vc$, but now vc is less, so the slope is 5, and profits will be more volatile regardless of the break-even point. Figure 10-3 compares the two profit equations; the difference in breakeven points is ignored. The shaded area indicates how much more extreme the variation in profits is under the

Table 10-2. Conditional Profit Example

Q	Profit	Partial Expectations
20	−100	−5
30	−50	−5
40	0	0
50	50	10
60	100	20
70	150	22.50
80	200	20.00
90	250	12.50

Expected value = $75.00 but σ = $90.14

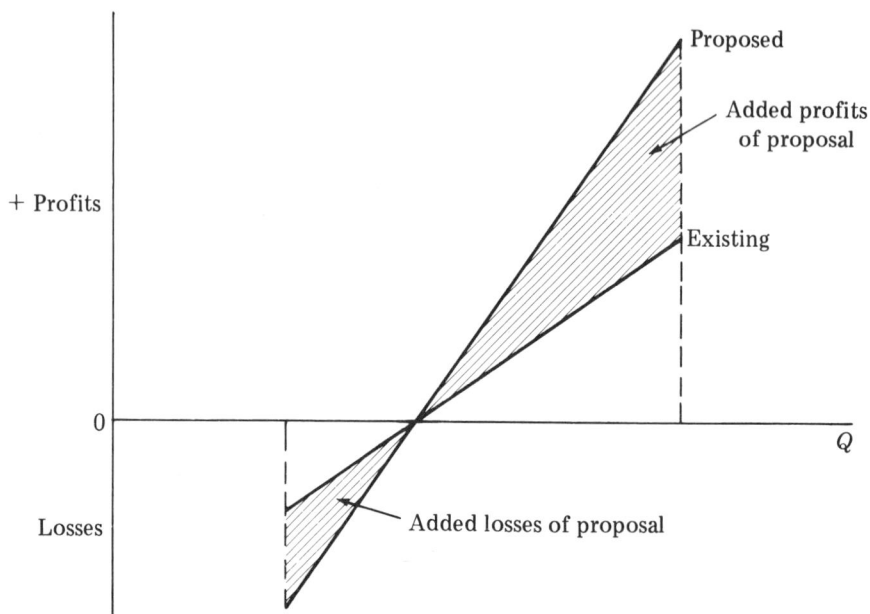

Figure 10-3
Impact of New Proposal on Possible Profits and Losses

proposed system. Hence, final decisions should not be based on break-even points alone.

This example demonstrates that breakeven analysis does not necessarily indicate the effect of a proposal on the firm's beta. The fact that earnings have a larger standard deviation with the new proposal implies that the rate of return (in which the growth of earnings and dividends are important) is more volatile. If the correlation between the firm's rate of return and the market yield does not change as a result of adopting the proposal, it is likely that adoption will increase the firm's beta.

This is not necessarily a criticism of the proposal. The issue is whether the shares, when discounted at the new required rate of return on equity, will have a value at least equal to the value before the proposal was adopted, when beta was lower.

Leverage Estimated from Income Statements

We can use breakeven analysis only when we are privy to what is usually confidential business information. Sometimes, however, outsiders need some insight into the volatility of a firm's earnings and response to revenue variations. For example, a financial institution considering a loan to a firm would be interested in the behavior of the applicant's profits as output varies. Suppliers offering trade credit terms to the firm would also be interested. Even customers of the firm may want to determine its stability, since they are concerned with its ability to fulfill promised deliveries. Fortunately, outsiders can make crude estimates of breakeven points and earnings' volatility by analyzing the components of the firm's income statement.

To make such an estimate, we start by dividing the cost elements of the income statement into fixed and variable costs. This distinction is more easily stated than accomplished, since income statements rarely give sufficient details to permit us to completely separate fixed elements from variable. To get around this problem, we assume that the variable costs are a constant percentage of revenues. This is similar to our previous assumption that variable costs per unit are constant. From this point on, the analysis is parallel to that of production breakeven analysis.

Total costs of a firm are

$$FC + vS$$

where v is variable costs per dollar of revenues and S is sales. At breakeven,

$$S - FC - vS = 0 \qquad\qquad (10\text{-}3)$$

or

$$S(1 - v) = FC \qquad\qquad (10\text{-}3a)$$

or

$$\overline{S} = \frac{FC}{1 - v} \qquad\qquad (10\text{-}3b)$$

Graphically, the income statement breakeven chart is similar to production leverage, except that revenue dollars are used instead of physical quantities.

Now let's look at a specific example. If revenues = $1000, total variable costs = $200, and total fixed costs = $400, then $\overline{S}$ = 400/ (1 − 200/1000) = $500. At $500 sales, variable costs are 20% of sales, or $100, fixed costs are $400, and profits are zero.

Since we have assumed that variable costs are a constant percentage of sales, and since the division made between fixed and variable expenses often has to be arbitrary, it is probably unwise to compare breakeven points for different firms. However, it may be valid to consider how a firm's breakeven sales level changes over time. Here we have assumed that the income statement classifications have remained the same, so any error made in separating variable from fixed costs has about the same effect on one breakeven sales estimate as it does on another.

Consider the data in Table 10-3, for example. Clearly, the breakeven level of sales has risen over the five-year period shown. However, the increase in the breakeven level of sales is not due simply to an increase in fixed costs. For years 3, 4, and 5, fixed costs are the same. During those years, the principal reason for the rise in the breakeven level of sales was an increase in variable costs. This increase might have

Table 10-3. Breakeven Level of Sales over Time

Year	1	2	3	4	5
S	100	150	120	80	100
FC	20	25	30	30	30
Other costs	40	50	50	40	60
$\overline{S}$	33.3	37.5	51.4	60	75

occurred because some of the variable cost elements were really fixed costs and so did not decline as sales declined, or simply because the ratio of variable cost to sales is not constant over time.

It is perhaps easier to see what has happened if we consider the ratio of actual sales to breakeven sales, and the difference between actual sales and breakeven sales.

Year	1	2	3	4	5
$S/\overline{S}$	3	4	2.3	1.3	1.3
$S - \overline{S}$	66.7	112.5	68.6	20	25

To some extent, the behavior of these ratios shows what happens to the breakeven level of sales over a business cycle. During the expansion phase, from year 1 to year 2, the profitability of the firm sharply increased despite a 25% increase in fixed costs. Some of this increase could well have reflected increased efficiency in the utilization of existing fixed plant because of the larger scale of operations during year 2. During the decline, shown in years 3 and 4, variable cost declined much less rapidly than sales, so that the breakeven sales picture deteriorated. The sharp increase in other costs or variable costs in year 5 did not weaken the breakeven picture because of the sharp increase in sales. The increase in variable costs may well reflect the inefficiencies a firm faces as it increases production from very low levels. It must train new workers and perhaps use equipment that is only marginally efficient. In general, the breakeven sales ratios tend to deteriorate during business recessions and improve during business expansions.

In other respects, income statement leverage behaves much the same as production leverage. The larger the difference $(1 - v)$, the more volatile are profits, as was the case in production leverage where the volatility of profits varied directly with the difference $(p - vc)$.

We should not make too much of the difficulties in distinguishing fixed from variable costs in the income statement. Though this inability weakens the analysis, the same problem often exists when the firm computes operating breakeven points with only rough estimates of fixed as compared to variable costs. Operating leverage is extremely useful in understanding why the earnings distributions of some firms vary more than others. Both production breakeven analysis and income statement breakeven analysis are useful tools in evaluating proposals and business situations. However, their usefulness is limited, since they concentrate primarily on breakeven points, which is only one point in the overall riskiness/profitability aspect of a firm or a business proposal. In short, breakeven analysis is a step in analysis, but not the final step.

The Degree of Operating Leverage

A more convenient way of expressing the leverage relationship from income statements is to measure the degree of operating leverage. This is based on the concept of the *elasticity* of the profit function. Elasticity measures the rate of change in profit given a rate of change in sales. By using the degree of operating leverage, we can move from the breakeven point, which may be irrelevant for firms whose scale of operations typically exceed breakeven. The degree of operating leverage is

$$\frac{\% \text{ change in profits}}{\% \text{ change in sales}} \qquad (10\text{-}4)$$

The change in profits is the change in sales less the change in variable costs. We also have

$$\text{sales} = pQ \quad \text{(the change in sales is } \Delta pQ)$$

$$\text{variable costs} = vQ,$$

$$\text{total profits} = pQ - vQ - FC$$

So equation (10-4) becomes

$$\frac{\Delta Q(p - v)/Q(p - v) - FC}{\Delta pQ/pQ} = \text{degree of operating leverage}$$

$$(10\text{-}4a)$$

The denominator can be stated as $\Delta Q/Q$, and the expression becomes

$$\frac{\Delta Q(p - v)/Q(p - v) - FC)}{(\Delta Q/Q)} = \frac{\Delta Q(p - v)}{(Q(p - v) - FC)} \frac{Q}{\Delta Q} \quad (10\text{-}4b)$$

This in turn is

$$(pQ - vQ)/(pQ - vQ - FC) = \text{degree of operating leverage}$$

$$(10\text{-}4c)$$

or

$$(S - vQ)/(S - vQ - FC) \qquad (10\text{-}4d)$$

Table 10-4. Operating Elasticity

Year	Degree of Operating Leverage = Profit Elasticity
1	1.5
2	1.33
3	1.75
4	4.0
5	4.0

In terms of the example just given, the elasticities for each of the years are shown in Table 10-4. The results show that profit elasticity increases as fixed costs become more important relative to sales. This is essentially what the breakeven diagram showed—the more significant the level of fixed costs, the more sensitive the profit to a change in volume.

We must remember that even though the degree of operating leverage may be more useful than the breakeven quantity or level of sales, it also assumes that price and per unit variable costs are constant as volume changes. And, of course, the answer is no better than the data used. When we cannot clearly and accurately distinguish variable from fixed costs, the estimate of the degree of operating leverage is equally inaccurate.

Summary

In addition to the risk added by the individual assets, the composition of the firm's assets contribute to the volatility of profits and hence to the standard deviation of the firm's rate of return, affecting beta for the firm. Measures of the impact are taken usually in terms of the breakeven point, that is, the point at which profits equal zero. The breakeven point emphasizes the importance of fixed assets relative to sales. The variables have been defined traditionally in terms of physical output, but it is not conceptually difficult to deal with breakeven in terms of dollar values. The difficulty lies in distinguishing fixed from variable operating costs.

Breakeven analysis, whether in volumes or dollar values, assumes constancy of price and per unit costs over the range of production. These assumptions limit its usefulness to what may be narrow ranges of production variations. The extent of the limitation depends on the degree of competition confronting the firm and the nature of its production process.

The breadth of operating leverage analysis is increased if one considers the degree of operating leverage. In those terms, one can analyze the impact of a relative change in sales on earnings before interest and taxes even when production is not near the breakeven point.

Review Questions

10-1   Discuss this statement: Increased operating leverage increases the value of the firm to its owners.

10-2   What is the typical relationship between (i) average revenue and average cost and (ii) marginal revenue and marginal cost at the breakeven level of output?

10-3   How might breakeven analysis be augmented to allow for risk?

Problems

10-4   The annual fixed costs for a firm are $40,000. It sells its product at $2.00 per unit, and the associated variable costs are $1.10 per unit.
   a. What is the breakeven point?
   b. What is the effect on the break-even point if fixed costs are decreased by $5000.

10-5   During 1974, total sales for XYZ Corporation amounted to $100,000, with a resulting profit after taxes of $4000. For the year, fixed costs amounted to $20,000. The company pays taxes at a 50% rate and sells its product for $25 per unit.
   a. What is the variable cost per unit for XYZ?
   b. What is the breakeven volume for XYZ?
   c. What is the effect on the breakeven volume if fixed costs increase by $1000?
   d. What is the degree of operating leverage (percentage increase in net operating income divided by the percentage increase in output) at the current level of sales?

10-6   The Small Corporation sells its product for $10 per unit. Variable costs for the firm are 60% of sales.
   a. For sales of $100,000, what is the firm's total variable cost? variable cost per unit?
   b. What level of fixed costs is consistent with an after-tax profit of $8000? The corporate tax rate is 50% and sales are $100,000.
   c. What is the breakeven level of sales for Small?
   d. If the variable cost per unit increases by $0.50, what is the impact on the firm's breakeven point?
   e. What effect does the increase in the variable cost per unit have on the degree of operating leverage for Small?

Glossary

Breakeven point	The level of output at which total costs equal total revenues, and accounting profits are zero.
Efficiency	The effectiveness with which resources are used. A process is efficient if it obtains the most output from a given level of input (including time and money).

Elasticity	A measure of the sensitivity of one variable to changes in another.
Financial leverage	The effect of fixed finchial charges (e.g., interest) on earnings per share or rate of return on equity.
Income statement leverage	A measure of the firm's leverage determined from income statement values.
Leverage	The relationship between profit volatility and fixed costs. Results because profits rise more quickly than revenues if the firm has fixed costs.
Margin	The price per unit less the variable cost per unit.
Operating leverage	The effect of fixed operating costs on earnings before interest and taxes.
Production leverage	See *operating leverage.*
Variable cost	A cost that varies directly with the level of output. Thus, it can be expressed as a constant amount per unit despite changes in the level of output. An example is the raw material used to make a product.

Bibliography

HOBBS, J. B., "Volume-Mix-Price Cost Budget Variance Analysis: A Proper Approach," *Accounting Review 39* (Oct. 1967), 905–913.

JAEDICKE, R. K., and A. A. ROBICHEK, "Cost-Volume-Profit Analysis, under Conditions of Uncertainty," *Accounting Review 39* (Oct. 1964), 917–926.

KELVIE, WILLIAM E., and JOHN M. SINCLAIR, "New Techniques for Breakeven Charts," *Financial Executive 36* (June 1968), 31–43.

MANES, R., "A New Dimension to Breakeven Analysis," *Journal of Accounting Research 4* (Spring, 1966), 87–100.

MAYER, R. W., "Analysis of Internal Risk in the Industrial Firm," *Financial Analysts Journal 15* (Nov. 1959), 91–95.

MORRISON, T. A., and E. KACZKA, "A New Application of Calculus and Risk Analysis to Cost-Volume-Profit Changes," *Accounting Review 44* (Apr., 1969), 330–343.

REINHARDT, U. E., "Breakeven Analysis for Lockheed's Tri Star: An Application of Financial Theory," *Journal of Finance 28* (Sept. 1973), 821–838.

WESTON, J. F., and EUGENE F. BRIGHAM, *Managerial Finance,* 5th Ed., New York: Holt, Rinehart & Winston, 1975.

Financial Leverage and the Variability of Earnings

11

Financial leverage reflects the impact of the fixed-return methods of financing (mortgages or bonds) on the returns to owners. If the rate of return on invested funds is larger than the interest rate promised on the fixed-return financing, the remainder of the earnings generated by the borrowed funds accrues to owners. Thus, in good times, the use of debt enhances the yield on equity. However, when the rate of return realized on investment is less than the interest rate promised creditors, the difference between the gross earnings and the interest charges is deducted from the owners' returns, reducing the rate of return on equity below the rate that the firm would have had without debt financing. Thus, debt financing levers the rate of return to owners in much the same way that fixed operating charges lever operating profits. And, as with operating leverage, the financial leverage can be either positive (when the overall rate of return exceeds the interest rate) or negative. Again, as with operating leverage, the more debt financing is used relative to equity, the more pronounced is the impact of financial leverage.

Leverage and the Rate of Return on Net Worth

As a result of financial leverage, the rate of return on net worth is much more volatile for firms that use debt financing than for similar firms that use primarily equity. High-debt firms therefore have a higher beta or risk premium, all else equal. As with operating leverage, this is not necessarily bad, since the firm may be able to earn, on average, a much higher rate of return with debt financing than it could with pure equity.

Although financial leverage results from the use of any debt, regardless of term, the use of long-term debt presents a different risk problem than does short-term debt. The firm with short-term debt can minimize negative leverage effects by repaying the debt in bad times if it has the money, whereas the firm with long-term debt does not normally have this option. Of course, the firm with short-term debt has a greater risk of technical insolvency if lenders do not refund the debt when it comes due.

If we ignore taxes, the general expression for the effect of debt financing on the rate of return to owners is

$$e = \frac{aA - d_1 D_1 - d_2 D_2 - \cdots - d_n D_n}{A - \Sigma D} \qquad (11\text{-}1)$$

where

e is the rate of return on book value (balance sheet values) of equity

a is the rate of return on book value of assets

A is the book value of assets

D is total liabilities

d_i is the interest rate on liability D_i, for $i = 1, \ldots, n$

$A - \Sigma D$ = book value of net worth

We can see how debt affects return on equity by looking at a specific example. If we have only class of debt, then equation (11-1) becomes

$$e = \frac{aA - dD}{A - D}$$

If $a = 10\%$, $d = 5\%$, and $A = \$100$, then $aA = \$10$, and we have the following range of returns on equity for different levels of debt:

D ($)	dD ($)	aA − dD ($)	e (%)
0	0	10	10.00
20	1	9	11.25
60	3	7	17.50
80	4	6	30.00
100	5	5	∞

In this case $a > d$, and the leverage is positive. The positive leverage function then looks like the curve shown in Figure 11-1. However, if $a < d$, the leverage is negative. Suppose $a = 4\%$ so that $aA = \$4$. Then

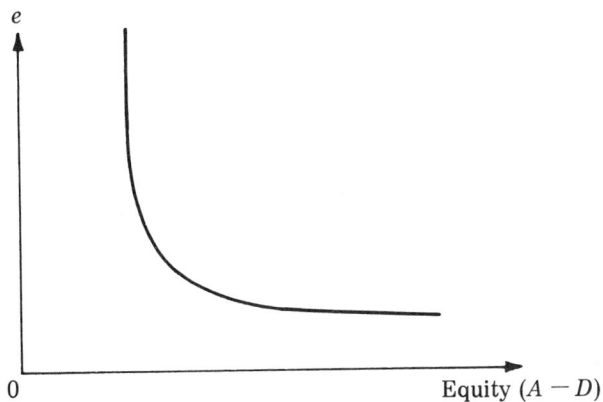

Figure 11-1
The Positive Leverage Function

the return on equity (e) looks like this, for a different level of debt (D):

D ($)	e (%)
0	4
20	2.75
60	2.50
80	0
100	$-\infty$

Figure 11-2 shows the shape of the negative leverage function.

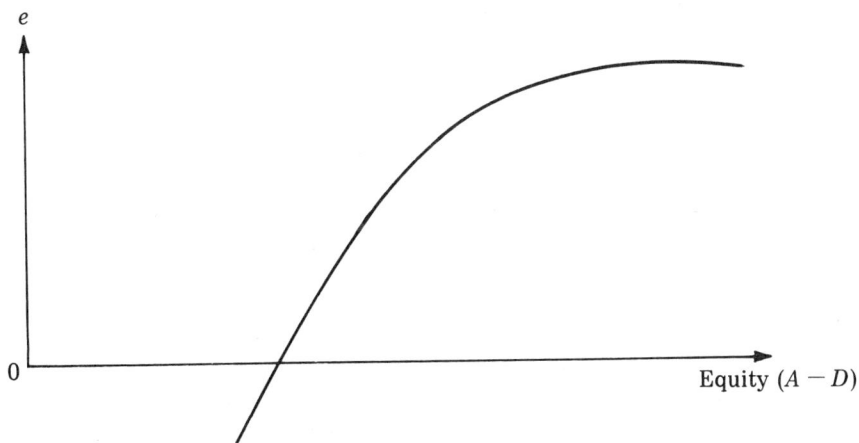

Figure 11-2
The Negative Leverage Function

In general, a is not fixed, but is a probability distribution. When that is true, adding debt increases the variability of the probability distribution. For example, suppose that $D = 0$ and a ($= e$) has the following probability distribution.

$a = e$ (%)	Probability
10	0.2
8	0.2
5	0.2
2	0.2
0	0.2

Then the expected return on equity ($\bar{e}$) is 5% and σ_e is 3.67%. However, if assets were $100, debt $25, and the interest rate 4%, we get the following values:

aA	$aA - dD$	e (%)
10	9	12
8	7	9.33
5	4	5.33
2	1	1.33
0	−1	−1.33

The rate of return or net worth is now 5.33% but the standard deviation of return is 4.92. If D is raised to $50, we have

$aA - dD$ ($)	e (%)
8	16
6	12
3	6
0	0
−2	−4

Now $\bar{e}$ is 7.5% and σ is 5.4%. So we see from these examples that the more debt, the stronger the leverage effect.

In general, if we ignore taxes, the financial leverage relationship is as shown in Figure 11-3. The points on the right show the conditional values of a, and the standard deviation of a is the basic asset risk of the firm. The spread moving to the left as debt is added shows how σ_e increases with financial leverage

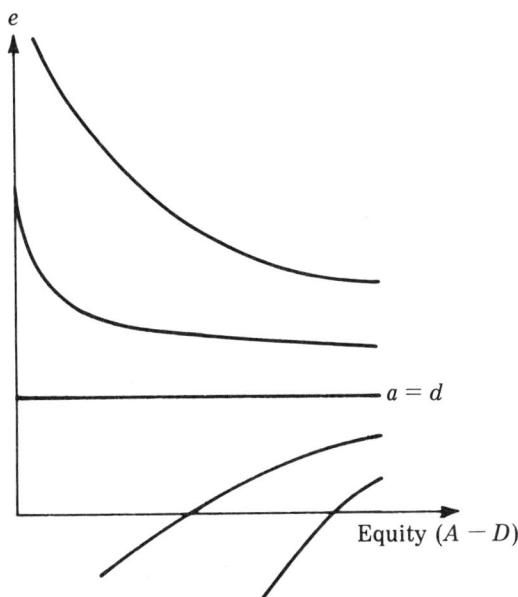

Figure 11-3
The Impact of Financial Leverage on Risk

Debt and Earnings per Share

Clearly, the use of debt increases the basic risk of the firm. We can view this in terms of breakeven analysis by considering the effect on earnings per share of different amounts of debt. Let's also examine the effect of taxation. Taxes are important in the analysis because interest payments can be deducted from taxable income, so the cost of interest to the firm is substantially less than the amount the firm pays to its creditors. On an after-tax basis, the cost of 10% debt is only 5% to the firm with a 50% tax rate.

To begin our analysis, let's define earnings per share as follows

$$eps = \frac{(aA - dD)(1 - t)}{N} \qquad (11\text{-}2)$$

where *eps* is earnings per share, t is the corporate tax rate, and N is the number of shares. Suppose that the company is choosing between equity financing, which will increase N to 10 shares, or debt, which will involve interest payments (dD) of $1.00 but an N of only eight shares. We'll let t be 50%. Table 11-1 shows the probability distribution of earnings before interest and taxes (EBIT). This table shows that the standard deviation of the distribution of earnings per share is larger with the debt option than with the equity option.

Table 11-1. Impact of Financing Alteration on Level and Volatility of *EBIT*

EBIT ($)	Probability	Option 1 (all equity) eps = [(EBIT)(1 − t)]/10	Option 2 (debt) eps = [(EBIT − dD)(1 − t)]/8
$12	0.2	$0.60	$0.69
11	0.2	0.55	0.63
10	0.2	0.50	0.56
9	0.2	0.45	0.50
8	0.2	0.40	0.44
		$\overline{eps}$ = $0.50	$\overline{eps}$ = $0.56
		σ_{eps} = $0.07	σ_{eps} = $0.097

Breakeven EBIT

It may also be useful to compute the breakeven level of earnings before interest and taxes at which earnings per share is the same with or without debt. In this case, the equality is

$$\frac{EBIT(1 - t)}{N} = \frac{(EBIT - dD)(1 - t)}{N'} \qquad (11\text{-}3)$$

Substituting the numbers from our example, we have

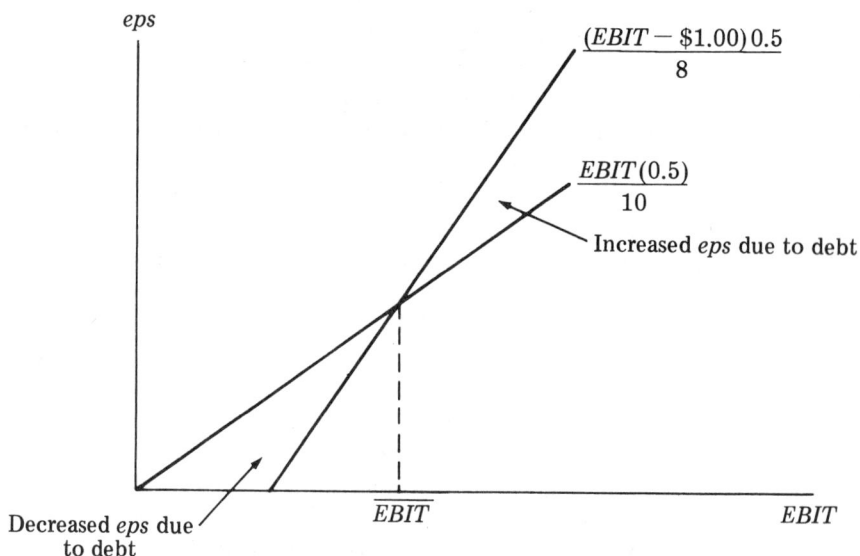

$$\frac{(EBIT - \$1.00)\,0.5}{8}$$

$$\frac{EBIT\,(0.5)}{10}$$

Increased *eps* due to debt

Decreased *eps* due to debt

EBIT

EBIT

Figure 11-4
Breakeven Level of EBIT

$$\frac{EBIT(0.5)}{10} = \frac{(EBIT - \$1.00)(0.5)}{8}$$

so the breakeven *EBIT* is \$5.00. Figure 11-4 shows this relationship graphically.

The figure clearly shows that the debt option increases earnings per share when *EBIT* exceeds \$5. However, when *EBIT* is less than \$5, *eps* is less with the debt option. The volatility of *eps* also increases with the debt option, but this would not worry the firm if they expected *EBIT* to be well above \$5. However, they would become concerned if *EBIT* was likely to be below \$5.

The Degree of Financial Leverage

Like asset or operating leverage, liability or financial leverage can also be expressed as an elasticity term. For financial leverage, the relationship is the effect of a percentage change in sales on the relative change in *EBIT*, given a debt structure. This relationship has the advantage of expressing the sensitivity of earnings to financial leverage at points other than breakeven.

For simplicity, we again assume just a single class of debt. Then we can derive the equation for the degree of financial leverage as follows:

$$EBIT = Q(p - v) - FC \qquad (11\text{-}4)$$

where the right-hand terms are defined as they were for operating leverage.

$$eps = \frac{(EBIT - dD)(1 - t)}{N} \qquad (11\text{-}5)$$

If dD is not changed, but other factors affect *eps*,

$$\Delta eps = \frac{\Delta(EBIT)(1 - t)}{N} \qquad (11\text{-}6)$$

As a percentage, the change is

$$\frac{EBIT(1 - t)/N}{(EBIT - dD)(1 - t)/N} = \frac{EBIT}{EBIT - dD}$$

$$= \text{financial leverage elasticity} \qquad (11\text{-}7)$$

Again we look at the specific values of the variables in our previous example: $EBIT = \$15.00$, $t = 0.5$, $dD = \$1.00$, and $N = 8$. Then the effect of financial leverage is $15/(15 - 1) = 1.07$. This means that *eps* rises by 1.07% for each 1% increase in *EBIT*.

Without debt, the ratio in our 10-share example is simply 1. This means that *eps* rises by 1% for each 1% increase in *EBIT*, which is the expected result in the absence of financial leverage.

Combining Financial and Operating Leverage

Since both operating and financial leverage affect the earnings return to shareholders, it is useful to combine these measures. This provides a combined measure of what we may refer to as the *balance sheet structure risk* of the firm.

Recall equation (11-4).

$$EBIT = Q(p - v) - FC$$

Substituting the term on the right-hand side of this expression into equation (11-7), we then find that

$$\frac{Q(p - v) - FC}{Q(p - v) - FC - dD} = \text{financial leverage elasticity} \qquad (11\text{-}8)$$

We can then express the combined effect of financial and operating leverage elasticities as the product of the two coefficients.

$$\frac{Q(p - v)}{Q(p - v) - FC} \frac{Q(p - v) - FC}{Q(p - v) - FC - dD}$$

$$= \frac{Q(p - v)}{Q(p - v) - FC - dD} \qquad (11\text{-}9)$$

This becomes

$$\frac{S - VC}{EBIT - dD} = \text{combined elasticities of balance sheet structure}$$

$$(11\text{-}10)$$

If $S = \$1000$, $VC = \$400$, and $EBIT = \$300$, then $FC = \$300$ and $dD = \$50$, so the coefficient for operating leverage is (from equation (10-2a))

$$\frac{S - VC}{S - VC - FC} = \frac{600}{300} = 2$$

The coefficient for financial leverage is

$$\frac{S - VC - FC}{S - VC - FC - dD} = \frac{300}{300 - 50} = 1.2$$

and the combined effort is

$$\frac{S - VC}{EBIT - dD} = \frac{600}{300 - 50} = 2.4 \qquad\qquad (11\text{-}11)$$

which is, of course, the product of the two coefficients.

This coefficient says that earnings per share will rise by 2.4 times the percentage increase in sales or, and equally important, *eps* will *fall* by 2.4 times a relative *decline* in sales.

Note that both operating leverage and financial leverage work in a *multiplicative* way, not simply an additive way, to make earnings per share sensitive to variation in sales, thus increasing *risk*. Well-managed, mature firms recognize this sensitivity. Thus, firms with technologies that require large proportions of fixed assets tend to have low financial leverage to offset their high level of operating leverage. This is true of many manufacturing firms. The reverse is also true. Financial institutions tend to have low levels of fixed assets, since even most of their long-term investments are more marketable than a manufacturer's plant and equipment. Since they have relatively liquid asset structures, financial institutions tend to use high levels of debt, that is, large amounts of financial leverage.

An exception to this tendency to balance operating leverage against financial leverage occurs among the public utilities. Because utilities are quasimonopolies, their asset portfolios are safe (except perhaps against the ravages of inflation). Thus they can use high levels of financial leverage. Even among utilities, however, adverse operating conditions combined with high levels of operating and financial leverage can result in a spectacular collapse. Witness the demise of the Penn Central. Even when failure seems remote, risk is present, and the remote can easily become real.

The Effect of Financial Leverage on Beta

Since the standard deviation of the rates of return on net worth increases as a result of financial leverage, the firm's beta or risk premium should also increase. What is the extent of the increase in the risk premium? The answer is not obvious because, so far, we have conducted the leverage analysis in terms of *accounting* values. However, the impact of the risk premium is on *market* values.

The answer depends on which theory of market valuation we apply. One approach, proposed originally by Modigliani and Miller (see references) and sometimes referred to as the *net operating income* (NOI) approach can be summarized in the following statements.

Proposition 1. The value of the firm as a whole, regardless of its capital structure, is determined by the riskiness of its asset portfolio.

Proposition 2. Increasing the risk or the return to owners through financial leverage does not change the value of the firm. Financial leverage merely increases the rate of return on net worth (because of the increase in risk premium).

The average rate of return for the firm as a whole is the weighted average of the rate of return on net worth and the interest rate. This is constant, regardless of capital structure. The argument is modified somewhat when corporate income taxes and the tax deductibility of interest are taken into account. Under those circumstances, the use of debt does permit some increase in the value of the firm, reflecting the effect of taxes.

According to this theory, the risk premium increases proportionately with the change in earnings per share, so the price of the stock is constant. This precise relationship relies on the assumption that all investors have free access to the capital markets. As a result, if firm A has leverage and firm B does not, the price of A's stock will not be higher than B's stock (ignoring taxes) because investors will buy B, using borrowed funds in the same proportion as in A's capital structure. When investors have access to funds on the same basis as firms, and if they are willing to undertake, as personal risks, the risk that A's shareholders take on as a limited liability, the following holds:

$$V_f = V + D \quad \text{where } V_f \text{ is the value of the firm,}$$
$$V \text{ is the market value of equity,}$$
$$D \text{ is debt}$$

We can also state V_f in terms of $EBIT$:

$$V_f = \frac{EBIT}{i_f} \tag{11-12}$$

where i_f is determined only by the risk of the *asset portfolio*, that is, i_f is the overall capitalization rate for a firm with only equity financing. We assume that i_f remains constant with respect to changes in capital structure. Hence,

$$V = \frac{EBIT}{i_f} - D \tag{11-13}$$

For example, if $EBIT$ = $100, and i_f = .1, then V_f = $1000 with 100 shares and no debt, $V = V_f$ = $1000, and the price per share (P) = $1000/100$ = $10. If we assume all earnings are paid out, then the rate of return on equity, R_j, is 10% ($100/$1000).

If we use $500 of debt at 5% interest instead, the number of shares falls to 50.

$$V = V_f - D, \quad = 1000 - 500 = 500, \quad P = \frac{500}{50} = \$10$$

But

earnings per share are $(EBIT - dD)/50$ or, in the example, $=$ $(100 - 25)/50 = \$1.50$ earnings per share.

and

R_j, the rate of return on equity, is $\dfrac{\$1.50}{\$10.}$ or $15\% \left(\dfrac{\$75}{\$500}\right)$

So this approach assumes that the risk premium rises proportionately with the changes in earnings per share.

At the other pole is the net income valuation method. This approach assumes that the use of leverage increases the value of common shares, as long as the interest rate is below the rate of return on assets. The value of the firm increases as a result of the use of leverage also. Basically, the assumption is that the rate of return on net worth is constant. So as earnings after interest and taxes increase because of financial leverage, the price of the shares also increases. This method of evaluation is sometimes called the *net income* (NI) *method* because the value of the firm is determined by capitalizing the net income ($EBIT$ less interest and taxes). The value of the firm is determined by adding the value of debt to the value of equity. For example, consider the following: Suppose $EBIT = 100$, the overall capitalization rate equals the equity capitalization rate ($i_f = R_j = 0.1$), without debt, and $N = 100$. Then

$$V = \$100/0.1 = \$1000, \qquad P = V/N = \$1000/100 = \$10$$

With $500 of debt at 5% interest, N drops to 50.

$EBIT$ = Net operating income	$100	
Less interest payments	25	
Equals EBT	$\ 75	

The value of equity is the capacity of earnings before taxes or $V = \$75/0.1 = \$750,$ $P = \$750/50 = \$15,$ $V_f = \$750 + \$500 = \$1250,$ raising the value of the firm.

To see this in somewhat more detail, consider the following examples of alternate capital structures under the two methods of valuation.

Suppose that a firm plans to acquire $100 of assets. With all equity financing, it anticipates $EBIT$ to be 10% of assets. If it borrows, the interest rate on debt (d) is 5%.

Under the net operating income method, the capitalization alternatives are given by ($i_f = 0.1$)

$$V_f = \frac{EBIT}{i_f} = \frac{10}{0.1} = \$100 \qquad\qquad (11\text{-}12)$$

D ($)	dD ($)	$V = V_f - D$ ($)	$R_j = (EBIT - dD)/V$ (%)
20	1	80	11.25
40	2	60	13.33
60	3	40	17.50
80	4	20	30.00

Under the net income method the alternatives are ($R_j = 0.1$) given by

$$V = \frac{EBIT - dD}{R_j} \qquad\qquad (11\text{-}13)$$

D ($)	dD ($)	$EBIT - dD$ ($)	$V = (EBIT - dD)/R_j$ ($)	$V_f = V + D$ ($)	$i_f = EBIT/V_f$ (%)
20	1	9	90	110	9.09
40	2	8	80	120	8.33
60	3	7	70	130	7.69
80	4	6	60	140	7.14

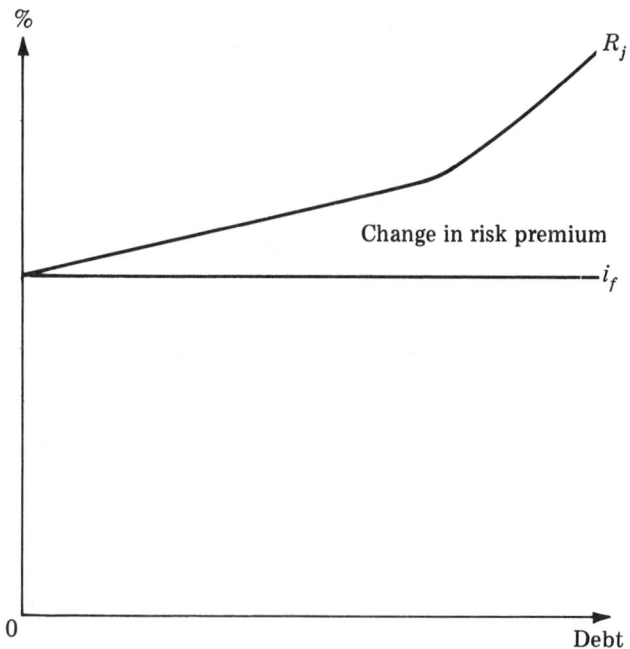

Figure 11-5
Impact of Debt on Capitalization Rates under NOI Method

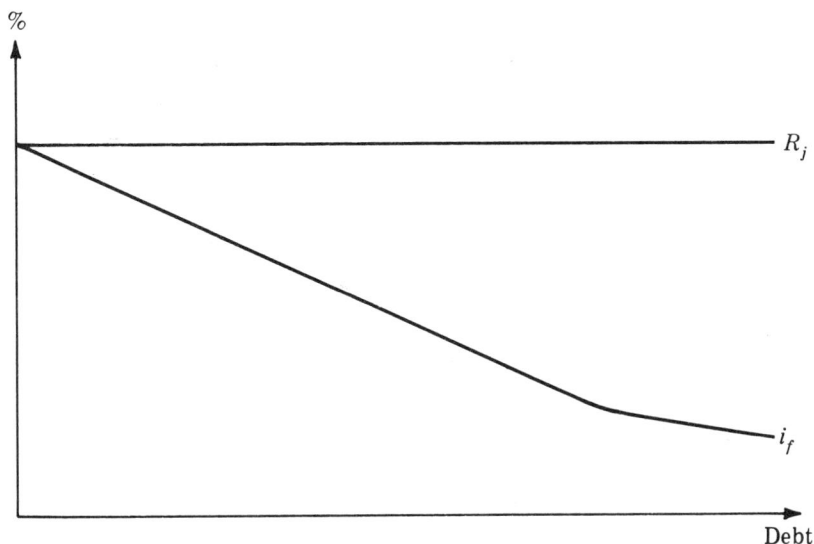

Figure 11-6
Impact of Debt on Capitalization Rates under the NI Method

Figures 11-5 and 11-6 show the relationship between i_f and R_j under the two methods.

Which of the two methods is correct? In general, probably neither is completely correct. Capital markets are not perfect, so it is unreasonable to expect that people can borrow at the same interest rates that are available to high-grade corporations. Further, in order to achieve Modigliani and Miller's results, an investor must be willing to buy stocks on margin. This is the equivalent to having personal financial leverage. However, when one owes money personally, the risk is far different than when a corporation in which one owns shares owes money.

Even if the Modigliani and Miller assumptions do not hold, it seems equally unreasonable to believe that investors ignore the potential pitfalls of negative financial leverage, no matter how rosy the current scene may appear. Were valuation of firms to increase substantially because of leverage, one would expect far more long-term debt in the balance sheets of corporations than is generally found. Further, to accept the net income method of evaluation is to reject the notion of risk premiums as formulated in the beta concept, and there is considerable evidence of a relationship between risk premiums and the variability of rates of return on net worth. This variability increases with debt, as we have seen.

A middle ground between the two methods of valuation is fairly comfortable, and not just because it is in the middle. One can agree that risk premiums increase as financial leverage increases. However, it does not follow that the risk premium rises so directly with earnings that share values remain constant. Nor does it follow that the rise re-

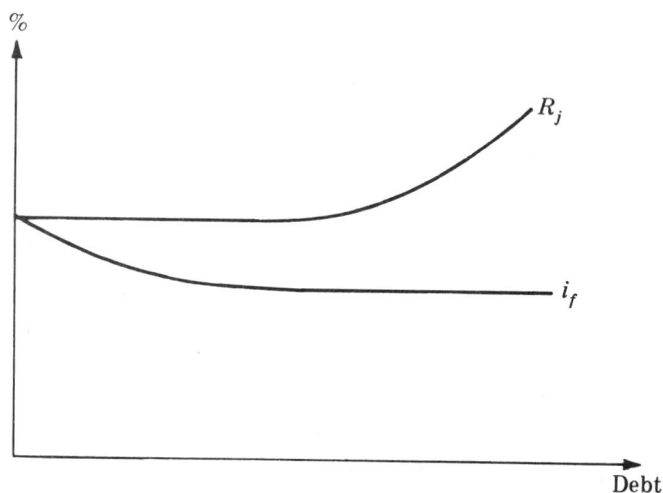

Figure 11-7
Compromise between NI and NOI Methods of Treating Debt

flects only the tax deductibility of interest payments. At almost all levels of analysis and investigation, the notion that risk premiums increase (though not necessarily proportionately), with financial leverage, seems acceptable, and it provides us with additional insights into the determination of the firm's beta. On the other hand, some increase in share value (less than proportional increase in beta) seems reasonable when the firm's debt/equity ratio is low relative to similar firms. This compromise does not satisfy hard-nosed theorists, but it does accord well with conventional wisdom. Figure 11-7 shows this compromise.

Hence, the equity capitalization rate is constant at relatively low levels of debt (the NI method), but rises as the debt level becomes large (the NOI method).

Taxes and Valuation

When we add taxes to the Modigliani and Miller approach, the difference between their conclusions and those of the NI school about the impact of debt on both the equity and the overall capitalization rates narrows. Specifically, if V_L is the total value of a levered firm, V_U the total value of an unlevered firm, D the amount of debt, and t the tax rate, then

$$V_L = V_U + Dt \qquad (11\text{-}14)$$

If we assume that the levered and unlevered firms are identical except with respect to capital structure, then the earnings after interest and taxes for the unlevered firm are

$$EAT_U = EBIT_U(1 - t) \qquad (11\text{-}15)$$

where EAT_U is earnings after taxes for the unlevered firm and $EBIT_U$ is its earnings before taxes. Interest, of course, is zero for the unlevered firm.

$$EAT_L = (EBIT_L - dD)(1 - t) \qquad (11\text{-}16)$$

However, total income (Y_L) for both creditors and owners of the levered firm is

$$Y_L = EAT_L + dD \qquad (11\text{-}17)$$

Now we can restate (11-17) and manipulate as follows

$$\begin{aligned} Y_L &= EBIT_L - dD - (EBIT_L)t + dDt + dD \qquad (11\text{-}17a) \\ &= EBIT_L - (EBIT_L)t + dDt \\ &= EBIT_L(1 - t) + dDt \qquad (11\text{-}17b) \end{aligned}$$

The first term in equation (11-17b) is identical to equation (11-15), and the second term, dDt, is the tax savings that occurs because interest is deductible for taxes. If we assume that the debt is risk free (a questionable assumption for borrowers; see Chapter 7), the value of the levered firm is

$$V_L = \frac{EBIT_L(1 - t)}{R_j} + \frac{dDt}{d} = \frac{EBIT(1 - t)}{R_j} + D_t \qquad (11\text{-}19)$$

However, $EBIT$ is the same for both levered and unlevered firms, so

$$V_U = \frac{EBIT(1 - t)}{R_j} \qquad (11\text{-}20)$$

and

$$V_L = V_U + Dt \qquad (11\text{-}14)$$

Hence the value of the firm rises as the amount of debt used increases, and the value of a levered firm is higher than that of an unlevered firm. Since the increase in value accrues to the shareholders, the price of the levered share is higher than that of the unlevered firms, which means that $R_{j_L} < R_{j_U}$. This is consistent with the direction of change suggested by the proponents of the net income method of valuation.

Summary

Just as the fixed charges associated with the asset portfolio result in variability (risk), so too do the fixed charges associated with the capital structure of the firm, known as financial leverage. High levels of debt are reflected in greater potential variations, both in the rate of return on book value of equity and in earnings per share of stock.

Breakeven analysis is one indicator of the sensitivity of the equity returns to changes in earnings before interest and taxes. Computing the elasticity of earnings per share to changes in *EBIT* is another, perhaps more useful, measure.

The combined effect on risk of the structure of the asset portfolio and the capital structure, that is, the structure of the balance sheet, can be computed by multiplying the operating leverage elasticity coefficient by that for financial leverage. Most mature firms tend to offset high levels of operating asset leverage (dictated by technology) by having low levels of financial leverage. The reverse is also true.

Both financial and operating leverage can affect beta. Thus, firms with high degrees of leverage should have higher betas than similar firms with low levels of leverage. Modigliani and Miller have argued that as financial leverage rises, the required rate of return on the *market* value of equity should rise proportionately (ignoring taxes). Thus, the total value of a firm using financial leverage should be equal to that of a firm with the same asset portfolio that does not use debt. Further, the market value per share of the two firms should be equal. The leveraged firm has a larger beta, and hence a larger required rate of return on equity, than the unlevered firm.

Others disagree. Since empirical tests have not really resolved this issue, it seems reasonable to compromise. Firms may increase share value by increasing debt proportions. However, as the level of debt rises, beta is likely to rise, increasing the required rate of return (or cost of equity capital) on equity and keeping share value from reflecting the effect of the leverage-induced increase in earnings per share.

In any event, much of the difference between the two schools disappears when taxes are taken into account. Then the value of the levered firm and the share values of the levered firm rise under both NOI and NI approaches.

Review Questions

11-1 The cost of equity financing will decrease as the firm employs more leverage. Is this statement correct? Discuss.

11-2 What financing strategy might a firm follow to protect itself from the possible effects of negative leverage? What costs are involved in this strategy?

11-3 What are the key assumptions of the net income and net operating income valuation models?

11-4 Under the net operating income approach, why might the use of personal leverage not be a perfect substitute for corporate leverage?

11-5 If an optimal capital structure does exist for a firm, what conditions in terms of the real costs of debt and equity financing exist for capitalizations that underutilize debt? Discuss.

Problems

11-6 A firm has liabilities of $40,000 and owners' equity of $60,000. Its interest cost of liabilities is 10% and its rate of return on equity (book value) is 12%. Determine the firm's rate of return on assets.

11-7 XYZ Company is considering the following alternative financing arrangements:

	A	B
Bonds (8%)	200,000	—
Common stock	400,000	600,000
Number of shares	4,000	6,000

They estimate that *EBIT* for this year will be $40,000, and they pay taxes of 50%. (Assume that the degree of economic risk associated with the sources of funds remains the same for both alternatives.)

a. Calculate the *eps* under both alternatives and decide which alternative you would select.

b. If *EBIT* doubles next year, what happens to *eps?*

c. Calculate the indifference level of *EBIT* for the two financing alternatives. Draw an *EBIT:eps* diagram showing both alternatives.

11-8 The Ace Widget Corporation sold 100,000 units last year at $11 each.

Ace Widget Corporation
Income Statement
(Year ending Dec. 31, 1977)

Sales		$1,100,000
Less: Variable costs	$550,000	
Fixed costs	150,000	700,000
EBIT		400,000
Less: Interest		50,000
Net income before tax		350,000
Income tax		175,000
Net income		175,000

a. Determine the degrees of financial leverage for Ace (at its current level of sales).
b. Determine the degree of combined leverage.
c. Under the NI approach, what would the valuation of Ace be if its future prospects were identical to those experienced during 1977? The cost of debt is 10%, and the shareholders of Ace require a 14% return (after corporate taxes).

Glossary

Balance sheet structure risk	The effect of both operating and financial risk. See *combined elasticity.*
Capitalization	Determining the present value of future income streams. In accounting, shifting amounts from retained earnings to the capital account in order to pay a stock dividend.
Combined elasticity	A measure of the total effect of operating and financial leverage

$$\frac{S - VC}{EBIT - dD}$$

S = sales
V = variable costs
$EBIT$ = earnings before interest and taxes
d = interest rate on debt
D = debt

Conditional value	An outcome that occurs with some probability less than 1.
EBIT *(earnings before interest and taxes)*	Total revenue minus all expenses except interest and taxes.
Earnings per share	Total earnings after taxes divided by the number of shares

$$eps = \frac{(aA - dD)(1 - t)}{N}$$

eps = earnings per share
t = corporate tax rate
a = rate of return on book value of assets
A = book value of assets
N = number of outstanding shares
d = interest rate on debt
D = debt

Equity financing	Obtaining funds by issuing stock.
Financial leverage	The effect of fixed financial charges on earnings.
Financial leverage elasticity	The sensitivity of earnings to different degrees of leverage (debt)

$$\frac{EBIT}{EBIT - dD}$$

$EBIT$ = earnings before interest and taxes
d = interest rate on debt (D)

Financial leverage sensitivity	See *financial leverage elasticity.*
Leverage function	The relation between return and equity at various levels of debt

$$e = \frac{aA - d_1D - d_2D_2 - \cdots - d_nD_n}{A - \Sigma D}$$

e = rate of return on book value of equity
a = rate of return on book value of assets
A = book value of assets
ΣD = total liabilities
d_2 = interest rate on liability D_2

Market value	The price at which an asset may be bought or sold.
Negative leverage effect	The interest rate exceeds the overall rate of return.
Net income (NI) approach	The valuation theory that states that the value of the firm is determined by capitalizing the net income. Thus as earnings after interest and taxes increase because of financial leverage, the price of the shares increases.
Net operating income (NOI) approach	The valuation theory that states that the value of the firm is independent of the capital structure, even though the return on net worth may be increased by the use of financial leverage.

Bibliography

ALTMAN, EDWARD I., "Corporate Bankruptcy, Potential Stockholder Returns, and Share Valuation," *Journal of Finance 24* (Dec. 1969), 887–900.

BAXTER, N. D., "Leverage, Risk of Ruin, and the Cost of Capital," *Journal of Finance 22* (Sept. 1967), 395–402.

BERANEK, W., *The Effect of Leverage on the Market Value of Common Stock,* Madison, Wisconsin: Bureau of Business Research and Service, University of Wisconsin, 1965.

BIERMAN, H., JR., "Risk and the Addition of Debt to the Capital Structure," *Journal of Financial and Quantitative Analysis 3* (Dec. 1968), 415–426.

BODENHORN, D., "A Cash-Flow Concept of Profit," *Journal of Finance 19* (March 1964), 16–31.

COHEN, K. J., and F. S. HAMMER, "Optimal Level Debt Schedules for Municipal Bonds," *Management Science 13* (Nov. 1966), 161–166.

DEARDEN, J., "The Case against ROI Control," *Harvard Business Review 47* (May/ June 1969), 124–135.

DONALDSON, G., *Corporate Debt Capacity,* Boston: Graduate School of Business Administration, Harvard University, 1961.

DONALDSON, GORDON, "Strategy for Financial Emergencies," *Harvard Business Review 47* (Nov./Dec. 1969), 67–79.

GHANDHI, J. K. S., "On the Measurement of Leverage," *Journal of Finance 21* (Dec. 1966), 715–726.

HASLEM, JOHN A., "Leverage Effects on Corporate Earnings," *Arizona Review 19* (March 1970), 7–11.

HUNT, PEARSON, "A Proposal for Precise Definition of 'Trading on the Equity' and 'Leverage,'" *Journal of Finance 16* (Sept. 1961), 377–386.

KRAUS, ALAN, and ROBERT LITZENBERGER, "A State-Preference Model of Optimal Financial Leverage," *Journal of Finance 28* (Sept. 1973), 911–922.

MILLER, M. H., and F. MODIGLIANI, "Some Estimates of the Cost of Capital to the Electric Utility Industry, 1954–57," *American Economic Review 56* (June 1966), 333–391.

MODIGLIANI, F., and M. H. MILLER, "The Cost of Capital, Corporation Finance, and the Theory of Investment," *American Economic Review 48* (June 1958), 261–297.

———, "Corporate Income Taxes and the Cost of Capital: A Correction," *American Economic Review 53* (June 1963), 433–443.

MORGAN, B. W., "Corporate Debt and Stockholder Portfolio Selection," *Yale Economic Essays 7* (Fall 1967), 201–259.

SARMA, L. V. L. N., and K. S. RAO, "Leverage and the Value of the Firm," *Journal of Finance 24* (Sept. 1969), 673–678.

STIGLITZ, J. E., "A Re-Examination of the Modigliani–Miller Theorem," *American Economic Review 59* (Dec. 1969), 784–793.

WESTON, J. F., and EUGENE F. BRIGHAM, *Managerial Finance,* 5th ed., New York: Holt, Rinehart & Winston, 1975.

WILLIAMS, EDWARD E., "Cost of Capital Functions and the Firm's Optimal Level of Gearing," *Journal of Business Finance 4* (1974) 78–83.

WIPPERN, RONALD F., "Financial Structure and the Value of the Firm," *Journal of Finance 21* (Dec. 1966), 615–634.

Dividend Policy

12

Dividends play a key role in any method of determining the value of a common share. After all, the reason for holding shares is to receive dividends. Stockholders may be willing to forego current dividends to enhance the firm's growth opportunities, but growth in the price of shares is determined by estimates of future dividends. If there is no hope of ever receiving dividends, there seems little reason to place any value on a share. The dividend valuation models discussed in Chapter 4 showed this. The value of a share is determined by both the current level of dividends and the expected growth rate of future earnings and dividends.

Review of Dividend Valuation Models

The effect of expected dividends on share value is so important that we shall review some of the salient points in Chapter 4 before examining other areas of dividend policy.

Constant Dividends

Basically, the value of a share is the present value of its expected dividends plus the expected value of the share at the end of the planning period. If the planning period is infinite and dividends are expected to be constant, then the price of the share is (if we ignore taxes)

$$P_j = D_j / R_j \qquad\qquad (12\text{-}1)$$

where P_j is the price of the jth firm's share, D_j is the dividend, and R_j is the required rate of return on the share. Using the material presented in Chapter 7, we can restate (12-1) as follows:

$$P_{jt} = \frac{D_j}{R_{F_t} + \beta_j(R_{M_t} - R_{F_t})} \qquad (12\text{-}1a)$$

where R_{F_t} is the risk-free rate at period t, R_{M_t} is the market index yield, and β_j is the risk coefficient for the firm. Thus, even with a constant dividend, the price of a share changes if interest rates or the risk coefficient changes.

As interest rates rise, the price of a share declines, all else constant. Even though this decline is due to factors beyond the firm's control, the firm is under pressure to at least partially offset the decline in share price. This pressure is stronger if the firm wishes to issue new shares. At the lower price, the firm has to issue more shares to attain a given amount of money than at the old higher price. Existing shareholders may be unhappy at this "dilution of equity," since a new shareholder is on equal footing with an old shareholder who paid more for the stock. One solution is to increase the proportion of earnings paid out as dividends. This, however, takes us beyond the single constant dividend model to reinvestment of earnings within the firm, with the aim of increasing share value by increasing expected dividends.

Growth

In general, we can view reinvestment as follows:

$$
\begin{aligned}
P_0 = {} & [E_0 + r_1 b_1(E_1 - D_1)] \frac{1}{1 + R_j} \\
& + [D_2 + r_2 b_2(E_2 - D_2)] \frac{1}{(1 + R_j)^2} \\
& + \cdots + [D_n + r_n b_n(E_n - D_n) + P_{jn}] \frac{1}{(1 + R_j)^n} \qquad (12\text{-}2)
\end{aligned}
$$

where r is the rate of return on reinvested earnings expected for each period, and b is the proportion of earnings retained in each period. Thus if $r > R_j$, the firm can increase share price by increasing b, the retained portion. On the other hand, if the rate the firm expects to earn on reinvested earnings is less than the required rate of return, the firm can increase share prices by increasing current dividends.

This dividend model is the general form for valuation. Simpler versions exist, but they are subject to limiting assumptions. For these simpler models to hold, the assumptions underlying the simplification have to be realistic. The most familiar of the simplifications is the constant growth model.

$$P_{j_0} = D_{j_0}/(R_j - G) \qquad (12\text{-}3)$$

where $G = br$. This model assumes that G is constant throughout; of course, no meaningful answer is possible if $G > R_j$. In addition, D must grow at the rate of G; otherwise the firm could maintain price by increasing the retention rate (b) when the rate of return on reinvestment (r) declines.

Under this simplification, changes in interest rate can affect dividend policies. If R_j rises because of a general increase in the market interest rate, price falls unless D increases by more than G or b increases due to an increase in r. Since an increase in r implies an increase in future dividends, the generalization that changes in interest rates can affect dividend policy even with constant growth still holds. For example, assume

$$P = \frac{\$1}{0.1 - 0.05} = \$20$$

If interest rates rise, so that R_j rises to 0.15 but all else remains unchanged in the firm, then

$$P' = \frac{\$1}{0.15 - 0.05} = \$10,$$

that is, the price has fallen by 50%.

If the firm cannot increase the rate of return on reinvested funds, it may want to reduce the rate of retention (b). If b was 0.33 and r was 0.1 before the interest rate changed, the firm was in equilibrium, since the rate of return on reinvested funds equalled the required rate of return (R_j). When the change in interest rate increases R_j to 0.15, the firm should eliminate all projects earning less than 15% and pay the difference as dividends. Suppose that this reduces b to 0.2 and increases D to \$2.40. Then the new price is

$$P'' = \frac{2.40}{0.15 - 0.03} = \$20 = P, \quad \text{the original price.}$$

Thus, without taxes, a firm that is maximizing share value retains only those funds that it can reinvest at R_j, the required rate of return on equity investment, or better.

Lagged Adjustments

In general, firms do not like to vary dividends (see Lintner reference). Even if interest rates or the expected yields on reinvested funds change, firms are not likely to change dividends until they believe that the new conditions are not simply temporary. Their hesitation partly reflects the belief that many changes in policy result in lower share prices than do stable policies. In any event, dividend changes tend to lag behind changes in the determinants of dividend policy.

So far, we have ignored the impact of taxation on dividend policy. If earnings are reinvested, the corporation must be reasonably certain that the reinvestment will enlarge the flow of future dividends, and hence increase the present value of the share. A stockholder who sells shares would then receive the increase in price. Since this increase is usually a capital gain, only half the gain is included in taxable income. Suppose that a taxpayer in the 30% bracket has $100 in capital gains. The tax on $50 (half the gain) at the 30% rate is $15. Effectively, the taxpayer pays only 15% on capital gains instead of the 30% due on $100 in dividends.[1]

Taxpayers in the 50% marginal tax bracket would pay taxes of $25 on the capital gain (50% of half of $100). Their effective tax rate on the $100 in capital gains is 25%, much less than the 50% they would pay if they received $100 in dividends. Thus, the larger the recipient's income, the more likely he or she is to prefer capital gains to dividend income.

The Effect of Taxes on the Cost of Capital for Retained Earnings

If a corporation believes that most of its shares are owned by people in upper income brackets, its dividend policy will be biased in favor of earnings retention and reinvestment. Of course, they must have profitable investment opportunities to justify the retention. However, the shareholders may find it profitable to reinvest earnings even when the investment opportunities offer a rate of return below the minimally acceptable rate. Let's see why this is true.

We can express the after-tax value of dividends to shareholders as $(1 - p)D$, where D is dividend per share and p is the tax paid by shareholders on dividends.

The value of capital gains to shareholders is

$$\frac{r(E - D)}{i} (1 - c)$$

where r is the rate of return after corporate taxes on reinvested funds, i is the cost of equity capital, E is earnings per share, and c is the capital gains tax rate. Thus, $E - D$ is the amount retained each year and $r(E - D)$ is the after-tax earnings each year. The capitalized value of these earnings, assuming a continuous flow of earnings on retained funds, is found by dividing by i. This capitalized value is the capital gain from retention received by the shareholder. Multiplying by $(1 - c)$ gives the after-tax value of the capital gain.

If financed solely by equity, the corporation should retain earnings as long as the after-tax value of capital gains exceeds the after-tax value

[1] This assumes the shareholder already has received $100 in dividend income ($200 in a joint return).

of dividends. We shall see in Chapter 13 that if the capital structure includes debt or preferred stock, the average weighted cost of all sources of capital generates the cut-off rate for expenditures. It seems intuitively reasonable that when capital gains taxation is less than the effective tax rate on dividends, shareholders may be better off if the firm retains earnings, even if they earn less than the required rate of return, that is, when $c < p$, or $r < i$. Since the firm should retain earnings as long as the value of the capital gains after personal taxes at least equals the value of dividends after personal taxes, we have

$$\frac{r(E - D)}{i} (1 - c) \geq (1 - p)D.$$

To illustrate, let's substitute these values

$$i = 10\%, \quad E = \$1.00, \quad D = \$0.50, \quad c = 25\%, \quad p = 50\%$$

Then we have

$$\frac{r(\$1 - \$0.50)}{0.1} (1 - 0.25) \geq (1 - 0.5)\$0.50 \quad \text{or} \quad r = 8\%$$

Thus, when capital gains are taxed at a lower effective rate than dividends, the firm can justify retaining earnings even if the rate of return on these earnings is 8% and the cost of capital is 10%.[2]

It is equally true that if dividends are taxed at a lower effective rate than capital gains, the rate of return on retained earnings should be above the minimally acceptable rate.

In setting dividend policy, the firm cannot ignore the effect of taxes.[3] If they believe that most shares are held by stockholders who pay a higher tax rate on capital gains than on dividends, they will be inclined to retain earnings. However, their decision is not easy, because all taxpayers are not in the same income tax bracket. Further, much stock is held in pension funds, which pay no taxes either on dividends or capital gains. To satisfy the needs of the pension plans, r would have to at least equal i.

Dividend Policy and Flotation Costs

When a firm issues stock, they usually have to prepare a registration statement for the Securities and Exchange Commission. This statement includes considerable detail about the issuing company and its pros-

---

[2] In Chapter 13, we will show that it is usually poor practice to use the cost of a single source of funds as the required rate of return. Rather, a weighted average of all sources should be used. However, the above oversimplification is adequate for illustrating the impact of taxation.

[3] The firm will be penalized if it retains earnings improperly, simply to gain advantage for stockholders in high tax brackets. However, it is up to the tax authority to prove the impropriety. See section 531 of the Revenue Act of 1954.

pects, thus requiring much work of engineers, accountants, lawyers, and the management. In addition, shares are usually issued through a distribution group of investment bankers and security dealers, who charge fees that depend on the size and quality of the issue as well as on market conditions (refer to Chapter 3 for a discussion of these fees). The combined costs are called *flotation costs*. These can be substantial, particularly for small issues.

As an alternative to issuing new shares, the company can retain earnings. This provides equity funds without incurring flotation costs. On a cost basis, this is better for both shareholders and the company. Of course, some shareholders may prefer dividends to capital gains. Further, retaining earnings may not satisfy all equity needs, particularly if the firm is growing rapidly. Nonetheless, avoiding flotation costs is a factor in determining dividend policy.

The Demand for Dividends

The shareholder who relies on dividend income may be unhappy when the firm retains earnings, even when the return on the internally invested earnings exceeds the required minimum rate. Will such shareholders sell off their shares and thereby reduce the value of the firm? If so, dividend policy is crucial, and a firm should reexamine the factors that bias dividend policy in favor of earnings retention. This is one aspect of what we may call "the clientele effect," which simply reflects the tendency of stockholders with particular desires, whether for dividends or capital gains, to gravitate to stocks with the qualities desired. Changes in dividend policy can adversely affect price, at least temporarily, if the policy affects the type of stockholder interested in the stock.

The "Dividends-Don't-Count" School

If the capital markets are perfect so that everyone has access to sources of funds without impediment, dividend policy should not affect the value of the firm. Shareholders who need liquidity can borrow against their shares values as long as the interest rate is less than or equal to the required rate of return on equity. Shareholders will not be any worse off. The retained earnings not paid out as dividends are earning at least the required rate of return, and the interest paid on funds borrowed by shareholders to meet their personal liquidity needs is less than that rate of return.

However, shareholders who receive dividends are subject to different risks than those who use shares as collateral for a loan. Ordinary shareholders who wish to borrow against their shares generally use their shares as collateral for what is referred to as a *call loan*. Should the value of the share decline because of general market movements, the lender will require the borrower to supply added collateral, pay off part of the loan, or sell the collateral. If the selling price of the share declines below the value of the loan for which it is collateral, the shareholder is liable for the difference. Thus, there is a very substantial difference in the risk undertaken by a shareholder who borrows in order to get some liquidity and a shareholder who receives a dividend.

Nevertheless, shareholders who need dividend income can sell their shares to those whose liquidity needs are less. Shareholders requiring dividend income can then concentrate on shares that pay high dividends. Thus, dividend policy makes a difference only if liquidity demand is very strong, so that stocks paying low dividends sell at a substantial discount. The implication of this condition is that shareholders do not have ready access to funds, which indicates that capital markets are not perfect. As we pointed out earlier, perfect capital markets are a necessary condition if dividends are not to count.

The "Dividends-Make-a-Difference" School

Observers of dividend policy believe that firms prefer to pay constant dividends and determine policy based on that preference. They tend to hold dividends constant when earnings increase until they are sure that the new level of earnings is permanent. When earnings decline, firms often do not cut dividends, allowing the payout ratio to rise. Some firms have paid dividends even when their current earnings were negative. Firms cut dividends when they are convinced that the decline in earnings is permanent.

Whether or not capital markets are perfect, most practitioners are convinced that dividend cuts *do* affect share values adversely and that dividend increases tend to increase share values. Some proponents of the "dividends-don't-count" school (the NOI group) agree that this relationship exists. However, they say that the change in share value is not a result of the dividend itself. They argue that the change occurs because the increase in dividend conveys information to the market about management's expectations. An increase in dividends indicates optimism, and a decrease implies pessimism. Hence, they say, share values increase when dividends increase because the information content of the dividend increases. Of course, this reasoning applies to dividend cuts also.

As in the case of debt, it is not easy to resolve these differences of opinion. It is tempting and probably accurate to say that both sides are correct. It is unlikely that all shareholders have such easy access to funds that they don't care whether they receive dividends or have to borrow money to achieve their liquidity needs. On the other hand, markets do exist, so those who need liquidity can generally sell their shares to those with lesser liquidity needs. Regardless of which theory holds, most managements behave as if dividends do count, whether this is because of imperfect capital markets or because of the information content of dividend changes.

Stock Dividends

Instead of paying cash dividends, the firm may issue stock dividends. These are shares of equity equal to some proportion of the shares outstanding. For example, a firm with 1,000,000 shares outstanding may declare a stock dividend of 100,000 shares, which is a 10% stock dividend.

Those who prefer cash to stock can then sell these dividend shares and have the cash proceeds. Of course, this reduces the proportion of the firm's equity owned by the shareholder. For example, a holder of 1000 shares would receive 100 shares if there were a 10% stock dividend. Selling these dividend shares reduces the stockholder's relative ownership from 0.1% of the shares outstanding to about 0.091% of the 1,100,000 shares outstanding.

When the firm issues a stock dividend, it is not only conserving cash; in effect, it is also capitalizing a portion of its retained earnings. The total value of the firm has not changed; all that has happened is that 10% more slices have been taken out of the same value pie. In principle, therefore, the value of each outstanding share should be 10% less after the stock dividend than it was before. For example, if each share in our example was worth $10 before the 10% stock dividend, the total value of the shares would have been $10,000,000. The 10% stock dividend does nothing to the total value of the shares, so the new value per share is $10,000,000/1,100,000, or $9.09 per share.

Whether share value actually changes like this depends on the size of the stock dividend. When stock dividends are large, they are referred to as *stock splits*. A firm may split its stock for various reasons. If it feels, for example, that the price of the share is so large that small stockholders are precluded from holding the stock, they may split the stock to reduce the price per share and provide a new market segment for the shares. In any event, the evidence suggests that with stock dividends or stock splits, the value of each share does change as one would expect unless it is accompanied by an increase in cash dividend or improved growth expectations.

Stock Repurchase

As an alternative to paying dividends or to increasing dividends, the firm may elect to repurchase stock. This can be done on the open market, by soliciting stockholders to tender their shares to the firm, or by purchasing blocks of shares directly from large holders. Repurchasing requires care, particularly if shares held by management are involved, because if the repurchase seems to favor one group of stockholders, other shareholders could initiate legal action.

From the seller's point of view, stock repurchase is advantageous since they pay tax only on the difference between the repurchase price and the price they originally paid for the stock. In addition, the tax on

Impact on Total Value of Shares

The arithmetic of share repurchase is deceptively simple. If total earnings available to shareholders have not changed, the stock repurchase reduces the number of pieces into which the earnings pie is cut, thus increasing earnings per share. However, increased earnings per share does not raise price if the cost of equity capital (R_j) also increases.

Suppose, for example, that the firm chooses to repurchase stock because there is no more profitable way to use funds. If they recognized the lack of profitable investment opportunities before the repurchase, stock price should not be affected. However, the announcement of the repurchase plans may create adverse expectations about the firm's future earning power, and this may result in a *decline* in price even though earnings per share rise.

Alternatively, the stock repurchase may be part of a larger plan to improve the firm's outlook. The repurchased stock is called *treasury stock*. It may be resold or it may be traded for shares in another company. If investors believe that this new investment enhances the outlook for the firm, share price may *rise*.

Note that this rise, like the decline we described earlier, results not from the repurchase of stock, but from the expectations that the stock repurchase generates.

There are, of course, many other situations in which stock repurchase can change share value by changing investors' expectations. However, stock repurchase in itself usually *reduces* total share value, although the price per share may rise.

Reduction in Cash

If the firm simply buys back stock without causing a change in expectations and uses available cash for the purchase, their liquidity declines. This can trigger an increase in beta (the risk coefficient) and hence in the cost of equity capital (R_j). Total value of stock should then fall, even though the price per share may rise if the decrease in the number of outstanding shares more than offsets the increase in R_j. If the decline in liquidity is severe, however, the price of the individual share may decline.

Recapitalization without Corporate Taxes

If the firm borrows funds and uses the proceeds of the loan to repurchase stock, it is increasing financial leverage. As we indicated in Chapter 11 (under the NOI method, ignoring taxes), the total value of shares declines, exactly offsetting the increase in debt. Under these conditions, the price of a single share remains unchanged.

Recapitalization with Corporate Taxes

However, this conclusion is based on the assumption of a world without taxes. As Modigliani and Miller recognized, the conclusions must be modified. If corporate taxes exist[4] and the firm substitutes debt for equity, value is affected. The firm is replacing a stockholder whose dividends must be paid in after-tax dollars with a creditor whose interest is paid in before-tax dollars. At a 50% tax rate, $1 in dividends requires $2 in before-tax earnings but $1 in interest payments in pretax terms.

Hence, replacing posttax dollar recipients with pretax dollar recipients increases earnings (after taxes) per share, not just because it reduces shares, but also because it substitutes pretax dollar claims for posttax dollar claims. As a result, the value of the levered firm exceeds that of the unlevered firm. If this was brought about by borrowing and using the proceeds to repurchase shares, both the total value of shares and the price per share rise.

Summary

Ultimately, dividends are the basis of share value, and it is the expectation of changes in future dividends that creates capital gains or losses in share prices.

Nonetheless, the more favorable taxes on personal capital gains encourage firms to retain and reinvest earnings instead of paying them out in dividends. Indeed, the stockholder whose personal tax rate is high may benefit even if the firm reinvests earnings in projects that yield less than the cost of equity capital. But not all stockholders are in high tax brackets, and some stockholders, such as pension funds, may not be taxed at all. Hence, most firms should be loathe to reinvest earnings if they cannot earn the required rate of return.

If profitable projects exist, should the firm retain earnings even if this affects dividends adversely? Ignoring the personal taxation aspect, we face two schools of thought. One says that dividends have no effect on stock price as long as the retained earnings are reinvested profitably. In a perfect capital market, stockholders who need cash can borrow, using their shares as collateral, or sell their shares and buy shares with high dividends. Though they admit that a change in dividends can change price, the proponents of the "dividends-don't-count" school of thought argue that the dividend changes affect price only because they reflect changes in the management's expectations for the firm.

On the other hand, imperfect capital markets can lead to lower

---

[4]Modigliani, F., and Miller, M. H., "Taxes and the Cost of Capital: A Correction," *American Economic Review* (June 1963).

prices for low-dividend stocks than for those with high payouts. At any rate, most managers seem to try to maintain stable dividends.

Stock dividends may be viewed as an alternative to cash dividends that permit the firm to retain earnings. However, stock dividends only increase the number of pieces that must be cut from the earnings pie. Hence, a 10% stock dividend should, and usually does, result in a 10% price decline.

Repurchasing stock reduces the number of shares and, if earnings are unchanged, increases earnings per share. However, the impact on price depends on the purpose of the stock repurchase plan. A firm that buys up its shares because it has no better use for its funds may signal adverse managerial expectations to the stock market, and price may fall. On the other hand, price may rise if the purpose of the repurchase plan is to enhance growth by providing the firm with treasury stock to swap for shares in promising companies. If the aim is simply to add financial leverage, stock prices in a world without corporate taxes remain unchanged. In the real world, however, the market may value the shares more highly because of the substitution of posttax claimants (stockholders) for pretax claimants (creditors).

Review Questions

12-1 What are possible explanations for a decrease in the rate of dividend payout by a corporation?

12-2 What dividend policy bias is introduced by the differential rate of taxation of capital gains and dividends? Discuss.

12-3 How would you justify the practice of paying a stock dividend?

12-4 In a world without taxes and in which the net operating income valuation model applied, how might dividend policy be established?

Problems

12-5 The ABC Steel Company expects its earnings per share to be $3 during the next year. Their dividend payout ratio has typically been 40%, and dividends have been paid annually. For this company, and the steel industry generally, the price/earnings ratio has been consistently near 9. If the stock is to yield 10% over the next year, what must its current price be?

12-6 In 1970 an investor bought some shares of XYZ Corporation at $8 per share. Today the stock sells at $12. A $1 per share dividend is expected in the near future.

    a. When this dividend is paid (the stock trades ex-dividend as defined in the glossary), what price change should the investor expect?

b. If XYZ declared a 6% stock dividend in place of the $1 dividend, what price effect should the investor expect?

c. The investor originally purchased 50 shares. What after-tax dollar return would the investor obtain by selling all shares received as a stock dividend? The investor is in the 30% tax bracket. Ignore brokerage expenses.

12-7 The common stock of XYZ Company currently sells at $30 per share, and they expect to pay a dividend of $4 per share to all those holding the stock at the end of the current week. What should happen to the stock price next week? If the company declares a 10% stock dividend in place of the cash dividend, what should happen to the price of the stock?

Glossary

Call loan	A loan for which the lender may demand repayment at any time, subject to such conditions as proper notice.
Dividend tax credit	A deduction from taxes payable because some of the income earned was in the form of dividends. The credit will be a function of the amount of dividend income.
Ex-dividend	Dividends are declared to be paid to holders at a given date. Anyone buying the stock after that date does not receive the dividend even though the dividend may not have been paid yet. Such stocks trade ex-dividend.
Insider shares	Shares held by the members of management.
Levered firm	A firm with debt in its capital structure.
Payout ratio	The proportion of total earnings that the firm distributes to stockholders in the form of dividends.
Stock dividend	A distribution to shareholders of additional stock in amounts reflecting their current relative holdings. Instead of paying cash, the firm capitalizes retained earnings and distributes new shares.
Stock split	An accounting action to increase the number of shares outstanding without changing the capital accounts. For example, in a 2-for-1 split, each shareholder receives two new shares for each one formerly held, and the total number of shares is doubled.
Tender	To offer in response to an invitation to submit shares for receipt of a specified price.
Treasury stock	Stock issued and formerly outstanding that has been repurchased by the firm.

Bibliography

BARKER, C. A., "Price Effects of Stock Dividend Shares, at Ex-Dividend Dates," *Journal of Finance 14* (Sept. 1959), 373–378.

BLACK, FISCHER, and MYRON SCHOLES, "Dividend Yields and Common Stock Returns: A New Methodology," in *Proceedings of the Seminar on the Analysis of Security Prices,* University of Chicago, Nov. 1970.

BRENNAN, MICHAEL, "A Note on Dividend Irrelevance and the Gordon Valuation Model," *Journal of Finance 26* (Dec. 1971), 1115–1123.

BRITTAIN, J. A., *Corporate Dividend Policy,* Washington, D.C.: Brookings Institution, 1966.

DAVENPORT, MICHAEL, "Leverage, Dividend Policy, and the Cost of Capital: A Comment," *Journal of Finance 25* (Sept. 1970), 893–897.

ELTON, E. J., and M. J. GRUBER, "Marginal Stockholder Tax Rates and the Clientele Effect," *Review of Economics and Statistics 52* (Feb. 1970), 68–74.

FAMA, E., L. FISHER, M. JENSEN, and R. ROLL, "The Adjustment of Stock Prices to New Information," *International Economic Review 10* (Feb. 1969), 1–21.

FAMA, E. F., and H. BABIAK, "Dividend Policy: An Empirical Analysis," *Journal of the American Statistical Association 63* (Dec. 1968), 1132–1161.

FAMA, E. F., "The Empirical Relationships between the Dividend and Investment Decisions of Firms," *American Economic Review 64* (June 1974), 304–318.

FRIEND, I. and M. PUCKETT, "Dividends and Stock Prices," *American Economic Review 54* (Sept. 1964), 656–682.

HARKAVY, O., "Dividends, Earnings, Leverage, Stock Prices and the Supply of Capital to Corporations," *Review of Economics and Statistics 44* (Aug. 1962), 243–269.

HAUSMAN, W. H., R. R. WEST, and J. A. LARGAY, "Stock Splits, Price Changes, and Trading Profits: A Synthesis," *Journal of Business 44* (Jan. 1971), 69–77

HIGGINS, ROBERT C., "The Corporate Dividend-Saving Decision," *Journal of Financial and Quantitative Analysis 7* (March 1972), 1527–1762.

———, "Dividend Policy and Increasing Discount Rate: A Clarification," *Journal of Financial and Quantitative Analysis 7* (June 1972), 1757–1762.

LINTNER, J., "Optimal Dividends and Corporate Growth under Uncertainty", *Quarterly Journal of Economics 78* (Feb. 1964), 49–95.

LOOMIS, C. J., "A Case for Dropping Dividends," *Fortune 77* (June 1968), 181–185ff.

MACDOUGAL, G. E., "Investing in a Dividend Boost," *Harvard Business Review 45* (July–Aug. 1967), 87–92.

MANNE, A. S., "Optimal Dividend and Investment Policies for a Self-Financing Business Enterprise," *Management Science 15* (Nov. 1968), 119–129.

MENDELSON, MORRIS, "Leverage, Dividend Policy and the Cost of Capital: A Comment," *Journal of Finance 25* (Sept. 1970), 898–903.

MILLAR, JAMES A., and BRUCE D. FIELITZ, "Stock-Split and Stock-Dividend Decisions," *Financial Management 2* (Winter 1973), 35–45.

MILLER, M. H. and F. MODIGLIANI, "Dividend Policy, Growth and the Valuation of Shares," *Journal of Business 34* (Oct. 1961), 411–433.

———, "Dividend Policy and Market Valuation: A Reply," *Journal of Business 36* (Jan. 1963), 116–119.

———, "Some Estimates of the Cost of Capital to the Electric Utility Industry," *American Economic Review 56* (June 1966), 333–391.

NORGAARD, RICHARD, and CORINE NORGAARD, "A Critical Examination of Share Repurchase," *Financial Management 3,* (Spring 1974), 44–50.

PETTIT, R. RICHARDSON, "Dividend Announcements, Security Performance, and Capital Market Efficiency," *Journal of Finance 27* (Dec. 1972), 993–1007.

PETTWAY, RICHARD H., and R. PHIL MALONE, "Automatic Dividend Reinvestment Plans of Nonfinancial Corporations," *Financial Management 2* (Winter 1973), 11–18.

TURNOVSKY, S. J., "The Allocation of Corporate Profits between Dividends and Retained Earnings," *Review of Economics and Statistics 49* (Nov. 1967) 583–589.

WALTER, J. E., *Dividend Policy and Enterprise Valuation,* Belmont, California.: Wadsworth, 1967.

WATTS, ROSS, "The Information Content of Dividends," *Journal of Business 46* (April 1973), 191–211.

WHITTINGTON, G., "The Profitability of Retained Earnings," *Review of Economics and Statistics 54* (May 1972), 152–160.

The Cost of Capital

13

In Chapter 11, a central question was whether debt affected the value of the firm and its ownership shares. More important than this issue, however, are the management issues that a firm faces in choosing its asset portfolio, since it is the asset portfolio that determines the size and stability of the *EBIT* flows. Thus the asset portfolio determines the fundamental profitability and risk of the firm, and so the criteria for selecting assets are critical.

A fundamental question in selecting an asset is whether its return is high enough. Although we may use net present value or internal rate of return methods to determine the rate of return, we cannot determine its adequacy unless the firm sets some target or required rate. In this chapter, we shall examine the procedures for establishing such a rate.

Setting Target Rates

Arbitrary Methods

Although the firm can set the required rate of return arbitrarily, this is usually undesirable. The firm may be overly ambitious and set too high a target rate of return, thus rejecting proposals that they would have accepted under a more reasonable rate. On the other hand, the firm may adopt an unnecessarily low target rate and fail to earn the return required by its owners under given capital market conditions. They may fail to earn the rate of return required when considering the risk-free rate, the rate of return available in the general market, and the risk of the firm itself. If the firm sets an unreasonably high rate, the value of its shares will be less than they would otherwise be, because the growth rate of the firm will be too low. On the other hand, with too low a rate of return, share values will also be too low, because too many unprofitable investments are included in the asset portfolio.

Determinants

To determine an appropriate rate of return, the firm must consider its investors' requirements. The return must meet the creditor's interest requirements as well as the owners' required rate of return. The return, of course, reflects both the risk of the asset portfolio and the risk of the capital structure (as measured, say, by debt/equity ratios). The creditors are concerned with the safety of their investment, so they review such measures as the ratio of *EBIT* to interest, and the debt/equity ratio.

The required rate of return is the firm's cost of capital, which we define as a weighted average of the costs of the firm's sources of funds. In analyzing the cost of capital, we shall consider the following questions:

How are the costs of individual sources of funds determined?
How are the weights to be used in calculating the average cost of capital determined?
Is there an optimal capital structure?

The Costs of the Components of the Cost of Capital

Taxation

Pretax costs differ substantially from posttax costs. Since interest costs can be deducted from taxable income while equity costs cannot, it is inappropriate to average the before-tax debt cost with the after-tax equity cost. Technically, it makes no difference whether we use before-tax or after-tax costs, as long as we are consistent. However, if the firm's objective is to maximize its share value, which is associated with after-tax costs, then we usually consider after-tax costs.

Cost of Common Shares

The cost of equity capital is familiar from our discussions of the capital market line. According to capital market theory, the required rate of return on equity capital is

$$R_j = R_F + \beta_j(R_M - R_F) \tag{13-1}$$

In addition to the capital markets line of approach, other methods of valuation of equity shares based on required rate of return are available. We used the constant growth model in Chapters 4 and 12. If we assume that both growth in earnings and dividends are constant, the following equation represents this approach:

$$R_j = D_0/p + G \qquad\qquad (13\text{-}2)$$

where D_0 is the current dividend expected this year, p is price, and G is expected growth in earnings. Note that without growth, the required rate of return would be the dividend yield.

Many other methods of generating required rates of return are available; they are based on different assumptions about the pattern of the firm's growth than either the capital market line approach or the constant growth model. In any event, to determine the cost of equity capital (R_j) we either have to consider the capital market and the risk of the firm (as in the capital markets line approach), or estimate future patterns of earnings and dividends and relate them to the market price of the firm (as in the constant growth model). The two methods are not so different, since the price of a share must reflect the alternative yields available in capital markets, the riskiness of the firm, and the expected growth of the firm.

Retained Earnings

As we pointed out in Chapter 12, firms do not pay out all their earnings in the form of dividends. They retain some earnings as a source of capital. Retained earnings are viewed as equity capital, since they are the part of earnings per common share that have not been distributed. If the firm were liquidated, the owners would receive the value of retained earnings, if assets could be disposed of at their balance sheet valuations.

Subject to the qualifications in Chapter 12 concerning taxes and flotation costs, the firm should earn the same rate of return on retained earnings as on externally generated equity capital (assuming the firm's function is to maximize share value). If the earnings had been paid out as dividends, stockholders could have reinvested the funds as freely as if they had sold their shares.

Depreciation

Another important source of funds is depreciation, or the amortization of capital costs. As we have pointed out, depreciation recaptures costs previously expended on capital goods. In the past, some firms have treated these funds as costless. Depreciation funds are certainly not earnings, but they are part of after-tax cash flow. As after-tax cash flow, they can be used just like cash. Hence, it seems inappropriate to treat these as costless funds. At the very least, they could be used to repay debt and save the firm interest costs. Or these funds could be used to increase dividend payouts and enhance the shareholders' dividend position.

Thus, when we look at the opportunity costs available for depreciation, we see that the cost associated with depreciation should not be zero. It is probably more appropriately the cost of equity capital. After all, the firm is supposed to be operated for the shareholders' interests, and so the recaptured capital costs are theirs. Further, the reinvestment of depreciation allows the firm to escape flotation costs.

Preferred Shares

Preferred shares are costed at their dividend yield. Since preferred dividends are not tax deductible, the cost of capital for preferred stock is its dividend yield.

Debt

Debt costs are interest payments adjusted for corporate income taxes. Thus, if the corporation is paying 40% in taxes, the after-tax cost of 8% interest is 4.8%, that is, $(1 - t)d$, where t is the marginal tax rate on the firm's income and d is the interest rate.

Short-Term Debt

A firm must provide for short-term as well as long-term debt. Even though short-term debt matures within one year, it is usually replaced with new short-term debt. For example, while the firm is paying off its old accounts payable, at the same time it is buying new inventory which creates new accounts payable. Even short-term bank loans can be "rolled-over" as they mature. Thus, many short-term debts are more permanent than their maturity implies.

For some short-term debt, the interest costs are quite clear, as in the case of bank loans with a stated interest rate. However, other kinds of short-term debt such as accounts payable, wages payable, and taxes payable have no explicit interest rate. Interest on these funds can be treated as zero.

The exception to this is accounts payable that are paid after the discount period has expired. Credit sales usually provide a discount for paying within a certain time. For example, if the terms of a credit sale are 2%, net 30, the buyer who pays within 30 days may deduct 2% from the bill. After 30 days the full amount is due. Thus, a firm that consistently fails to pay within the discount period is incurring an interest cost of 24% annually on its trade credit. Such funds are not costless, and the cost should be included in the cost of capital. In most cases, firms borrow from banks to avoid such high interest charges.

Long-Term Debt Yields

An interesting question is whether to value d at its coupon rate or yield to maturity. This has become more important in recent years because of wide variations in interest rates. It is of particular concern to regulated firms such as public utilities, since their required rate of return (cost of capital) determines their prices.

On the one hand, using the coupon rate is reasonable, since this is the actual interest rate paid by the firm, regardless of market interest rates. When the firm has to refinance, new and perhaps higher rates will be reflected.

On the other hand, we can justify using market rates even though the coupon rate may be lower (or higher). After all, if the firm makes investments assuming one cost of capital (of which interest is a part) and then finds itself having to refund at very different interest rates, the old assets being refinanced may not yield enough to cover the higher rates. Or if the actual interest rate is less than coupon, the firm might have expanded more rapidly, providing more service.

The firm is actually less concerned with the current market rate than with the rate likely to prevail when refunding will be necessary. Since no one can predict future rates with certainty, firms may attempt to match the maturities of their funding with the expected lives of their assets. Hence, if prices do not cover increased interest costs, they can avoid refunding by not replacing the asset.

Perhaps as a result of attempts to match the maturities of funds with the expected lives of major assets, the use of the coupon rate in the cost of capital calculation is common. However, one can justify market yields, particularly if major new funding is anticipated. Ideally, the firm would like to use a geometric mean of future rates at which funding will be necessary (similar to the use of the geometric mean in term structures in Chapter 4). Since this ideal is not practical, both current market rates and coupon rates are acceptable compromises. The same arguments apply to the cost of capital of preferred stock when the coupon rate differs from the market rate.

Weights for the Cost of Capital

To orient our discussion, it is probably useful to consider the relative importance of the different sources of funds that nonfinancial corporations have used recently. These are shown in Table 13-1.

Perhaps the most startling revelation of this table is the importance of internally generated funds. Although the importance varies from year to year, about half the funds invested by business corporations come from internal sources. Thus, our comments about costing both retained earnings and capital consumption allowances now seem far more important than may have appeared earlier in the chapter. Since these funds are so important, it is clear that financial managers need some means of forecasting internal flows, such as cash budgets and statements of sources and uses of working capital.

Generally, the relative importance of retained earnings tends to be less stable than that of capital consumption allowances, since retained earnings reflect total earnings, which vary from good to bad times. The

Table 13-1. Private Nonfinancial Corporation Financial Flows

	1973	1972	1971
Additions to Retained Earnings	9%	10%	10%
Capital Consumption Allowance	38	43	47
Total Internal Financing	47%	53%	57%
Net New Share Issues	2	7	10
Corporate Bonds	7	8	15
Mortgages	12	11	9
Other Sources including Short-term	32	21	9

SOURCE: Board of Governors of the Federal Reserve System.

importance of capital consumption allowances, however, is somewhat surprising. It is also significant for policy, since government sometimes increases capital consumption allowances to stimulate investment and sometimes cuts them back to reduce inflationary pressures.

Other shifts in the relative importance of different sources of funds reflect business conditions. Retained earnings become less important during recessions and more important during periods of recovery. Early in a recovery period, firms can finance their expansions largely by internally generated and short-term sources of funds. Firms tend to avoid long-term debt when interest rates are high, even though short-term debt levels are already very high.

The issuance of stock appears to be last in order of priority. Although capital spending rose from $101 billion to $114 billion between 1972 and 1973, new stock issues declined from $10.4 billion to $5.7 billion.

The aggregate figures shown in Table 13-1 provide an important perspective on the relative importance of different sources of funds, but they are less useful in determining the weights of an individual firm's cost of capital. The capital structures of individual firms may be very different from the aggregate relationships shown in Table 13-1.

Choosing the appropriate weights for the weighted cost of capital may seem trivial, but it is quite important. As the aggregate figures show, the relative importance of the actual components of the capital structure can shift rapidly. The shifting weights may reflect opportunistic adjustments by firms to market conditions. For example, a firm may issue debt even if it feels that its debt/equity ratio is too high, because it believes that current interest rates are low relative to expected future interest rates. The firm would thus be borrowing ahead of its actual needs. Under other conditions, it may prefer to wait before issuing equity if its current equity needs are quite small, in order to keep issue or flotation costs at a reasonable level.

A firm's capital structure also reflects its stage of development. Young firms usually have only limited access to equity funds except for those of the entrepreneur. For these firms, debt, especially the more easily acquired short-term debt such as accruals and trade payables, is important. As the firm matures, retained earnings become more important. Later, it can choose external equity, long-term debt, or other appropriate means of funds. Clearly, the capital weights for firms at different stages are not constant.

Current Weights

If current weights are used, the weighted average cost of capital changes over time. To the extent that these weights represent opportunistic shifting, caused by market conditions for example, using them is undesirable, because investments accepted in one year might have been rejected in another year, simply because of shifting weights.

For example, suppose that the interest rate is 8% and the required rate of return on equity is 12%. With a 50% tax rate, the cost of capital is 8% if debt and equity are equally weighted. However, suppose that debt is 30% of the capital structure, perhaps reflecting a large issue of equity that year or the opportunistic postponement of a debt issue until interest rates are more favorable. Then the cost of capital rises to 9.6%. An investment generating $100 per annum for 15 years with a cost of $855.90 would be acceptable with equal weights, but would be rejected with 70% equity weight. Figure 13-1 shows this change.

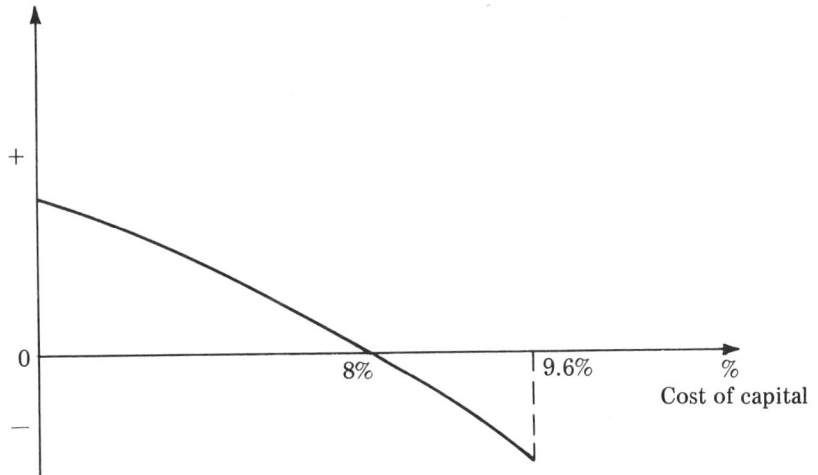

Figure 13-1
Relationship of Cost of Capital to Net Present Value

Target Weights

A firm can avoid the effects of these opportunistic shifts in the cost of capital, and hence in the acceptability of particular projects at different times, by using target capital structure ratios as weights. This ratio reflects the capital structure proportions *desired* by the firm and the firm's policies on debt, dividends, and so on. If the firm has not made such target estimates or policies, it can use average weights over time, thus removing some of the static caused by transient shifts in capital structure weights.

Exceptions to the Weighted Cost of Capital

Under some circumstances, it is sensible for the firm to define its discount rate as something other than the overall weighted cost of capital. Real estate firms, for example, may finance virtually all their assets by mortgages. In addition, they may incorporate each asset separately to reduce the firm's risk by minimizing the impact of one failure on its total holdings. In that case, the mortgage rate seems a more appropriate rate than the overall weighted cost of capital.

Similarly, government may encourage a firm to build a plant in an economically disadvantaged area by lending money for the total cost at a low interest rate. In this case, using the overall cost of capital might give the plant a negative net present value, which is probably the reason that the government offered the low-cost loan in the first place. It makes more sense to use the interest rate offered by the government.

When the mortgage or the government finances less than the full amount so that the firm must invest either sources of debt funds or equity, they should develop a separate cost of capital that includes the weights applicable to the specific projects. In these exceptions, the capital structure for the special projects is permanently different from the capital structure for the firm as a whole.

Marginal versus Average Costs

Some argue that firms should calculate the short-run marginal cost of capital when they evaluate a project. This would reflect the costs and relative importance of sources for that project. Except for the cases that we discussed, the short-run marginal cost of capital should *not* be used, since the actual capital structure of the firm at any time reflects a variety of factors, for example, taking advantage of temporarily favorable rates, or using debt until equity needs are large enough to justify an equity issue. Thus, the short-run marginal cost of capital often reflects temporary expedients, and the longer-run methods of financing are better measured by using the overall or average weighted cost of capital.

The main difference between the short-run and the long-run marginal cost of capital is that the latter reflects the firm's optimal capital structure, whereas the short-run marginal cost reflects monetary opportunities, or the "lumpiness" of particular kinds of funds, such as the costs of flotation that make small issues of equity expensive.

What is the difference between the long-run marginal cost of capital and the average weighted cost of capital? If the costs of the individual sources do not change, they should be identical, given an optimal capital structure for the firm. This is illustrated in Figure 13-2, which shows the long-run marginal cost of capital, the weighted average cost, and how these interact with an investment demand schedule for capital projects to determine the level of investment. Short-run marginal cost schedules are also shown. The curve labeled SRC_1 assumes that low-cost debt is used, while SRC_2 is the short-run marginal cost schedule assuming equity was issued in the particular short run. Note that in the former instance, the firm would "overinvest" and would "underinvest" with the high-cost equity financing. However, marginal cost of capital can be used, provided that it is the *long-run* marginal cost of capital that is being used.

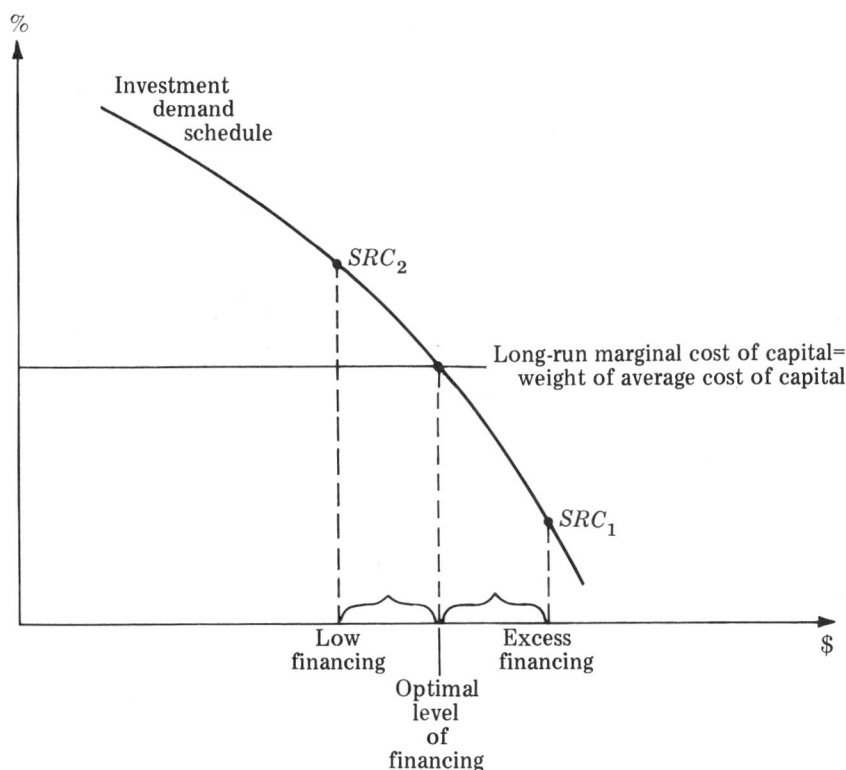

Figure 13-2
Different Levels of Financing Caused by Using Short-Run Marginal Cost of Capital Rather than Long-Run Marginal or Weight of Average Cost of Capital

Is There an Optimal Capital Structure?

An optimal capital structure would be one consistent with maximizing the value of shares. For example, under the net income method of valuing the firm, the ratio of debt to equity is extremely high, because debt lowers the cost of capital, and the value of the equity residual increases substantially despite the increase in risk.

However, under the net operating income method, debt has no effect on the value of shares, except for the impact of taxation. The overall cost of capital for the firm remains unchanged. Under these conditions, the firm's debt proportion makes essentially no difference, since share value does not change.

Even with the net operating income method, there may be reasons to prefer one capital structure to another. For example, the interest charges on debt may require the firm to hold larger average cash balances than it otherwise would, thus reducing the amount of capital that it can profitably invest. Short-term debt may require larger average cash balances than long-term debt or equity financing, since the firm must be able to renew short-term loans when they come due, and there may be some time gap between the expiration of one loan and the start of a new loan.

We cannot easily dismiss optimal capital structure despite the net operating income approach to valuation. The linear capital market line may not apply even though risk premiums rise as debt is incurred.

The required rate of return on equity and beta may be positively, but not linearly, correlated, as Figure 13-3 shows.

The upper section of the graph is the capital market line under three assumptions. The familiar capital market line is a straight line rising to the right, associated with the net operating income method of evaluation. The net income method shows the required rate of return when equity does not respond to increases in risk, and debt is treated as a proxy for changes in beta. Between these is the alternative capital markets line. This follows the net income method for small increases in debt. The required rate of return on equity does not change. However, as the amount of debt increases, the market demands a higher required rate of return and risk premium, resulting in a line that rises fairly steeply.

The bottom half of the graph relates the value of the firm to changes in debt. The net operating income method assumes that the value of the firm does not change as debt increases, if we ignore taxes. Hence, there is no optimal capital structure in terms of maximizing share value.

However, with taxes included, as shown in Chapter 11, the value of the firm increases with debt. Hence, the optimal capital structure would be 100% debt despite practical consequences.

Under the net income method, the value of the firm rises linearly with the increases in debt, because the risk coefficient does not increase. So the value of shares increases. In this case, the optimal capital structure is approximately 100% debt, identical to the ultimate under NOI with corporate taxes. In both the upper half and lower half of Figure 13-3, the NOI curves would shift toward the NI curves.

If the alternative capital market's line shown in the top half of the graph holds, the curved line labeled "alternative" in the bottom half of the graph shows a relationship between the value of the firm and the amount of debt. When debt is OP, value of the firm is at a maximum. Beyond that point, the value of the shares declines as risk is reflected in market valuation. Thus, an optimal capital structure and debt/equity ratio can exist if the market line is not strictly linear, or if practical concerns about the increasing possibility of insolvency are recognized.

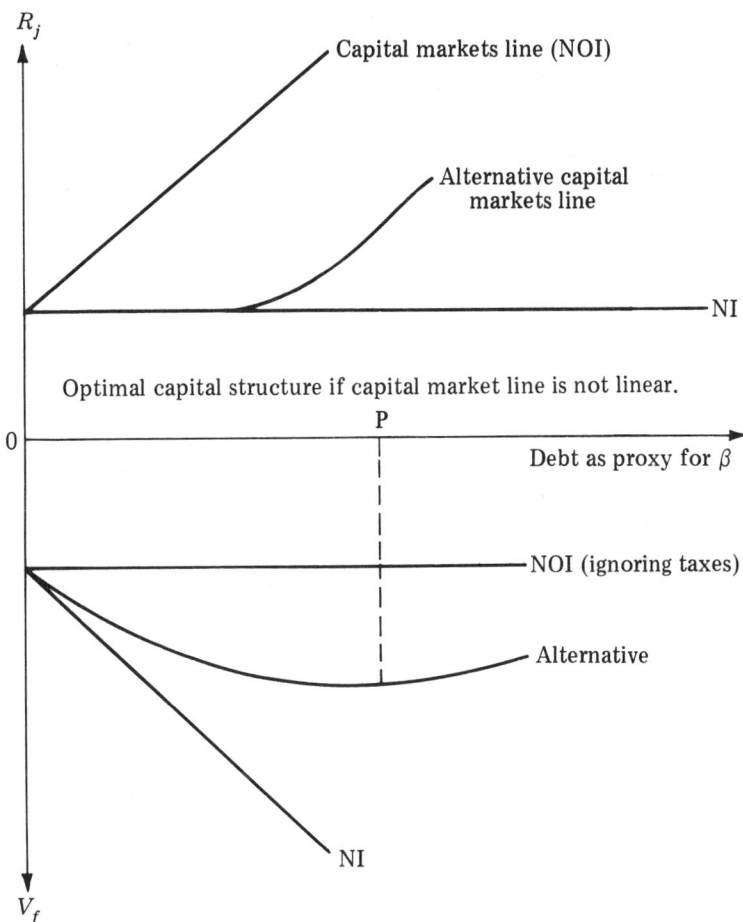

Figure 13-3
Comparison of Optimal Capital Structure Implications of NOI and NI Methods of Valuation

Summary

The target rate of return, or cost of capital, is an essential element in maximizing the value of the firm. If the rate is too low the firm may adopt investment projects that it should reject. If the rate is too high, the firm may overlook opportunities it should seize.

In general, the cost of capital that a firm uses should be a weighted average of all sources of funds, including internal sources. The cost of equity can be calculated by using various valuation models, depending on the firm's outlook. Whatever method a firm uses, they should give adequate consideration to risk and the capital market.

Retained earnings are costed as equity, since these funds could have been distributed to the shareholders. Thus, they should earn at least the rate of return that shareholders require.

Depreciation is an important source of funds and should not be treated as costless. Since the firm operates for the shareholders' financial interests, the recaptured capital costs are theirs and it seems reasonable to assign the cost of equity funds to depreciation.

Preferred shares are costed at their dividend yield. No adjustment is made for taxes, since preferred dividends are paid from after-tax income.

Interest costs, on the other hand, are paid before taxes; hence, the interest rate should be reduced to reflect its after-tax equivalent. Though most of the emphasis is on long-term debt, short-term debt is important, since it is not necessarily temporary. Short-term debt can be renewed, and thus it actually becomes as permanent as long-term debt. For short-term loans, the after-tax interest rate equivalent is used. However, many kinds of short-term debt have no interest cost. These funds are therefore treated as costless. Accounts payable may also be costless if the firm pays them during the discount period. Failure to pay within the discount period makes this source of funds very expensive indeed.

With long-term interest rates, coupon rates can differ from market rates. Either coupon rates or market rates can be used, depending on when the debt is due. If the debt is due soon, it is better to use the market rate since it may more nearly approximate the actual cost of the debt in the near future. However, if the debt does not mature for many years, the market rate is no better an approximation of future interest rates than the coupon rate. For this reason, it is not uncommon for firms to use coupon rates, adjusted for taxes, of course, as the debt cost of capital, even though current market rates are quite different.

The appropriate weight to be assigned each source of capital is not obvious either. Firms use different sources of funds at different stages of the business cycle and also at different stages of their development. The "now" capital structure may thus be a momentary matter, but it could affect the selection of projects if current weights are used. If the firm has a target structure, this is appropriate. If not, an average of past capital structures may be more appropriate than simply taking what may be a very transient current capital structure.

Although there are exceptions, firms should generally use the average cost of capital in assessing projects. The marginal cost of the funds actually used is, for a particular project, a matter of chance. The project may be rejected if it happens to be proposed when the firm is raising expensive sources of funds. Under some conditions, however, particular sources of funds, such as mortgages or incentive loans, may be tied to particular projects. In such instances, use of the marginal cost of funds is appropriate.

As a matter of theory, there appears to be no unique capital structure for the firm. Under the net operating income method of valuation, the value of the firm is not affected by its capital structure. One capital structure is as good as another, except for considerations such as the amount of liquidity required by one structure over another. However, when corporate taxation is considered, the firm's value increases with the proportion of debt in the capital structure. This leads to the conclusion that the optimal capital structure should contain all debt, a conclusion that few managers would accept.

The simplest form of the net income approach to valuation also leads to the conclusion that an all-debt capital structure maximizes the firm's value. However, most proponents of the net income approach recognize that risk becomes increasingly important if imprudently large proportions of debt are included in the capital structure. Theoretical factors can lead to an optimal capital structure under the net operating income approach also, if the capital market line is not strictly linear.

Review Questions

13-1 When a firm employs too low a cost of capital in making capital budgeting decisions, how is the attainment of the firm's objective affected?

13-2 If a new project is financed with funds borrowed at a bank, should the bank lending rate be employed when evaluating the project?

13-3 Do you expect that the costs of various types of financing are independent of one another for a firm?

Problems

13-4 Given the accounting data below for the ABC Corporation, calculate a weighted average cost of capital.

		Market value
Bonds, 9% coupon	$5,000,000	$98
Preferred stock, 8%	2,000,000	90
Common stock (100,000 shares)	1,000,000	40
Retained earnings	2,000,000	

Dividends are expected to remain fixed at $300,000, and earnings are expected to grow 5% per year. The firm pays taxes at the rate of 40%.

13-5 The common stock of ABC Manufactures Ltd. is currently selling for $20 per share. New shares can be sold at a 5% discount. Earnings are expected to grow 8% per year for the forseeable future. The firm has a steady payout policy, and the dividend for the current year is expected to be $1.25 per share. What is the firm's marginal cost of equity capital?

13-6 The total assets of Ace Corporation are expected to increase by $10 million during the upcoming year. The firm has no short-term liabilities and has the following (optimal) capital structure.

Debt (8% coupon bonds)	$ 6,000,000
Preferred stock (10%)	4,000,000
Common stock ($1 par value)	1,000,000
Retained Earnings	14,000,000
	$25,000,000

Bonds with a 9% coupon can be sold at par, and 10% preferred can be sold at a 5% discount from par. New common stock can be sold at a 10% discount from its current price of $30 per share. The risk-free rate is 8% and the return on the market is 12%. The beta for the common stock of Ace is 1.3 (assumed to be unaffected by the expansion). Ignore depreciation flows. The corporate tax rate is 40%. Retained earnings for the year are expected to be $3 million. Compute an average cost of capital for Ace for funds raised during the year.

13-7 BPI Limited has reason to believe that its current capital structure of 50% debt and 50% equity is optimal in a valuation sense. The firm pays 8% on its debt and estimates its cost of equity to be 12%. The firm pays taxes at a 40% rate.

a. What is the weighted cost of capital for BPI?

b. If marginal financing can be arranged so that the cost of debt increases by 0.5% (above 8%) for each $100,000 of debt raised and the cost of equity increases by 1% (above 12%) for each $100,000 of equity raised, how much extra financing should the firm secure if they can earn 9.7% on available projects? Assume that the current capital structure is optimal.

Glossary

Debt/equity ratio	Debt divided by equity. Sometimes debt is restricted to long-term debt.
Discount period	The time during which the debtor may take a discount to reflect prompt payment.

Average cost of capital	The cost of all the firm's sources of funds, weighted by relative importance.
Permanent financing	Long-term debt and equity plus the level of short-term debt that the firm will maintain even at low levels of activity.
Weighted cost of capital	A cost of capital for the firm calculated by weighing the cost of each source of funds by its proportion of the total market value of the firm (including the market values of debt and equity).
Marginal cost of capital	The cost of the additional funds required to finance the project under consideration.

Bibliography

ADLER, MICHAEL, "On the Risk–Return Trade-Off in the Valuation of Assets," *Journal of Financial and Quantitative Analysis* (Dec. 1969), 493–512.

ALBERTS, W. W., and S. H. ARCHER, "Some Evidence on the Effect of Company Size on the Cost of Equity Capital," *Journal of Financial and Quantitative Analysis 8* (March 1973), 229–245.

ANG, JAMES S., "Weighted Average versus True Cost of Capital," *Financial Management 2* (Autumn 1973), 56–60.

ARDITTI, F. D., "Risk and the Required Return on Equity," *Journal of Finance 22* (March 1967), 19–36.

———, "The Weighted Average Cost of Capital: Some Questions on its Definition, Interpretation and Use," *Journal of Finance 28* (Sept. 1973), 1001–1007.

ARDITTI, FRED D., and MILFORD S. TYSSELAND, "Three Ways to Present the Marginal Cost of Capital," *Financial Management 2* (Summer 1973), 63–67.

BAUMOL, W. J., "On the Social Rate of Discount," *American Economic Review 58* (Sept. 1968), 788–802.

BAUMOL, W. J., and B. G. MALKIEL, "The Firm's Optimal Debt–Equity Combination and the Cost of Capital," *Quarterly Journal of Economics 81* (Nov. 1967), 547–802.

BLUME, MARSHALL E., "On the Assessment of Risk," *Journal of Finance 26* (March 1971), 1–10.

BLUME, MARSHALL E., and IRWIN FRIEND, "A New Look at the Capital–Asset Pricing Model", *Journal of Finance 28* (March 1973), 19–34.

BONESS, A. JAMES, ANDREW H. CHEN, and SAM JATUSIPITAK, "On Relations among Stock Price Behavior and Changes in the Capital Structure of the Firm," *Journal of Financial and Quantitative Analysis 7* (Sept. 1972), 1967–1982.

BOOT, JOHN C. G., and GEORGE M. FRANKFURTER, "The Dynamics of Corporate Debt Management, Decision Rules, and Some Empirical Estimates," *Journal of Financial and Quantitative Analysis 7* (Sept. 1972), 1956–1966.

BREWER, D. E., and J. MICHAELSON, "The Cost of Capital, Corporation Finance, and the Theory of Investment: Comment," *American Economic Review 55* (June 1965), 516–524.

DONALDSON, GORDON, "New Framework for Corporate Debt Capacity," *Harvard Business Review 40* (March–Apr. 1962), 117–131.

ELTON, E. J., "The Effect of Share Repurchases on the Value of the Firm," *Journal of Finance 23* (March 1968), 135–150.

ELTON, EDWIN J., and MARTIN J. GRUBER, "Valuation and the Cost of Capital for Regulated Industries," *Journal of Finance 26* (June 1971), 661–670.

HAMADA, ROBERT S., "Portfolio Analysis, Market Equilibrium and Corporation Finance," *Journal of Finance 24* (March 1969), 13–32.

HAUGEN, ROBERT A., and JAMES L. PAPPAS, "Equilibrium in the Pricing of Capital Assets, Risk-Bearing Debt Instruments, and the Question of Optimal Capital Structure," *Journal of Financial and Quantitative Analysis 5* (June 1971), 943–954.

HEINS, A. JAMES, and CASE M. SPRENKLE, "A Comment on the Modigliani–Miller Cost-of-Capital Thesis," *American Economic Review 59* (Sept. 1959), 590–592.

HIGGINS, ROBERT C., "Growth, Dividend Policy and Capital Costs in the Electric Utility Industry," *The Journal of Finance 29* (Sept. 1974), 1189–1201.

HIRSHLEIFER, JACK, "Investment Decisions under Uncertainty: Applications of the State-Preference Approach," *Quarterly Journal of Economics* (May 1966), 252–277.

JENSEN, MICHAEL C., "Risk, the Pricing of Capital Assets, and the Evaluation of Investment Portfolios," *Journal of Business 42* (Apr. 1969), 167–247.

KEENAN, MICHAEL, "Models of Equity Valuation: The Great Serm Bubble," *Journal of Finance 25* (May 1970), 243–273.

KROUSE, CLEMENT G., "Optimal Financing and Capital Structure Programs for the Firm," *Journal of Finance 27* (Dec. 1972), 1057–1072.

LEWELLEN, W. G., *The Cost of Capital,* Belmont, California: Wadsworth, 1969.

LINTNER, JOHN, "The Aggregation of Investors' Judgments and Preferences in Purely Competitive Security Markets," *Journal of Financial and Quantitative Analysis 4* (Dec. 1969), 347–400.

MILLER, M. H., and FRANCO MODIGLIANI, "Cost of Capital to Electric Utility Industry," *American Economic Review 56* (June 1966), 333–391.

MODIGLIANI, FRANCO, and M.H. MILLER, "The Cost of Capital, Corporation Finance and the Theory of Investment," *American Economic Review 48* (June 1958), 261–297.

———, "The Cost of Capital, Corporation Finance and the Theory of Investment: Reply," *American Economic Review 49* (Sept. 1958), 655–669. "Taxes and the Cost of Capital: A Correction," *American Economic Review 53* (June 1963), 433–443. "Reply," *American Economic Review 55* (June 1965), 524–527.

MOSSIN, JAN, "Security Pricing and Investment Criteria in Competitive Markets," *American Economic Review 59* (Dec. 1969), 749–756.

MYERS, STEWART C., "A Time–State Preference Model of Security Valuation," *Journal of Financial and Quantitative Analysis 3* (March 1968), 1–34.

———, "Interactions of Corporate Financing and Investment Decisions—Implications for Capital Budgeting," *Journal of Finance 29* (March 1974), 1–25.

———, "The Application of Finance Theory to Public Utility Rate Cases," *Bell Journal of Economics and Management Science 3* (Spring 1972), 58–97.

REILLY, RAYMOND R., and WILLIAM E. WECKER, "On the Weighted Average Cost of Capital," *Journal of Financial and Quantitative Analysis, 8* (Jan. 1973), 123–126.

RESEK, ROBERT W., "Multidimensional Risk and the Modigliani–Miller Hypothesis," *Journal of Finance 25* (March 1970), 47–52.

ROBICHEK, A. A., and S. C. MYERS, "Problems in the Theory of Optimal Capital Structure," *Journal of Finance and Quantitative Analysis 1* (June 1966), 1–35.

ROBICHEK, ALEXANDER A., "Risk and the Value of Securities," *Journal of Financial and Quantitative Analysis 4* (Dec. 1969), 513–538.

ROBICHEK, ALEXANDER A., J. G. MCDONALD, and R. C. HIGGINS, "Some Estimates of the Cost of Capital to Electric Utilities, 1954–1957: Comment," *American Economic Review 57* (Dec. 1967), 1279–1288.

SCHWARTZ, ELI, and J. RICHARD ARONSON, "Some Surrogate Evidence in Support of the Concept of Optimal Capital Structure," *Journal of Finance 22* (March 1967), 10–18.

SCOTT, DAVID F., JR., "Evidence on the Importance of Financial Structure," *Financial Management 1* (Summer 1972), 45–50.

SOLOMON, EZRA, *The Theory of Financial Management,* New York: Columbia University Press, 1963.

STIGLITZ, JOSEPH E., "A Re-Examination of the Modigliani–Miller Theorem," *American Economic Review 59* (Dec. 1969), 784–793.

TINSLEY, P. A., "Capital Structure, Precautionary Balances, and Valuation of the Firm: The Problem of Financial Risk," *Journal of Financial and Quantitative Analysis 5* (March 1970), 33–62.

VICKERS, D., "The Cost of Capital and the Structure of the Firm," *Journal of Finance 25* (March 1970), 35–46.

WESTON, J. FRED, "Investment Decisions Using the Capital Asset Pricing Model." *Financial Management 1* (Spring 1973), 25–33.

WHITMORE, G. A., "Market Demand Curve for Common Stock and the Maximization of Market Value," *Journal of Financial and Quantitative Analysis 5* (March 1970), 105–114.

WIPPERN, R. F., "Financial Structure and the Value of the Firm," *Journal of Finance 21* (Dec. 1966), 615–634

Leasing Assets and Merger Policy

14

Leasing

Almost all fixed assets from typewriters through machinery to land and plant can be leased. Manufacturers, distributors, builders, and real estate companies offer their goods and services on lease terms as well as through straight purchase. Although the kinds of equipment that can be leased have greatly increased since World War II, certain kinds of leases have existed for many years. Leasing of land and buildings is, of course, quite old. Leasing of transportation equipment is traditional in the railroad industry. Bus companies and airlines commonly lease their vehicles.

Those who sell products and services may offer leases directly or through subsidiary leasing companies. In the direct lease, the lessor may be willing to take more risk or offer better terms than an independent leasing company or other financial institution would, for the same reason that sellers are willing to accept trade credit risks that banks and other financial institutions would not consider. Manufacturers, however, may offer lease terms if they believe they can sell the lease to a financial institution or use them as security for loans. In that case, the manufacturer has to apply the same credit standards that the financial institution would use.

The lessor acts as an intermediary between the user of the equipment, the lessee, and financial institutions. The lessor uses the lease agreement, the physical assets, and the lessor's general creditworthiness as a basis for borrowing from banks, insurance companies, pension funds, and other financial institutions. The user who buys equipment can borrow directly, using the asset and his own general creditworthiness. Leasing companies can offer the financial institution a diversified group of leases and thus better creditworthiness than the lessee. The asset portfolio of the leasing company may be superior to that of the lessee because the leasing company can spread leases over several firms and often among many industries. Hence, if one firm or industry should face misfortune, the leasing company can count on its holdings in other firms or industries to keep its income stable.

In addition, the lease company has two assets to serve as security for loans. It can make short-term loans using near-term lease payments as collateral, and it can borrow on the physical assets that have been leased. If the user purchases the equipment, it can use only the physical asset as security for loans, although this limitation is not important for a user who can borrow on an unsecured basis.

The decision to buy or lease assets is relatively complex. There is no reason to believe that either decision is correct in all cases. We shall use an example to illustrate the differences between leasing and buying and to demonstrate an analytic technique for arriving at the correct decision.

Purchase

The asset costs $100 and has an expected life of three years. It generates $90 annually before expenses. Of the expenses, $20 is a cash outlay, so cash flow before depreciation and taxes, but after all other operating expenses, is expected to be $70 per year. If the firm buys the asset, it will depreciate 0.5 of the asset's original cost the first year, 0.33 second year, and 0.17 the last year. Using the sum of the year's digit method of calculating depreciation, the firm thus depreciates three-sixths of the asset the first year, two-sixths the second, and one-sixth the third year. Assume that the asset is worthless at the end of three years and that the tax rate is 48%.

If the firm buys the asset, it will finance the acquisition by a three-year 6% unsecured loan, to be repaid in three annual installments with interest and principal amounting to $37.41 per year. We derive this figure by dividing the 6% factor for three years shown in Table B of Chapter 2 into the $100 loan value, that is, $100/2.673 = $37.41. The division between interest and principal annually is shown in Table 14-1. If we ignore the flotation costs, then we have the after-tax cash flow shown in Table 14-2. In this case, we have deducted the loan payments from the cash flow, and since the firm used the loan for full financing, the initial outlay for the asset is zero. If they had financed half the asset by debt, then we would subtract the debt payments from the after-tax cash flow and C would be $50. We reduce the original cost of the asset by the amount of the debt repayment, not interest, which has been deducted from the cash flow, to avoid counting the cost of the asset twice—once when purchased with borrowed money and once again when repaid. In this case, the present value of the after-tax cash flow is the net present value. At a cost of capital of 0.10, it is $43.53.

Table 14-1. Principal and Interest Components of Fixed Repayment Financing

End of Year	Interest	Principal	Total
1	$ 6.00	$ 31.41	$ 37.41
2	4.11	33.30	37.41
3	2.12	35.29	37.41
Totals	$12.23	$100.00	$112.23

Lease Alternative

Lease payments are usually made in advance. Assume that we have a lease involving three equal annual payments of $35.30. This provides the lessor with a 6% return. The firm would pay $35.30 at the beginning of each year. Table 14-3 shows the annual cash flow for the lessee under this arrangement. The lessee does not deduct depreciation because the lessor owns the asset. Interest and debt repayment are not separated because both are tax deductible when a legitimate lease exists. If the lease is not written carefully, the tax authorities may treat the arrangement as a conditional sales agreement. This would require a complete recalculation of the tax liability under the assumption that the lessee becomes the owner. To be legitimate, a lease must extend no longer than 30 years, it must provide the lessor a reasonable rate of return, between 6 and 10%, and its price must reflect a reasonable market value if the lessee has the option of purchasing the asset at the end of the lease.

In this example, we have not deducted the lease payment in the third year because payments are made in advance. The third year payment occurs at the end of the second year and is deducted at that point. The cost C of the leased asset is the cost of the first year's lease payment adjusted for taxes, that is, $0.52 \times \$35.30 = \$18.36$, since this is paid before cash inflows are received at time zero. At a cost of capital of 0.10, the gross present value of the after-tax cash flow is $58.64. The net present value is $58.64 − $18.36 = $40.28. In this case, the firm would buy, because the net present value of buying the asset is $3.25 more than leasing it. Note that, merely by shifting the lease payments from the beginning of each year to the end of each year gives a net present value of $44.85 for leasing, slightly more valuable than the purchase net present value.

Other slight changes in the leasing agreement would make it more profitable than the purchase. One variable in which slight changes would make little difference is the interest rate used for both leasing and buying. The lessor would have to charge less than half the 6% interest rate charged for the three-year loan before leasing would be superior to buying.

Table 14-2. Debt Financing Alternative

Year	(1) Gross Flow	(2) Less Depreciation	(3) Less Interest	(4) Equals Income Before Taxes	(5) .52 of (5) Equals Income After Taxes	(6) Less Debt Repayment	(7) Plus Depreciation	(2) + (5) – (6) After Tax and Debt Repayment Cash Flow
1	$70	$50	$6.00	$14.00	$ 7.28	$31.41	$50	$25.87
2	70	33	4.11	32.89	17.10	33.30	33	16.80
3	70	17	2.12	50.88	26.46	35.29	17	8.17

Table 14-3. Lease Financing Alternative

Year	(1) Gross Flow	(2) Lease Payment	(3) = (1) − (2) Before Tax Flow	(4) = 0.52(3) After Tax Flow
1	$70	$35.30	$34.70	$18.04
2	70	35.30	34.70	18.04
3	70	35.30	70.00	36.40[a]

[a](70)(0.52) = $36.40.

Other Factors

When a firm leases or buys assets, it becomes involved in a fixed obligation, and the magnitudes of both are similar. If it buys an asset, it shows the three-year loan in its liabilities. The liability is as large under the lease. However, most firms do not show the lease obligation as a liability on the balance sheet, although footnotes to the operating statements should show the lease payments. Thus, the balance sheet appears to have less debt, which may please creditors and owners. However, if capital markets are even moderately perfect, the ability to disguise debt by leasing should be very limited.

When a firm owns an asset, any gain in disposal value of that asset accrues to the firm. If it leases the asset, the capital gain goes to the lessor. For most equipment, salvage value usually does not result in a capital gain; indeed, obsolescence may result in a capital loss. With land and buildings, however, capital gains are quite possible. To offset this advantage, the lessee and lessor can negotiate lower lease payments for assets that seem likely to result in capital gains. But not all capital gains can be foreseen, and the resale value of an asset may soar because of a large windfall gain. Thus, a firm may prefer to own an asset rather than lease it.

The lease in our example is called a *net lease*. Under a net lease, the lessee pays taxes, maintenance, and other expenses directly associated with the leased asset. The lessor's function is purely financial, and the lease is a financial instrument similar to a bond. The lessor often provides other services as well as the financial service and includes the cost of these services in the lease rental.

Frequently, however, the lessor cannot perform services such as paying property taxes on the leased asset any more efficiently than the lessee. Sometimes the lessor can provide maintenance separate from a lease by entering into a maintenance service contract when buying the asset. Even if the lessor cannot perform the gross lease services more efficiently than the lessee, the lessor may be able to provide the services more cheaply if it has access to cheaper sources of funds. The only way to decide between owning and taking a gross lease is to compare the net present value of an asset purchase with the net present value of a gross lease.

Leasing assets when the lessee can cancel the lease with no side payments may enable the firm to use assets with little risk. If the assets turn out to be unprofitable, the firm can return them to the lessor. In effect, the lessee shifts the asset risk to the lessor. Since free insurance is, to say the least, uncommon, the rentals in leases that can be canceled contain an insurance premium. The lessee must then ask whether the insurance premium is less than if the cost of purchasing the asset and taking the risk on a "self-insurance" basis.

The lessor can assume risks at a lower cost than the lessee under at least two conditions.

First, if many firms use the asset, the lessor may be able to transfer the asset from one firm to another at minimal cost. Computer equipment is an example. One firm may decide to transfer the equipment to some other firm. The transfer can be effected at less cost than if the original lessee had owned the equipment and tried to sell it on the secondhand market, because the lessor has better knowledge of the secondhand market and can offer lease terms to a new user.

Second, even if the leased asset is highly specialized and there is no substantial secondhand market for it, the lessor may be able to absorb the loss of a canceled lease more easily than the user could absorb the loss of an unprofitable asset. The argument here is based purely on insurance principles. Since some cancelable leases will, in fact, be canceled, the lessor will spread the cost of the anticipated losses due to cancellation among all the lease agreements. Unless everyone cancels their leases, the cancellation premium included in the rental payments will most likely be less than the loss the firm would suffer if it owned the asset.

Summary of Leasing

There is no a priori reason for believing leases to be more or less costly than purchases of assets. Each case must be analyzed separately, with all relevant services and costs included in the cash flows. The firm should buy if the net present value of the after-tax cash flow for purchasing assets exceeds the net present value of the after-tax cash flow for leasing. Otherwise, it should lease.

Mergers

To increase its asset portfolio, a firm usually either buys assets from another firm whose business is selling such assets, or it builds them. In addition, a firm can increase its assets by acquiring another firm that already has the desired assets. Such acquisition can take a number of forms. If the acquiring firm simply absorbs the other firm and the identity of the acquired firm is lost in the acquisition, the form is called a *statutory merger*. If both acquiring and acquired firms lose their identities in a new firm, the form is called a *statutory consolidation*. Finally, if the acquired firm retains its identity but control passes to the acquiring firm, the acquired firm becomes a *subsidiary* and the acquiring firm is referred to as the *parent corporation.* A *holding company* is a parent firm whose asset portfolio consists almost completely of the stocks of its subsidiaries. We shall refer to the acquisition of one firm by another, whether by merger, consolidation, or a holding company device, as a merger. Despite the inaccuracy, the usage is common and is justified for the sake of simplicity.

The model for the merger decision is the same as that used for fixed assets. In fact, the alternative to merger is often normal plant and equipment acquisition. If the risks of the alternatives are equal, the firm chooses the one with the higher net present value. Where the risks differ, the firm chooses the alternative that provides the more desirable combination of risk and return. Thus, a firm considering a merger must compare its advantages to those of other means of acquisition.

Reduction in Competition

Merging may be better for the buying firm than the ordinary means of increasing assets. It may reduce competition, if the acquired firm was or could have been a competitor. Acquiring assets by merger is likely to be more profitable and/or less risky than acquiring them by other means.

Mature Acquisition

Another advantage of merging is that the assets of the absorbed firm constitute a going concern. The absorbing firm buys not only the assets, but the experience, administrative organization, and so on, of the old firm. In some cases, these may be liabilities, but they are more likely to be assets, when the absorbing firm is adding to its product mixture, moving into a new market, or developing some other new function instead of just expanding existing operations. In addition, acquiring a going concern may provide the absorbing firm with more accurate estimates of costs and demand than it would have if it started from scratch with new assets. This should work to reduce the variance of estimates, reducing risk.

Still another advantage of merger is that the cost may be lower than for buying new assets, or the income stream may be greater. Several factors make either of these possibilities highly probable.

Taxation. The effects of taxation on the price of a firm or the income stream to be derived from acquiring a firm usually make merger more desirable than the normal means of acquiring assets. The value of the absorbed firm is presumably the present value of its expected future returns. If the owners of the firm choose to remain as owners, they realize these returns. But the returns are subject to normal corporate taxation, and the dividends generated are taxed as ordinary income. However, if the owners sell the firm, they receive the present value of the firm's expected future returns, but taxed as a capital gain, that is, at half the tax rate of normal income.

Taxation favors merger when firms are sustaining losses, providing that the losses are not expected to continue indefinitely. Such a firm may be more valuable to another firm than to the existing owners. Current losses can be carried forward to reduce any taxable profits made within five years after the loss is incurred. When a losing firm merges with a profitable firm, the two firms can present consolidated operating statements for tax purposes, and the losses of one can reduce the tax liability of the other immediately. For example, let's assume a corporate tax rate of 40%. A firm that generates a $1 loss today can reduce its taxable income by the loss providing it earns income within five years of the loss. If it earns profits next year, today's loss will reduce next year's income tax liability by 40% of the loss, so today's loss of $1 saves $0.40 next year. Assume that the firm sustaining the loss expects the 40% rate to apply next year. Nonetheless, the present value of today's loss is less than $0.40, because the firm has to wait a year. At a discount rate of 10%, the present value of $0.40 next year is less than $0.36. But the value of the loss to the profitable firm is the full $0.40, since it can deduct the loss today. The scene for a merger is set when the absorbing firm's maximum price is less than $0.40 per dollar of loss and the absorbed firm's minimum price is $0.36 or more. The further off or the less certain future profits are, the greater the gap between the price that a profit-making firm is willing to pay for the loss-taking firm and the minimum price that the loss-taking firm is willing to accept.

To be a desirable candidate for merger, the loss-taking firm does not even have to show a real prospect of profit. At the right price, the gross present value of the tax reductions resulting from their losses could make the merger profitable to the absorbing firm. If a portion of the losses result from depreciation, the losing firm is an even better buy, for then the actual cash flows resulting from the combination of depreciation with the tax saving are even larger. For example, at a 48% tax rate, a $1000 loss results in a $480 tax saving for the profit-making firm. If $700 of the loss is depreciation, the profit-making firm realizes a $1180 cash inflow from the combination of tax saving and depreciation.

The chance to convert loss to gain is not the only, nor necessarily the major, reason for mergers. A relatively undiversified firm, even if highly profitable, may be willing to be absorbed by a larger, more diversified firm in order to reduce risk. In this instance, the income stream of the smaller firm is more valuable to the larger firm, because the stream is less risky after the merger than before.

Economies of Scale. Other factors that lead small firms to merge with larger ones are economies of scale—perhaps in production, marketing, management, or finance. Because of economies of scale, merging may increase the present value of a small firm.

Means of Exchange. The actual medium of exchange in a merger may be cash, stock, other securities, or some combination of these. In a statutory merger, the absorbing company may exchange its stock for the stock of the absorbed firm. In a statutory consolidation, both firms may exchange their stock for the stock of the new corporation. Even if there is a simple sale of assets, payment for the assets may be in securities. The buying firm may prefer using securities as a medium of exchange because doing so conserves cash. The selling firm may also prefer securities, since this postpones capital gains tax payments. In addition to such payments, the absorbing firm may offer managerial contracts to the officers of the absorbed corporation, particularly when it is absorbing a small, new firm. These contracts provide the absorbing firm continuity of management, and they may be an important factor in convincing the officers of the absorbed corporation to agree to the merger.

Determining Value

Whatever medium of exchange is used, the major problem in merging is determining the value of the absorbed corporation. When securities are exchanged, the problem of valuation extends to the absorbing firm as well. The question is; How many shares of Corporation A stock equal one share of Corporation B stock? Basically, the problem is solved by bargaining, and the results reflect not only the value of the merger to each party, but also the abilities of the bargainers.

Presumably, the market value of each company's stock determines the values relative to each other. However, such is not always the case. If one company's stock is not actively traded, or is, perhaps, held by a closed group so that it is not traded at all, it is quite difficult to determine fair values. Even when the stocks are actively traded, one party can always argue that current market price is temporarily low (or temporarily high, depending on who is arguing). Such arguments cannot be easily disproved, and they may well be true. The mere rumor of an impending merger could raise the price of a firm's stock beyond its real value. Other valuation methods, such as calling in professional appraisers, are not foolproof, since the valuations can and do vary from appraiser to appraiser.

Valuation is particularly important in statutory mergers or consolidations. Not only must the officers of the corporation agree that the valuation is fair, but most of the stockholders of both firms also have to agree. The law usually requires two-thirds of the stockholders of both corporations to agree to a proposed merger or consolidation. Even then, the dissenting stockholders may have to be bought out. The value of their shares can be set by voluntary agreement or by the courts. When valuation is high or dissentors numerous, the cost of purchasing dissenting shares may make the merger infeasible.

The purchase of assets without statutory merger provides the buying firm the chance to buy only the assets it wants. Further, it does not have to absorb the liabilities of the selling firm. This may be quite important if the selling firm got into difficulties because of an inappropriate capital structure. In addition, only the stockholders of the selling firm have to agree to a purchase of assets.

Public Policy

Mergers are affected by public policy if they substantially lessen competition. However, the definition of substantially lessening competition is determined by judicial decision on a case-by-case basis.

Summary of Mergers

Mergers are another way of acquiring assets. Hence, they too should be analyzed by using net present value. Among the advantages of merging are reduced competition, and the acquisition of a "going concern," which may reduce the problems of initiating successful operations. Economies of scale may encourage small firms to merge with other firms.

Taxation is an important factor in some mergers. Selling entitles the owners of the absorbed firm to more favorably taxed capital gains whereas operating the company subjects their dividends and wages to normal tax rates.

If the firm happens to be losing money, the absorption of that loss into the income stream of the absorbing firm results in a tax saving. The actual cash flow may exceed the tax saving alone if depreciation is one of the operating expenses contributing to the loss.

The purchase of another firm may be paid for in cash, stock, other securities, or some combination of these. Of course, valuation is important and often difficult to achieve in a mutually satisfactory way. Even market values of the respective firms' shares may have been distorted if rumors of the proposed merger have been spread.

Finally, for large firms, merger may result in a violation of the anti-trust laws.

Review Questions

14-1 Why would the leasing of a piece of equipment, as opposed to buying, be attractive to a firm that is untaxed or expected to be generating significant losses during the life of the equipment?

14-2 Discuss the shortcomings of a present value (PV) comparison of lease and debt financing.

14-3 The shareholders of ABC Limited are meeting to discuss a potential merger with a corporation which is, for part of its business, a direct competitor. As a director of ABC, what arguments might you bring in support of the merger?

Problems

14-4 The Ace Corporation is considering the acquisition of a $30,000 machine that would have a three-year life with no salvage value. The machine could be financed with a three-year term loan at 12%, repayable at $12,490 per year, or by a lease calling for payments at the start of each year of $12,800. The machine would be depreciated on a straight line basis. The corporation is in the 40% tax bracket and has a cost of capital of 16%.

a. Do a present value analysis of the financing alternatives.

b. Determine an internal rate of return estimate for the leasing alternative that is comparable to the after-tax cost of debt.

14-5 Firm X is studying the possible acquisition of firm Y by way of merger. The following data are available:

Firm	After-tax earnings	Number of common shares outstanding	Price/share
X	$10,000,000	2,000,000	$75
Y	3,000,000	500,000	60

a. If the merger goes through by exchange of common shares where the exchange ratio is set according to the current market prices, what is the new eps for firm X?

b. Firm X wants to be sure that its eps is not diminished by the merger. What maximum exchange ratio is consistent with this requirement?

14-6 The We-Lease-Everything Company requires an 8% after-tax return on its investments. BPI Limited requires a minicomputer for a period of seven years (the estimated useful life of the machine). The scrap value of the machine at the end of seven years is estimated to be $5000, and its current cost is $145,000. What annual (in advance) lease charge should BPI be quoted? The lessor pays taxes at a 50% rate and would depreciate the machine on a straight-line basis over seven years.

Glossary

Asset risk	The risk associated with the asset itself, such as the risk of damage or obsolescence, as opposed to the risk that the lessee fails to make payments.
Capital gain (loss):	An excess of the selling price over the purchase price (or vice versa) for a capital asset as opposed to inventory.

Conditional sale	A sale for which the buyer's credit is secured by the seller's claim on the asset (contingent on default).
Credit-worthiness	The borrower's willingness and ability to repay.
Going concern	An established and functioning (however poorly) firm.
Holding company	A parent firm whose asset portfolio consists almost entirely of the stocks of its subsidiaries.
Intermediary	An institution whose major function is channeling money from individuals or firms with funds to invest to those with a need for the funds. The widespread activities of the intermediary permit a diversification of risk not possible if the investors place their money in the borrowers projects directly.
Lessor/lessee	The lessor owns the asset; the lessee rents it from the lessor.
Legitimate lease	A lease regarded as a lease, and not a conditional sales agreement, by the law, and especially by the tax authorities.
Net lease	A lease under which the lessor's function is purely financial; the lessee pays taxes, maintenance, and any other expenses associated with the asset.
Statutory consolidation	Both the acquiring and acquired firms lose their identities in the newly established firm.
Statutory merger	The acquiring firm absorbs the other, and the identity of the acquired firm is lost in the acquisition.
Subsidiary	An acquired firm that retains its identity but loses control to the acquiring firm (the parent).
Sum of the year's digits depreciation	The ordinal value of the years of life is added and then each year a fraction of the asset's original cost, equivalent to the year (counting in reverse) over the total of years, is taken as depreciation. For example, if the asset has a life of five years, the denominator is $1 + 2 + 3 + 4 + 5 = 15$. The depreciation in each year is the original cost times

$$5/15 \text{ in year } 1$$
$$4/15 \text{ in year } 2$$
$$3/15 \text{ in year } 3$$
$$2/15 \text{ in year } 4$$
$$1/15 \text{ in year } 5$$

Bibliography

ALBERTS, W. W., and J. E. SEGALL (eds.), *The Corporate Merger,* Chicago: University of Chicago Press, 1966.

AUSTIN, DOUGLAS V., "The Financial Management of Tender Offer Takeovers," *Financial Management 3* (Spring 1974), 37–43.

BEECHY, T. H., "Quasi-Debt Analysis of Financial Leases," *Accounting Review 44* (Apr. 1969), 375–381.

BOWER, R. S., F. C. HERRINGER, and J. P. WILLIAMSON, "Lease Evaluation," *Accounting Review 41* (Apr. 1966), 257–265.

BRILOFF, A. J., "The Funny-Money Game," *Financial Analysts Journal* (May-June 1969), 73–79.

COHEN, M. F., "Takeover Bids," *Financial Analysts Journal 26* (Jan.-Feb. 1970), 26–29ff.

GORDON, MYRON J., "A General Solution to the Buy-or-Lease Decision: A Pedagogical Note," *Journal of Finance 29* (March 1974), 245–250.

GORT, MICHAEL, and THOMAS E. HOGARTY, "New Evidence on Mergers," *Journal of Law and Economics 13* (Apr. 1970), 167–184.

HELFERT, E., *Valuation: Concepts and Practice,* Belmont, California: Wadsworth, 1966.

HOGARTY, T. F., "The Profitability of Corporate Merger's *Journal of Business 43* (July 1970), 317–327.

JOHNSON, L. R. E., ELI SHAPIRO, and J. O'MEARA, JR., "Valuation of Closely Held Stock for Federal Tax Purposes: Approach to an Objective Method," *University of Pennsylvania Law Review 100* (Nov. 1951), 166–195.

JOHNSON, ROBERT W., and WILBUR G. LEWELLEN, "Analysis of the Lease-or-Buy Decision," *Journal of Finance 27* (Sept. 1972), 815–823.

KELLY, E. M., *The Profitability of Growth through Mergers,* University Park, Pa: Pennsylvania State University, 1967.

KITCHING, J., "Why Do Mergers Miscarry?" *Harvard Business Review 45* (Nov.-Dec. 1967), 84–101.

LARSON, KERMIT D., and NICHOLAS J. GONEDES, "Business Combinations: An Exchange-Ratio Determination Model," *Accounting Review 44* (Oct. 1969), 720–728.

LEV, BARUCH, and GERSHON MANDELKER, "The Microeconomic Consequences of Corporate Mergers," *Journal of Business 45* (Jan. 1972), 85–104.

LEVY, H., and M. SARNAT, "Diversification, Portfolio Analysis, and the Uneasy Case for Conglomerate Mergers," *Journal of Finance 26* (Sept. 1970), 795–802.

LEWELLEN, W. G., "A Pure Financial Rationale for the Conglomerate Merger," *Journal of Finance 26* (May 1971), 521–537.

LORIE, J. H., and P. HALPERN, "Conglomerates: The Rhetoric and the Evidence," *Journal of Law and Economics 13* (April 1970), 149–166.

MACDOUGAL, GARY E., and FRED V. MALEK, "Master Plan for Merger Negotiations," *Harvard Business Review 48* (Jan.-Feb. 1970), 71–82.

MANNE, H. G., "Mergers and the Market for Corporate Control," *Journal of Political Economy 73* (Apr. 1965), 110–120.

MELICHER, RONALD W., "Financing with Convertible Preferred Stock: Comment," *Journal of Finance 25* (March 1971), 144–147.

MELICHER, RONALD W., and DAVID F. RUSH, "Evidence on the Acquisition-Related Performance of Conglomerate Firms," *Journal of Finance 29* (March 1974), 141–149.

MELICHER, RONALD W., and THOMAS R. HARTER, "Stock Price Movements of Firms Engaging in Large Acquisitions," *Journal of Financial and Quantitative Analysis 7* (March 1972), 1469–1475.

MITCHELL, G. B., "After-Tax Cost of Leasing," *Accounting Review 45* (Apr. 1970), 308–314.

NANTELL, TIMOTHY J., "Equivalence of Lease-versus-Buy Analyses," *Financial Management 2* (Autumn 1973), 61–65.

PETTWAY, R. H., "Interest Rates on Direct Leases and Secured Term Loans," *National Banking Review 3* (June 1966), 533–537.

REINHARDT, UWE E., *Mergers and Consolidations: A Corporate-Finance Approach* Morristown, N.J.: General Learning Press, 1972.

ROENFELDT, RODNEY L., and JEROME S. OSTERYOUNG, "Analysis of Financial Leases," *Financial Management 2* (Spring 1973), 74–87.

SARTORIS, WILLIAM L., and RONDA S. PAUL, "Lease Evaluation—Another Capital Budgeting Decision," *Financial Management 2* (Summer 1973), 46–52.

SCHALL, LAWRENCE D., "The Lease-or-Buy and Asset-Acquisition Decisions," *Journal of Finance 29* (Sept. 1974), 1203–1214.

SHICK, RICHARD A., "The Analysis of Mergers and Acquisitions," *Journal of Finance 27* (May 1972), 495–502.

SEGALL, J., "Merging for Fun and Profit," *Industrial Management Review 9* (Winter 1968), 17–29.

SHAD, J. S. R., "The Financial Realities of Mergers," *Harvard Business Review 47* (Nov.–Dec. 1969), 133–146.

SILBERMAN, H., "A Note on Merger Valuation," *Journal of Finance 23* (June 1968), 528–534.

SMITH, K. V., and J. C. SCHREINER, "A Portfolio Analysis of Conglomerate Diversification," *Journal of Finance 24* (June 1969), 413–428.

SPRECHER, C. RONALD, "A Note on Financing Mergers with Convertible Preferred Stock," *Journal of Finance 26* (June 1971), 683–686.

VANCE, J. O., "Is Your Company a Take-Over Target? *Harvard Business Review 47* (May–June, 1969), 93–98.

WESTON, J. FRED, KEITH V. SMITH, and RONALD E. SHRIEVES, "Conglomerate Performance Using the Capital Asset Pricing Model," *Review of Economics and Statistics* (Nov. 1972), 357–363.

WESTON, J. FRED, and SURENDRA K. MANSINGHKA, "Tests of the Efficiency of Conglomerate Firms," *Journal of Finance 26* (Sept. 1971), 919–936.

WOODS, DONALD H., and THOMAS A. CAVERLY, "Development of a Linear Programming Model for the Analysis of Merger/Acquisition Situations," *Journal of Financial and Quantitative Analysis 4* (Jan. 1970), 627–642.

Some Macrofinancial Issues

IV

In the first two parts of this book, we emphasized the financial problems confronting individuals, private firms, and public agencies. Now we shall consider broader topics centering on financial markets.

Chapter 15 considers the process of financial intermediation. Then, in Chapter 16, we treat the impact of inflation on yields. In that chapter, we analyze the determination of the inflation premium attached to debt and stock yields. Finally, in Chapter 17, we consider two related topics in international finance: How can financial managers protect themselves against exchange rate risk in international trade? Can countries maintain independent monetary policies with the current system of exchange rates?

Financial Intermediation and the Sources of Funds

15

The flow of funds from ultimate savers to those needing funds is quite complex. For example, a firm may use its accounts receivable as collateral for a loan from a commercial finance company. The commercial finance company, in turn, may have received its funds from commercial banks and from foreign short-term investors. The commercial bank may have received its funds partly from deposits by individuals and partly by selling some of its assets to the Federal Reserve Bank. The foreigners, in turn, may have received their U.S. currency from a foreign bank, which in turn received the U.S. currency from a foreign manufacturer who had sold goods to the United States. Though this seems quite complex, the actual flows may be considerably more so.

Sectoral Surpluses and Deficits

It is useful in understanding the flows to divide separate groups or similar institutions into sectors. We can then distinguish sectors that typically supply savings to the economy from sectors that typically have to acquire additional funds to finance their activities. We can define saving as the total of capital consumption allowances and net saving (retained earnings, for example).

Surplus sectors are those whose gross savings exceed their capital expenditures. After having met their real current and capital expenditures, they invest the surplus in financial assets or use it to reduce liabilities. *Deficit* sectors are those whose gross savings are inadequate to finance capital expenditures. They have to finance their deficits externally. For the economy as a whole, savings must equal capital expenditures, so total surpluses must also equal total deficits. However, the process of rotating surplus to deficit sectors is the heart of financial markets. Obviously, financial managers must know where to obtain funds and how to invest excess funds.

The sectoral data represent the net effect of the many portfolio and capital structure decisions made by the individual entities within the sector. Even though the sector may have a net surplus, entities within the sector may have deficits. Of course, the opposite is also true.

Economic Impact of Surpluses and Deficits

Accounting Relationships

Most of you are familiar with the gross national product accounting system, the system that measures the dollar value of output for the economy. In this system, estimates are made of capital expenditures (in GNP terms, net investment plus capital cost allowances) and savings (income less current expenditures). The ways that parts of the economy dispose of their surpluses or finance their deficits picks up where the GNP leaves off.

Reflecting this, the sectors, their surpluses and deficits, and the ways in which they invest surpluses or finance deficits form another part of the national system of accounts, called the *flow of funds,* published by the Board of Governors of the Federal Reserve System. We are not going to examine the details of the flow-of-funds accounting system (though it does not differ that much from flow-of-funds or sources-and-uses accounting for the firm). Nor will we examine specific data, since they would soon be outdated because of the continuing shift in importance of various sources and uses. However, we have already presented the underlying theory in principle. This theory is based on adjusting the balance sheet to maximize value or (in the case of households) maximize utility.

Households

It is useful, however, to be aware of typical surplus and deficit sectors. The household sector usually has a surplus. In effect, this means that their savings exceed their capital spending on consumer durables, housing, and so on. The size of the surplus reflects the complex relationships that determine household income, consumption, and household capital spending. Further, all these must be considered in the context of the overall economy because what households do simultaneously reflects the condition of the economy and helps to create those conditions.

Firms

Firms, on the other hand, are typically deficit sectors, having run down their holdings of financial assets or added to their liabilities to finance their acquisitions of plant, equipment, and inventory. Again, the level of the deficit both reflects and affects the conditions of the overall economy.

Governments

Governments, whether federal, state, or local, may be either surplus or deficit sectors. In accounting for the government sector, we usually count capital expenditures, such as highway construction, as current expenditures. Gross savings are tax receipts less current expenditures. Hence, governments often show negative gross saving. This is the same as saying that the capital spending of governments (treated as current expenditures) exceeds tax collections less true current expenditures of government.

With the existence of built-in cyclical stabilizers (such as unemployment insurance and the progressive income tax), the economy determines whether government operates at a deficit or surplus. However, the economy is also affected by tax cuts or increases in government spending, and these in turn are reflected by the government's surplus or deficit.

Rest of the World

Since the United States trades with other nations, the effects of that trade must be included. The flow-of-funds accounts shows this as the rest of the world. We will discuss the financial impact of this sector in more detail later. For now, we'll just say that the saving of this sector reflects the *balance of trade.*

If the United States has an overall favorable balance of trade (including the so-called invisible trade items such as transportation and other services), the rest of the world shows a deficit in its flow-of-funds accounts. This means that foreigners must either reduce financial assets or increase liabilities owed to the United States in order to finance the deficit.

On the other hand, when the balance of trade is unfavorable for the United States, the rest of the world shows a surplus which permits it to increase its holdings of U.S. financial assets (in part, by providing trade credit to U.S. importers) or reduce foreign liabilities held by U.S. organizations.

As with the other surpluses and deficits, the balance of trade both reflects and affects the state of the U.S. economy. However, since foreign trade accounts for about 5%–7% of GNP, the balance of trade probably reflects U.S. conditions more than it affects them. Nonetheless, the balance also reflects and affects economic conditions abroad. Despite the relative lack of importance of trade in the U.S. economy, for many countries the ability to ship goods to the United States makes the difference between prosperity and recession.

The Impact of Surpluses and Deficits on Yields

After the fact, the accounts have to show that the total of surpluses equals the total of deficits. This is necessary by the logic of accounting. However, planned surpluses and deficits may *not* be equal. Much of the dynamics of yield determination occurs in this area.

If everyone wants to spend heavily on capital goods in relation to savings, planned surpluses may well be less than planned deficits. The result is a shortage of funds at given interest rates. If the money supply is constant, the imbalance causes interest rates and stock yields to rise.

With higher interest rates, the net present values of some planned investments are no longer positive. This reduces capital spending, which in turn reduces deficits relative to surpluses. Some households also avoid the consumer durable market because of higher rates and less ready access to credit. Again, deficits fall relative to surpluses.

If planned spending is reduced because of the higher interest rates, the economic outlook appears less bright. This reflects the reduction in capital spending by firms and consumer spending by households. The decline in economic expectations causes planned spending to fall even more.

The adjustment continues until planned deficits equal planned surpluses. When this occurs, pressure on interest rates ceases, since the supply of funds (measured roughly by total surpluses) equals the demand for funds (measured, again roughly, by the total of deficits).

Financial Intermediation

When individuals or nonfinancial business make loans and investments to other nonfinancial sectors or within their own sector (one business buys stock in another business, for example), they are involved in direct investment. The transaction is directly between two nonfinancial sectors. However, a significant amount of lending and investing is done indirectly. A nonfinancial sector buys a claim on a financial sector, and the financial sector then lends to a nonfinancial sector.

It may even be less direct. For example, a person deposits money in a bank, which is a financial obligation of the bank. The bank then buys sales finance paper, which is the obligation of another financial institution. And, finally, the sales finance company buys a consumer debt obligation, which is a claim on a nonfinancial sector.

As a result of such financial transactions, the total of all financial claims is so large relative to measures of real economic activity that the careless observer worries about the solvency of the entire system. Instead of indicating solvency, the size of financial claims indicates the significance of *intermediation,* which is a measure of the sophistication of the financial system. Underdeveloped countries have little intermediation, their ratio of total financial claims to GNP is low, thus indicating the lack of sophistication in their financial systems.

Why Intermediation?

Financial intermediaries tend to increase the flow of saving and make increased borrowing possible. Since this borrowing mainly finances capital expenditures, the process enhances economic growth.

The flow of saving is increased because financial intermediaries offer a wide range of financial assets for surplus sectors to hold. Without financial intermediaries, the surplus sectors could acquire only the bonds, stocks, and short-term claims offered by other nonfinancial sectors. These are sometimes illiquid and risky. Financial intermediaries offer claims that are sometimes more liquid, often safer, and frequently provide a service to encourage savers. Banks, for example, offer checking and savings accounts to people who might not be interested in investing directly in business loans. Savings banks and savings and loan associations provide savings accounts to those who want safety and liquidity without having to invest directly in mortgages. A life insurance policy is probably more attractive to savers than a mortgage, stock, or bond in which the life insurance company invests. Thus, the claims sold by financial institutions are designed to promote savings. Where the degree of intermediation is extensive, the claims are very different from the assets in which the financial intermediary invests the proceeds from the sale of its obligations.

The degree to which the intermediary can issue claims that are different from the financial assets purchased by the intermediary indicates the success of intermediation. For example, although policyholders may switch from permanent life insurance policies to term policies when interest rates rise, they do not eliminate insurance completely in favor of direct investment. A life insurance policy is obviously different from a portfolio of bonds, mortgages, and stocks. On the other hand, mutual funds provide little distinction between the claims they sell and the assets they buy. As a result, when the public becomes disenchanted with the stock market, they redeem their mutual funds shares.

Intermediaries can more closely structure the nature of their claims to the borrowers' needs than borrowers could if they approached surplus sectors directly, partly because some intermediaries can attract more long-term funds by selling attractive obligations, and partly because intermediaries operate on a large scale and can therefore diversify their asset portfolios to a far greater degree than an individual saver, thus lessening risk. For example, banks can make relatively risky consumer and business loans and still offer highly liquid claims to surplus sectors.

This ability is due to diversification and the economies of scale, but it is also due to two other factors. Institutions such as banks and savings institutions insure their deposit liabilities through agencies of the federal government. Further, in the case of banks, the Federal Reserve is an ultimate source of liquidity if many depositors want to withdraw their deposits all at once. Thus banks have more leeway in making investments than if they had to hold enough cash to cover "runs" by depositors.

Table 15-1. Proportion of Corporate Bonds, Stocks and Nonfarm Residential Mortgages Outstanding Held as Assets by Financial Institutions

	Corporate Bonds Bonds	Corporate Stock	Nonfarm Residential Mortgages
1900	35%	3%	46%
1929	35	2	59
1933	35	1	66
1945	65	4	69
1958	84	9	85
1972	77	24	95

SOURCE: Data for 1900–1958 from Goldsmith, Lipsey, and Mendelson, *Studies in the National Balance Sheet of the United States,* Vol. II, Princeton University Press, 1963, pp. 276, 288, 309, 310, 314, 318. Data for 1972 from *Flow-of-Funds Accounts, 1945–1972,* Board of Governors of the Federal Reserve System, 1973.

To further protect purchasers of financial obligations government regulations usually control the debt/equity ratios and asset investments of intermediaries. In addition, there is Federal Reserve support for commercial banks and deposit insurance for deposits in banks and other thrift institutions.

Without intermediaries, direct borrowers would have to pay higher yields on their obligations in order to attract buyers. Hence, direct borrowers' demands for funds would probably be less than with intermediation.

Measuring Changes in the Rate of Intermediation

As we have already suggested, the importance of financial intermediation should grow with the level of economic development. Raymond Goldsmith has developed long-term measures of the significance of financial intermediation. Table 15-1 demonstrates the long-term growth of financial institutions.

In recent years, shareholdings have increased sharply. Two facts emphasize this increase. Institutions are commonly attributed with accounting for more than half of all trading on the New York Stock Exchange, and they have continually been net purchasers of common stock for the past ten years. For example, although only $57.1 billion[1] of corporate equities were issued between 1968 and 1973, financial institutions purchased $76.4 billion of equities. Most of the difference was accounted for by the sale of stocks by households to institutions.

[1] See *Flow of Funds,* Division of Research and Statistics, Board of Governors of the Federal Reserve System.

Summary

We can divide the economy into sectors of similar economic entities. In the simplest division, we have households, firms, governments, and the rest of the world.

Each of these sectors can have a financial surplus or deficit, depending on whether their gross savings are sufficient to finance their capital expenditures. Households typically have surpluses, and firms usually have deficits. The rotation of surpluses to finance deficit sectors creates financial markets.

Actual surpluses must equal actual deficits. However, planned surpluses may exceed planned deficits. In this event, the demand for funds does not equal the supply, since the surpluses can be viewed as supply and the deficits as the basis for demand. Interest rates change, and this change, in turn, alters the level of planned surpluses and deficits. As a result of the changes in spending and saving plans, income also changes, further affecting the desired levels of surpluses and deficits. Finally, equilibrium is reached when planned surpluses equal planned deficits.

Financial intermediaries are extremely important in the process of rotating surpluses to deficit sectors. They can offer savers greater liquidity or more safety than the saver could have by investing directly, because the intermediary offers economies of scale and diversification that the ultimate borrower cannot achieve. Further, government institutions have been developed to enhance the safety and liquidity of financial instruments. For example, deposit insurance covers the deposits in banks and savings institutions, and the operations of the Federal Reserve maintain the liquidity of the banking system.

The degree of financial intermediation is one measure of the degree of a country's economic development. The data indicate that over the past 70 years, U.S. economic development as measured by the degree of financial intermediation has been substantial. Intermediary holdings of the direct obligations of corporations (bonds and equities) and households (residential mortgages) have grown markedly since 1900, to the point where institutions now hold most of the bonds and residential mortgages outstanding. Their share of equity holdings also appears to be growing rapidly.

Review Questions

15-1 What is the basic difference between the ways that physical goods and financial instruments appear in accounting statements?

15-2 For upcoming periods, planned surpluses often do not equal planned deficits. Describe the process by which the system reaches an equilibrium.

15-3 Under what circumstances are the services of a financial intermediary required? Discuss.

15-4 What is meant by financial "disintermediation"? Under what circumstances would you expect to observe it?

15-5 Why is the process of financial intermediation relevant to the overall level of output achieved by the economy?

15-6 How are portfolio effects relevant to the financial intermediary?

Glossary

Balance of trade	Exports minus imports.
Built-in cyclical stabilizer	A government activity that, to a certain extent, results in a desirable course without an overt policy change. For example, unemployment insurance payments, and thus government expenditures, rise during the trough of the business cycle.
Closed economy	A country or economy that does not trade with other countries or economies.
Deficit	A sector has a deficit if its nonfinancial capital expenditures exceed its gross saving.
Demand for funds	Is measured approximately by the total deficits of deficit sectors.
Direct borrower	A nonfinancial sector that borrows from another nonfinancial sector without the aid of a financial intermediary.
Direct investment	A loan from one nonfinancial sector to another, or the same, nonfinancial sector. Also, an investment by one nonfinancial sector to another.
Equilibrium	A state in which the economy does not tend to change because the planned surpluses equal the planned deficits.
Financial intermediary	An organization whose main activity is channeling the savings of surplus sectors to the financing of the deficit sectors.
Flow of funds	A representation of the composition of the surplus and deficits of the sectors, and the manner in which the surpluses are invested and the deficits are financed.
Gross national product	A measure of the dollar value of the output of the economy. It is the sum of capital expenditures (net investment plus capital cost allowances) and savings (income less current expenditures).

Gross savings	The total of capital consumption allowances and net saving (for example, retained earnings).
Invisible trade item	An export or import that is not a physical good, such as tourism.
Money supply	A measure of the liquidity in the economy, for example, M_1 is defined as currency plus demand deposits, and M_2 as M_1 plus time deposits.
Nonfinancial sector	One whose primary activities deal with real factors. For example, households or business firms are nonfinancial sectors, while banks are financial.
Sectors	Divisions of the economy, such as households or private business firms.
Supply of funds	Is measured approximately by the total surpluses of sectors.
Surplus	A sector has a surplus if its gross saving exceeds its nonfinancial capital expenditures.

Bibliography

BAIN, A. D., "Flow of Funds Analysis in the Formulation of Economic Policy," *Transactions of the Manchester Statistical Society,* Session 1972-3.

———, "Surveys in Applied Economics: The Flow of Funds Analysis," *Economic Journal* (Dec. 1973), 1055-1093.

BENSTON, G. J., and C. W. SMITH, JR., "A Transactions Cost Approach to the Theory of Financial Intermediation," *Papers and Proceedings of the American Finance Association,* 1975.

BOSWORTH, J., and J. S. DUESENBERRY, "A Flow of Funds Model and Its Implications," *Federal Reserve Bank of Boston,* Conference Series No. 10, June 1973.

BOSWORTH, J., "Patterns of Corporate External Financing," *Brookings Papers on Economic Activity 2* (1971), 253-284.

BRAINARD, W., and J. TOBIN, "Pitfalls in Financial Model Building," *American Economic Review 58* (May 1968), 99-122.

COHEN, J., "Copeland's Moneyflows after Twenty-Five Years: A Survey," *Journal of Economic Literature* (March 1972), 1-25.

———, "Integrating the Real and Financial, via the Linkage of Financial Flows," *Journal of Finance 23* (March 1968), 1-27.

COPELAND, M. A., "A Study of Moneyflows in the United States," *National Bureau of Economic Research,* 1952.

———, "Some Illustrative Analytical Uses of Flow of Funds Data," in National Bureau of Economic Research, *Studies in Income and Wealth 26: The Flow of Funds Approach to Social Accounting,* Princeton, N.J.: Princeton University Press, 1962.

DAWSON, J. C., "A Cyclical Model for Post-War United States Financial Markets," *American Economic Review* (Supplement) *48*(May 1958), 145-157.

DORRANCE, G. S., "Financial Accounting: Its Present State and Prospects," *International Monetary Fund Staff Papers 13* (July 1966), 210-227.

_____, "The Role of Financial Accounts," *Review of Income & Wealth 15*(June 1969), 198–228.

_____, "A Framework for the Determination of Central Banking Policy," *International Monetary Fund Staff Papers 17* (July 1970), 192–212.

DUESENBERRY, J. S., and BOSWORTH, J., "Policy Implications of a Flow-of-Funds Model," *Journal of Finance* (May 1974), 17–46.

FREUND, W. C., and E. ZINBARG, "Sources and Uses of Funds Analysis," Chapter 23, in Murray E. Polakoff, et al., *Financial Institutions and Markets,* Boston: Houghton Mifflin, 1970.

FURNESS, E. L., "Income Flows and Financial Asset Holdings," *Oxford Economic Papers,* New Series, *21* (March 1969).

GOLDFIELD, S.M., "An Extension of the Monetary Sector," in J. Duesenberry (ed.), *The Brookings Model: Some Further Results,* New York: Rand McNally, 1969.

GOLDSMITH, R. W., *Financial Intermediaries in the American Economy, Since 1900, National Bureau of Economic Research,* Princeton, N.J.: Princeton University Press, 1958.

_____, *The Flow of Capital Funds in the Postwar Economy,* New York: Columbia University Press, 1965.

GOLDSMITH, R. W., and R. E. LIPSEY, *Studies in the National Balance Sheet of the United States, National Bureau of Economic Research,* Princeton, N.J.: Princeton University Press, 1963.

GURLEY, J. G., and E. S. SHAW, *Money in a Theory of Finance,* Washington, D.C.: Brookings Institution, 1960.

HENDERSHOTT, P. H., "A Flow-of-Funds Model of Interest Rate Determination: Theoretical and Institutional Underpinnings, Krannert School of Industrial Administration Institute Paper No. 259, Oct. 1969.

_____, "A Flow-of-Funds Model: Estimates for the Nonbank Financial Sector," *Journal of Money Credit and Banking 3* (Nov. 1971) 815–832.

HOLLAND, D. M., *Private Pension Funds: Projected Growth,* New York: National Bureau of Economic Research, 1966.

HOMER, S., "Stocks versus Bonds: A Comparison of Supply and Demand Factors," *Institutional Investor* (Aug. 1968), 77–81.

KENDRICK, J., *Economic Accounts and their Uses,* New York: McGraw-Hill, 1972.

KHATKHATE, D. R., "Analytic Basis of the Working of Monetary Policy in Less Developed Countries," *International Monetary Fund Staff Papers 19* (Nov. 1972).

LAFFER, M., and L. RANSOM, "A Formal Model of the Economy," *Journal of Business 14* (July 1971), 247–273.

LINTNER, J., *Finance and Capital Markets,* New York: National Bureau of Economic Research, 1972. In *Economics Research; Retrospect and Prospect,* Finance and Capital Markets, Fiftieth Anniversary Colloquium II (National Bureau of Economic Research, General Series, 96).

MEISELMAN, D., and E. SHAPIRO, *The Measurement of Corporate Sources and Uses of Funds,* New York: National Bureau of Economic Research, 1964.

MEISELMAN, D., Review of R. Goldsmith, "Flow of Capital Funds in the Postwar Economy," *American Economic Review 57* (1967), 72–92.

PEARSON, G., "A Framework for Analysis of the Financial Sector," Harvard Institute of Economic Research, Discussion Paper No. 194, June 1971.

RITTER, L. S. "The Flow of Funds Accounts: A Framework for Financial Analysis,"

New York University Graduate School of Business Administration, *Bulletin of the Institute of Finance 52* (Aug. 1968).

ROE, A. R., "The Case for Flow-of-Funds and National Balance Sheet Accounts," *Economic Journal 83* (June 1973), 27–48.

RUGGLES, N., and R. RUGGLES, *The Design of Economic Accounts,* Economic Research General Series No. 89, New York National Bureau of Economic Research, New York: Columbia University Press, 1970.

SHAPIRO, R., "Financial Intermediaries, Credit Availability and Aggregate Demand," *Journal of Finance 21* (Sept. 1966), 459–478.

SHATTO, G., and L. STERN, "The Portfolio Adjustments by Corporations and the Role of Liquid Financial Assets," *Economic Business Bulletin 22* (Spring/Summer 1970), 77–84.

SILBER, W. L., *Portfolio Behavior of Financial Institutions,* New York: Holt, Rinehart & Winston, 1970.

SMITH, G., *Estimating a General Disequilibrium Model of the Financial Sector,"* unpublished Yale University Ph.D. Dissertation, 1971.

SMITH, P. F., *Economics of Financial Institutions and Markets,* Homewood, Ill.: Irwin, 1971.

SOLDOFSKY, R. M., and R. L. MILLER, "Risk Premium Curves for Different Classes of Long-Term Securities," *Journal of Finance 24* (June 1969), 429–446.

STONE, R., "The Social Accounts from a Consumer's Point of View," *Review of Income & Wealth 12* (March 1966), 17–28.

TICE, H. S., "Report of a Conference on the Proposals for Revision of the United Nations System of National Accounts," *Review of Income & Wealth 13* (March 1967), 36–101.

TINBERGEN, J. *Business Cycles in the United States of America, 1919–1932,* Geneva: League of Nations, 1939.

_____, "A Model for a Flow of Funds Analysis of an Open Country," *Rivista Internazionale de Scienze Economiche e Commerciali 12* (March 1965), 1–25.

TOBIN, J., "A General Equilibrium Approach to Monetary Theory," *Journal of Money, Credit and Banking 1* (Feb. 1969), 17–34.

UNITED NATIONS, Department of Economics and Social Affairs, *A System of National Accounts, Studies in Methods,* Series F, No. 2, New York: United Nations, 1968.

WALLICH, H. G., "Uses of Financial Accounts in Monetary Analysis," *Review of Income & Wealth 15* (Dec. 1969), 321–334.

Inflation and Yields

16

It is often argued that since inflation reduces the purchasing power, or real value of investment returns, yields should reflect inflation, so that

$$i = p + k, \qquad (16\text{-}1)$$

where i is the nominal yield, p is the expected annual rate of inflation, and k is the real yield, that is, the yield without any inflation. For example, if the real yield desired in the absence of inflation were 4% and the expected rate of inflation were 10%, the nominal yield would be 14%.

If we compare the inflation rate to interest rates, the actual interest rate does not fully reflect inflation changes, although there usually is a rough similarity of movements. When inflation is increasing, interest rates rise but not as fast. Similarly, when inflation cools, the decline in interest rates may be almost indiscernible.

The relevant comparison is between interest rates and *expected* rates of inflation. We could treat the expected rate of inflation as some average of past realized rates. This would smooth the inflation curve and result in closer correspondence between interest rates and inflation rate changes. But nominal yields would probably still not equal $p + k$ precisely.

Our purpose in this chapter is to provide a more complete treatment of the effect of inflation on yields. First we shall consider the impact of inflation on fixed return instruments, such as bonds. Next we shall consider the effect inflation has on common stock yields. Finally we shall consider its effect on real asset investment.

Fixed-Return Instruments

The Demand for Debt Instruments

What is the present value or maximum price an investor would pay for a note that pays $1050 in one year, if the interest rate is 5%? We can answer this question by using the following equation.

$$V = S \frac{1}{1 + i}, \qquad\qquad (16\text{-}2)$$

where V is the present value or maximum price, S is the value of the note in one year, and i is the nominal interest rate. Using the data, we find that

$$V = \$1050(0.9523) = \$1000$$

However, if we expect the inflation rate to be 10% over the year, the real value or purchasing power in current prices of the $1050 is

$$S \frac{1}{1 + p} = \text{real value} = \$1050 \, (0.90909) = \$954.55 \qquad (16\text{-}3)$$

Since the investor would be receiving $954.55 of real value for making an investment at $1000, the real yield would be negative. A rational investor would not accept such an investment. We can find a more appropriate value of the investment by including the expected inflation rate in the calculation of the investment's present value.

$$V = S \frac{1}{(1 + k)(1 + p)} \qquad\qquad (16\text{-}4)$$

If 5% is the real rate of return, the investor should pay no more than

$$V = \$1050 \frac{1}{(1.05)(1.1)} = \$1050 \, (0.8658) = \$909.09$$

At this price the nominal yield is

$$\frac{\$1050}{\$909.09} - 1 = 15.5\%$$

We can also get this result from

$$(1 + k)(1 + p) - 1 = (1.05)(1.10) - 1 = 15.5\% \qquad (16\text{-}5)$$

At the beginning of this chapter we defined the nominal rate as the sum of the real rate and inflation. The more correct definition of the nominal rate is the product of the real rate and the expected inflation rate. The difference, however, is only of slight significance, although it becomes more important as the rate of inflation increases.

If the security has several years to mature and the inflation rate is constant, the value of the investment is

$$V = \frac{S_1}{(1 + k)(1 + p)} + \frac{S_2}{(1 + k)^2(1 + p)^2}$$
$$+ \cdots + \frac{S_n}{(1 + k)^n(1 + p)^n} \qquad (16\text{-}6)$$

The nominal yield is still equal to $(1 + k)(1 + p) - 1$. However, this simple computation becomes more complex if the expected inflation rate is not the same for each year. Though more complex, the principle of the relationship is the same.

Reservation Prices

The present value of an investment represents the maximum price that an investor is willing to pay for that investment. We can define this as the investor's reservation price. The yield of the investment acquired at the reservation price is the reservation yield, that is, it is the lowest yield the investor is willing to accept.

In general, the reservation yield is then

$$(1 + k)(1 + p) - 1 = i. \qquad (16\text{-}5)$$

If all investors have the same desired real rate of return and identical inflation expectations, does every investor have the same nominal reservation yield? The answer is Yes if all investors are in every way equal. In the real world, however, investors differ in many ways. Two important exceptions are pension funds and life insurance companies.

Pension Funds. Pension funds do not pay taxes on investment income. Nor do most beneficiaries pay taxes on their contributions to pension funds. Instead, the beneficiaries pay taxes on pension receipts after retirement, when the personal tax rate is usually lower than when they were working.

The pension fund must earn enough so that contributions to the plan plus the investment income are sufficient to provide for the specified level of pension benefits. The level of contributions required to achieve a workable pension program depends on the investment yield assumed. The minimum yield necessary for contributions to generate sufficient income to support the payments is the *actuarial* yield. Since the actuarial yield determines the required level of contributions, the actuarial yield must be set at the time the plan is adopted. After that the actual yield must be at least equal to the actuarial yield. It follows that the actuarial yield will be set in a conservative fashion to assure the viability of the plan. It is unlikely that the actuarial yield will equal available current yields. Hence, when actual yields are 7–10% actuarial yields may be 4–6%.

Pension plan managers invest at the best yield available, subject to the constraints of risk. Since they do not earn even the actuarial yield on idle funds, however, they may be willing to invest even if the nominal yield does not cover fully the expected rate of inflation, as long as they earn at least the actuarial yield.

If pension funds are not always invested at yields that include the expected level of inflation, why do people participate in pension plans? After all, employees are foregoing consumption when they contribute to the pension. If the rate of return is not high enough—it may not even yield a positive *real* return—they would be better off withdrawing from the plan and providing for their own retirement.

One reason that employees may participate is that they may not have the right to withdraw from the plan; this is clearly true for Social Security. Another is that belonging to the plan entitles employees to the benefit of contributions made by employers. Perhaps most important is the tax factor. For example, an employee in the 40% marginal tax bracket has the benefit of only 60% of what would otherwise be a pension contribution. Suppose that the employee wanted a nominal return of at least 15.5%. What is the lowest rate the pension plan could earn that would yield the same investment proceeds as investing 60% of the pension contribution? If the pension fund contribution is $1000, we can find the answer as follows:

$$0.6(0.155)(\$1000) = \$1000x$$

The left-hand term represents the investment proceeds that the employee could earn by withdrawing from the plan and reinvesting the money at 15.5%. The right-hand term is the minimum rate of return required of the pension fund for its earnings to be equivalent to the earnings available to the employee. In this case, the return is 9.3%.

Thus pension funds can accept rates of return that do not fully compensate for inflation effects. Indeed, if inflation is expected to be 10 percent, the 9.3% result implies that a negative real return would nonetheless be acceptable to the employee.

To the extent that pension funds are important in the demand for fixed-return securities, the market rate (which reflects all demands) may not fully reflect the expected rate of inflation. Between 1945 and 1973, private pension plans grew at an annual rate of 25%, more than double the 11% growth rate for all financial institutions. Hence they have had a relatively increasing impact on market demands.

Life Insurance. Life insurance companies may also be able to invest their reserves at rates of return that do not fully reflect expected inflation. To see why let us first consider the source of investment funds for life insurance companies.

Recall our earlier example of the determination of life insurance premiums. We assumed that 10% of a particular age group were expected to die within the next year. If 100,000 people are in the group and each wants a $10,000 policy effective for one year, then (if we ignore administration costs), the death payments equal $100,000,000 for the group. The cost per insured must then equal $100,000,000/100,000 = $1000. Since the probability of dying increases with age, the premium for the following year would be greater than $1000 and would increase for each successive year.

The company could offer a policy covering more than one year with a constant premium throughout by charging more than the premium for a one-year policy in the early years of the policy and investing the excess premium from the early years. Thus the proceeds of investing the excess premium would make up for the smaller premiums in the later years of the policy. The excess premiums represent the reserves of the life insurance company.

For example, assume the following one-year premium per $10,000 policy.

Year	One-Year Premium ($)
1	1000
2	1200
3	1400
4	1600
5	1800

What is the flat premium for a five-year policy? When it sets the premium, the company must estimate the rate of return on the invested excess premium or reserve. This estimated return is an actuarial yield, similar in concept and purpose to the actuarial yield of pension funds. Suppose the yield is 6%. Then the present value of the premiums at 6% is

$$5799.27 = \frac{1000}{1.06} + \frac{1200}{(1.06)^2} + \frac{1400}{(1.06)^3} + \frac{1600}{(1.06)^4} + \frac{1800}{(1.06)^5}$$

To arrive at a constant annual payment that would have the same present value, we have to solve the following equation.

$$\$5799.27 = S \sum_{i=1}^{5} \frac{1}{(1.06)^5} \quad \text{or} \quad \frac{\$5799.27}{\sum_{i=1}^{5} \frac{1}{(1.06)^5}} = S$$

Using Table B in Chapter 2, we get

$$S = \frac{\$5799.27}{4.212} = \$1376.84$$

With this annual charge, the prepayment of premium in years 1 and 2 of $376.84 and $176.84, respectively, and the 6% interest earned on the investment of these reserves would offset the underpayment in the last three years.

With a fixed yield, the insurance company can undertake investments that do not fully reflect the effects of inflation, as long as the yields equal or exceed the actuarial yield. However, if the companies consistently fail to reflect the effects of inflation in the actuarial yield, the number of policyholders who choose long-term policies at flat rates will decline. After all, the policyholders can buy one-year term policies and reinvest the difference between the cost of the one-year and the cost of longer-term policies at interest rates above the actuarial yield. This leaves them better off than they would be by purchasing a longer-term policy.

However, there is an important *caveat*. The purchase of short-term insurance policies and reinvestment of "saved" premiums requires a self-discipline that not all policyholders have. They may be tempted to consume the "saved" premium. As a result, some policyholders choose the less demanding and less rewarding path of buying long-term policies. That is why life insurance companies have long-term reserves that they can invest at yields less than the rate that reflects the full effects of expected inflation.

Market Demand

Figure 16-1 presents the effects of inflation and the impact of institutions, such as pension funds and life insurance companies, that make fixed payments on their obligations. The three demand curves for securities rise to the right because yields are measured on the vertical axis. Remember that yields and prices vary inversely so that a demand curve measuring prices of securities would fall to the right, as is traditional for demand curves.

The curve labeled D is the demand curve that would prevail with no inflation. D_p is the demand curve that fully reflects the inflation effect. D_a is the demand curve that includes the effects of institutions such as pension funds and life insurance companies and reflects only part of the effect of expected inflation. The perpendicular curve labeled S is a supply curve, assumed to be perfectly inelastic for simplicity.

k is the real rate of return determined by the intersection of D with S. $(1 + k)(1 + p) - 1$, the yield that reflects the full effect of inflation, is determined by the intersection of D_p and S. The middle yield i in-

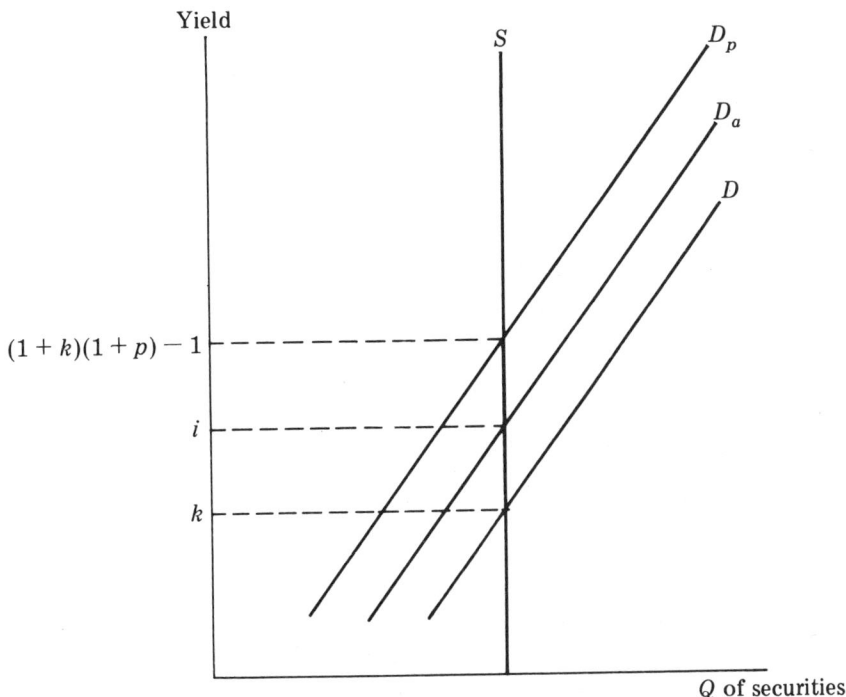

Figure 16-1
Demand for and Supply of Securities with and without Inflation

cludes partial effects of inflation because not all investors demand the inflation premium. It is determined by the intersection of D_a and S.

The Supply of Debt Instruments

Inflation reduces the real burden of debt to borrowers because it reduces the purchasing power of interest and redemption payments. A borrower who can afford to borrow $100,000 for one year at 5% without inflation has a smaller real debt burden if inflation rises 10% per year. The $105,000 interest and redemption payment have a real value of $95,454.55 ($105,000/1.1), in terms of the price level prevailing at the time the loan is made.

At a 5% interest rate, the borrower can borrow $110,000 and have the same real debt burden. This is formulated as follows:

$$\$105,000 = 1.05X/1.1, \quad X = \$110,000$$

where X is the debt that generates a debt burden whose real cost is $105,-000. As a result, borrowers increase the supply of debt instruments if they expect inflation, raising interest rates as the market supply curve shifts to the right as shown in Figure 16-2. In the figure, S is the supply

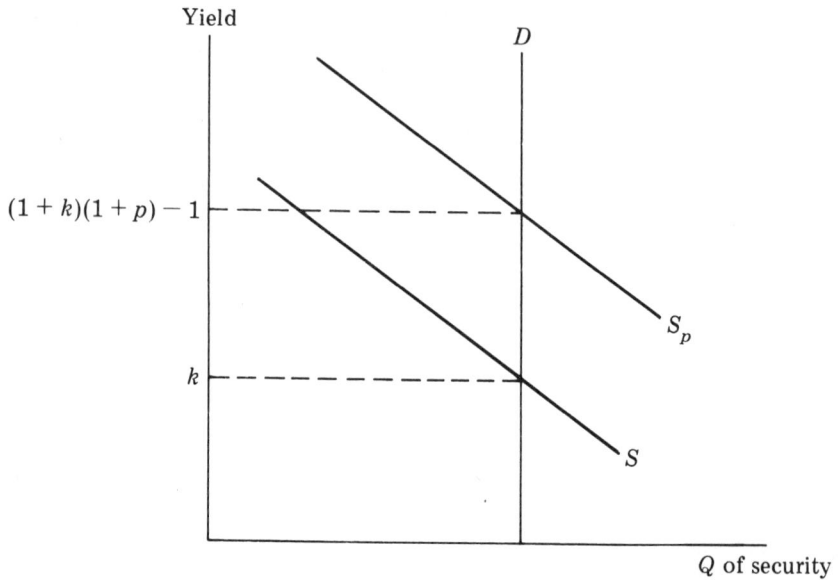

Figure 16-2
Effects of Inflation Expectation on the Supply of Securities by Borrowers

curve with no expected inflation and S_p is the supply curve with expected inflation. For simplicity, the demand curve is shown as perfectly inelastic.

As the supply curve shifts, the nominal rate of interest rises until $i = (1 + k)(1 + p) - 1$. If the real interest rate is 5% and inflation of 10% is anticipated, the supply curve shifts until the nominal rate is 15.5%. At this rate the person who borrows \$100,000 has a debt burden at the end of a year of \$15,500 in interest and \$100,000 in redemption, for a total of \$115,000. The real burden of this is \$115,500/1.1 = \$105,000, which is the same real burden the borrower would have been willing to accept had there been no inflation.

Cash Flow Inelasticity to Inflation

Implicit in the preceding example is the assumption that the cash flows of the assets being financed by the borrowings increase with the rate of inflation. If this assumption is not true and cash flows increase less rapidly than inflation, the borrower may not want \$100,000 if the interest rate moves to 15.5%. Some of the investments that had a positive net present value at a 5% interest rate have a negative net present value when the interest rate is 15.5%. Thus if cash flows are sticky, the shift in the supply curve shift does not reflect the full increase due to inflation, and

Some Macrofinancial Issues

$$i < (1 + k)(1 + p) - 1. \hspace{4cm} (16\text{-}5a)$$

Sticky cash flows may shift supply less than that warranted by the expected rate of inflation. This can happen when very large borrowers whose charges are subject to regulation want to increase their charges. Regulators may move slowly in permitting rate increases even when interest rates have increased. Thus the inflation rate on which the new prices are based are historic rather than expected, which is adverse to the borrower when inflation rates are rising. In addition, political factors may keep increases lower than the rate of inflation.

Sticky cash flows may also affect supply when domestic firms are competing with foreign firms either in the domestic or foreign markets. Firms in countries with a lower rate of inflation can charge less than U.S. firms because the foreign cost structures have smaller increases due to inflation. As a result, U.S. firms cannot increase their cash flows by raising prices by the full amount of the inflation experienced elsewhere.

Still another example involves firms selling to customers on fixed incomes. Retired persons, for example, have incomes that do not increase with inflation. Hence firms selling to them cannot raise prices by the full extent of the inflation.

Market Supply

When we discussed the factors that keep demand for securities from reflecting the full effect of inflation, we cited pension funds and life insurance companies as the two major examples. In the case of supply, the examples are more numerous; regulated companies are important suppliers of debt securities and foreign competition has been becoming more significant in key industries. It seems likely that the factors that keep supply from fully reflecting the effects of expected inflation are more important than the those that affect demand. A reduction in the supply of debt instruments reflects a reduction in capital expenditures and ultimately productivity of the economy.

The range of combined demand and supply effects is shown in Figure 16-3. The upper limit reflects the full effect of inflation; D_p and S_p intersect and the nominal yield equals $(1 + k)(1 + p) - 1$. At the lower limit inflation has no effect at all, and the interest rate is the required real rate of return k. The figure also shows what happens to capital spending when the supply shift is less pronounced than the demand shift for the extreme case in which demand fully reflects inflation (D_p) and supply reflects no inflation effect (S). Although the nominal yield at this intersection is less than $(1 + k)(1 + p) - 1$, borrowing is sharply reduced, reflecting the decreased rate of capital expenditures.

This is of course only a partial equilibrium solution. If the total rate of real capital spending is reduced, both real and nominal GNP are affected. However, inflation can still persist if the source of inflation is exogenous to the economy.

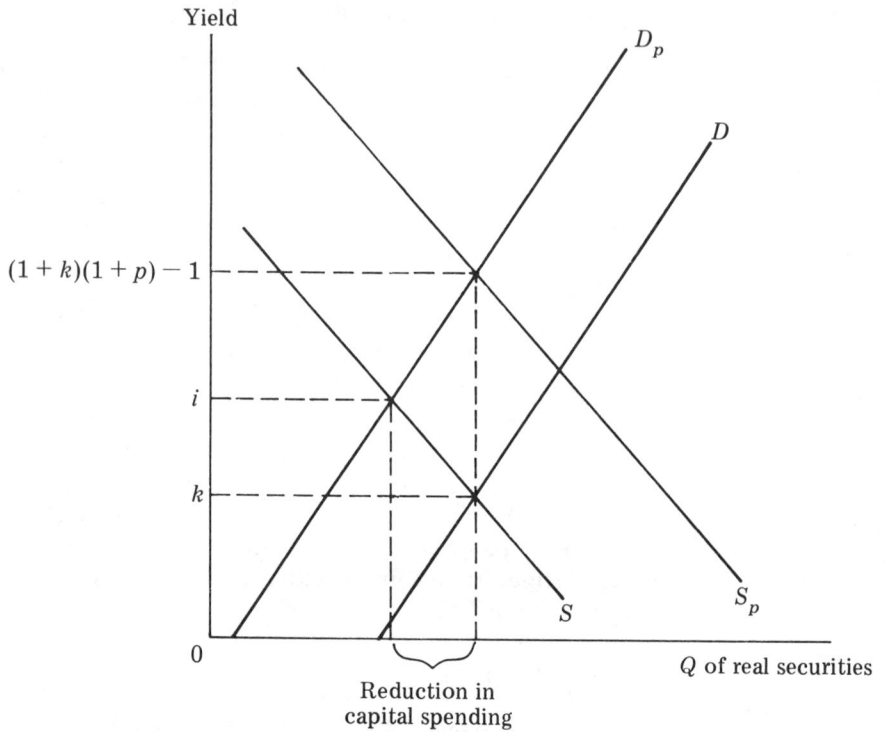

Figure 16-3
Reduction in Capital Spending Caused by Inflation

Variable Return Instruments

The same factors that affect the supply of and demand for fixed-return instruments with inflation apply also to equity shares. Demand for shares shifts upward as investors demand higher yields on equities. The shift is moderated because some investors such as pension funds do not require the full inflation premium on yields. Supply also shifts upward, depending on the extent to which firms can capture the effect of inflation in their cash flows. If cash flows increase by more than the inflation rate, the shift in supply is very sharp. On the other hand, the supply shift is weak if cash flows to the corporations increase at less than the inflation rate.

Yield Effects

If we let K_e be the real rate of return on equities and R_j be the nominal yield, we have

$$R_j = (1 + K_e)(1 + p) - 1 \tag{16-7}$$

when demand and supply curves for equity shares shift to reflect fully the rate of expected inflation.

Underlying any change in nominal yields are shifts in debt markets, particularly in the market for risk-free assets, and shifts in overall stock market yields. Using the formula developed in Chapter 7, we have

$$R_j = R_f + \beta_j(R_m - R_f) \tag{16-8}$$

where R_f is the nominal risk-free rate, R_m is the nominal rate of return on the stock market portfolio, and β is the firm's risk coefficient.

Although the risk coefficient may change with inflation, it is convenient for now to hold it constant. Further let us define K_{rf} as the real risk-free rate and K_{rm} as the real rate of return on the stock market portfolio. If inflation is fully reflected in the shifts of the supply and demand curves for risk-free securities, then

$$R_f = (1 + K_{rf})(1 + p) - 1 \tag{16-9}$$

Further, if the supply and demand curves for the stock market portfolio also shift to reflect the full effect of inflation, then

$$R_m = (1 + K_{rm})(1 + p) - 1 \tag{16-10}$$

Then

$$R_j = (1 + K_{rf})(1 + p) - 1$$
$$+ \beta_j[(1 + K_{rm})(1 + p) - 1 - (1 + K_{rf})(1 + p) - 1] \tag{16-11}$$

Now suppose that $K_{rf} = 0.04$, $K_{rm} = 0.10$, and $\beta = 1.2$. Without inflation, we have

$$K_e = 0.04 + 1.2(0.1 - 0.04) = 0.112$$

With inflation of 10% expected, we have

$$R_j = (1.04)(1.1) - 1 + 1.2[(1.1)(1.1) - 1] - [(1.04)(1.1) - 1]$$
$$= 0.2232$$

Note that this is the same as

$$R_j = (1 + K_e)(1 + p) - 1 = (1.112)(1.1) - 1 = 0.2232$$

However, if either R_f or R_m does not fully reflect inflation, the nominal yield on equity is less than $(1 + K_e)(1 + p) - 1$. Suppose that only 75% of the expected inflation rate is reflected in the supply and demand curves for equity shares. Then if $p = 0.1$ and $K_e = 0.112$,

$$R_j = (1.112)(1 + 0.75(0.1)) - 1 = 19.54\%,$$

less than the yield on the equity share when inflation is fully reflected in the supply and demand curves.

Price Effects

Inflation affects share prices differently than it does fixed-return instruments such as bonds. When inflation increases the required rate of return on fixed-return instruments, the prices of the instruments fall because their interest payments are fixed. However, the price of common shares can increase if firms can increase dividends and earnings in response to inflation. As a result, share prices may not fall even if the required rate of return on equity rises. If dividends rise at the inflation rate, share prices also rise at the inflation rate.

The simplest example is a firm that anticipates no growth and therefore pays out all its earnings as dividends. The dividend stream is constant; for simplicity, assume that it is also perpetual. Hence the value of the dividend stream is the value of a perpetual annuity, that is,

$$V_j = D_j/R_j \qquad\qquad (16\text{-}12)$$

Assume that the dividend is $1 annually and that the required rate of return without any anticipated inflation is 10%. The value of the share is then $1.00/0.1 = $10. If anticipated inflation is 10%, then $R_j = (1 + K_e)(1 + p) - 1$, so R_j is 21%.

The earnings stream rises with expected inflation. Assume that the earnings stream also rises by the inflation rate. The shareholder expects the dividend at the end of the coming year to rise to $1.10. With inflation continuing at 10%, the dividend expected in two years is $1.21, that is,

$$D_2 = D_0(1 + p)^2 \qquad\qquad (16\text{-}13)$$

Thus the expected dividend stream rises in nominal terms at the compounded rate of inflation. However, the first increase in the dividend is not expected for one year and, hence, its present value is less than it would be if the $1.10 were paid immediately. On the other hand, R_j has already risen. As a result, the price of the stock rises gradually as the time for the next dividend increase approaches (and hence its present value increases) and continues rising over the years until the price reaches $11. The price adjustment is not immediate because the price reflects the *present value* of the expected dividends. At $11, the adjustment is complete and the shareholder's price is $11 nominal terms but $10 in real terms. At the end, the dividend is $2.31. Capitalizing this by the inflation adjusted rate of return gives $2.31/0.21 = $11.

The adjustment path is shown in Figure 16-4. Note that even though

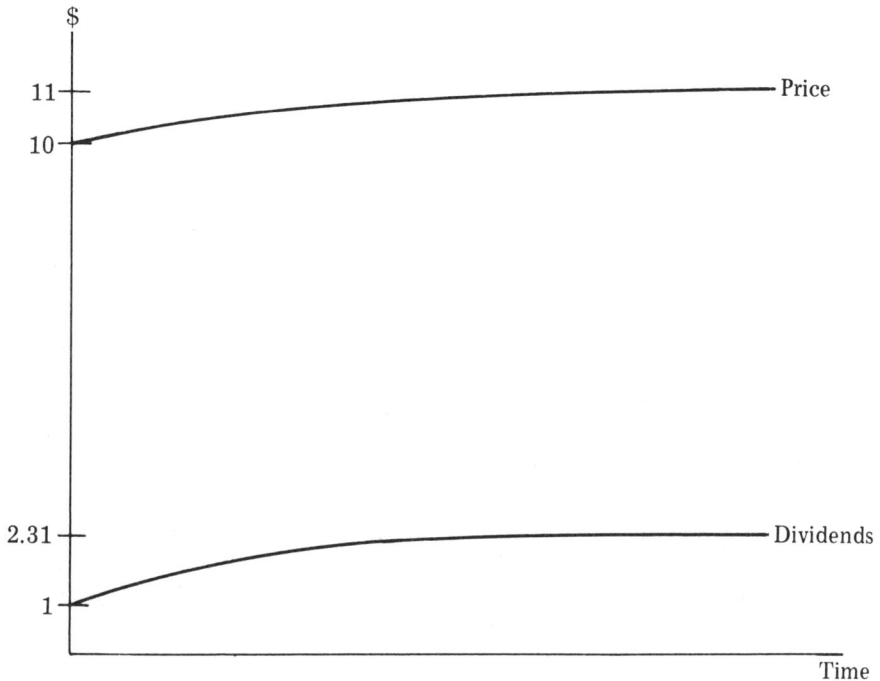

Figure 16-4
Impact of Inflation on Dividends and Stock Prices over Time for a Zero-Growth Company

dividends and prices are changing, the shareholder is earning 21% return at each price shown.

Illusory Effects

If the expected rate of inflation is less than the actual rate, inflation tends to increase the earnings of a firm that has leverage. If it has operating leverage, the fixed charges remain fixed (until the asset must be replaced) and *EBIT* rises. So, too, with financial leverage. Here, fixed interest charges on long-term debt do not change with the inflation rate until the debt has to be refinanced. Thus, until debt is refinanced or assets replaced, unanticipated inflation gives the illusion of increased profitability and encourages a company to retain a larger proportion of earnings.

Other factors may also appear to increase profits during periods of inflation. For example, if the firm uses a FIFO inventory system (first in, first out; that is, the first item brought into inventory is the first one sold), the cost of old inventory items charged against sales to determine profit is lower than the cost for identical but newer inventory units.

Inflation-generated gains such as these occur because inflation has not been accurately foreseen. Had everyone foreseen the inflation rate, sellers of fixed assets would have demanded and received higher profits, lenders would have required and received higher interest rates, and all other suppliers to the firm would have charged more. When inflation is perfectly foreseen, neither the firm nor anyone else benefits in terms of real values. Of course, if economic conditions change from price stability to inflation, there are temporary bookkeeping gains for firms with operating and financial leverage. However, as soon as they must replace the assets or refinance the funds, their advantage disappears. Hence if they anticipate inflation, investors foresee that the advantage is only temporary and are willing to pay less for the advantage than if they think that the earnings rise is permanent.

This explains why common stocks have not been as good "hedges" against inflation as they were once thought to be. Generally their price rises faster than inflation only when the inflation is unforeseen. Once the participants in the economic process correctly anticipate the inflation, the shareholders' windfall gain disappears.

As we pointed out earlier, not all firms can increase earnings and dividends with the expected inflation rate; thus the price of their stock rises less than the inflation rate; indeed, it may decline in nominal terms if the earnings response is very weak. Hence, only stocks whose earnings stream can respond by at least the rate of inflation should be viewed as "hedges" against inflation.

Reductions in the Inflation Rate

Just as unforeseen inflation increases may lead to mistakes in treating nominal changes in earnings as if they were real, unforeseen declines in inflation may also reduce the firm's nominal value of sales and operating and financial leverage work to shrink nominal earnings. A FIFO system of inventory value further shrinks earnings.

As a result, share prices may decline in *real* terms because the expected inflation rate exceeds the actual. When the expected rate of inflation adjusts to the new lower level, price adjustments take place, bringing the nominal values to a point where the real value of the dividends and shares are correctly treated.

Financial Management Decisions. Shareholders are not the only ones who may be wrong in their estimate of expected inflation. With actual inflation rising above expected, firms may view the inflation-generated increases in earnings as if they were real changes. The no-growth firm used in the earlier inflation illustration could view its increased earnings as if they showed real growth. As a result, they would reduce dividends or hold them constant in nominal terms, reinvesting earnings to bolster the sudden growth shown by the firm. If shareholders are making the same incorrect estimate of inflation, this bolsters management's confidence in its decision by pushing share price up well above the path shown in Figure 16-4.

Once inflation expectations are corrected (and this may take considerable time), the share price is revalued correctly. This has been a factor in the sharp slumps and recoveries shown from time to time in stock prices during conditions of inflation. The problem is even more severe when both actual and expected rates of inflation are changing.

Hence, although it is not easy to forecast inflation correctly, substantial gains appear possible for those who can make such forecasts accurately. Unfortunately, the record in this regard is not reassuring. Thus, a desirable condition is an economic environment in which the inflation rate is stabilized so that actual and expected rates coincide and the errors that contribute to stock market volatility are reduced.

Effects of Inflation on Capital Budgets

Discount Rates

The rate at which a firm discounts its cash flow reflects financial market rates. If the firm were to finance itself purely through equity, the appropriate discount rate would be

$$R_j = R_f + \beta_j(R_m - R_f) \qquad (16\text{-}8)$$

The cost of debt is included in the discount rate to the extent to which debt is used. As we pointed out earlier, the use of either coupon yields or yields to maturity can be justified.

Using i as the nominal discount rate and K as the real value, we have

$$i = (1 + K)(1 + p) - 1 \qquad (16\text{-}14)$$

assuming that the effects of inflation are fully reflected in yields. If inflation is not fully reflected in the yields,

$$i = (1 + K)(1 + tp) \qquad (16\text{-}15)$$

where t equals unity when inflation is fully reflected in yields, and less than 1 if inflation is only partially reflected.

Cash Flows

Inflation also affects the cash flows of the firm. However, the flows may expand more rapidly or less than the inflation rate. If m is the proportion of inflation affecting cash flows (where $m \gtrless 1$), and S is the real value of cash flows, then the nominal cash flows are

$$S(1 + mp) \qquad (16\text{-}16)$$

Given accepted accounting procedures, we expect that m is more likely to be less than unity than to exceed unity. For example, depreciation for tax purposes is based on original cost. Thus, the depreciation charges do not reflect inflation, and to the extent that depreciation is significant in cash flows, cash flows do not increase as rapidly as inflation.

Capital Budgeting Equation

The present value of the cash flows can be found as follows:

$$V = S_1 \frac{1 + mp}{(1 + K)(1 + p)} + S_2 \frac{(1 + mp)^2}{[(1 + K)(1 + p)]^2}$$
$$+ \cdots + S_n \frac{(1 + mp)^n}{[(1 + K)(1 + p)]^n} \qquad (16\text{-}17)$$

If the firm can increase cash flows as rapidly as the inflation rate, then $m = 1$ and $(1 + mp) = (1 + p)$. These terms cancel and

$$V = S_1 \frac{1}{1 + K} + S_2 \frac{1}{(1 + K)^2} + \cdots + S_n \frac{1}{(1 + K)^n} \qquad (16\text{-}17a)$$

Such firms only have to recognize that $m = 1$, and they can ignore inflation.

However, other firms have to adjust cash flows by $(1 + mp)$. If m exceeds one, present values of investments increase as a result of inflation, encouraging capital expenditures.

If m is less than one, the effect of inflation is to reduce the present value of cash flows. As a result, capital expenditures are retarded.

The firm does not have to adjust the nominal yield, since market forces adjust nominal rates to include inflation factors. Even if nominal rates do not fully reflect inflation expectations, the discount rate is automatically

$$(1 + K)(1 + tp) - 1 \qquad (16\text{-}14a)$$

So the major change is to adjust cash flows so that they reflect inflation.

If a firm fails to make such adjustments, actual returns are less than expected if

$$(1 + mp) < (1 + tp). \qquad (16\text{-}18)$$

If this is the case, the firm may undertake some investment projects that it would have rejected if they had considered inflation.

Actual returns exceed expected returns if

$$(1 + mp) > (1 + tp), \tag{16-19}$$

and the firm has not adjusted cash flows to reflect inflation. In this case, the firm rejects investments that would have been undertaken with appropriate inflation adjustments.

Summary

Inflation tends to increase nominal yields by some proportion of the expected inflation rate. However, market yields may not fully reflect the rate of expected inflation because some investors, such as pension funds, feel less pressure than ordinary investors to earn the full inflation premium. Further, not all borrowers may be able to pay the full inflation premium, particularly borrowers who have to compete with foreign firms either in domestic or foreign markets, regulated borrowers, and borrowers who serve customers whose incomes do not fully reflect the inflation rate.

Since equity yields are variable, they are often claimed to be good "hedges" against inflation. However, even if earnings do rise, inflation also increases the rates at which equity earnings are capitalized. The result is that unless earnings rise as rapidly as the rate of inflation, the effects of inflation on capitalization rates tend to overpower the effects on earnings, and share prices fall.

Whether earnings can grow more rapidly than the rate of inflation depends on whether the inflation has been foreseen. If it has not, the firm's cheap fixed assets and low-cost funds provide favorable leverage to increase accounting earnings more rapidly than the rate of inflation. Under these circumstances, share prices can rise as the effect of inflation on earnings becomes greater than the effect on capitalization rates. Once the rate of inflation is correctly anticipated, investors realize that the growth in earnings is temporary and will disappear once the firm has to replace assets and refinance debt. As a result, investors are willing to pay only a small inflation premium, if any, for the temporary increase in accounting earnings. The reverse is true when the expected rate of inflation is unrealistically high. The solution is to have an economic environment with a stable rate of inflation. This would work to reduce volatility of stock prices.

Firms should adjust cash flows of proposed capital investments to reflect the extent to which those cash flows respond to the expected rate of inflation. Failure to do so may lead firms either to accept proposals that they should reject, or to reject proposals that they should accept. However, nominal yields do not require adjustment since these already include the effects of inflation. If the firm attempts to adjust both expected cash flows and the capitalization rate to expected inflation rates, it will be guilty of "overkill" with respect to treating inflation.

Review Questions

16-1   If funds can be borrowed at 10% when inflation is running at 12%, what does this imply for loan demand and for the real cost of loans?

16-2   As a pension fund manager, what (if any) differences would there be in your analysis of a bond issue if you are considering holding it in your personal portfolio or in the pension fund?

16-3   It is generally accepted that yields and prices vary inversely. Typically, as the rate of inflation increases, so do yields. In such circumstances can you think of a case where the price of a security might rise along with its yield?

Problems

16-4   An investor is considering purchasing a 5%, $1000 bond with one year to maturity (the interest payment comes at the end of the year). The investor requires a 5% return in real terms. What maximum price should the investor offer for the bond if the consumer price level is expected to be 3% higher at the end of the year?

16-5   A pension fund is required to make unconditional payments of $25,000 per year for 5 years; the first payment is due in 11 years. Annual contributions of $8000 will be made to the fund for the next 10 years. What is the actuarial yield of the pension fund?

16-6   The Data-Set Corporation requires a real return after taxes of 8% on its investments. A project is available that requires an outlay of $14,000 today and will generate annual after-tax cash inflows of $2,000 (in today's dollars) for the next 10 years. Over the next 10 years, the annual rate of inflation is expected to be 6%. The cash inflows from the project will be affected by inflation; it is estimated that they will expand at a rate one-third above the inflation rate. Should the project be undertaken?

16-7   BPI Limited has just decided to undertake a project requiring an outlay of $100,000. The project will be productive for three years, and the after-tax cash flow from the project is expected to be $38,128 (measured in today's dollars) at the end of each of the three years. Inflation is expected to run at 6% per year for the next three years, and the cash flows for the project are expected to expand at 50% of the rate of inflation. What real rate of return is BPI earning on this project?

Glossary

Actuarial yield   The minimum yield necessary for contributions to an insurance plan to generate sufficient income to support the promised payments.

Excess premium	The excess of the straight-life premium over the premium for a one-year term policy.
Nominal cash flows	Stated or monetary cash flows, not adjusted for changes in the price level.
Nominal yield	The yield in monetary terms, not adjusted for changes in the price level.
Real burden	The cost of debt in real terms, i.e., the price effects removed.
Real value/ yield	The yield adjusted for changes in the price level.
Reservation price	The maximum price an investor is willing to pay for an investment, equivalent to the present value of the investment. Also, the minimum the issuer of a security is willing to accept.
Reservation yield	The lowest yield the investor is willing to accept; the yield of the investment is acquired at the reservation price. Also the maximum yield the issue is willing to pay.
Perfectly inelastic	Elasticity equal to zero. Quantity is entirely insensitive to changes in prices.

Bibliography

ANDERSON, L. C., and CARLSON, K. M., "A Monetarist Model for Economic Stabilization," *Federal Reserve Bank of St. Louis,* Apr. 1970.

_____, "The State of the Monetarist Debate," *Federal Reserve Bank of St. Louis,* Sept. 1973.

BIGER, N., "Portfolio Selection and Purchasing Power Risk—Recent Canadian Experience," *Journal of Financial and Quantitative Analysis* (June 1976), 221–230.

_____, "The Assessment of Inflation and Portfolio Selection," *Journal of Finance* 30 (May 1975), 165–194.

BIGER, N., and YEHUDA KAHANE, "Purchasing Power Risk and the Performance of Non-Life Insurance Companies," *Journal of Risk and Insurance 43* (June 1976), 243–256.

BIGER, N., and J. BAESEL, "Inflation and Pension Plan Linkage of Benefits to the Cost of Living Index," *Financial Review of the Eastern Finance Association* (Fall 1976), 206–215.

_____, "The Allocation of Risk: Some Implications of Fixed Versus Index-Linked Mortgages," *Journal of Finance,* forthcoming.

CHEN, A. H. and J. A. BONESS, "Effects of Uncertain Inflation on the Investment and Financing Decisions of a Firm," *Journal of Finance 30* (May 1975), 77–88.

GORDON, M. J. and P. J. HALPERN, "Bond Share Yield Spreads under Uncertain Inflation," *American Economic Review* (Sept. 1976), 385–400.

KERAN, MICHAEL, W., "Expectations, Money and Stock Market," *Federal Reserve Bank of St. Louis,* January 1971.

KLEIN, L. R., and K. BRUNNER, "Commentary on: The State of the Monetarist Debate," *Federal Reserve Bank of St. Louis,* Sept. 1973.

LINTNER, J., "Inflation and Common Stock Prices in a Cyclical Context," 53rd Annual Report, NBER, Sept. 1973.

———, "Inflation and Security Returns," *Journal of Finance* (May 1975), 135–146.

LONG, J. B., JR., "Stock Prices, Inflation and the Term Structure of Interest Rates," Working Paper Series No. 7310, Graduate School of Management, University of Rochester (April 1973).

PATINKIN, D., *Money, Interest and Prices,* 2nd ed., New York: Harper and Row, 1965.

ROLL, R., "Assets, Money and Commodity Prices Inflation under Uncertainty," *Journal of Money, Credit and Banking* (September 1973), 340–351.

SARGEANT, T. J., "Rational Expectations, the Real Rate of Interest and the Natural Rate of Unemployment," *Brookings Papers on Economic Activity 2* (1973), 429–472.

SARNAT, M., "Purchasing Power Risk, Portfolio Analysis and the Case of Index-Linked Bonds," *Journal of Money Credit and Banking* (Sept. 1973), 205–217.

Some Aspects of International Finance

17

Any analysis of finance limited to domestic aspects increasingly runs a serious risk of being inadequate and erroneous. The existence of the multinational enterprise (MNE) with access to capital markets around the world is an indication of the inadequacy of a national approach to finance. Further, even as large a country as the United States can be forced to modify its approach to international finance, as was dramatically shown when President Nixon stopped international redemption of U.S. currency into gold.

The Balance of Trade and the Balance of Payments

The trade balance reflects the purchases and sales of goods and services between the United States and the rest of the world. This constitutes the balance of trade plus remittances made by U.S. residents to foreigners, for example, immigrants sending money to their families in their native countries.

The balance of payments shows the process by which the trade balance is financed. If the balance is favorable to the United States, foreigners have to liquidate their holdings of U.S. financial assets, sell foreign credit obligations to U.S. firms, or reduce their holdings of international reserves. Changes in holdings of international reserves may be viewed simply as a transfer of gold holdings from foreign countries to the United States, transfer of acceptable foreign exchange, or transfer of SDRs (special drawing rights) which are a form of international money held by countries as part of their deposits in the International Monetary Fund. The latter is an international agency whose purpose is to facilitate the financing of international trade deficits and the recycling of funds from nations with trade surpluses to nations with trade deficits.

Recycling Payments

The last function has become a major problem with the increased price of oil. Members of OPEC (an association of oil exporters) have had their trade surpluses increased enormously as a result of the increased price of oil. Almost all nations have been affected. If OPEC reinvests the surpluses they receive from each country, such reinvestments would provide the means for the oil-importing country to finance its oil purchases. For example, suppose an oil-importing country imported $1 million of oil from Venezuela and exported $700,000 of goods and services to Venezuela. The $300,000 deficit would be no problem if Venezuelans were willing to invest that amount in the oil-importing country. The foreign net financial investment would exactly equal the Venezuelan surplus from trade.

If the Venezuelans were not interested in the investment opportunities offered by the oil-importing nation, the deficit would have to be financed by exports to other countries, attracting investment funds from other countries, by selling financial claims on foreigners and using this to pay the Venezuelans, or by reducing holdings of international reserves by transferring ownership of gold or of some acceptable foreign currency to Venezuela.

Recycling becomes a problem when the OPEC countries do not reinvest the surpluses into the oil-deficit countries, and the deficit countries cannot attract more export business or foreign investment. Then, it is just a matter of time until they run out of international reserves. The day of doom can be postponed if the oil-importing country receives loans and grants from countries with surpluses or from the International Monetary Fund. The recycling can be indirect. For example, the International Monetary Fund may interest OPEC countries in buying debt obligations of the IMF. These funds are then loaned to the IMF to finance the unfavorable balance of trade of the oil importer.

The recycling problem illustrates functions of the balance of trade, that is, the changes in financial assets and holdings of U.S. liabilities by foreigners. In this fashion, a developing country that has little to export yet may run a trade deficit financed by financial investment of foreigners in the liabilities of the deficit country. Or, a surplus country can use its surplus profitably instead of holding it in the form of international reserves that do not yield interest. Similarly, mature countries that are running temporary deficits (perhaps because of bad crops or a war) can finance temporary deficits by using their holdings of international reserves or by borrowing from the IMF or other countries.

The variety of financial claims and international institutions makes international finance a very complex subject, but this complexity is required in order to achieve the benefits of international trade without continual disruption of the international economy.

Can the United States Have an Independent Monetary Policy?

To view a problem in international finance with more domestic content, let us attempt to decide whether the U.S. can maintain an independent monetary policy. Like most important questions, this one has supporters on both sides. The current international financial situation may no longer allow U.S. monetary policy to be independent of monetary policies applied elsewhere, although this statement would have seemed ludicrous following the end of World War II.

We can assess the degree of independence that the U.S. monetary policy may have by considering the independence of U.S. interest rates from the interest rates of other countries. If the United States has an independent monetary policy, one would expect U.S. interest rates to move independently of those in other countries. However, many countries have capital restrictions on the convertibility of their currencies into a different country's currency. Fortunately, we need not look far to find a country that has no such restrictions. Canada is not only the United States' largest trading partner, but is also the host country for many U.S. MNEs.

Virtually free capital markets exist between Canada and the United States. Recently, the interest equalization tax was removed. This tax was imposed by the United States on investment in foreign securities and, although new issues of Canadian securities were exempt from its provisions, older issues were affected. Further, the very existence of this tax undoubtedly affected the willingness of U.S. investors to buy Canadian securities. However, barriers no longer exist between Canada and the United States for either short- or long-term capital investment. As a result, Canadian and U.S. interest rates should be identical for the following reasons:

1. If the United States tried to induce economic growth by keeping low interest rates at the same time that Canada is trying to raise interest rates, U.S. funds would flow to Canada in order to take advantage of the higher interest rates available there.

   As a result, there would be a surplus of funds in the Canadian short-term market, which would depress Canadian rates. Canadian rates would continue to fall until U.S. investors who wish to buy Canadian securities no longer have an advantage.

2. If the United States were attempting to take a more restrictive position with respect to monetary growth than Canada, U.S. interest rates would rise above Canadian rates. U.S. investors would have no incentive to invest in Canada, but Canadian investors would find U.S. rates attractive.

The flow of funds from Canada to the United States would affect Canadian rates by decreasing the supply of funds in Canada. As supply decreases, interest rates will rise in Canada and will fall in the United States until the differential between Canadian and U.S. rates is so reduced that Canadian investors no longer find American rates relatively attractive.[1] Hence, the interest rate effect of monetary policy would be blunted.

Are Canadian and U.S. Interest Rates Movements Similar?

If the reasoning we have just presented is valid, one would expect U.S. and Canadian interest rates to move in much the same direction for securities of the same risk. It is difficult to find securities of identical risk in the two countries, if only because Canadian markets in general are less liquid than American markets. However, high-grade commercial paper is often issued by Canadian subsidiaries of American companies and may be treated as the equivalent of commercial paper in the United States. Table 17-1 shows the behavior of U.S. and Canadian 90-day maturity commercial paper on a monthly basis over a sample period.

During this period U.S. commercial paper rates tended to be above Canadian rates, shown by the positive differences. Certainly, there is no perfect relationship between U.S. and Canadian rates. Even the argument that a small difference would be tolerated between the rates, because it is troublesome and costly to move funds internationally, does not seem to hold. In July and August of 1973, the interest rate differentials of 200 and 250 basis points were so large that it was impossible to understand why substantial amounts of Canadian funds did not flow to the United States. On this basis, one is tempted to argue that Canadian and U.S. commercial paper rates have not moved closely enough together to justify the notion that the United States cannot have an independent monetary policy.

However, one should not move too rapidly to that conclusion. Consider Figure 17-1. Although the relationship between the rates in the United States and Canada is not perfect, clearly there is a tendency for the rates of the two countries to move together. This is what underlies the arguments of those who hold that Canadian and U.S. interest rates are not independent.

That the interest rate differentials do not adjust more rapidly is troublesome. After all, modern technology permits the transfer of large amounts of funds from one market to another on the basis of a telephone call. Modern communications make rate differentials immediately obvious to people throughout the world. So, despite the crude positive relationship between U.S. and Canadian rates, the existing evidence hardly proves that the United States cannot maintain some degree of in-

---

[1]Realistically, the Canadian capital market is too thin to permit enough diversion of U.S. funds to affect measurably U.S. interest rates. However, let us ignore this for purposes of illustration and analysis.

Table 17-1. 90-Day Commercial Paper (%) Yields in Canada and the U.S., Jan. 1973–Feb. 1974.

End of	U.S.	Canada	Difference (U.S.–Canada)
January, 1973	6	$5\frac{1}{4}$	$\frac{3}{4}$
February	$6\frac{1}{2}$	$5\frac{1}{8}$	$1\frac{3}{8}$
March	$7\frac{1}{4}$	$5\frac{1}{4}$	2
April	$7\frac{1}{8}$	$6\frac{1}{8}$	1
May	$7\frac{5}{8}$	$6\frac{3}{8}$	$1\frac{1}{4}$
June	$8\frac{3}{8}$	7	$1\frac{3}{8}$
July	$9\frac{5}{8}$	$7\frac{5}{8}$	2
August	11	$8\frac{1}{2}$	$2\frac{1}{2}$
September	$9\frac{3}{4}$	$8\frac{3}{4}$	1
October	$9\frac{1}{8}$	$9\frac{1}{4}$	$-\frac{1}{8}$
November	$9\frac{1}{4}$	$9\frac{1}{4}$	0
December	$9\frac{1}{4}$	$10\frac{1}{4}$	−1
January, 1974	$8\frac{7}{8}$	$9\frac{1}{2}$	$-\frac{5}{8}$
February	$8\frac{3}{4}$	9	$-\frac{1}{4}$

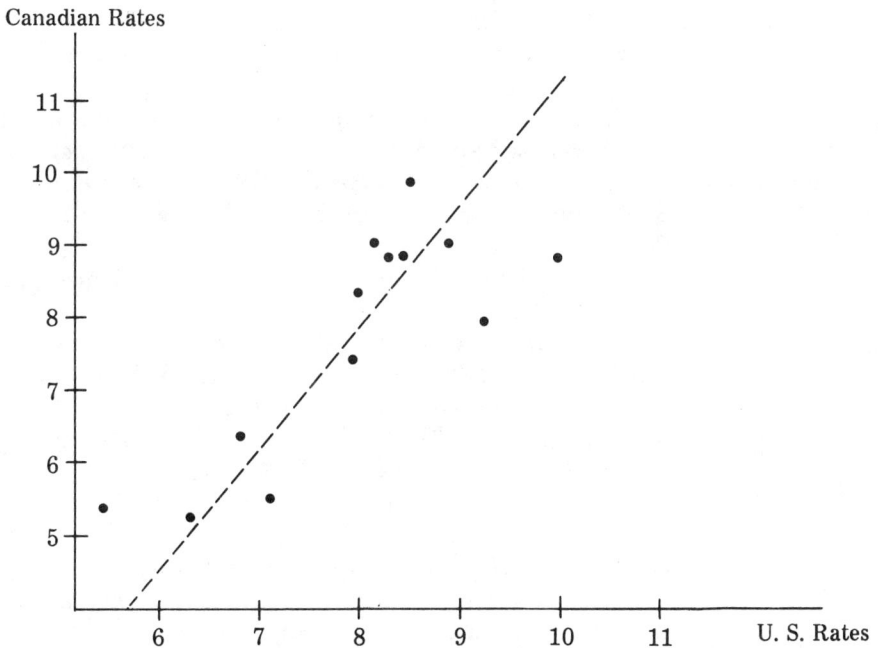

Figure 17-1
Comparison of U.S. Rates and Canadian Short-Term Rates, Jan. 1973–Feb. 1974

dependence in its monetary policy. Further, we have to answer troublesome questions of why large differences can persist between Canadian and U.S. commercial paper rates. To answer this question, we have to analyze the arguments of those who believe that the United States can have an independent monetary policy, even under current world conditions.

Exchange Rate Hedging as an Equilibrium Mechanism

Investors operating internationally face the risk that the international value of the foreign investor's currency may decline between the time the foreign investment is made and the time it matures. The decline in the international value of the investor's currency reduces the net yield on the foreign investment and may result in a negative yield.

To offset this risk, the investor can insure an exchange rate for the time that the foreign investment proceeds have to be converted. However, this is usually done at a cost. The cost of hedging against foreign exchange rate risk is a direct function of the advantage to foreign investment. When foreign interest rates are much higher than domestic rates, the cost of insuring against foreign exchange rate risk tends also to be quite high. When the insurance or hedging cost is very high, it is not profitable to invest in a foreign country. Hence, foreign interest rates can be substantially above domestic interest rates, and the differential remains as long as the cost of insuring against the exchange rate risk is also high. To see this more clearly, let us consider some specific numeric examples and then relate the analysis to the realities of Canadian and U.S. interest rates.

Suppose that a corporation with excess cash, or a financial institution, purchased 90-day Canadian commercial paper selling at a 9% annual interest rate. The mechanical steps in the investment are moderately complicated. The corporation has to convert its U.S. dollars into Canadian dollars to make the investment. The currency conversion is usually handled by a bank, or an investment dealer working in cooperation with a bank.

When the investment matures, the proceeds are in Canadian dollars. The U.S. investor faces the risk that the exchange rate may be different when the investment matures. If the value of the U.S. dollar has risen, the Canadian dollar proceeds buy fewer U.S. dollars than they would have bought at the earlier exchange rate. For example, if the exchange rate was at par when the investment was made, $100 U.S. convert into $100 Canadian. Invested for 90 days at a 9% annual interest rate, the Canadian proceeds are approximately $102.18. However, if the value of the U.S. dollar rose during the period, so that a Canadian dollar is worth only 99¢ in U.S. dollars, the U.S. proceeds are

$$\text{U.S. } \$0.99 \times \text{C\$102.18} = \text{U.S. } \$101.16$$

The actual net interest rate earned by the U.S. investor turns out to be approximately 4.7% on an annual basis, rather than the 9% the investor had hoped for. Hence, if U.S. interest rates were 4.7% or more, the investor would have been at least as well off staying in the United States. If, for example, the U.S. interest rate was 8% when the investment was made, the investor would receive $101.94 as the proceeds from investing $100 in the U.S. investment, that is, $(1.08)^{1/4} \$100 = \$101.94$.

We have to recognize that the value of the U.S. dollar may have declined; in that case, the U.S. investor would have made a gain in coming back to U.S. dollars. However, the future direction of the value of the dollar is never clear. An investor gambling that the value of the U.S. dollar will decline is involved in speculation, an activity quite different from investment. Many investors, particularly those involved in fixed-return instruments, do not like speculating.

It is possible to protect against exchange rate risk. In the previous example, the U.S. investor would have to arrange for future delivery of U.S. dollars at a set price. The arrangement would be made at the same time that the Canadian dollars were purchased in order to make the investment. Thus, the investor would know exactly what the net or covered yield would be before making the investment. The contract for future delivery of U.S. dollars is called a *futures contract.* These operate to remove exchange rate risk by replacing an unknown and uncertain cost with a certain cost.

The exchange rate implied in the futures contract is not necessarily the same as the current or spot rate. The future rate is determined by supply and demand for future deliveries of currency. If many U.S. investors wish to buy contracts for future delivery of U.S. dollars, as would be the case if Canadian interest rates were substantially above U.S. interest rates, the future rate of the Canadian dollar would decline, which is the same as saying that the future rate or value of the U.S. dollar would rise. Hence, the investor would be receiving fewer U.S. dollars when it came time to convert the Canadian proceeds back into U.S. dollars. The investor will make the investment if the net yield from investing in the hedged foreign investments exceeds the yield available on domestic investments.

The supply and demand for future delivery of foreign exchange reflect a variety of things.

1. In international trade, buyers of goods for future payments in foreign currencies and sellers who agree to receive such payments in foreign currencies protect themselves or *hedge* against exchange rate risk.
2. Investors wish to protect against foreign exchange rate risk, as in our example.
3. Speculators, who believe one currency is likely to rise in value against another, buy contracts for future receipt of a currency expected to rise in value. They sell contracts for future delivery of what they expect to be a weak currency. Thus, when the United States dollar was

weakening in 1970, speculators added to the weakness by selling contracts to deliver U.S. dollars spot (immediately), and bought contracts for future receipts of German marks, which were expected to rise in value.

All these forces determine the future rate. However, our major interest is not determining the future rate, but indicating how, given a future rate, the covered yield of an investor considering foreign investment is affected.

To focus more clearly on the investor's decision, let us examine the following decision-making model.

The investor moves funds to a foreign country if he expects his yield, covered for exchange rate risk, to be equal to or greater than the yield on investing at home.

The proceeds on Canadian investment are

$$C\$(1 + i_C)^{1/4}, \tag{17-1}$$

where C\$ are the result of converting U.S. dollars to Canadian dollars and i_C is the annual rate on 90-day paper in Canada.

$$C\$ = U.S.\$/r_s \tag{17-2}$$

where U.S.\$ is the amount to be invested as U.S. currency, and r_s is the spot or current value of the Canadian dollar in terms of the U.S. dollar. Hence, the proceeds from the investment, in terms of Canadian dollars, are

$$\frac{U.S.\$}{r_s}(1 + i_C)^{1/4} \tag{17-3}$$

If the investor hedges against exchange rate risk by buying a futures contract for receipt of U.S. dollars in 90 days, the U.S. dollar proceeds from the investment are

$$\left[\frac{U.S.\$}{r_s}(1 + i_C)^{1/4}\right]/r_f \tag{17-4}$$

where r_f is the future value of the Canadian dollar in U.S. dollars. This becomes

$$U.S.\$ (r_f/r_s)(1 + i_C)^{1/4} \tag{17-4a}$$

The proceeds from a U.S. 90-day investment are

$$U.S.\$(1 + i_{U.S.})^{1/4} \tag{17-5}$$

where $i_{\text{U.S.}}$ is the annual yield on 90-day commercial paper in the United States. Hence, to move to Canada

$$\text{U.S.\$ } (r_f/r_s)(1 + i_C)^{1/4} \geqq \text{U.S.\$}(1 + i_{\text{U.S.}})^{1/4} \qquad (17\text{-}6)$$

or dividing both sides by U.S.\$ and by $(1 + i_C)^{1/4}$, we get

$$\frac{r_f}{r_s} \geqq \left(\frac{1 + i_{\text{U.S.}}}{1 + i_C}\right)^{1/4} \qquad (17\text{-}6a)$$

Assume a 9% Canadian rate, $r_s = 1.00$, and $r_f = 0.99$. Then funds move to Canada if

$$\frac{0.99}{1.00} \geqq \left(\frac{1 + i_{\text{U.S.}}}{1.09}\right)^{1/4}$$

Solving for $i_{\text{U.S.}}$, we find that the U.S. rate needed to hold the money in the United States is 4.7%. If the actual U.S. rate is higher, no funds move to Canada.

It is common to talk about the difference between the forward rate of exchange and the spot rate of exchange $(r_f - r_s)$ as the *forward rate spread*. Clearly, this reflects supply and demand in both spot and futures markets, underlying which are a host of trade, investment, and speculative factors. Nonetheless, if the U.S. rate in the previous example were less than 4.7%, U.S. investors would wish to invest in Canada. This would increase the demand for spot Canadian dollars. It would also increase the supply of future Canadian dollars (and the demand for future U.S. dollars). As a result, the forward rate spread would shrink, that is, the future value of the Canadian dollar would decline relative to its spot value. Indeed, the forward rate spread could become negative. The forward rate spread adjusts until the short-term capital flows cease. In other words, changes in forward rate spread would allow a differential to exist between Canadian and U.S. interest rates.

To see this more clearly, let us return to the previous example. Suppose that the U.S. interest rate is 1%. Allow the spot rate to be at par. Then the forward rate becomes

$$r_f \geqq \frac{(1 + i_{\text{U.S.}})^{1/4}}{1 + i_C} r_s$$

or

$$r_f \geqq \frac{(1.01)^{1/4}}{1.09} (1.00) = 0.981$$

and the forward spread is $0.981 - 1 = -0.019$. Thus, the forward spread is the equilibrium mechanism that permits the countries to have independent interest rates and, hence, independent monetary policies.

Do the facts support the notion that the forward rate spread operates as an equilibrium mechanism? One can test this in a simple fashion by contrasting the differences between interest rates in the United States and Canada with the forward rate spread. The larger the difference between Canadian and U.S. 90-day commercial paper rates, the more

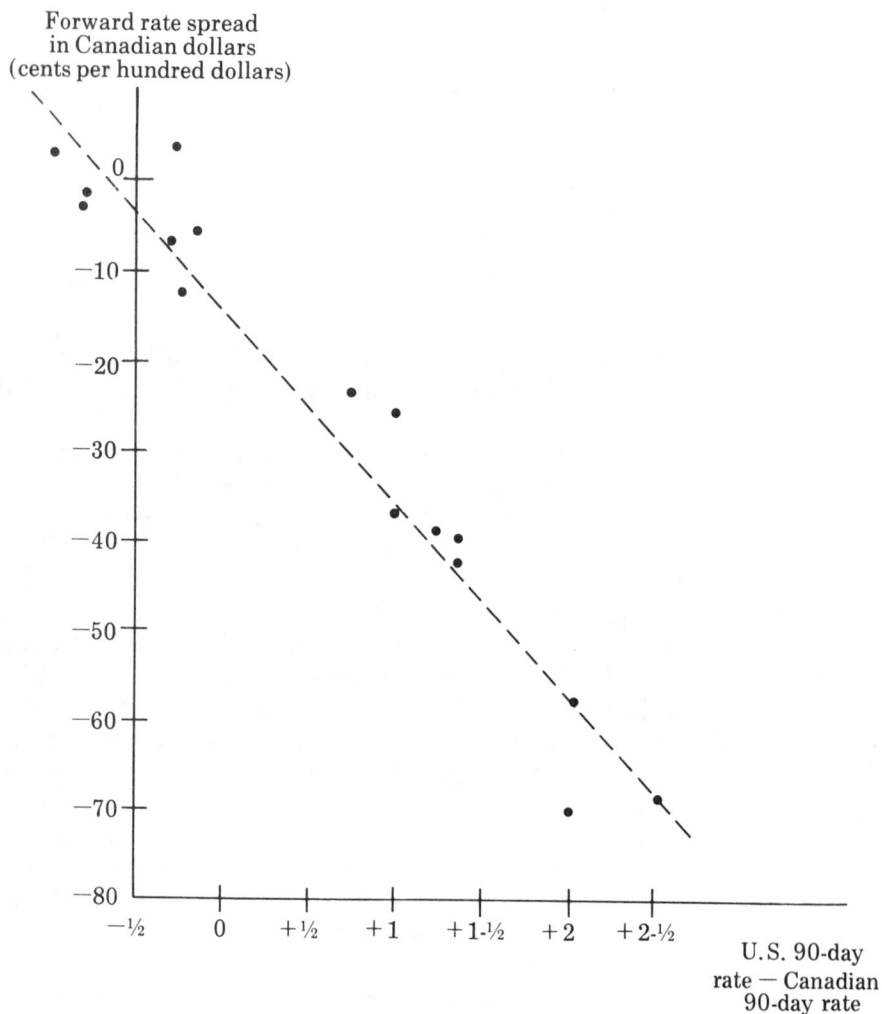

The negative slope in the graph shows that as U.S. short-term interest rates rise above Canadian, the future demand for Canadian dollars (= future supply of U.S. dollars) will rise, reducing the future value of the U.S. dollar in terms of the Canadian dollar. As a result, the forward rate spread will be negative. The larger the interest rate difference, the larger the forward exchange rate spread as shown by the graph.

Figure 17-2
Forward Rate Spreads as a Function of Interest Rate Differentials: Monthly Data from End of Each Month Jan. 1973–Feb. 1974

money should flow to Canada. In turn, this should result in a declining or negative forward rate spread.

Figure 17-2 compares the differentials in the end-of-month interest rates with the forward rate spread. Although there is a scatter, clearly the slope of the relationship is negative, and this is what we would expect if the forward rate spread operates as an equilibrium mechanism. The larger the interest rate difference, the larger the forward exchange rate spread. In this case, it is a negative spread in Canadian dollars, or a positive spread in U.S. dollars, because U.S. rates tended to exceed Canadian rates.

Although the relationship between the foreign exchange rate spread and the interest rate differential has the proper slope for the forward exchange rate spread to be working as an equilibrium mechanism, there is a positive relationship between changes in Canadian and in United States interest rates. Hence, it is clear that while the forward exchange rate spread does adjust to interest rate differentials, it is not sufficient to stop short-term capital flows. Thus, we can see a correspondence between Canadian and U.S. short-term interest rates.

Policies Creating Interest Rate and Monetary Policy Dependence

There were some special reasons for the failure of the forward rate spread to stop short-term capital flows during the period we have been considering. For the system to work, there must be variations in the spot rate. Although Canada was ostensibly on a flexible exchange rate during this period, the range of variation in the spot value of the Canadian dollar had been very narrow. For ten months of 1973, the variations were one-half percent or less. If one is sure that the value of the Canadian dollar is not going to depreciate, there is no reason for a Canadian investor to fear exchange rate risk. Similarly, if the value of the Canadian dollar is not to depreciate because of government policy, there is no reason for an American investor to hedge against investments in Canada.

During most of the period under consideration, and particularly during the period of the largest U.S./Canadian interest rate differentials, the spot value of the Canadian dollar tended to rise in terms of the U.S. dollar. Hence, investors were willing to gamble on the exchange rate. If the movement reversed, they could always hedge later, so that they would earn the full interest rate differential for at least part of their holding period.

The Role of Multinational Enterprise

Multinational enterprises (MNEs) can frustrate the results of money market hedging in at least two ways. One way is fairly trivial and the other is fundamental to both an understanding of capital market forces and of the operations of multinational enterprises.

On a trivial basis, MNEs can take advantage of interest rate differentials between countries by speeding or delaying payments. Thus, if Canadian rates are higher than U.S. rates, a U.S. MNE with a subsidiary operation in Canada can speed an advance to its subsidiary (the ultimate purpose of which is to add to the Canadian subsidiary's fixed assets) so that the funds can be invested at the favorable Canadian rate until the subsidiary actually has to spend the advance. If U.S. rates are higher than Canadian rates, the MNE could have the subsidiary make a profit remittance or return advances earlier than usual. In this case, the subsidiary could actually make a short-term loan in Canada to finance the early payment to the parent MNE in the United States.

Thus, the MNE can ignore exchange rate risk to some extent and take advantage of interest rate differentials even when the forward rate spread exactly offsets the interest rate advantage, if we assume that the transaction is hedged in the traditional manner. Of course, funds can flow from the United States to any country in this way, even to countries that restrict currency conversion. In such cases, the fund movements into the foreign country represent payments that would have been made in any event. With a favorable interest rate spread, the payment is simply made to the subsidiary earlier than otherwise. The extra profits are no more difficult to reconvert into U.S. dollars than the normal profits earned by the subsidiary.

Eurodollars

Indeed, the dollar balances made available to subsidiaries, as well as other payments made to foreigners, form the basis for the Eurodollar market. These represent dollar payments made abroad that have not been sent back to the United States for conversion. Instead, the recipient receives local currency by lending the dollars directly or, more usually, indirectly through a financial intermediary to someone who needs U.S. dollars to make payments to others who will accept U.S. dollars as payments for goods and services.

The latter recipients may not be U.S. residents but others for whom U.S. dollars are viewed as an international reserve currency. These recipients may deposit the U.S. dollars in a foreign financial institution (or the foreign branch of a U.S. bank), receiving interest on the deposit. The funds may then be reloaned, resulting in the Eurodollar interest rate, which can and does deviate from domestic dollar interest rates.

The internationally dominant role of the U.S. dollar has shrunk in recent years. Foreigners now perfer German marks or Swiss francs on the grounds that these are more stable than dollars. Eurodollars have been gradually repatriated so that the Eurodollar market is considerably smaller today than it was in the late 1960s. Of course, should the U.S. dollar sometime in the future be viewed as more stable than other currencies, the Eurodollar market would expand.

Asset Hedging

Even with large interest rate differentials, MNEs can take only limited advantage by making or receiving advance payments. However, they have devised techniques for avoiding foreign exchange risk that are far more effective than traditional hedging.

Consider the problem caused by foreign exchange risk for a large MNE. It has assets all over the world, and these can rise or fall in value not only because of normal business fluctuations, but also because of fluctuations in currency values. Thus, the assets open to foreign exchange rate risk are far larger than the amount that they would move to take advantage of money market rate differentials.

Further, these assets are to a large extent long-term assets, including plant, equipment, and real estate. For such assets, traditional hedging by purchasing forward currency contracts is not available. To receive U.S. dollars ten years hence, someone has to be willing to deliver dollars in ten years. In practice, most contracts are written for one year or less. There is a very thin market in contracts extending beyond one year up to five years. However, the nature of thin markets is that any increase in demand or supply causes disproportionate fluctuations in price.

Without some sort of protection against foreign exchange risk, MNE's would be extremely unsafe operations. However, they have two methods of hedging.

The first applies to MNEs that operate in several countries with approximately equal investments in each country. When the value of one currency falls, the value of other currencies, by definition, rise. So the MNE can offset losses on its assets in the country with a declining international value by gains made in the appreciation of assets in other countries. This reflects a form of diversification. However, the diversification is effective only if the MNE has assets in countries whose currencies appreciate when the currencies of others depreciate. And they must be holding similar quantities of assets in the various countries.

The second method, if feasible, is more effective. This method involves not only buying assets in the foreign country, but financing the assets in the same country's currency. Hence, the value of both the MNE's assets and its liabilities reflect shifts in the exchange rate. If the foreign currency falls in value, the value of the MNE's assets in that country also falls. However, so do the value of the liabilities as measured in U.S. dollars. If there is perfect matching of assets and liabilities, the MNE is completely hedged by its foreign balance sheet.

Unfortunately, this is not completely practical. Obviously, if the MNE is to own the subsidiary, it must invest some of its own capital. Further, capital in less developed countries may be scarce and far too expensive. Hence, matching assets and liabilities provides only a partial solution to the problem of foreign exchange rate risk.

In practice, MNEs use all these methods. They use forward contracts to cover relatively short-term commitments. They attempt to diversify among countries. They also attempt to forecast short-term exchange rate movements and appraise the policies of the different countries with respect to longer-term prospects. They then attempt to shift their assets from countries with weak currencies to countries with strong currencies. One complication is that assets in strong currency countries may be sufficiently less profitable than those in weak currency countries to offset the exchange rate risk. Indeed, under equilibrium conditions, one would expect the probable losses due to exchange rates to be offset by the probable superiority in return—another example of compensating investors for taking risk.

In any event, the MNE does have a variety of ways of moving funds to take advantage of international interest rate differentials so that their exposure to exchange rate risk is very low even though they do not use traditional hedging techniques. Since they can do this, they can work to frustrate monetary policy by partially or completely offsetting the attempts of a given country to use monetary policy to adjust its interest rates so that they are appropriate for its goals. Instead, interest rates tend to be similar (for similar risk), and this similarity is at least partly due to the operations of the MNEs.

Summary

Balance of payments reflects the means by which international trade balances are financed. The payments consist of the purchase and sale of financial instruments that are normally used to finance deficits. However, foreign exchange reserves, which include foreign currencies, gold, and SDRs, are also involved. Balance of payments problems arise because nations with a trade surplus do not recycle their surpluses into the international economy so that the deficit nations can finance their deficits. Even when the surplus nations do put their surpluses into international circulation, a particular deficit country may not be the beneficiary. The rise in oil prices has aggravated this inadequate redistribution of surpluses and deficits among the nations.

International finance can also undermine the goals of a nation's monetary policies. If a nation tightens money supply, interest rates usually rise. Then investors from other nations may take advantage of the better yields, increasing the supply of funds and thwarting the monetary policy of the country. This tendency is at least partially offset by the need of international investors to protect themselves against the risk that the value of the currency in which they are investing may decline during the period of investment. They can buy future contracts to deliver currency to protect against exchange rate fluctuations. However, as the demand for these rises, so does their price. The price, a form of insurance, rises until the extra cost offsets the interest rate advantage.

However, the existence of multinational enterprises can thwart the forward rate spread's equilibrating force. MNEs can speed advances to subsidiaries in countries with high interest rates and speed payments from countries with low interest rates. Since these payments would have been made in any event, the risk of a decline in currency value does not exist.

MNEs can also hedge their longer-term assets in foreign countries by diversifying over countries so that losses in one country are offset by gains in another. Further, they can hedge balance sheets by financing foreign assets in the host country's currency. Hence, a decline in the exchange rate leads to losses in the value of the foreign assets that are at least partially offset by gains due to the reduction in the U.S. value of foreign currency liabilities.

These devices have made it increasingly difficult for nations to establish independent monetary policies. There has been a growing tendency for interest rates to move more closely together than was the case before the rapid growth of MNEs in recent years.

Review Questions

17-1 The United States usually runs a trade surplus with respect to Canada. What, if any, are the implications for Canadian monetary policy of such a trade position?

17-2 The financial vice-president of New York Metals Ltd., who is considering commercial paper as a potential investment for the company's surplus cash, notices that the rates on the paper of Canadian firms are running roughly 1% above those for United States firms. Is this sufficient justification for purchasing Canadian commercial paper?

17-3 Why are the recent oil price increases potentially disruptive to the international economy as well as to national economies?

Problems

17-4 A U.S. investor with funds to invest for 90 days is considering two investment alternatives: a U.S. Treasury Bill with an annual yield to maturity (90-days) of 8%, or a Canadian government treasury bill with an annual yield to maturity (90-days) of 8.86%. The price of the Canadian treasury bill is C$979, and the spot exchange rate is U.S. $1.02.

    a. What is the U.S. dollar price of the Canadian treasury bill?

    b. Assuming that the investor decides to purchase the Canadian treasury bill, what are the U.S. dollar proceeds of the investment at maturity if the spot exchange rate remains constant at $1.02 U.S.? What is the annual yield on his investment?

    c. Recalculate the U.S. dollar proceeds at maturity and the annual yield on the investment assuming the spot exchange rate 90-days hence falls to U.S. $1.01.

17-5 As a risk-averse investor, you decide to weigh the alternatives of purchasing the Canadian treasury bill described in Problem 17-4 on a "fully hedged" basis against purchasing the U.S. treasury bill. The spot exchange rate is still U.S. $1.02, and the 90-day forward exchange rate is U.S. $1.00.

a. What is the covered yield on this investment?

b. Suppose that the 90-day forward rate rises to U.S. $1.04. What is the covered yield on this investment?

17-6 For the most recent 12-month period look up end-of-month rates on 90-day commercial paper for both the United States and Canada. Is there evidence that these rates move together? For those months when the differences in the rates is greatest, what evidence can you gather that might explain the differences?

Glossary

Appreciation	An increase in the value of one currency relative to another or several other currencies.
Asset hedging	The attempt to hedge assets against foreign exchange risk by borrowing in the same currency.
Balance of trade	Exports minus imports. The balance of trade is often considered unfavorable if imports exceed exports (a deficit).
Capital restrictions on convertibility	Limits that a country may place on the ability of individuals and firms to change that country's currency into or from another currency.
Covered (net) yield	The yield on a hedged transaction.
Depreciate	To decline in value vis-à-vis another currency.
Equilibrium mechanism	A device or variable that adjusts to permit equilibrium despite differences between two other variables that would seem inconsistent. For example, the forward rate spread can adjust to permit differences between interest rates in different countries.
Eurodollar market	The market for dollars (generally expatriate U.S. dollars) in Europe. Dollars not sent back to the U.S. for conversion.
Exchange rate	The price of one currency in terms of another.
Fixed exchange rate	An exchange rate at which a country stands prepared to trade its currency. The country has to insure that value by buying or selling foreign exchange to remove market pressures on the rate.

Flexible exchange rate	An exchange rate that the country does not support. Most countries are not content to leave the value of their currency entirely to market forces and thus have a "managed" or "dirty" float.
Foreign exchange rate risk	The risk of a change in the exchange rate.
Forward rate	The exchange rate available in the forward market today on currency that will not be delivered until some future point in time. The current price of future foreign exchange.
Forward contract	A contract for the future delivery of foreign exchange at a price established today.
Forward rate spread	The difference between the forward rate and the spot rate.
Futures contract	The contract for future delivery of foreign exchange at a fixed price.
Hedging	The arrangement to buy or sell foreign exchange in the future to guarantee the future price of foreign exchange sold or bought today, or needed in the future.
Interest equalization tax	A tax imposed by the U.S. on investment in foreign securities. One purpose is to prevent firms from other countries from issuing obligations in the U.S. market to take advantage of lower interest rates.
Interest rate differential	A difference between the yields on comparable assets in different countries.
International monetary fund	An organization that serves as the central bank for the central banks of most countries. Its purpose is to facilitate the financing of international trade deficits and the recycling of funds from nations with trade surpluses to nations with trade deficits.
International reserves	The gold, other currencies (foreign exchange), and SDRs held by a country, often by the central bank or a foreign exchange fund.
Matching	A company's liabilities match its assets if they are of the same amount and have the same distribution of maturities.
Monetary growth	Growth of the monetary aggregates such as M_1 (currency and demand deposits).

Multinational enterprise	A company that conducts operations (including production) in more than one country.
Negative spread	The spot rate exceeds the forward rate.
Net interest rate	The interest earned less the cost of hedging (or exchange losses).
Recycling	An investment or purchase of goods by a country with a trade surplus from the country suffering the trade deficit.
Special drawing right (SDR)	A form of international money held by countries as part of their deposits in the International Monetary Fund.
Spot rate	The current foreign exchange rate.

Bibliography

"A Common Currency for the Common Market," The International Monetary System: Status and Prospects.

ADLER, M. and R. HOERSCH, "The Relationship among Equity Markets: Comment," *Journal of Finance* (Sept. 1974), 1311–1317.

ANBROM, R. K., "Top-Level Approach to the Foreign Exchange Problem," *Harvard Business Review* (July/Aug. 1974), 26–35.

BACK, "Problems of the International Monetary System and Proposal for Report 1944–70," *Federal Reserve Bank of St. Louis,* May 1972.

COHEN, R. and J. PRINGLE, "Imperfections in International Financial Markets: Implications for Risk Premium and the Cost of Capital to Firms," *Journal of Finance* (March 1973), 264–287.

DUFEY, G., "Corporate Finance and Exchange Rate Variations," *Financial Management* (Summer 1972), 170–185.

EITEMAN, D. K., and A. I. STONEHILL, *Multinational Business Finance,* Reading, Mass.: Addison-Wesley, 1973.

"Eurodollars—An Important Source of Funds for American Banks," *Business Conditions* (June 1969), 9–20.

DEFARO, C. and J. J. JUCKER, "The Impact of Inflation and Devaluation on the Selection of an International Borrowing Source," *Journal of International Business Studies* (Fall 1973), 121–133.

FLOYD, J., "International Capital Movements and Monetary Equilibrium," *American Economic Review* (Sept. 1969), 472–490.

FRIEDMAN, M., "The EuroDollar Market: Some First Principles," *Morgan Guaranty Survey,* Oct. 1969.

GAILLOT, H., "Purchasing Power Parity as an Explanation of Long-Term Changes in Exchange Rates," *Journal of Money, Credit and Banking* (Aug. 1970), 221–256.

GRUBEL, HERBERT, G. and K. FADNER, "The Interdependence of International Equity Markets," *Journal of Finance* (March 1971), 89–94.

————, "Internationally Diversified Portfolios: Welfare Gains and Capital Flows," *American Economic Review,* Dec. 1968, pp. 1299–1314.

HEBERMAN, D., "The Exchange Risks of Foreign Operations," *Journal of Business* (Jan. 1972), 3–17.

HELBLING, H. H., "International Trade and Finance under the Influence of Oil," *Federal Reserve Bank of St. Louis,* May 1975.

KEMP, D., "Balance of Payments Concepts—What Do They Really Mean?" *Federal Reserve Bank of St. Louis,* July 1975.

LAFFER, A., "Balance of Payments and Exchange Rate Systems," *Financial Analysts Journal* (July/Aug. 1974), 64–67.

LESSARD, D., "World, National, and Industry Factors in Equity Returns," *Journal of Finance* (May 1974), 379–391.

LEVY, H. and M. SARNAT, "International Diversification of Investment Portfolios," *American Economic Review* (Sept. 1970), 668–675.

MAKRIDAKIS, S. G. and S. C. WHEELWRIGHT, "An Analysis of the Interrelationships among the Major World Stock Exchanges," *Journal of Business Finance and Accounting* (Summer 1974), 195–215.

MILLER, N. C. and M. V. N. WHITMAN, "Alternative Theories and Tests of U.S. Short-Term Foreign Investment," *Journal of Finance* (Dec. 1973), 1131–1147.

————, "A Mean-Variance Analysis of United States Long-Term Portfolio Foreign Investment," *Quarterly Journal of Economics* (May 1970), 175–196.

NORTH, C., "The Future of a Currency: A Four-Step Procedure for Forecasting Change," *Business Horizons* (June 1972), 97–102.

PIPPENGER, J., "Balance of Payment Deficits: Measurement and Interpretation," *Federal Reserve Bank of St. Louis* (Nov. 1973), 120–131.

ROBBINS, S. M. and R. B. STOBAUGH, *Money in the Multinational Enterprise: A Study in Financial Policy,* New York: Basic Books, 1973.

RODRIGUEZ, R. M. and E. E. CARTER, *International Financial Management,* Englewood Cliffs, N.J.: Prentice-Hall, 1976.

SOLNIK, B., *European Capital Markets,* Lexington, Mass.: D. C. Heath/Lexington Books, 1973.

————, "The International Pricing of Risk: An Empirical Investigation of the World Capital Market Structures," *Journal of Finance* (May 1974b), 365–378.

————, "An International Market Model of Security Price Behavior," *Journal of Financial and Quantitative Analysis* (Sept. 1974a), 537–554.

WALLINGFORD, B. A. H., II, "Discussion: The International Pricing of Risk," *Journal of Finance* (May 1974), 392–395.

WESTON, J. F. and B. SORGE, *International Managerial Finance,* Homewood, Ill.: Irwin, 1972.

WILLMS, H., "Controlling Money in an Open Economy: The German Case," *Federal Reserve Bank of St. Louis,* April 1971.

Index

Accounting data, 148
Accounts payable, 44, 222
Accounts receivable, 131, 146, 151, 152, 153, 155
Accounts receivable turnover, 155, 169
Acid-test (quick) ratio, 156, 169
Accruals, 44, 57, 151, 225
Accumulated depreciation, 157, 169
Actuarial yield, 267–68, 269, 270, 282
Actual interest rate (*see* Yield to maturity)
Advertising, 146
After-tax cash flows, 34, 35
Amortization, 50, 51, 52, 57, 221
Analysis:
    breakeven, 174–78, 181, 189
    flow-of-funds, 156–59, 169
    fundamental, 129–30, 137
    income statement leverage, 178–81
    production breakeven, 174–78, 181
    regression, 132
    risk, portfolio, 129–33
    technical, 129–30, 138
Annual reports, 156
Anomaly, 91, 92, 96
Appreciation, 297, 300
Arbitrage, 86, 96
Arditti, F. D., 103
Asset hedging, 297–98, 300
Asset risk, 242, 247
Assets:
    buying, 237–38, 239, 241, 242, 243, 245–46
    current, 155, 156
    financial, 119, 121, 131, 137, 253, 255
    fixed, 237, 243, 278
    gross fixed, 157, 169

    individual, 131
        risk of, vs. portfolio risk premium, 124–26
        and risk premiums, 145
    leasing, 237–38, 239–42
    liquid, 4, 14, 151–53, 155, 156
    mergers (*see* Mergers)
    net fixed, 157, 170
    nonfinancial, 119, 137
    nonliquid, 151, 152, 170
    operating, 151, 170
    quick, 155, 156, 170
    real, 121, 130–33
    risk-free, 120, 123–24, 127, 130
Atlantic Acceptance Corporation, 54
Average cost of capital, 220, 225, 226–27, 233
Average return, 36, 38
    calculating, 22–27
    payback period, 28–29
    significance of, 20–21
    timing, 27–29

Balance of payment, 285–87
Balance sheet, 153, 154, 156, 169
Balance sheet management, and earnings variability, 146–47
Balance sheet structure risk, 192, 202
Balance of trade, 255, 260, 285–87, 300
Balloon payment, 50, 51, 57
Bank deposits, 146
Bank loans, 222
Banks, 85, 91, 257, 258, 290
Bank stocks, 72
Basis points, 50, 57, 120
Beaver, W., 148

Benefit-cost ratio, 20, 31–35, 36, 39
Benefits, calculating, 33–34
Beta, 127–29, 130, 131–33, 136, 144, 147,
    148, 173, 178, 185, 197, 213, 228
    financial leverage effect on, 193–98
Bid, takeover, 9, 15
Bond points, 46, 57
Bonds, 44, 45–50, 91, 185, 257
    callable, 52–53, 57
    coupon, 93–94
    extendible, 54, 58
    flower, 55, 58
    government, 72
    inflation, effect on, 265, 276
    long-term, 85, 88, 93–94
    market value, 46
    mortgage, 45, 52, 59
    retractible, 54, 59
    short-term, 88, 93–94
    sinking fund, 52–53, 60
    tax-exempt, 55, 60
    warrants, 65
    yield to maturity, 45, 46
    yields, 55
    yield tables, 46, 47, 48, 49
Bookkeeping return (see Average return)
Book value, 157, 169
Borrower, direct, 258, 260
Breakeven analysis, 181, 189
    as measure of risk, 174–78
Breakeven charts, 175, 179
Breakeven EBIT, 190–91
Breakeven point, 174, 176, 177, 178, 179,
    180, 181, 183
Breakeven sales ratios, 180
Breen, W. J., 148
Budgeting, cash, 159–66, 169, 279–81
Buildings, leasing, 241
Built-in cyclical stabilizer, 255, 260
Bull market, 148
"Buy-and-hold" strategy, 130

Callable bonds, 52–53, 57
Call loans, 210, 216
Call price, 52–53
Canada, monetary policy, 287–95
Capital:
    average cost of, 220, 225, 226–27, 233
    cost of (see Cost of capital)
    marginal cost of, 226–27, 233
    restrictions on convertibility, 287, 300
    weighted cost of, 220, 223–26, 227, 233
    working (see Working capital)
Capital asset pricing model (CAPM), 129,
    147–49
Capital budgeting, 31, 39, 112–13, 145
    equation, 280–81
Capital consumption allowances, 223–24,
    253
Capital cost allowances, 34–35, 39
Capital gains, 208–209, 210, 213, 241, 244,
    245, 247
Capital goods, 3, 13, 146, 221

Capitalization, 195, 198, 202
Capital loss, 241
Capital market line, 122–24, 125, 126, 128,
    129, 136, 220, 221, 228, 229
Capital structure, 144, 147, 150, 224, 225,
    226, 227, 228–29
Cardinal instability, 133, 136
Cardinal value, 12, 13
Carrying charges, 146, 150
Cash, 131, 153, 155, 213, 221, 228
Cash budgeting, 159–66, 169, 279–81
Cash flows:
    after-tax, 34, 35
    and inflation, 272–73, 279–81
    nominal, 279, 283
Checking accounts, 153, 257
Closed economy, 260
Coefficient of variation, 102, 103, 115
Collateral, 45, 50, 57, 210, 211
Collection period, 146, 150
Combined elasticity, 192, 193, 202
Commercial paper, 45, 54–55, 57, 146, 152,
    288, 289, 290, 292, 293, 294
Common equity, 63
Common shares, 63
Common stocks, 45, 53, 58, 64
    constant dividend, 66–67, 205–206
    constant growth, 67–69, 70, 206–207
    cost of, 220–21, 224
    cost factors, 72–74
    inflation, effect on, 265, 278
    price/earnings ratio, 70–71
    risk analysis, 119, 121
    super-growth, 69–70
    valuation, 70–71
    warrants, 65
    yield:
        determining, 66–70
        and standard deviation, 103
Competition:
    imperfect, 7–9
    and mergers, 243, 246
    perfect, 6–7
Compound interest, 22, 39
Computers, and efficient portfolios, 121
Conditional sale, 239, 248
Conditional value, 188, 202
Consolidation, of firms (see Mergers)
Constant dividend, 66–67, 205–206
Convertible debentures, 53, 58
Convertible preferred stocks, 64–65
Convertibility, capital restrictions on, 287,
    300
Corporate earnings, 173, 180–81
    variability, and balance sheet manage-
        ment, 146–47
Corporate form, 8
Corporations, as deficit sector, 254–55
Correlation, 107–109, 110, 112, 113, 115,
    120–21, 131, 148
    serial, 138
Cost of capital, 13, 21, 27, 39, 147, 219–29
    and capital structure, 228–29

common shares, 220–21, 224
components costs, 220–27
current weights, 225
debt, 222, 225, 228, 229
depreciation, 221–22
long-term debt, 222–23, 224, 225, 228
marginal costs vs. average costs, 226–27
and net present value, 225
preferred stock, 222, 223
retained earnings, 208–209, 221, 223, 224, 225
short-term debt, 222, 224, 225, 228
taxation, 220
weighted, 220, 223–26
Costs:
calculating, 33–34
fixed, 173, 174, 179, 180, 182
fixed operating, 147, 173
flotation, 72, 73, 76, 209–210, 222, 227
variable, 174, 179–80, 181, 182
Coupon bonds, 93–94
Coupon interest rate, 45, 46, 47, 48, 49, 58, 93, 222, 223
Covariances, 109, 110, 115, 121, 122, 126, 127, 130, 131, 132
market, 122, 137
Covenant, 44, 58
Covered (net) yield, 291, 292, 300
Credit:
customer, 146
trade, 155, 170, 178, 222, 255
Credit conditions, 4, 13
Creditors:
general, 52, 59
secured, 44, 60
Credit worthiness, 237, 248
Cumulative dividends, 63, 76
Current assets, 155, 156
Current liabilities, 151, 155, 156, 169
Current ratio, 156, 169
Current yields, 45, 58

Debentures, 44, 45, 58
convertible, 53, 58
subordinated, 44
Debt, 225, 229
as cost of capital, 222
and earnings per share, 189–90
long-term, 4, 14, 222–23, 224, 225, 228, 277
real burden, 271, 272, 283
short-term, 4, 15, 222, 224, 225, 228
Debt/equity ratio, 220, 224, 229, 232
Debt instruments, 43–44, 50, 53, 58
cost factors, 72–74
demand for, 266–67
supply of, 271–72
tax treatment, 71
warranties, 65
yields on, 45–55
Default risk, 83, 84, 96, 123, 136
Deficits, 253, 254–56, 260
trade, 286

Demand curves, 7, 270, 272, 285, 286
Demand for funds, 258, 260
Demand schedules, 119, 120, 227
Democracy, 12
Deposits, term, 153
Depreciate, 295, 297, 301
Depreciation, 20, 33–34, 35, 39, 159, 173, 239, 280
accumulated, 157, 169
as cost of capital, 221–22
sum of the year's digits, 238, 248
Dictatorship, 12
Direct borrower, 258, 260
Direct investment, 256, 257, 260
Discount basis, 54, 58
Discount period, 222, 232
Discount rates, 131, 132, 279, 280
Diversifiable risk, 126, 136, 137
vs. systematic risk, 121–22
Diversification, 107–110, 112, 115, 121–22, 125–26, 128, 129, 130, 137, 146, 257, 297, 298
Dividend payout ratio, 71, 76
Dividends, 8, 13, 45, 144, 145, 147, 148, 149
and capital gains, 208–209, 210
common stock, 66–70
constant, 66–67, 205–206, 211
constant growth, 67–69, 70, 206–207, 221
cumulative, 63, 76
cuts, 211
demand for, 210–11
"dividends-don't-count" school, 210–11
"dividends-make-a-difference" school, 211
flotation costs, 209–210
and inflation, 276–77, 278
lagged adjustments, 207–208
models, 206–208
policy, 205–215
preferred stock, 64
risk, 210, 211
stock, 212
stock splits, 212
taxation, 208–209
valuation, 205–208
Dividend tax credit, 216
Dividend yield, 64, 76, 221, 222
Dominate, 111, 116
Dow Jones, 123

Earnings:
corporate, 173, 180–81
retained, 71, 76, 147, 210
as cost of capital, 208–209, 221, 223, 225
variability:
and balance sheet management, 146–47
and financial leverage, 185–99
Earnings before interest and taxes (EBIT), 189–91, 194, 195, 199, 202, 219, 220, 277
Earnings per share, 189, 202
Earnings/price ratio, 70–71, 76

EBIT, 189–91, 194, 195, 199, 202, 219, 220, 277
Economies of scale, 7, 244, 257
Efficiency, 180, 183
Efficient frontier, 112, 152
Efficient portfolios, 111–13, 114, 116, 121, 123, 124, 128
Efficient portfolio line, 111–12, 116, 120, 124, 125, 126, 129
Elasticity, 181, 182, 184
  combined, 192, 193, 202
  financial leverage, 191, 192, 203
Equilibrium, 256, 260, 273
Equilibrium mechanism, 293, 294, 295, 298, 300
  and exchange rate hedging, 290–95
Equipment, 173
  leasing, 237–38, 241, 242
Equity:
  common, 63
  financial leverage and, 185–89
Equity financing, 189, 203
Equity fund, 119, 137
Equity instruments, 43, 44–45, 53, 58
  yield on, 63–74, 274–76
Eurodollar mechanism, 296, 300
Excess premium, 269, 283
Exchange rate, 290, 291, 293, 295, 297, 298, 300
  fixed, 300
  flexible, 295, 301
  forward, 293, 294, 301
Exchange rate risk, foreign, 290, 291, 292, 295, 296, 297, 298, 301
Ex-dividend, 216
Expected value, 10, 11, 12, 13–14
Extendible bonds, 54, 58

Federal Reserve Bulletin, 132
Federal Reserve System, 254, 257, 258
FIFO inventory system, 277, 278
Finance company paper, 44, 54, 58
Financial assets, 119, 121, 131, 137, 253, 255
Financial intermediary, 257, 260, 296
Financial leverage, 147, 148, 149, 150, 174, 184, 186, 203, 277, 278
  debt, and earnings per share, 189–90
  degree of, 191–92
  effect on beta, 193–98
  and operating leverage, 192–93
  and rate of return on net worth, 185–89
  risk and, 185–89, 193–94
  and stock repurchase, 213–14
  and taxation, 198–99
  and variability of earnings, 185–89
Financial leverage elasticity, 191, 192, 203
Financial leverage sensitivity, 191, 192, 203
Fixed assets, 237, 243, 278
Fixed costs, 173, 174, 179, 180, 182
Fixed exchange rate, 300
Fixed operating costs, 147, 173
Fixed-return instruments, and inflation, 266–71, 276

Fixed-term savings certificate, 146, 150
Flexible exchange rate, 295, 301
Flotation costs, 72, 73, 76, 209–10, 222, 227
Flower bonds, 55, 58
Flow of funds, 253, 254, 255, 260
  analysis, 156–59, 169
Forecasting, 130, 279
Foreign exchange rate risk, 290, 291, 292, 295, 296, 297, 298, 301
Forward contract, 297, 298, 301
Forward rate, 293, 294, 301
Forward rate spread, 293, 294, 295, 296, 301
Freedom of entry, 6, 7
Fundamental analysis, 129–30, 137
Funds:
  flow of, 253, 254, 255, 260
  sources of, 253–58
    corporations, 254–55
    deficit sector, 253–56
    governments, 255
    households, 254
    surplus sector, 253–56, 257
    world, 255
  supply of, 256, 261
Futures contracts, 291–92, 301

Gambling, 104, 106
General creditors, 52, 59
Geometric mean, 87
Going concern, 243, 248
Gold, 285, 286
Goldsmith, Raymond, 258
Gonedes, M. J., 148
Gross fixed assets, 157, 169
Gross national product (GNP), 131, 254, 255, 256, 260, 273
Gross savings, 253, 255, 261

Hamada, R. S., 148
Hedging, 295, 301
  against inflation, 278
  asset, 297–98, 300
  exchange rate, as equilibrium mechanism, 290–95
Holding company, 243, 248
Holding period yield, 50, 59, 64, 66, 69
Households:
  as deficit sector, 254
  financial objectives, 4–6

Income statement, 154, 155, 156, 160–61, 162, 165, 169
Income statement leverage, 178–81, 184
Indifference curves, 5, 6, 105, 116, 124
Inefficient portfolios, 111–13, 116, 123, 124, 129
Inflation, 4, 148, 224
  cash flow inelasticity to, 272–73
  and cash flows, 279–80
  and discount rates, 279, 280
  effects on capital budgets, 279–81
  effects on yields, 265–81
  fixed-return instruments, 266–71, 276

forecasting, 279
"hedges" against, 278
and market supply, 273–74
rate reductions, 278–79
and supply of debt instruments, 272–73
Insider shares, 216
Insolvency, technical, 3–4, 15, 159, 186
Instruments:
  debt (*see* Debt instruments)
  fixed-return, and inflation, 266–71, 276
  variable return, and inflation, 274–79
Insurance premiums, 242, 269–70, 273
Interest equalization tax, 287, 301
Interest rate differential, 288, 293, 294, 295, 296, 297, 298, 301
Interest rate risk, 123, 137
Interest rates:
  Canadian vs. U.S., 287–90, 291, 292–95
  high, 4
  international, 287, 290–98
  long-term, 88
  net, 291, 302
  short-term, 88
Intermediary, 237, 248
  financial, 257, 260, 296
Intermediation, financial, 256–58
Internal rate of return, 29–31, 36, 39, 46, 50, 219
  calculating, 29–31
  limits to, 31
International Monetary Fund (IMF), 285, 286, 301
International reserves, 285, 296, 301
Inventory, 151, 152, 153–55
  FIFO system, 277, 278
  investment, 145–46
  value, 131
Inventory turnover, 155, 170
Investment, direct, 256, 257, 260
Investment bankers, 72, 76, 210
Investment tax credits, 34, 39
Invisible trade items, 255, 261
Iterative approach, 30, 46

Kettler, P., 148

Land, leasing, 241
Latané, H., 101
Leases (*see also* Leasing)
  legitimate, 238, 248
  net, 241, 248
Leasing:
  assets, 237–38, 239–42
  equipment, 237–38, 241, 242
  payments, 239–41
  services, 241
Legal entity, 8, 14
Legitimate lease, 238, 248
Lerner, E. M., 148
Lessee, 237, 238, 239, 241, 242, 248
Lessor, 237, 238, 239, 241, 242, 248
Lev, B., 148

Lever, 65, 76
Leverage, 173, 184, 277, 278
  financial (*see* Financial leverage)
  income statement, 178–81, 184
  negative effect, 185, 186, 187, 197, 203
  operating (*see* Operating leverage)
  positive, 186, 187
  production, 173, 179, 180, 184
  and rate of return on net worth, 185–89
Leverage function, 186–87, 203
Levered firm, 214, 216
Liabilities, 173, 174, 191, 241, 243, 253, 255
  current, 151, 155, 156, 169
Liens, statutory, 44, 60
Life insurance companies, 50, 85, 91, 92, 107
  inflation, effect on, 267, 269–70
Life insurance policies, 257
  borrowing on, 91
Life insurance premiums, 242, 269–70, 273
Liquid assets, 4, 14, 151–53, 155, 156
Liquidation, 44, 59
Liquidity, 4, 14, 151, 170, 210, 211, 213, 257
  management of, 151–69
  measurement of, 153–56
  risk and, 151–53
Liquidity policy, 147, 148, 149, 150
Liquidity premium, 88, 96
Liquidity squeeze, 51, 59
Listed stocks, 63, 76
Loans:
  bank, 222
  call, 210, 216
  policy, 91, 96
Long end, of market, 84, 89, 91
Long-term debt, 4, 14, 222–23, 224, 225, 228, 277
Losses, 6, 9, 14

Maintenance service contracts, 241
Managerial contracts, 245
Managers:
  corporate, 8, 143
  functions of, 3
  public, 143
Margin, 175, 176, 184
Marginal cost of capital, 226–27, 233
Marginal rate of substitution, 105, 116
Marginal revenues, 7, 14
Marginal risk, 112, 116
Market:
  long end, 84, 89, 91
  role of, 119–22
  secondary bond, 88
  short end, 84, 85, 91, 97
Marketable securities, 151, 153, 155, 170
Market covariances, 122, 137
Market index, 122
Market portfolios, 123, 124, 125, 127, 128, 137
Market rate of interest, 45, 46, 59, 223
Market segmentation, 85, 91–92, 96
Market supply, and inflation, 273–74
Market value, 193, 203

Markowitzian-efficient portfolios, 123, 125
Matching, 297, 301
Maturity, 45, 46, 47, 48, 49, 50, 54, 59
Mean:
  geometric, 87
  weighted, 110, 117
Mergers:
  advantages of, 243–44
  competition, 243, 246
  economies of scale, 244
  mature acquisition, 243–45
  means of exchange, 245
  public policy, 246
  securities, 245
  stocks, 245–46
  statutory, 242, 245, 248
  taxation, 243–44
Michaelson, J. B., 103
Midwest Stock Exchange, 63
Miller, M. H., 193, 197, 198, 214
Mining exploration, 146
Modigliani, F., 193, 197, 198, 214
Moment, 102, 116
Monetary growth, 287, 301
Money supply, 256, 261
Monopolies, 7–8
Mortality tables, 107
Mortgage bonds, 45, 52, 59
Mortgagee, 50
Mortgages, 44, 45, 50–52, 59, 91, 185, 257,
    258
  interest tables, 51–52
  payment table, 51
  value of, 51–52
Mortgagor, 50
Multinational enterprise (MNE), 285, 287,
    302
  role of, 295–98
Mutual funds, 119, 137, 257
Mutually exclusive alternatives, 24, 27, 31,
    39

Negative leverage effect, 185, 186, 187, 197,
    203
Negotiable instruments, 51, 59
Negotiable securities, 131
Net fixed assets, 157, 170
Net income (NI) approach, 195, 196, 197,
    198, 199, 203, 228, 229
Net interest rates, 291, 302
Net lease, 241, 248
Negative spread, 293, 295, 302
Net operating income (NOI) approach, 193,
    195, 196, 197, 198, 203, 211, 228, 229
Net present value (NPV), 27, 32, 36, 39, 219,
    225
Net receipts, 43, 59
Net worth, 6, 8, 14, 144, 147
  leverage and the rate on return, 185–89
New York City, 3–4, 55
New York Stock Exchange, 63, 258
Nixon, Richard M., 285

Nominal cash flows, 279, 283
Nominal yields, 144, 150, 265, 266, 267, 268,
    273, 274, 275, 280, 283
Nonfinancial assets, 119, 137
Nonfinancial sector, 256, 257, 261
Nonliquid assets, 151, 152, 170
Nonprofit organizations, 19
Normal return, 6, 7, 14
Notes, 45, 50, 59, 83, 84, 266

Objectives, financial:
  household, 4–6
  management, 3–9
  public sector, 12
Oil, 286
Oligopolies, 7–8
OPEC, 286
Operating assets, 151, 170
Operating leverage, 147, 148, 149, 150, 173–
    84, 192–93, 277, 278
  degree of, 181–82
  income statements, 174–78
  production breakeven analysis, 174–78,
    181
  and risk, 174–78
Organizations, public, 8–9, 14
Original cost, 20, 39
Over-the-counter market, 63, 76

Parent corporation, 243
Par value, 55, 59, 64
Payables, 44, 57
Payback period, 28–29, 36, 39–40
Payout ratio, 211, 216
Penn Central, 54, 193
Pension funds, 91, 119, 143, 209
  inflation, effect on, 267–68, 270, 273, 274
Perfect knowledge, 129, 130, 137
Perfectly inelastic, 270, 272, 283
Permanent financing, 222, 233
Plants, 173
Pledges, 52, 59
Policy loan, 91, 96
Portfolios, 100–101, 102, 105, 257, 275
  beta value, 127–29, 133
  capital market line, 122–24, 125, 126, 128,
    129, 136
  covariances, 121, 122, 127, 130
  demand schedules, 120
  diversification, 121–22, 125–26, 128, 129,
    133
  efficient, 111–13, 114, 116, 121, 123, 124,
    128
  financial assets, 121
  inefficient, 111–13, 116, 123, 124, 129
  management, 92–94, 119
  market, 123, 124, 125, 127, 128, 137
  Markowitzian efficient, 123, 125
  real assets, 121
  risk analysis, 129–33
  risk-free assets, 120, 123–24

risk premiums, 120–22
  vs. risk of individual assets, 124–26
  variance of, 101, 103–104, 106, 107–108,
    109, 110, 111, 116, 121–22
  zero beta, 123
Portfolio composition, 120, 121, 122, 137
"Portfolio-peculiar," 121
Positive leverage function, 185, 186, 187
Preference curves, 105, 106, 116
Preferred shares, 63
Preferred stocks, 45, 59, 63, 64, 222, 223
  convertible, 64–65
  cost factors, 72–74
  tax treatment, 71
  warrants, 65
  yield, 64
Present value, 11, 14, 21, 29, 34, 39, 46
  calculating, 22–27
  net, 27, 32, 36, 39
  tables, 25–26
Price/earnings (P/E) ratio, 70–71, 76
Price index, of stocks, 123
Principal (maturity) value, 45, 59
Probability distribution, 10, 100–101, 102,
    113, 145, 146, 188, 189
Product differentiation, 7, 14
Production leverage, 173, 179, 180, 184
Profits, 14
  breakeven analysis, 174, 175, 176, 177, 178
  elasticity, of profit function, 181–82
  maximizing, 6, 7, 8, 9–12, 19
    vs. share value maximizing, 8, 9–12
Profitability index, 32, 40
Promissory notes, 50
Prospectus, 72, 74, 76
Proxy fights, 8–9
Proxy statements, 8, 14
Public exchange, 63, 76
Public organization, 8–9, 14
Public ownership, imperfect competition of,
    8–9
Public stocks, 63, 72, 76
Public utilities, 143, 146, 193, 223
Pure expectations theory, 85–88, 96

Quadratic programming, 121, 137
Quick assets, 155, 156, 170

Random walk, 130, 138
Rational investor, 123, 137, 266
Real assets, 121
  beta, 130–33
  inflation, effect on, 265
Real burden, of debt, 271, 272, 283
Real value, 266, 271, 278, 279, 283
Real yield, 265, 266, 283
Recessions, 146–47
Recycling, 285–86, 302
"Red-herring" prospectus, 72
Refinance, 4, 15, 51, 59, 223, 277
Regression analysis, 132

Required rate of return, 145, 147, 209, 220,
    221, 223, 228
  setting target rates, 219–20
Required yield, 11, 15, 68, 69, 71, 76
Reservation price, 267–70, 283
Reservation yield, 267, 283
Retained earnings, 71, 76, 147, 210
  and cost of capital, 208–209, 221, 223, 225
Retention rate, 71, 76
Retirement pension funds (see Pension
    funds)
Retractible bonds, 54, 59
Return, normal, 6, 7, 14
Return on capital, 6, 7, 14
Returns, average (see Average returns)
Risk, 9–10, 11, 12, 14, 15
  analysis, 99
    breakeven, 174–78, 181
  asset, 242, 247
  balance sheet structure, 192, 202
  coefficient of variation, 102, 103
  default, 83, 84, 96, 123, 136
  defined, 100
  diversifiable, 126, 137
    vs. systematic risk, 121–22
  dividends, 210, 222
  financial leverage and, 185–89, 193–94
  interest rate, 123, 137
  and liquidity, 151–53
  low, 147
  managing, 99, 107, 110
  marginal, 116
  market price of, 119–33
  probability distribution, 100–101, 102
  ratio of, 102
  systematic, 126, 127, 137, 138, 148
    vs. diversifiable, 121–22
  underwriting, 72
  variability as measure, 101–104
Risk analysis, 119, 122
  portfolio, 129–33
Risk aversion, 101, 103, 105, 116, 124, 138
Risk-free rate, 120, 124, 125, 127, 132, 138,
    144, 275
Risk-free security, 106, 116
Risk management, 99, 107–110, 116
Risk premiums, 103, 116, 119–20, 129, 138,
    148, 173, 174, 185, 193, 194, 195, 197,
    198
  competition, 121–22
  estimating, 120–22
  individual assets and, 145–46
  individual determinants, 104–106
  portfolio, vs. risk of individual assets,
    124–26
  for securities, 126–29
Risk/return ratio, 145, 150
Roll overs, 4, 15, 83, 84, 96, 222

Sales, 131
Sales finance paper, 54, 55, 256
Salvage, 241

Savings, 253, 254
  gross, 253, 255, 261
Savings accounts, 257, 258
Savings and loan associations, 257
Scholes, M., 148
Sectors, 253–56, 257, 261
  corporations, 254–55
  deficit, 253–56
  government, 255
  household, 254
  nonfinancial, 256, 257
  surplus, 253–56, 257
Secured creditors, 44, 60
Securities:
  analysis for selecting, 129–30
  beta value, 128–29, 130, 133
  fundamental analysis, 129–30
  government, 55, 72, 83–85
  long-term, 85–88, 103
  marketable, 151, 153, 155, 170
  in mergers, 245
  negotiable, 131
  risk-free, 106, 116, 127
  risk premiums, 126–29
  short-term, 85, 86–88, 103
  technical analysis, 129–30
  U.S. Treasury, 83–85, 103
  yield, consistency of, 90
Securities Act of 1933, 72
Securities and Exchange Commission, 63,
  72, 209
Serial correlation, 138
Shareholders, 9, 258
  classes of, 8
Shares:
  common, cost of, 220–21, 224
  dividends (see Dividends)
  earnings per, and debt, 189–90
  insider, 216
  preferred, 63, 222, 223
  prices, 276–77, 278–79
  valuation of, 143–45, 173, 205–208,
    213–14
  values, maximizing, 228
    vs. profit maximizing, 8, 9–12
Shares of stock, 63
Short end, of market, 84, 85, 91, 97
Short-term debt, 4, 15, 222, 224, 225, 228
Sinking fund bonds, 52–53, 60
Social Security, 268
Sources, and uses of funds (see Flow-of-
  funds, analysis)
Special drawing rights (SDR), 285, 302
Speculation, 291
Spot rate, 291, 292, 293, 295, 302
Standard deviation, 10, 11, 15, 101–104, 108,
    109, 120, 123, 126, 133, 144, 145,
    146, 152, 173, 176, 177, 188, 189
Standard and Poor's Index, 123, 132
Statistical tests, 130, 131
Statutory consolidation, 242, 245, 248
Statutory lien, 44, 60
Statutory merger, 242, 245, 248

Stock dividends, 212, 216
Stockholders (see Shareholders)
Stock options, 65
Stocks, 8, 257, 258
  bank, 72
  beta value, 127–29, 130, 133
  common (see Common stocks)
  convertible preferred, 64–65
  cost factors, 72–74
  diversification, 122, 133
  dividends (see Dividends)
  and inflation, 278–79
  listed, 63, 76
  in mergers, 245
  preferred (see Preferred stocks)
  price effects, 276–77
  prospectus, 72, 74
  public, 63, 76
  registration statements, 72, 74, 209
  repurchase, 212–14
  shares of, 63
  treasury, 213, 216
Stock split, 212, 216
Subordinated debentures, 44
Subsidiary, 237, 243, 248
Sum of the year's digits depreciation, 238,
  248
Super-growth, 69–70, 77
Supply, market, and inflation, 273–74
Supply curves, 271–72, 275, 276
Supply and demand, 119–20, 124
Supply of funds, 256, 261
Surpluses, 253, 254–56, 257, 261
  trade, 286
Survival, 3–4, 6, 7
Systematic risk, 126, 127, 137, 138, 148
  vs. diversifiable risk, 121–22

Takeover bids, 9, 15
Taxation, 143
  capital gains, 208–209, 210, 213, 241, 244,
    245, 247
  and cost of capital, 220
  of debt instruments, 71–72
  of dividends, 208–209
  financial leverage and, 198–99
  and interest payments, 189, 194, 198
  and leasing, 241
  mergers, 243–44
  pension funds, 268
Tax credit, 71, 77
  dividend, 216
Taxes:
  corporate, 208–209, 213–14
  estate, 55
  inheritance, 55
  interest equalization, 287, 301
Taxes payable, 44, 222
Tax-exempt bonds, 55, 60
Technical analysis, 129–30, 138
Technical insolvency, 3–4, 15, 159, 186
Tender, 212, 216
Term deposits, 153

Terminal price, 77
Term structure, 83, 84, 85, 90, 91, 92, 93,
    97, 99, 103
  pure expectations theory, 85–88
Thompson, D. J. 148
Trade, foreign, 255
Trade balance, and balance of payments,
    285–87
Trade credit, 155, 170, 177, 222, 255
Trade deficits, 286
Trade surpluses, 286
Trade payables, 225
Treasury bills, 54, 55, 83, 84, 97, 123, 132,
    152
Treasury stock, 213, 216
Trust companies, 91

Uncertainty, 9–10, 15, 100
Uncertainty premium, 88–89, 97, 103
Underwriting, 72, 73, 77
United States, monetary policy, 287–88
United States Treasury, 83, 84
Utility, 5–6, 7, 15
Utility function, 6, 12, 15
Utility maximization, household, 4–6

Value:
  conditional, 188, 202
  expected, 10, 11, 12, 13–14
  present (see Present value)
Variable costs, 174, 179–80, 181, 182
Variable return instruments, and inflation,
    274–79
Variances, 11, 15, 119, 126, 127, 131, 132,
    144, 145
  of a portfolio, 101, 103–104, 106, 107–108,
    109, 110, 111, 116, 121–22
Voting rights, 8, 15

Wages payable, 44, 151, 222
Warrants, 65, 77
Weighted cost of capital, 220, 223–26, 227,
    233
Weighted mean, 110, 117
Wells Fargo, 133
Working capital, 155, 156, 159, 170
  changes, analysis of, 156–59
World Bank, 83

Yield curves, 87, 88, 89, 91, 92, 93, 97
Yields, 11, 15
  actuarial, 267–68, 269, 270, 282
  common stock, 66–70
  consistency of, 90
  covered (net), 291, 292, 300
  current, 45, 58
  deficits, impact on, 256
  dividend, 64, 76, 221, 222
  equity instruments, 63–74, 274–76
  holding period, 50, 59, 64, 66, 69
  inflation, effect on, 265–81
  nominal, 144, 150, 265, 266, 267, 268, 273,
    274, 275, 280, 283
  real, 265, 266, 283
  required, 11, 15, 68, 69, 71, 76
  reservation, 267, 283
  surpluses, impact on, 256
  term structure of, 83–94
Yield spread, 97
Yield to maturity, 45, 46, 55, 60, 222–23,
    279
  tables, 47, 48, 49

Zero beta portfolios, 123